BARRON'S

HOW TO PREPARE FOR THE

AP®
EUROPEAN HISTORY

ADVANCED PLACEMENT EXAMINATION

3RD EDITION

James M. Eder
Former Social Studies Teacher,
Northport High School
Northport, New York

BARRON'S

Dedication

To the students at Northport H.S.

All inquiries should be addressed to:
Barron's Educational Series, Inc.
250 Wireless Boulevard
Hauppauge, New York 11788
http://www.barronseduc.com

Library of Congress Catalog Card No. 2002027682
International Standard Book No. 0-7641-2020-4

Photo credits: pp. 42, 268—French Government Tourist Office

Library of Congress Cataloging-in-Publication Data

Eder, James M.
    How to prepare for the advanced placement examination. AP
European history / James M. Eder.—3rd ed.
        p.   cm.
    Includes index.
    ISBN 0-7641-2020-4
    1. Europe—History—Examinations, questions, etc.   I. Title:
AP European history.   II. Title.
D21 .E24   2003
940'.076—dc21   2002027682
                                                      CIP

PRINTED IN THE UNITED STATES OF AMERICA
9 8 7 6 5 4

Contents

PART ONE INTRODUCTION

SECTION A Using This Book

This book is designed primarily to prepare students of European history for the Advanced Placement Examination in European History. It provides

Systematic Methods for Studying History

A Guide to the Advanced Placement Examination in European History

Review chapters including sample and practice questions on the various periods of European history

A complete model Advanced Placement Examination and answers

TO THE TEACHER AND THE STUDENT

This volume can be a useful supplement to classwork and study materials.

Part One Section B offers *systematic methods for studying history*—how to recognize the logical order of history materials; how to pre-read; how to frame the big picture; how to read, take notes, and highlight; and how to connect events by using chronology.

Part One Section C is a guide to the Advanced Placement Examination in European History—exam's duration and number of questions; subject matter; historical time span; grading; multiple-choice section with *hints, types,* and *samples;* interpreting the essay questions; the document-based question with *hints, don'ts,* and a *sample;* the thematic essay questions with the *frequency of themes* and *hints.*

Part Two consists of fifteen chapters of *review* of the major historical periods covered on the Advanced Placement Examination in European History along with *sample and practice* thematic essays and multiple-choice questions and answers.

Part Three is two model Advanced Placement Examinations in European History with multiple-choice questions, thematic essays, and a document-based question and suggested answers.

A SUGGESTED APPROACH FOR USING THIS BOOK

1. Peruse the Systematic Methods for Studying History section.
2. Study the Guide to the Advanced Placement Examination in European History.
3. Study any or all of the review chapters and do the sample and practice questions.
4. Try the model exams.

TO THE TEACHER

The various review chapters can be used as year-long supplements to sum up or reinforce a particular teaching unit and homework assignments. The historical review section of each chapter helps students to frame the big picture; the sample and practice essays and multiple-choice questions reinforce the learning.

Part Two, the review section, can be used near the end of the year to pull the course work together and to prepare students for the exam.

It's often helpful for students to study Part One at the beginning of the course to help them to study history and to give them an idea of what the exam at year's end will be like. Knowing what they will face is both a motivator and method of organizing the course's information.

TO THE STUDENT

This volume can be used independent of a prescribed course in European history or it can be used along with assigned materials to sum up, pull together, clarify, and review.

It's best to use it at the beginning of the year and to read Part One right away. That will help you to study better in and out of class, and it will give you an idea of what's ahead if you decide to take the Advanced Placement Exam. Use the appropriate chapters in Part Two right before you start each topic in class to "frame the picture" and to help fit everything into place in your mind. Or go to the appropriate chapter after studying that unit in class in order to pull it all together.

If you intend to use the book as review and practice for the Advanced Placement Exam, don't wait until late April or May. Instead of getting nervous and wasting energy on test anxiety, put time aside in late March or early April to study review chapters and to do sample questions on content you have already covered in class and in homework. Save the model Advanced Placement Exams for early May, then use them to fill in any gaps in your understanding.

SECTION B Systematic Methods for Studying History

What follows are some time-tested methods for studying history. Although there is no substitute for being an involved student in a challenging history course, these suggestions will help you with homework, supplementary reading, and preparation for the Advanced Placement Examination in European History.

How to Recognize the Logical Order of History Materials

Most history readings—especially texts—are organized logically:

Facts support a theme: The Magna Carta, the Puritan Revolution, and the personalities involved help trace the development of constitutional government in England.

Great events define an era: The French Revolution colored the political, social, cultural, and diplomatic life of Europe for over a hundred years after it happened.

Cause-effect relationships are ascertained: The outbreak of World War I in August 1914 was caused by long-term trends, such as nationalism and imperialism, that stretched back decades into the 19th century.

The influence of individuals on an age is identified: The totalitarian dictatorships of Hitler and Stalin impacted on the entire planet before and long after World War II.

In reading history materials, the object is to focus on this inherent logical order. This can be done by *pre-reading* and by *framing the big picture.*

How to Pre-read

Before tackling the text itself, be sure to skim the chapter by reading each of the following *in order:*

1. The chapter heading
2. The introductory paragraph
3. Focus questions at the beginning of the chapter
4. Subheadings

5. The concluding paragraph
6. Review questions at chapter's end
7. Bold print or italics within the text

It is better to concentrate on the reading at this point than to try to take notes.

How to "Frame the Big Picture"

During both the *pre-reading* and the *reading of the text,* pose the following questions as a natural way of keeping the mind's eye on the main story, on the *logical order* of the material:

1. What is the theme of the chapter? (What is it about? What is the author trying to prove?)
2. What are main events? (What happened and what caused it?)
3. Who are the principal personalities? (Who did what, and why?)
4. What are the important results? (New ideas? Significant changes? Power shifts?)

Remember: "Don't lose the forest for the trees."

How to Read the Text

Once you have *pre-read* the material and *framed the big picture,* you are ready to attack the text itself. Certain difficult material deserves a "straight read" before you try to highlight, underline, or take notes; most readings allow you to do both simultaneously as long as you have *pre-read.*

If You Own the Book

HIGHLIGHTING OR UNDERLINING

Advantages: easy, quick, neat; has visual appeal; the text itself provides an instant condensation.

Disadvantage: too much highlighting/or underlining defeats the purpose.

MARGINAL NOTES

Advantage: making notes in the margin of the book requires a synthesis that is itself a learning tool.

Disadvantages: time-consuming; often illegible, messy, or incomplete.

If You Don't Own the Book

Notetaking and outlining on separate paper are traditional and effective methods of condensing and synthesizing a reading. Notetaking has the advantage of requiring critical thought for the condensation, the disadvantage of often being jumbled and confusing.

Sample Reading with Underlining, Accompanying Notes, Brief Outline

Underlined Passage

Early 19th-Century <u>industrialization</u> in England depended upon <u>steam engines</u> made of iron and fueled by coal. Steam-powered <u>textile mills</u> created a <u>factory economy</u> and a new <u>working class</u>. Steam-powered railway <u>trains</u> moved people and products speedily over great distances, <u>concentrating populations</u> into expanded cities and linking the sources of raw materials with the centers of manufacturing. Functional <u>new architectural designs</u>—using structural steel—reflected the practical needs of the new society. <u>Class conflict</u>, brought on by disparities of wealth, extremes of poverty, and the unexpected difficulties of industrialization, raged throughout most of the century.

Notes

Industrialization, 19th-Century England
   Coal-fueled, iron steam engines powered textile mills = factory economy + new working class.
   Speedy steam-powered railroads = expanded cities; links raw materials + factories.
   New steel architecture; class conflict because of income differences + effects of industrialization.

Brief outline

19th-Century Industrialization in England
   I. Steam power, the essential element
      A. Iron engines fueled by coal
      B. Textile factories, new working class
      C. RRs move masses: people, products
   II. Effects of industrialization
      A. Expanded cities
      B. New architecture
      C. Class conflict: disparities of wealth

Summary for How to Read History Material

1. *Pre-read:* Skim the chapter *heading, first and last paragraphs, subheadings.*
2. *Focus* on the logical order of the reading—*themes, events, cause-effect relationships, personalities*—by *framing the big picture.*
      What is the chapter's theme?
      What are the main events, causes, personalities, results?
3. *Read* the text; highlight or take notes; outline.
4. Be able to answer the questions you posed while *framing the big picture* and any *review questions* in the text.

How to Connect Events by Using Chronology

A consistent problem in studying history is the failure to appreciate that significant trends are often concurrent, that influential people are sometimes contemporaries. For instance, the Reformation and the Age of Exploration shared the 16th century, and the personification of absolutism, Louis XIV, reigned while the greatest scientist of the Enlightenment, Isaac Newton, formulated his theories of gravitation.

An excellent method for *connecting* events, trends, and personalities of history is to *identify their century*. History is not a series of separate strands but rather a fabric of causes, effects, and interwoven influences.

15th Century: The Renaissance; the fall of Constantinople to the Ottoman Turks; the voyages of Portuguese explorers and Columbus. Contemporaries: Leonardo da Vinci, Sulieman the Magnificent, Guttenberg, Henry the Navigator.

16th Century: The Reformation and Catholic and Counter-Reformations; the Age of Exploration; the growth of national monarchies. Contemporaries: Luther, Henry VIII, Loyola, Holy Roman Emperor Charles V, Copernicus, Elizabeth I, Phillip II.

17th Century: The Age of Colonization; the Commercial Revolution and the rise of capitalism; the rise of modern science; the Thirty Years' War; the Age of Absolutism and the rise of constitutionalism. Contemporaries: Descartes, Galileo, Newton, the Stuart kings and Cromwell, Grotius, Locke, Mazarin, the Romanovs, Louis XIV.

18th Century: The growth of capitalism; the Age of Enlightenment and of Reason; the Age of Benevolent Despotism and of Revolution. Contemporaries: Adam Smith, Voltaire, Rousseau, Frederick the Great, Maria Theresa, Catherine the Great, Louis XVI, George III, Robespierre, George Washington.

19th Century: The Age of Napoleon; the Age of Metternich; the Age of Romanticism; the Age of Nationalism and Unification; the Age of "ISMs"; the Age of Imperialism; the Age of Progress. Contemporaries: Talleyrand, Metternich, Wordsworth, Goethe, Bismarck, Cavour, Marx, Darwin, Cecil Rhodes, Teddy Roosevelt, Gregor Mendel, Louis Pasteur.

20th Century: The Age of Violence; the Age of Technology; the Nuclear Age; the Age of Information; the Age of Anxiety; the Age of Totalitarianism; the Age of Democracy. Contemporaries: Kaiser Wilhelm, Clemenceau, Lenin, Wilson, Stalin, Hitler, Gandhi, Churchill, Freud, Einstein, Franklin Roosevelt, Hirohito, Mao, Adenauer, De Gaulle.

When studying a historical event, personality, or trend:

1. Determine its century (or centuries).
2. Make up an open-ended chart of the centuries, and make it a habit to place events, people, and trends in the appropriate time frame.

SECTION C A Guide to the Advanced Placement Examination in European History

Time Allowed for Each Part

The exam lasts a total of 3 hours and 5 minutes.

1. *55 minutes* will be allowed for *80 multiple-choice* questions.

2. *130 minutes* will be allotted for the *free-response* section.

3. *15 minutes* will be allowed for a mandatory reading period to analyze the *document-based question* (DBQ) documents and to consider choices of thematic essays.

4. *45 minutes* will be allowed to answer the DBQ.

5. *70 minutes* will be allotted to answer two thematic essays (*5 minutes* planning and *30 minutes* writing recommended for each of the thematic essays).

Themes

Political-diplomatic history of Europe: The nation-state; nationalism; political parties; ideologies; revolution and reform; political rights; colonialism and imperialism; diplomacy and war (30–40 percent of questions).

Economic-social history of Europe: Social classes; cultural values; industrialization; urbanization; demography; family and gender; economic systems; commerce and markets; life-styles; race and ethnicity (30–40 percent of questions).

Cultural-intellectual history of Europe: Religion; science and technology; literature and art; intellectual developments; political, social, and economic thought; secularization, education; cultural developments (20–30 percent of questions).

Span

The history of Europe from the Renaissance (1450) to contemporary times.

Multiple-Choice Questions: One half of the questions pertain to the period from the Renaissance to the French Revolution and Napoleon (1450–1815); one half pertain to the period from 1815 to the present.

Free-Response Questions: The two essays will be on subjects of significance during this period; the document-based question (DBQ) will draw on evidence pertaining to this period.

No questions in either the multiple-choice or free-response sections use pre-Renaissance information.

Grading

Section 1 (multiple choice) = one half of the grade

9

Section 2 (free response) = one half of the grade

The DBQ will be 45 percent of Section 2;

The two thematic essays will count for 55 percent of Section 2 scoring, and they will be weighted equally.

SCORES

5, extremely well qualified, is accepted by most colleges for either course credit or placement into a higher level section.

4, well qualified, is accepted by a majority of colleges.

3, qualified, is accepted by many colleges.

2, possibly qualified, is accepted by a few colleges for either credit or placement.

1, no recommendation, is not accepted anywhere.

Some colleges require additional documentation about course work.

Students may choose to suppress a score on the Advanced Placement Examination once it has been reported to them. They may also cancel the test within a certain time after they have taken it but before the score has been reported.

Multiple-Choice Questions

Eighty questions, each with five answer choices; 60 minutes; 30 to 40 percent on political-diplomatic history; 30 to 40 percent on economic-social history; 20 to 30 percent on intellectual-cultural history.

Generally, *50 percent* of the multiple-choice questions must be answered correctly and the free-response section completed acceptably in order to qualify for a score of 3 ("qualified").

HINTS FOR THE MULTIPLE-CHOICE QUESTIONS

1. Don't guess blindly. Each incorrect answer is penalized one fourth of a point.
2. The more incorrect answers you eliminate, the greater the odds of gaining a point.
3. Be methodical. Even on questions you are sure of, put a line through the letters of the incorrect answers as they are eliminated. Circle the number of any question you are unsure of so you can return to it if you have the time.
4. Go with your intuition. Your first choice is usually correct, so change an answer only if you are absolutely certain.
5. Underline the key idea in each question.
6. Try reading the answer choices from E back to A.

TYPES OF MULTIPLE-CHOICE QUESTIONS
Identification; analysis; quotation; interpretation of a picture, art object, cartoon, or photo; map study; graph or chart.

Samples of Identification Questions

Identification requires very specific information to link things like an idea with a thinker; a style with an artist; a dogma with a religion or ideology; a social, economic, cultural, or political environment with a geographic location, or a development with an era.

Of the multiple-choice questions, 35 to 40 percent tend to be *identification*.

---

1. Machiavelli's *The Prince* (1513) was primarily
   - (A) a secular handbook on modern statecraft
   - (B) a guide to courtly etiquette
   - (C) a scathing critique of the New Monarchies
   - (D) a glorification of the independent city-states of Renaissance Italy
   - (E) a pious testament to the secular role of the Popes

2. The belief that only a small portion of humanity has been elected, since the beginning of time, for eternal salvation was fundamental to
   - (A) Lutheranism
   - (B) Roman Catholicism
   - (C) Calvinism
   - (D) all Protestant sects
   - (E) the Society of Jesus

3. Which best describes the 18th century *philosophes*?
   - (A) They used their satiric skills to support the *ancien régime*.
   - (B) They believed in the primacy of emotion in human affairs.
   - (C) They argued for social improvement based on piety and prayer.
   - (D) They believed in the inevitability of human progress based upon natural law.
   - (E) They rejected empirical science as incompatible with Deism.

4. Which describes the political situation in Germany in 1800, prior to Napoleon's conquests?
   - (A) Thirty-nine separate and independent states
   - (B) Over 300 independent political entities
   - (C) A unified empire of all the German-speaking peoples in Europe
   - (D) A confederation of the Northern German states
   - (E) Part of the Hapsburg Empire

Answers   1. A   2. C   3. D   4. B

Comments   *Identification* questions are answerable primarily if you know the information. Analysis is applicable in eliminating inappropriate choices, but very specific information is required to zero in on the one correct answer.

If you don't have the requisite information and elimination through analysis is not possible, don't answer the question!

Question 1 is the "purest" form of identification in that it requires knowledge of the significance and context of *The Prince.* Choices B, C, and E can be eliminated only if you know the basic subject matter of the book, that Castiglione wrote the classic on etiquette, that the New Monarchies supported Machiavelli's ideas. Choice D is incorrect because Machiavelli's reason for writing the book was to correct the political chaos that had been caused by disunity in the Italy of his day.

Question 2 also demands very specific information, but it is easier because the concept of the Elect or the Saints is central to Calvinism's distinguishing belief in predestination.

Question 3 allows more analysis than the previous two. Since the philosophes were critics of society before the French Revolution and the ancien régime was the existing form of government, choice A can be eliminated. Since the concept of the primacy of emotion is part of the Romantic movement that followed the French Revolution, choice B is out. Most of the philosophes were Deists, so choice C is inaccurate. Choice E is wrong because Deism is an outgrowth of the findings of empirical or natural science.

Question 4 allows some of the answers to be eliminated by applying some general understandings of German history. Choice C is easily eliminated because there has never been "a unified empire" of all the German-speaking peoples in Europe. Choice E is out because, even at its height in the early 16th century, the Hapsburg Empire did not include all of Germany. Since the North German Confederation was a creation of Bismarck just prior to the unification of Germany in the latter third of the 19th century, choice D can be eliminated. Choices A and B are left. You would have to know that Napoleon tended to consolidate independent states after his conquests in both Italy and Germany to pick choice B as the correct answer.

Analysis lends itself to working out the answer with more general understandings or less specific information by considering cause and effect relationships or sorting out the chronology.

Twenty to 25 percent of the multiple-choice questions tend to be *analysis.*

Samples of Analysis Questions

1. Which of the following did NOT contribute to bringing about the Industrial Revolution?
   (A) The supremacy of Parliament in 1688, which favored the interests of large landowners
   (B) The improvement of food production, which occurred after the enclosure movement
   (C) The shift of the rural population to cities and towns
   (D) The widespread employment of the internal combustion engine
   (E) The use of steam power

2. Which best describes the nature of German military tactics in 1940?
    (A) Use of highly mobile armored forces with air support
    (B) Establishment of "impregnable" fortresses on the borders
    (C) Use of mazes of trenches to consolidate military gains
    (D) Massed infantry attacks across a broad front
    (E) Use of "terror weapons" such as V-2 rockets

3. A major result of the Treaty of Utrecht in 1714 was
    (A) that French became the "universal tongue" in Europe
    (B) the restoration of the "balance of power" on the continent
    (C) an end to the Wars of Revolution
    (D) the ascension of Louis XIV to the French throne
    (E) an end to absolutism in France

Answers   **1.** D   **2.** A   **3.** B

Comments   *Analysis* questions let you eliminate some answers if you can figure out that one thing could not cause another because it came later in time. Knowing the general time frame of events and developments helps immeasurably.

It is worth the trouble and time to try to figure out the answer to this type of question.

Question 1 is a classic cause-effect problem. Beware of "not." If you can determine the sequence of events, you can eliminate certain choices. Since the Enclosure Acts were passed by a Parliament that represented the interests of the rich landowners, and since they led to the migration to cities of small farmers displaced by the fencing off of common pasture lands, a labor force was created. This cause-effect relationship eliminates choices A, B, and C as factors that did not contribute to the Industrial Revolution. Even if you did not know that the use of steam power to pump water seepage from mines, to run textile mills, and to move transport was a crucial factor in industrialization, you can eliminate it if you consider the time frame of the other choice. The internal combustion engine is a late 19th century invention; the Industrial Revolution occurred from 1780 to 1830.

Question 2 can be answered by determining the general time frame of each tactic. If you did not know that the infamous *Blitzkrieg* or "lightning war" was the German tactic employing fast armor and air support that was used to defeat France during the spring of 1940, you can still use the process of elimination. Choices C and D were tactics of the "war of attrition" during the First World War. Choice E was used by the Germans near the end of World War II as a desperation measure. Choice B was a World War I tactic that was employed by the victors, the French, and would not have been used by the losers, the Germans. Winners tend to play the game the way they won; losers change the rules.

Question 3 can be answered primarily by determining time sequence. Choice C is out because the Wars of Revolution happened after the French Revolution began in 1789. Choice E is out because absolutism ended in France because of the French Revolution. Choice D is out because Louis was king during the wars that ended with the Treaty of Utrecht. He took the throne in 1647. Choice A can be eliminated because the long and illustrious reign of Louis XIV helped make French the language of diplomacy and refinement.

Sample of a Quotation Question

Quotation analysis, like most analysis questions, can be done with less specific information than identification requires. Again chronology and cause-effect help in the process of elimination.

About 10 percent of the multiple-choice questions tend to be *quotation* analysis.

"Not only was he accused of imprisoning and torturing or murdering his enemies, but he set into place the whole apparatus of totalitarian repression. He denied basic human rights in pushing forward his policy of industrialization, and the human cost can be measured in the deaths of tens of millions of his own countrymen. His detractors also accuse him of governing according to a 'cult of personality.'"

The individual referred to is
- (A)   Napoleon
- (B)   Lenin
- (C)   Hitler
- (D)   Stalin
- (E)   Mao Zedong

Answer and Comments

(D) Choice A is incorrect because totalitarianism is an invention of the 20th century and because Napoleon neither effected industrialization nor killed millions of his countrymen. Choice B is out because Lenin did not rule long enough to do this and because the description does not seem to fit his character. Choice C is out because although Hitler murdered 12,000,000 people as part of his racist policies, they were not all his countrymen. Choices D and E would seem to fit. "Cult of personality" is the key. It was the phrase used by Nikita Khrushchev in his "de-Stalinization" speech a few years after the death of Stalin.

Chronology was the prime sorter here. A specific bit of information was the last piece of the puzzle.

Sample of an Interpretation Question

Interpretation can involve identifying the artist, style, subject, or period of a work of art; it may require interpretation of a cartoon, photo, or picture. Unless you know enough about it to identify what is required or unless you can apply analysis to figure out what is required, it is best to skip this type of question.

Less than 10 percent of the multiple-choice questions are this type.

What innovation in painting was developed by Renaissance artists?

(A)   The use of color
(B)   The use of religious themes
(C)   The illusion of depth
(D)   The use of symbolism
(E)   The use of abstract geometric figures

Answer and Comments

(C) Perspective, or the illusion of depth, was a technical innovation of the Renaissance painters. Religious themes and symbolism were used by the medievals; color was used even by the ancients. Abstract art belongs to the 20th century.

Sample of Map Interpretation Question

Map interpretation questions require very general map skills and less general information to work out. They are worth the time and trouble.

Less than 10 percent of the multiple-choice questions are map interpretations.

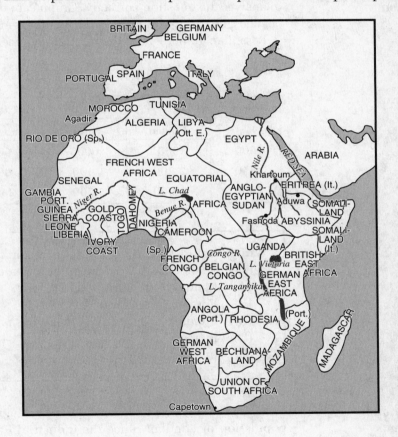

The map on the previous page represents Africa in what year?
- (A)   1880
- (B)   1914
- (C)   1939
- (D)   1946
- (E)   1975

Answer and Comments

(B) Go for the obviously incorrect choices first. Choice E is out because the map does not show most of the nations of contemporary Africa. Choices D and C are incorrect because the Italian and German colonies would certainly have been lost after the defeats in World War II, and the German colonies were seized after World War I. That leaves choice A, which is wrong because Africa was terra incognita before the start of imperialism in 1880, and choice B, which is correct because it marks the highwater period of imperialism.

Sample of a Chart Question

Graphs and charts frequently provide all the information necessary in order to answer the question correctly. Graphs are diagrams representing successive changes; charts are information sheets that employ tables or graphs.

Less than 10 percent of the multiple-choice questions are of this type.

POPULATION OF CITIES IN THOUSANDS

Year	Cities				
	London	Paris	Antwerp	Berlin	Moscow
1800	960	600	60	170	250
1850	2,700	1,400	90	500	360
1900	6,500	3,700	280	2,700	1,000

Which would be the most likely explanation for the population rise between 1800 and 1900 in the cities included on the chart above?
- (A)   Malthusian "unbridled lust"
- (B)   Foreign immigration
- (C)   Population shift from other cities
- (D)   Increase in the average life span
- (E)   Industrialization

Answer and Comments

The clue to the correct answer is in the early, nearly sevenfold increase of the population of London. Since the Industrial Revolution caused a mass movement from the countryside to the cities and since it began in Britain then caught on later in the rest of Europe, the answer is choice E, industrialization.

Free-Response Section

This section includes

Two thematic essay questions on two major topics out of a choice of six; the essays are in two groups, and you must choose one from each group.

One document-based essay (DBQ), which uses historical sources to measure the ability to work with evidence.

A 15-minute required reading period for analyzing the documents in the DBQ, for outlining the answer, and, if time allows, for looking over the thematic essay choices; *45 minutes* for the DBQ; *70 minutes* for the thematic essays.

Interpreting the Essay Questions

In both the thematic essay and the document-based question (DBQ), it is necessary to understand the way in which the answer is to be presented. In order to do this, you must interpret the *key term* in the question.

Examples of Key Terms

1. *Defend or refute* (argue for or against a specific statement by framing an essay that uses *factual support*)
   Sample:
   "World War II was the inevitable result of a failure of the democracies to confront aggression by totalitarian dictatorships."
   Defend or refute this with factual evidence from the diplomatic history of the 1930s.
2. *Analyze* (examine in detail; determine relationships; explain)
   Sample:
   Analyze the ways in which the Protestant Reformation fostered both the growth of capitalism and the rise of modern science.
3. *Evaluate* (judge the worth of; discuss advantages and disadvantages, pluses and minuses)
   Sample:
   Evaluate both the domestic policies and the foreign involvements of the government of France during the reign of Louis XIV.
4. *To what extent and in what ways* (how and how much?)
   Sample:
   "*To what extent and in what ways* did Napoleon carry out the ideals of the French Revolution?"
5. *Assess the validity* (judge the value of; determine the truth)
   Sample:
   "The religious wars of the 16th and 17th centuries were more the result of the territorial ambitions of rival states and the economic interests of competing factions than of doctrinal differences."
   Assess the validity of this statement.

6. *Contrast and compare* (show differences and examine for similarities)
   Sample:
   "Contrast and compare the art and architecture of the Renaissance with that of the Romantic period and explain how each reflected the prevailing culture."

7. *Explain* (offer the meaning, the cause, the reason for; make clear; detail)
   Sample:
   "Explain how the theories of Copernicus, Galileo, Kepler, and Newton impacted the religious beliefs and intellectual trends of the 17th and 18th centuries."

8. Discuss (consider various points of view; write about; examine)
   Sample:
   "Discuss the accomplishments of the various governments in France during the French Revolution."

9. Describe (tell about; offer an account or a word picture)
   Sample:
   "Describe the life-style of noble women in Italy during the Italian Renaissance. Refer to family life, political status, and economic conditions."

Additional sample and practice free-response questions will appear in the review chapters and in the sample Advanced Placement Examination in European History.

The Document-Based Essay Question (DBQ)

The DBQ is designed to test your ability to analyze documentary materials and to use these materials to support an essay. *It is not a test of prior knowledge.* Although it requires skills similar to those used by historians interpreting primary source materials, the documents appear in an order that facilitates answering the accompanying essay question.

DBQ Do's

1. Read and interpret the essay question.
2. Read and analyze each of the documents in turn.
3. Remember that none of the documents is irrelevant to the issue, but some are more pertinent and revealing than others.
4. Determine which of the documents are more important to the issue and make a mark in order to return to them.
5. Identify the point of view of the source—where the author stands and possible biases.
6. Return to the more important documents for further evaluation.
7. Outline an essay that incorporates an interpretation of the documents into an original essay.
8. No one answer is right. By using various documents, you can make a strong case from any number of points of view.
9. It is not necessary to cite all of the documents.

10. *The documents must be integrated into the essay response.* Refer to the documents in making your case by summarizing or briefly quoting, but not by simply giving the number.

DBQ Don'ts

1. Don't *simply* list or *simply* summarize each or any of the documents.
2. Don't forget to draw on the documents to support your essay.
3. Don't fail to answer the question in your effort to incorporate the documents.
4. Don't parrot the points of view reflected in the documents.

Come back to the DBQ Do's and Don'ts after you have looked over the sample DBQ.

Sample DBQ

Answer the essay below by analyzing the documents that follow and integrating this analysis into your answer. Other pertinent references, not included here, may be used.

"Contrast and compare the literary freedom available to novelists and other fiction writers in the Stalinist U.S.S.R. and the United States after World War II."

Document A

SOVIET LITERARY CREATIVITY ABOUNDS

This year, six fictional works have been published in the U.S.S.R. which depict the heroic struggle of the Soviet People against the fascist war machine from 1941 to 1945. Each novel is a gritty, realistic portrayal of combat, of personalities, of human sacrifice. Never before has fiction been so close to truth.

Press release to the Western Media,
Soviet Bureau of Information. (Nov. 7, 1948)

Document B

Memo: To all fiction writers.

Re: Acceptable references in works about the recent war.

Date: 3 January 1947

Hereafter, World War II is to be referred to as "The Great Patriotic War." Any fictional depictions of the events from June 1941 to May 1945 must conform to the following prescriptions:

1. Any portrayal of Soviet citizens must emphasize patriotic commitment to the Anti-Fascist Crusade.

2. Any representation of the peoples' enemies must stress inhuman characteristics and bestial atrocities.

3. Any references to the former allies of the U.S.S.R. (such as the U.S.A. or Great Britain) must emphasize the Capitalist/Imperialist conspiracy.

Union of Communist Novelists

Document C

27 July 1949

Vladimir vanished a week ago today. Rumor has it that he has already been shipped to the Gulag. Not so much as a hearing! Neither his publisher nor the members of his writer's cell are talking. He has disappeared hardly a month after his short story, critical of the role of "Comrade S" in the horrific losses of the early days, was circulated in handwritten copies. A coincidence? I am sure now that the man following me for the last two days is a member of the MKVD.

Personal diary of a Soviet novelist smuggled to the West
after her mysterious death in the fall of 1949.

Document D

The worldwide communist conspiracy, whose headquarters are in the Kremlin, has targeted all free expression for a slow but painful death. Droves of Soviet dramatists, novelists, and journalists have been executed for failing to follow the party line. Reports, smuggled to the Free World, indicate that the teaching of literature has been banned in Soviet schools so that the reading and writing of fiction will disappear within a generation. Not content with controlling the print media in Russia, the Reds have used selective assassination and intimidation to silence writers in the West who have had the courage to reveal their plan for global dominance, engineering their placement with "pinko fellow-travelers" who are critical of the United States.

Excerpt from *Monolithic Communism,* a book published in 1951
by J. Ed Garr, former advisor to Senator Joseph McCarthy's
Senate Sub-committee on Government Operations.

Document E

SECRET

From: Special *ad hoc* assistant to House Un-American Activities Committee

To: Administrative Staff of the Committee.

Re: Hearings in Hollywood, October 1947.

A list of screen-writers, actors, and directors, whose Communist leanings or past affiliation with the Communist Party render them unfit to make films for the American public, will be forthcoming. Every effort will be made to "encourage" studio and broadcasting executives to comply with a *blacklist* to bar these individuals from future employment in the entertainment industry.

Document F

Go with the proven formula! A little sex. A fight or two. A laugh here and there. And Americanism, Americanism, more Americanism. That's what sells.

The Wisdom of Moguls, a study of the studio system in the film industry.

Comments on the DBQ

Refer to "DBQ Do's and Don'ts" on pages 18–19.

Read and interpret the question: To "contrast and compare" requires that you show differences and examine for similarities. You must determine and make clear to what extent writers in the U.S.S.R. and in the United States were free to write and publish after World War II. Was there censorship? If so, what was its nature and how and by whom was it enforced?

Read and analyze each of the documents in turn: Are they all pertinent to your answer? Are some more useful than others? What is their total effect? Do they "cancel each other out"? Do you get a "big picture"?

Read the question again and relate specific documents to framing an answer: What is the relative veracity of an official government release compared to a personal diary? How does one document tend to contradict another? To which would you lend the most credence?

Outline your essay: Interpret the documents in order to analyze and determine how fiction writers in the Soviet Union fared under Stalin and how they fared in the United States during the "Red Scare" of the late 1940s and 1950s. Refer to anything else that you know about the period that is relevant to your answer. You may cite all or some of the documents. Be sure not to cite them by number or to simply summarize them. USE THEM TO ANSWER THE QUESTION!

Before writing the essay: Read the question again. Glance through the documents. Check your outline to make sure it addresses the question.

Sample Answer for the DBQ

The Stalinist Soviet Union was one of the most terrible totalitarian dictatorships of the 20th century. The collapse of the U.S.S.R. has revealed horrors that not even the most rabid anti-Communist Cold Warrior could have imagined. While suspicions of the state-sponsored extermination of tens of millions of Soviet citizens has been confirmed by archival evidence, new truths about the habitual, deliberate, large-scale violation of every human right have emerged. Few in the West except the most self-delusionary or rigidly dogmatic were shocked to learn that the Communists under Stalin inflicted famine on its own people, sent dissenters to the Gulag, miscalculated and mishandled the threat of foreign invasion, and wreaked havoc on every basic freedom including that of expression.

It is easier to see evil in one's enemies, but much harder to detect our own faults. America—"land of the free," the world's first and most successful deliberately designed constitutional democracy—also systematically denied freedom of expression to its people. It was not with the efficient and odious apparatus of a dictatorial government but rather with the tyrannies of fear and prejudice. No writers were shot by the secret police but some were driven to suicide. None were shipped off to Siberia, but many were denied the right to publish or produce. "Freedom of the press" and artistic creativity in the United States may not have been crushed by a Soviet-style state-sponsored censorship, but they were restrained and thwarted by "blacklisting" and crass commercialism.

Soviet Literary Creativity Abounds says the puffed-up headline of the self-congratulatory press release by the Soviet Bureau of Information. "Gritty, realistic portrayal(s)" are promised in the works of Soviet fiction that depict the war against the Nazis. The memo to all fiction writers from the Union of Communist Novelists puts this promise into another light. Rules. The rules of the totalitarian state to make sure that the rulers look good because their people were united, their enemies were evil incarnate, and their allies were plotters. It is very significant that the memo predated the press release.

"Vladimir vanished" and "I am sure now that the man following me is a member of the MKVD" completes the picture of brutal repression. The implication of the memo from the Union of Novelists is that if you want to be published, you have to belong and if you want to belong you have to follow the party line. The diary is much more ominous: if you try to write the truth, the secret police will find out and you may well disappear.

McCarthyism is what history refers to as the witch-hunting Red Scare of the early Cold War. A pompous senator and opportunistic congressmen—supported by legions of the ignorant—played on fears of nuclear war and a world-wide Communist conspiracy to destroy personal lives, to impugn the reputations of revered and powerful public figures, and to instill popular suspicion of our basic institutions by simply making unsubstantiated accusations. "There were Communist spies in government, in the military, in the schools everywhere." In this context, the excerpt from the book by one of the McCarthy Sub-committee's advisors is an example of the pot calling the kettle black. The underlying idea of McCarthyism, whether practiced by the senator and his cohorts or by the House Un-American Activities Committee (a curious name considering that the very nature of Americanism, diversity, renders difficult the designation of what is "Un-American") seems to be that it is acceptable for certain Americans to deny other Americans freedom of expression in order to prevent the Communists from doing it. The "blacklist" probably rarely appeared on paper; word of mouth was enough to destroy reputations and end illustrious careers. "There is nothing more frightening than ignorance in action" said a poet. The power to censor—by blacklist or secret police—is the power to enslave.

"The proven formula." This alone is enough to make *"The Wisdom of Moguls"* a contradiction in terms. How many worthy pieces of writing, good ideas, fragments of the truth have been lost to "the bottom line," the "ratings system," the mass appeal mentality of the publishing, broadcasting, and film industries? More insult added to the injury of "blacklisting."

Literary freedom was significantly denied in both the Stalinist Soviet Union and the democratic United States in the postwar period of the late forties and the fifties. The methods were different, though, and the effects varied. In the U.S.S.R., the institutions of the police state—the secret police, the government-controlled unions—enforced censorship. In the United States, public fears and prejudices were played upon by ruthless politicians who intimidated or destroyed writers in the name of American orthodoxy, and the almighty dollar limited the free flow of ideas to the narrow stream of the "least common denominator to appeal to the biggest possible audience." American writers were not silenced by execution or exile as were their Soviet counterparts. Freedom of the press and of speech in America eventually righted the excesses and injustices of McCarthyism. But in both great nations, truth was denied and truthtellers were punished.

Comments on the Sample Answer for the DBQ

5—Extremely well qualified

This essay demonstrates how the DBQ should be answered. It avoids the major "Don'ts."

It does not simply list, refer to by number, or summarize the documents.

It does not forget to draw on the documents, if not necessarily all of them, to support its answer.

It does not fail to address the question in its effort to incorporate the documents.

The essay is well-written; it draws on the documents appropriately; it adds relevant references to the period:

"....state-sponsored extermination...." in the U.S.S.R.

"....tyrannies of fear and prejudice...." in the United States under McCarthyism

It is a well-balanced consideration of the assaults on freedom of expression in the U.S.S.R. and the United States after World War II, drawing on the documents and supporting its argument with relevant additional information.

Thematic Essay Question

The thematic essay part of the free-response section requires you to answer two interpretive questions that measure both knowledge and analytical skills. They are designed to test your understanding of the events and trends of the political-diplomatic, economic-social, and cultural-intellectual history of Europe from 1450 to contemporary times. Like any essay question, they are open to subjective interpretation both in answering and in evaluating the answer. It helps to be a good writer, to interpret the question accurately, to design an approach, to marshal relevant data, to present it all clearly. The essays require a broader and deeper understanding of the history than the multiple-choice section does, but they can be a showpiece for a good grasp of the subject.

Hints for Answering the Thematic Essay Questions

1. Read all the choices before deciding on which two to do.
2. Your primary consideration should be *how much you know about the specific subject*. This may seem obvious, but it is easy to pass over a question if you are confused about what it asks. Read. Reread those questions that encompass areas you have focused on in class or in your studies.
3. Interpret the *key terms*. (See pages 17–18.)
4. Make your choice by *mentally framing* the argument of your essay. (The "argument" is the point of view, the proof, the statement, the thesis, the core of your essay, and you should follow your intuitions since they flow from what you know most about.)
5. Read the question again and *jot down anything* that comes to mind.
6. Organize your essay by *outlining* your argument. Don't fret over format; you are the only one to see or use the outline.
7. *Gather facts* to support your argument. (If you are not certain of a fact—a date, an event, a cause, a person—*don't use it.*)
8. *Check for consistency.* What seems like supporting evidence may actually contradict your assertions.

9. Now, you are ready to write. Make a *clear statement of the intent* of your argument in the introduction, a *clear summary* of your argument in the conclusion.
10. *Reread! Rewrite!* Delete. Add. "Substance takes precedence over neatness." Don't be afraid to cross out words, sentences, whole paragraphs, whole pages.

How to Write an Essay

It is a lot easier than you think.... if you pick the right question, interpret the terms correctly, and follow a few simple procedures. The tricks to picking the right question and interpreting its terms are given in the preceding section.

What then are these "simple" procedures?

THE ESSENCE OF YOUR ESSAY IS THE BODY

It is here that you do your job of showing "to what extent and in what ways," or of "assessing the validity," or of "contrasting and comparing," or of "explaining," and so on. The introduction simply points out the direction your argument will take. The conclusion simply summarizes your argument. What you have to do is write a clear, convincing argument in your essay. (Remember, an "argument," as used here, is whatever you write to answer the question.)

The Simple Procedures

First, ask yourself what the question wants to know.

Second, ask yourself what you know about it.

Third, ask yourself how you put it into words.

Sample Question

> *To what extent and in what ways* did Napoleon carry out the ideals of the French Revolution?

First, what does the question want to know?

"How and how much did Napoleon, an autocrat, fulfill the democratic aims of the Revolution?"

Second, ask yourself what you know about it?

Napoleon was a dictator and an emperor and both are generally undemocratic roles.

He made domestic reforms in the law, education, and government that furthered democracy. He carried the ideals of the Revolution—"liberty, equality, fraternity"—to other countries during his conquests. He had personal reasons for trying to change the "old order."

Third, how should you put it into words?

Write about the historical irony: one of history's "bad guys"—a dictator, conqueror, and vainglorious emperor—actually helped the experiment in democracy, called the French Revolution, get put into practice.

Use the *Simple Procedures* to plan the body of every essay.

Use the *Hints for Answering the Thematic Essay Questions* to do the actual writing.

PART TWO REVIEW SECTION

CHAPTER 1 The Italian Renaissance, The Northern Renaissance (1450–1550)

Overview

The term "Renaissance," a rebirth, is misleading. It implies that the 15th and 16th centuries marked a distinct awakening for Europeans from the "darkness" of the Middle Ages. Actually, the medieval period gave rise to the basic institutions of Europe, its laws, languages, economics. The elite culture that developed during the *quattrocento* (Italian for 15th century) in the city-states of the Italian peninsula, though, not only borrowed from the ancient cultures of Greece and Rome but also expressed a new conception of humankind—individualism—through innovative art and literature. It was in these independent domains, governed by a merchant class, despots, or republicans, that pure secularism (a belief that life was more than a preparation for the hereafter) first appeared in the modern world.

Humanism (a literary movement that was truly modern in that a class of nonclerical writers concerned themselves with secular issues) rose in Italy in the 14th and 15th centuries and found a special affinity with classical Greek and Roman culture. In Northern Europe, the "pagan" humanism of the Italian Renaissance was rejected in favor of a blend of religion and classical literature. Christian humanists, such as Erasmus and Thomas More, tried to recapture the moral force of early Christianity by studying the Greek and Hebrew texts of the Bible and the writings of the Church Fathers.

Whether or not the Renaissance marks the beginning of the modern age, it provided a conception of the role and destiny of humankind vastly different from that of the Middle Ages, and its artistic achievements influenced the culture of all of Europe.

Since the Renaissance is defined less by specific events than by individual accomplishments and ideas, the following review focuses on significant personalities, achievements, and concepts. First, though, a few words about the setting for one of the most creative periods in all of human history.

The Italian Renaissance

The Italian City-States By the 15th century, certain Northern Italian towns—which had been trade centers of the Roman Empire—had expanded into independent city-states that ruled wide areas of the surrounding countryside.

"Geography is destiny" proved true for the Italians of the 14th and 15th centuries. Fragmented as a nation since the fall of Rome, a battleground for the more unified peoples of Europe, they took advantage of their proximity to the sea and applied the energy that springs from being always at the focus of crisis to establish a seagoing trade with the peoples in the eastern Mediterranean. They became the "middlemen" of Europe.

THE MAJOR CITY-STATES

Republic of Florence (considered the cultural center of the Italian Renaissance; often compared to ancient Athens for its utter brilliance over a brief period)

Republic of Genoa

Duchy of Milan

Rome, the Papal states

Naples, Kingdom of the Two Sicilies

Venice, Venetian Republic

Venice, Genoa, and Pisa (in the Republic of Florence) used their strategic locations on the Mediterranean to control the European trade with the Middle East and Asia; Florence, and, to a lesser extent, Rome, Naples, and Milan thrived as manufacturing and market centers. Bankers from all of these prosperous cities made profitable loans to the popes and to the monarchs of Europe and financed successful commercial ventures.

This powerful middle class of merchants and bankers controlled the governments of the city-states and served as patrons to the artistic geniuses of the times. Their newfound wealth encouraged appreciation of earthly pleasures and diminished dedication to the pious traditions of the Middle Ages. It was not that most were irreligious, but rather that accidents of history and geography presented them with great wealth, far beyond any expectations of the subsistence feudal economy that had ruled Europe for a thousand years. Money is meant to be spent. It just so happened that the more they spent on the beautiful handiwork of the skilled artisans in their cities, the more beautiful things were made for the buying. Beauty for its own sake, and art for art's sake, values lost to Europeans with the end of the ancient world, replaced the medieval notion that art not dedicated to God is irreverent. To these people, the world could be changed without the help of God. "Money is power" was never more true. Secularism was born. The rich nurtured it; the lower classes copied it.

The Medici Family

This was the most famous dynasty of those merchants and bankers who used their vast wealth both to govern the city-states and to patronize illustrious creators in the arts.

Giovanni De'Medici (d. 1429): Merchant and banker of Florence, founder of the dynasty. He could be considered one of the world's first modern people, an ultimate adapter who ignored the church's prohibitions of lending for interest to provide the necessary funds for a changing world economy. Although his son and great-grandson were the ones who brought glory to the family name by spending the fortune that he established, his originality is reflected in his deeds rather than his ideas, and he is one of the people of Europe whose restless genius molded the modern world.

Cosimo De'Medici (1389–1464): Son of Giovanni who used the family fortune to fill the vacuum of power created by the lack of a national monarchy. Allied with other powerful families of Florence, he became unofficial ruler of the republic.

Lorenzo the Magnificent (1449–1492): Cosimo's grandson, not only the republic's ruler but a lavish patron of the arts. He personified the Renaissance attitude of living life rather than waiting for its fulfillment after death. His genius was his recognition and support of the creative talent in his city; his luck was to be surrounded by geniuses.

The Medici family ruled the Grand Duchy of Tuscany, of which Florence was the principal city, well into the 18th century. Two popes, many cardinals, and two queens of France belonged to the family.

Individualism, A New Conception of Humankind

"Man is the measure of all things." A sense of human power replaced religious awe. Pleasure and accomplishment superseded the medieval dedication to the cloistered life of the clergy. Instead of the disdain for the concerns of this world that the piety of the Middle Ages had fostered, people now valued involvement, a life of activity.

Virtu: Literally, "the quality of being a man"; possible for a woman to express, but expected among aggressive males, the "movers and shakers" of the day; whatever a person's pursuit—in learning, the arts, or even in war—it meant living up to one's highest potential and excelling in all endeavors. The Renaissance man was an all-around man, as comfortable with the pen or the brush as with the sword; lover, poet, painter, conversationalist.

The Arts as an Expression of Individualism

Before the Renaissance, the Church was the greatest patron of the arts. Painters and sculptors labored anonymously to fill the churches and cathedrals of the Middle Ages with figures of the saints that lacked the proportions and animation of real human forms or faces. During the Renaissance, the new commercial class and the governments of the city-states supported the arts. Even though the art was religious in nature, the forms were anatomically proportional, the faces filled with emotion, and the artists reveled in their individuality of style.

Architecture adapted Greco-Roman symmetry, classical columns, arch, and dome. Architects such as *Filippo Brunelleschi* (1377–1446) and *Leon Battista Alberti* (1404–1472) studied ancient Roman buildings and used their principles of design to build cathedrals.

Sculpture was freestanding, not designed to fit in niches of churches, and showed nude subjects in the Greek tradition in both religious and mythological representations. *Lorenzo Ghiberti* (1378–1455) sculpted a set of bronze doors for the Florentine baptistry with not only crowds of human figures but the illusion of depth.

Painting was primarily religious in theme but radically different from medieval art because of the invention of oil paints and because of the illusion of three dimensions created by precise variation of size (perspective). All art was less symbolic, more representational, depicting real people in recognizable settings and glorifying the beauty of the corporeal world. *Giotto* (1267–1337) painted on walls in Florentine buildings and created the illusions of depth and movement. *Massaccio* (1401–1428) used light and shadow, nude figures, and the illusion of perspective. *Sandro Botticelli* (1444–1510) painted themes from classical mythology such as his *Birth of Venus. Raphael* (1483–1520) is considered one of the greatest painters of any era; his portraits and Madonnas epitomize the Renaissance style.

The Greatest of the Great

Leonardo Da Vinci (1452–1519): personification of the "Renaissance man." Painter, sculptor, architect, engineer, writer, scientist—the versatility of his genius marks the last time that a single human could command virtually all the realms of knowledge and create masterworks in several areas of competence. His *Mona Lisa* and his *Last Supper* rival any of the world's great paintings for the perfection of their execution and for their sheer beauty.

Michelangelo Buonarroti (1475–1564): Primarily a sculptor whose *Pieta*, Mary mourning the limp body of Christ across her lap, is often considered the most perfect marble carving. His awesome statues of *Moses* and *David* are unrivaled masterpieces that reflect religiosity and real human emotion. His paintings on the *Sistine Chapel* in Rome, over which he labored for four years, portray biblical and allegorical figures with power, grace, and human clarity. He glorified God by depicting the beauty of his earthly creations.

Humanism

This was a literary movement distinct from the writing of the late Middle Ages in both its subject matter (it dealt with issues of politics and personal concern outside the realm of religion) and in its practitioners (laypeople who considered writing a profession rather than a pursuit of the clergy). They drew on antiquity, which ironically had been preserved by monks doing the laborious copying of ancient manuscripts by hand. They wrote in Italian rather than Latin, and thereby created the first European vernacular literature. The works of the great poet *Dante,* especially the *Divine Comedy*, and the speech patterns of Florence became the standard form of modern Italian.

Petrarch (d. 1374): Considered the first "modern" writer, he wrote sonnets in Italian, other works in Latin, and he used writing to consider the ebb and flow of his life and the human condition itself.

Boccaccio (1313–1375): A contemporary of Petrarch and like him a Florentine, his most famous work is the *Decameron,* entertaining tales that reflected upon the human condition.

Bruni: A chancellor of the Republic of Florence in the late 14th century, he wrote perhaps the first modern history, an account of the development of Florence, using narrative, drawing on authentic sources, and introducing new historical periods.

Baldassare Castiglione (1478–1529): Offered a manual for the manners of the modern gentleman, *The Book of the Courtier:* A gentleman is trained for polite company, poised and well dressed, skilled in arms and sports, capable of making music and conversation, a reader of the classics, a social mixer who is good humored, lighthearted, and considerate of others' feelings. It was a civilized antidote to the crude social habits of the day in which even the wellborn spit on the floor, wiped noses on sleeves, ate without utensils, shrieked, and sulked. Prosperity had bred civility.

Niccolo Machiavelli (1469–1527): *The Prince* is the first political science work, an observation of how governments actually rule without moral judgment or exhortation. It is one of the most maligned and misinterpreted books of modern times, called "cynical and ruthless," the "handbook of dictators," and the origin of the concept "The end justifies the means." Machiavelli discovered that the successful governments of his times— whether Italian city-states or national monarchies—acted in their own political interests, making war or keeping the peace, true to their word or deceitful, benevolent or brutal when it was useful. Religion had virtually ceased to influence the process of governing as the rise of the nation-state became the ultimate goal, and *The Prince* (1513) offers keen insights. It was meant as a guide to the survival of the separate and independent city-states of Italy, which were vulnerable to the predatory powers in the north.

The Northern Renaissance

The Renaissance in the north of Europe reached its greatest fruition in Germany, France, Switzerland, the Low Countries (Holland and Belgium), and England. It differed from the Italian Renaissance primarily because it emphasized religion. The pagan humanism of Italy glorified the non-Christian culture of the ancient world; the Christian humanism of the north drew upon the Hebrew and Greek texts of the Bible and the writings of the Church Fathers to invigorate Christian tradition.

Germany

On the eve of the Reformation, at the turn of the 16th century, Germany was at the heart of European progress. Politically diverse (the German-speaking world included most of central Europe, Switzerland, and parts of the

Netherlands), its economy thrived anyway. Towns sprouted, grew, traded. Banking expanded: the Fuggers and other German families controlled more capital than the Italian bankers and all other Europeans combined.

Science and Technology

Gutenberg (d. 1468) invented the first movable-type *printing press* around 1450.

Regiomontanus (Johann Muller, 1436–1476) and *Nicholas of Cusa* (1401–1464) laid the foundations for modern mathematics and science in the 15th century.

Behaim and *Schoner* developed the era's most accurate maps. *Copernicus* (1473–1543) upset the time-honored *geocentric view* (that heavenly bodies revolved around the earth) of astronomy with calculations that offered proof of a *heliocentric* (sun-centered) system.

The notion that humankind could understand and control nature evolved from the work of these Germans.

Mysticism

This involved the belief that an individual, alone, unaided by church or sacraments, could commune with God. The mystics—such as *Meister Eckhart* (d. 1327) and *Thomas à Kempis* (1471), author of the inspirational *Imitation of Christ*—pursued religious depth rather than rebellion. They stayed true to the Church, but sought to offer, to the few faithful who could understand, a substance that transcended traditional religiosity.

Gerard Groote, a Dutch lay preacher, organized the *Brothers of the Common Life* in the late 14th century, a religious organization that stressed personal virtues of Christianity rather than doctrine. Its movement of *modern devotion* preached Christ-like love, tolerance, and humility.

Both mysticism and the basic religious devotion of many laypeople contrasted, ominously, with the worldliness and smugness of the clergy.

Desiderius Erasmus, "The Christian Gentleman" (1456–1536) personified Christian humanism. A man of letters, he disdained the Middle Ages, ignored hard philosophy, admired antiquity, and wrote on humanist issues in purified Latin. The ultimate moderate, he championed gradual reform, ridiculed hypocrisy among the powerful, distrusted the fickle opinions of common people, and abhorred violence. He satirized the worldliness of the clergy in *The Praise of Folly*; he offered a model of practical Christian behavior in *Handbook of a Christian Knight*; he wrote new Greek and Latin editions of the Bible. A confidant of kings and a critic of church abuses, he aimed at gentle reform of the Church from within. He was the most famous and influential intellectual of his times, and he used his writings and his example to preach peace, reason, tolerance, and loving reform. It is a convincing notion that had Martin Luther not pushed for radical reform in the early 1600s, the *Erasmian spirit* might have corrected the abuses of the Church while maintaining its structure. (This is a *hypothesis contrary to fact*. Since it did not indeed happen, there is no way we can know what would have followed if it had.)

England

The Renaissance here coincided with, and was fostered by, the reign of *Elizabeth I* (1558–1603). An era of intense nationalism, produced by the resolution of dynastic rivalries and religious turmoil, it gave birth to perhaps the greatest vernacular literature of all time. The dramatist *Christopher Marlowe,* the poet *Edmund Spenser*, and the scientist *Francis Bacon* helped form modern English during the *Elizabethan Age*. The greatest writer in English—maybe in any language—*William Shakespeare* reflected the influence of the dramatists of the ancient world and also the writers of the Italian Renaissance. He single-handedly set the standard for the English language.

During the reign of Elizabeth's father, *Henry VIII*, a contemporary of Erasmus, *Sir Thomas More*, had fostered the Erasmian spirit in his *Utopia,* a book that criticized the correctible abuses of various institutions and that offered the blueprint for a perfect society. A devout Roman Catholic, he was beheaded for not supporting the king against the Pope during the English Reformation.

France

After the *Hundred Years' War* (1337–1453), the monarchy in France was strengthened by a renewal of commerce, which expanded and enriched the middle class. Government was centralized because the nobility had been weakened by a century of warfare and the bourgeoisie provided an ample source of revenue for the royal treasury. Through the late 15th and early 16th centuries, a succession of strong kings—*Louis XI, Charles VIII, Louis XII*—reduced the power of the nobility, firmed up the structure of the modern nation-state, and brought the middle class into government as advisors. *Francis I* (1515–1547) not only inherited a strong monarchy but extended its power by establishing a taille (a direct head tax on all land and property). During his reign and that of his successor, *Henry II* (1547–1559), the Renaissance took hold in France.

> *Rabelais* (1494–1553), a priest and a classicist, attacked the failings of French society and the Church in his *Gargantua and Pantagruel* while advocating rational reform.

> *Montaigne* (1533–1592) penned his *Essays,* which preached open-mindedness and rational skepticism and offered an urbane, modern view of life.

Spain

Locked into Catholic orthodoxy by centuries of warfare against the Moslems (Moors), who had conquered much of the Iberian peninsula, the Spanish reached the height of their expansion in the 16th century through exploration and overseas colonization. Xenophobia and rigidity diluted the impact of Renaissance individualism and humanism. In 1492 (when Aragon and

Castille united to form modern Spain), the Jews and Moslems, the nation's educated middle class, were expelled. *Miguel de Cervantes* (1547–1616) satirized his society's anachronistic glorification of chivalry and medieval institutions in one of the world's greatest novels, *Don Quixote*.

The century from 1550 to 1650 marks the "Golden Age" of Spanish culture. *Lope de Vega* wrote hundreds of dramas; *Bartolomé Estaban Murillo, Doménikos El Greco,* and *Diego Velázquez* painted magnificent pictures on religious themes; and the Jesuit *Francisco Suárez* wrote widely admired works on philosophy and law.

Sample Essay Question

The sample thematic essay questions presented in this chapter are types found in the Advanced Placement History Exam.

Sample Question

> "The secular humanism of the Italian Renaissance reflected the modern world while the Christian humanism of the Northern Renaissance compromised between medievalism and modernity."
>
> *Defend or refute this statement.*

Comments on the Sample Question

Follow the "Simple Procedures" for writing an essay. (See page 24.)

First, *What does the question want to know?* The best way to approach a question like this—laden with terms and concepts—is to identify each of them, and, then and only then, determine whether the statement can be more easily defended or refuted.

What was the Italian Renaissance? Did it occur before or after the Northern Renaissance? Did one influence the other? What did they have in common? How did they differ?

What is "secular humanism"? How did it draw on ideas from the ancient world while adapting them to the unique historical circumstances of 15th century Italy?

What is "Christian humanism"? How was it influenced by secular humanism and by Christian tradition?

What is meant by "medievalism" and "modernity"? Do the attitudes expressed in secular humanism come closer to the attitudes of our world than those of Christian humanism? Is an idea that "reflects" a future development one of its causes?

Second, *What do you know about it?* Once you have answers to these questions, the choice of whether to defend or refute the statement is actually made for you. If the secular humanism of the Italian Renaissance is significantly different from the Christian humanism of the North, you can measure which more closely reflected the world that followed and then you can build a strong case for defense or refutation of the statement.

Third, *How would you put it into words?* Remember, since history rarely offers "either/or" simplicities, sometimes the best approach to a *defend or refute* question is to argue both sides. Be careful, though, not to make your essay a circle of contradictions. State your defenses and refutations clearly, and let your evidence point to the sophistication of your understanding.

Sample Answer

A defense of the statement would be both expected and easy. History—or at least the teaching of it—is full of convenient generalizations. "The Italian Renaissance was pagan in tone"; "the Northern Renaissance was religious." All labels are limiting. The trouble with the terms "secular humanism" and "Christian humanism" is that there was no absolute distinction between the religiosity of the Italian and Northern Renaissance because the men of both were Christians by birth, belief, and practice.

It is a question of emphasis, then. What is meant by "reflected the modern world"? That attitudes, interests, and activities were similar to those in our times or a cause for them?

At first glance, it would be tempting to assume that our secular age had its start in the literary movement, humanism, that began in Renaissance Italy and that departed from the literature of the Middle Ages in that it dealt with issues other than law, philosophy, and theology. True, nonclerical writers such as Castiglione and Machiavelli wrote about social manners or politics without arguing their cases from a theological base, but the cultured Italian courtiers and ruthless princes would have been shocked had they been accused of being irreligious.

The glorification of the culture of the ancients by the so-called "pagan humanism" of the Italians (a term that was probably derisively applied by the self-righteously pious Northern Europeans) did not cancel out their Christianity. "Secularism" in the modern world applies, not necessarily to atheism or a disbelief in religion, but rather to a network of attitudes, interests, and activities that do not include religion. This network has been expanded in our times far beyond that of the Middle Ages and even of the Renaissance.

What caused the growth of secularism? The Italian humanists may have been the first to write in the vernacular and about nonreligious issues—politics and the human condition—but secularism in our world grew from our reliance on the findings of science rather than on the mysteries of religion. The rise of science took place in Northern Europe in the 16th and 17th centuries.

The Northern humanists did much more than use Hebrew and Greek versions of the Bible or the writings of the Church Fathers like St. Augustine to revitalize tradition-bound Christianity. If Erasmus was the "Christian gentleman" who tried to reform the church from within, he also championed social reform. While Meister Eckhart and Thomas à Kempis were mystics who preached that people should commune directly with God, this emphasis on personal religious experience was an early expression of "individualism," which has reached its ultimate expression in our world. Gerard Groote also stressed individualism by arguing for personal virtue over reliance on religious dogma. The approaches of these "Christian humanists" were far removed from the traditionalism of the medieval world.

In France, the writings of Montaigne reflected skepticism, a very modern attitude, and those of Rabelais criticized the existing social structure. In England, Thomas More wrote of a utopian society more modern than medieval, and the great Shakespeare captured the human condition in his dramas. All these men would undoubtedly have counted themselves as religious Christians.

The humanism of the Northern Renaissance included writers who were concerned with religious issues but in radically new dimensions from that of the authority-bound religiosity of the Middle Ages. Many Northern humanists wrote of very earthy issues and with very secular outlooks. To call the work of the "Christian humanists" a compromise between medievalism and modernity is to dilute the potency of their very modern individualism and secularism. To classify the Italian humanists as "pagan" or "secular" is to diminish their commitment to Christianity. It is imperative in history as in human affairs not to allow generalization to degenerate into stereotyping.

NOTE: Long essays are not necessarily the best; how well the question is answered determines the quality.

Evaluate the Sample Answer

1. Did it have a clear introductory statement?
2. Did it reflect an understanding of the terms and the intent of the question?
3. Did it *defend* or *refute* the statement definitively? If not, did it offer balanced support for both sides?
4. Did it offer factual support for its argument—specific references to historical persons, events, dates, ideas?
5. Were the references accurate? Abundant? Interesting? Relevant?
6. Was the argument one-sided and simplistic? Was the position vague?
7. Did the concluding paragraph sum up the position—*defense* or *refutation* or a *case for both*.
8. Was the essay long enough? Clearly written? Easy to understand?

Rater's Comments on the Sample Answer

5—Extremely well qualified

This is a well-crafted, logical, and abstract approach to a question whose difficulty rests in its generalities and its terminology. This essay reflects an understanding of the various shadings of any great development. The tack it took—to refute what on the surface seems a very defensible statement—adds originality to the substantial argument. "All labels are limiting" is the essay's focal point, and it supports this point clearly, convincingly, and with specific factual references.

Perhaps the only significant weakness of the essay is its interpretation of terms. Is "modernity" measured by "secularism" and "individuality"? Is "medievalism" equivalent to "religiosity" and "tradition"?

Practice Essay Questions

The questions that follow are samples of the various types of thematic essay questions that appear on the Advanced Placement Examination in European History. The review chapters in this section (Part Two) will have samples of the major types of thematic essays: Defend or refute, Analyze, Evaluate, To what extent and in what ways, Assess the validity, Contrast and compare, Explain.

> 1. To what extent and in what ways did the Italian Renaissance result from Italy's geographic advantage in the world trade of the 15th century?

Comments on Question 1

"Geography is destiny." So it is said. And the strategic location of Italy, a peninsula jutting into the Mediterranean, gave it advantages in the world trade of the 15th century. "How and how much" are the questions to answer here. The clues are inherent in the geography. With what parts of the world did the Europeans carry on trade at this time? Why did Italy have an advantage? What were the rewards of that advantage? How were those rewards instrumental in fostering the greatest brief period of creativity in history?

> 2. "Although the term "Renaissance" is misleading, the modern world began with Renaissance secularism and individualism." *Assess the validity* of this statement.

Comments on Question 2

"To judge the value" or "determine the truth" of this statement, you must ascertain why the term "Renaissance" may be misleading and what the "modern world" is. Then you must determine whether or not the modern world began with secularism and individualism. Can we claim that any era, especially one so complex, began at a specific time or with a few ideas? Did these concepts affect other developments—the Reformation, for instance? This abstract question requires careful thought and organization to answer.

> 3. *Explain* why Machiavelli's *The Prince* is both one of the most misinterpreted books of modern times and the first modern treatise in political science.

Comments on Question 3

"Explain" offers no choice. You must "make clear," "detail," and "offer meanings, causes, reasons for." The essence of the book is in the phrase "The welfare of the state justifies everything...." Is this equivalent to arguing that the end justifies the means? What was Machiavelli's purpose in writing the book? How did his methods of observation and his arguments make it the "first modern treatise in political science"? Would medieval philosophers have considered the same issues? If so, what would their arguments be based upon?

> 4. *Contrast and Compare* the Italian and the Northern Renaissance.

Comments on Question 4

"Show differences"; "examine similarities." In showing the differences, consider how each began, which influenced which, how their emphases differed, how they interpreted common concepts differently, how they expressed their differences. How did the art and literature of each differ? How did the personalities vary—who was the "ideal Renaissance man" in Italy, in Northern Europe? What were the accomplishments of each?

In examining similarities, consider common concepts such as "individualism" and "secularism"; look for similarities in their religious commitments, in their artistic and literary techniques and themes, in their approaches to defining human life.

---

5. Analyze how the Northern Renaissance gave rise to two diverse trends: *religious mysticism and revival* and *science and technology*.

Comments on Question 5

In this case, *analyze* means primarily to "determine the relationships" between the Northern Renaissance and two glaringly different approaches to the human condition: religion and science. How did the study of ancient texts—specifically Hebrew and Greek versions of the Bible and the writings of the early Church Fathers—revitalize religious devotion? How did the concept of "individualism" encourage the very personal religious experience of mysticism? How did "individualism" and "skepticism" give rise to modern science?

Why did the revival of religion and the growth of mysticism occur primarily in Northern Europe? Was Italian religious devotion centered on the arts? Did the papacy have less sway in the North?

Why did Northern Europe give birth to modern science? Was the desire to understand and control nature the Northern counterpart to Italian virtu or richness of the human spirit? Was it a tradition that began with the mathematician Regiomontanus and evolved into the Copernican formula for a heliocentric universe?

Practice Multiple-Choice Questions

(These represent the different types of questions that appear on the exam.)

1. The term "Renaissance," a rebirth, is misleading because
   (A) the *Quattrocento* gave rise to an elite culture
   (B) the Middle Ages saw the development of Europe's basic institutions
   (C) it borrowed from the cultures of ancient Greece and Rome
   (D) it developed outside the heart of Europe in the Italian peninsula
   (E) it was supported, in part, by patronage from despots

2. "Geography is destiny" proved true for the Italians of the 14th and 15th centuries for all of the following reasons EXCEPT
   (A) their proximity to the Mediterranean
   (B) their establishment of overland trade with Asia
   (C) their role as the "middlemen" of Europe
   (D) their ability to adapt to victimization by more united peoples
   (E) their seagoing trade with the eastern Mediterranean

3. Which of these city-states is said to have been the cultural center of the Renaissance and has been compared to ancient Athens for its burst of creativity over a relatively short time span?
    (A) Venice
    (B) Milan
    (C) Rome
    (D) Genoa
    (E) Florence

4. The powerful middle class that developed in the independent city-states of Renaissance Italy was involved in all of the following EXCEPT
    (A) making profitable loans to popes and monarchs
    (B) financing commercial ventures
    (C) patronizing the arts
    (D) encouraging manorialism
    (E) controlling the governments of the city-states

5. Which dynasty of merchants, bankers, and despots of Florence used its wealth to patronize the great creative artists of the day?
    (A) Petrarch
    (B) Bellini
    (C) Medici
    (D) Sforza
    (E) Condottieri

6. Which of these concepts was NOT valued by Renaissance thinkers?
    (A) Humans as the measure of all things
    (B) The cloistered life
    (C) A life of activity
    (D) Excellence in all human endeavors
    (E) Living up to one's individual potential

7. Before the Renaissance, which was the greatest patron of the arts?
    (A) The Church
    (B) The middle classes
    (C) European monarchs
    (D) The nobility
    (E) The governments of the city-states

8.   Michelangelo's *David* displays which thematic innovation of Renaissance artists?

    (A)   The depiction of religious personages

    (B)   Accurate human anatomy

    (C)   The use of wood as a material

    (D)   The portrayal of enigmatic expressions

    (E)   The depiction of classical costumes

9. The sculpture of the Renaissance differed from that of the Middle Ages in all the following ways EXCEPT
    (A) the forms were anatomically proportional
    (B) the faces expressed emotion
    (C) the figures expressed animation
    (D) the artists prided themselves on the individuality of style
    (E) the subject matter was nonreligious

10. All of the following were painters during the Renaissance EXCEPT
    (A) Botticelli
    (B) Raphael
    (C) Bruni
    (D) Buonarroti
    (E) Massaccio

11. The so-called pagan humanism of the Italian Renaissance differed from the so-called Christian humanism of the Northern Renaissance primarily because
    (A) the art of the Italian Renaissance depicted only classical themes
    (B) the literature of the Northern Renaissance drew upon the Hebrew and Greek texts of the Bible and the writings of the Church Fathers
    (C) Italian Renaissance writers were often antireligious
    (D) The merchant-princes who ruled the Italian city-states resisted the influence of the Church in civic affairs
    (E) The Northern churches were the biggest patrons of the arts

12. Which of the following was NOT an important development of the Northern Renaissance?
    (A) The use of the first movable-type printing press in Europe
    (B) The formulation of the heliocentric view
    (C) The establishment of a brilliant English vernacular literature
    (D) Mysticism's assertion that an individual could commune directly with God, unaided by the Church
    (E) The invention of the banking system

13. The "Prince of Humanists," who attempted through satiric writings to reform the Roman Catholic Church while remaining loyal to it was
    (A) Sir Thomas More
    (B) Erasmus
    (C) Luther
    (D) Cervantes
    (E) Rabelais

"It was a literary movement that reflected a new way of looking at the human condition. The writers were laymen, not clergy, who examined secular issues such as politics and the emotional life of the individual. While they drew on the themes of the ancient classics and often wrote in classical Latin and Greek, they also laid the foundations for modern language and literature by writing in their mother tongues."

14.   The literary movement described above is
  (A)   secularism
  (B)   individualism
  (C)   classicism
  (D)   humanism
  (E)   *virtu*

15.   Which of the following are considered writers of the literary school described in the above passage?
  (A)   Petrarch, Boccaccio, Erasmus
  (B)   Boccaccio, Erasmus, Brunelleschi
  (C)   Erasmus, Castiglione, Thomas Aquinas
  (D)   Castiglione, Machiavelli, Thomas Aquinas
  (E)   Petrarch, Giotto, Castiglione

Answers and Answer Explanations

1. B	**2.** B	**3.** E	**4.** D	**5.** C
6. B	**7.** A	**8.** B	**9.** E	**10.** C
11. B	**12.** E	**13.** B	**14.** D	**15.** A

1.   (B)   This is an analysis question. Choice C is the reason it would be a rebirth. Choices A, D, and E are largely irrelevant to the concept that the term is misleading.

2.   (B)   Analysis demonstrates that all the other choices support the idea.

3.   (E)   This is identification. If you did not know that Florence was the "center of the Renaissance," it would be difficult to work it out.

4.   (D)   Manorialism was a feature of feudalism, and the shift in power from the feudal nobility to the middle class eventually ended it because money took precedence over land.

5.   (C)   Again, this is largely identification. You could have eliminated Petrarch, the writer; Bellini, the painter, and *condottieri,* mercenary soldiers of the period. The Sforza family ruled Milan.

6.   (B)   The cloistered life was the dedication to piety, solitude, chastity, and poverty of the medieval monk.

7.   (A)   This is the kind of analysis that "makes good sense" when you think about the medieval preoccupation with religion. By the way, it was local churches and cathedrals, not simply the papacy, which patronized the largely anonymous artists of the Middle Ages.

8.   (B)   Accurate and proportionate representations of anatomy was a Renaissance "innovation" reintroduced from classical sculpture.

9.   (E)   The people of the Renaissance were devout Roman Catholics and that dedication to faith is reflected in their art.

10.   (C)   Bruni was one of the first modern historians, who divided chronicles into distinct periods. He summed up a goal of the Renaissance person with his statement, "The whole glory of man lies in activity."

11.   (B)   The key term in the question is "so-called." It demonstrates the limitations of the terms "pagan" and "Christian."

12.   (E)   Banking developed in Europe in Italy among the "merchant princes" who sought to invest their surplus capital by lending, for profit, to the popes and monarchs.

13.   (B)   "Prince of Humanists" is the giveaway. In his day, Erasmus was one of the most famous people in Christendom.

14.   (D)   Humanism was primarily a development of the secular writers of the period who looked at human life from another perspective than that of the medieval clerics. It involved "classicism," a study of ancient writings; it encouraged individualism, the glorification of individual experience and value; it resulted in secularism, the consideration of nonreligious issues. Virtu was a quality of extreme individualism.

15.   (A)   Brunelleschi was an architect; Aquinas was a medieval philosopher; Giotto a painter.

CHAPTER **2** Protestant Reformation, Catholic and Counter-Reformations, Wars of Religion (1517–1648)

Overview

Historians generally agree that the Protestant Reformation marks the beginning of modern Europe and that it influenced the development of Western civilization. What began as an attempt to reform the Roman Catholic Church resulted in the destruction of the religious unity of Western Europe and in the subjection of Europeans to bitter wars of religion.

Protestantism was adopted by the growing nation-states of the north as they were about to replace Italy and Spain as leaders of modern Europe. It inherited and adapted the concept of *individuality* from the Renaissance, and it influenced monumental developments in Western civilization: nationalism, capitalism, democracy, science.

The Catholic and Counter Reformations were responses of the Roman Catholic Church to both the criticisms of the reformers and the spread of Protestantism. The Council of Trent redefined the doctrines of the Church; the Jesuits propagated them; the Inquisition enforced orthodoxy. The Inquisition in Spain was designed to encourage a sense of national unity based on Catholicism. The Moslem Moors and the Jews—the educated groups in Spanish society—were either driven into exile or forcibly converted. The Inquisition was later adapted in Spain and in Spanish territories to combat Protestantism, and it was imported to Italy for the same purpose. Protestantism, though, dominated most of Northern Europe, and the continent suffered devastating disruptions during the wars of the 16th and 17th centuries.

CAUSES OF THE REFORMATION

1. Corruption of the Roman Catholic Church during the Renaissance
      Sale of church offices (simony); nepotism; sale of indulgences
      Decline of morality among the clergy
2. Impact of Renaissance *humanism,* which questioned Church traditions
      Humanist "glorification of humanity" contradicted the Church's emphasis on salvation
      Prosperity brought the "virtue of poverty" into disrepute and the Church lost the "spirit" of Christ's message and was out of touch with the mass of believers

3. Declining prestige of the papacy

Babylonian Captivity of the Church in the 14th century when popes, subservient to the French king, took up residence in Avignon and lost prestige in the rest of Christendom.

The *Great Schism* beginning in 1378, when French and anti-French cardinals elected two popes—one of whom lived in Rome, the other in Avignon—and lasting over forty years.

Moral decline of the Renaissance popes bred cynicism

Papal involvement in secular politics fostered contempt

4. Influence of religious reformers, such as Wycliffe and Huss

Stressed personal communion with God

Diminished the importance of the sacraments

Weakened the influence of the clergy

5. Resentment of secular rulers over the power of the popes and clergy

Monarchs of growing nation-states resisted papal supremacy over national churches

Resentment over vast landholding of the Church within national boundaries

6. Invention of the printing press, allowing dissenters to spread their ideas throughout Europe and making the Bible available to the common people

Chronological Overview of Events, Personalities, Ideas

1517

Johann Tetzel (1465?–1519), a wandering friar, was authorized by *Pope Leo X* to sell *indulgences* (which guaranteed the remission of sins), the proceeds of which would be used to rebuild St. Peter's Church in Rome and to provide funds to local dioceses.

Martin Luther (1483–1546), a Roman Catholic priest, Augustinian monk, and theologian at the University of Wittenburg in Germany, condemned these sales as impious expediencies. Tormented by obsessions of his own damnation, despite a life dedicated to holy service, he came to believe that the traditional means of attaining salvation (*Good works,* such as the sacraments, prayer, and fasting) were inadequate. He nailed his *95 Theses* to the door of the Wittenburg church (his day's equivalent of calling a press conference), listing the points of his opposition to the indulgences and inviting debate.

1519–1520

When an appeal to Pope Leo for reform of this abuse went unanswered, Luther began to formulate the tenets of his beliefs, ideas that he had been mulling over for nearly a decade.

Tenets of Lutheranism as published in a series of tracts:

1. *Salvation by faith alone:* Good works (the sacraments and such) cannot guarantee salvation but rather are an outward manifestation of the faith that a loving God will grant that salvation. This concept was inspired by Luther's reading, many years earlier, of a passage from Romans I; 17; in which St. Paul says " the just shall live by faith. . . ."

2. *The Bible is the ultimate authority:* Neither the Pope nor church councils can define Christian doctrine; every believer should read and interpret the Bible, and the faithful will be divinely guided.

3. *The grace of God brings absolution:* Neither indulgences nor confession can bring forgiveness of sins; the individual is freed of sin only by the Grace of God; pilgrimages, veneration of saints, fasts, and worship of relics are useless.

4. *Baptism and communion are the only valid sacraments:* The Roman Catholic Church regarded seven sacraments (baptism; confirmation; eucharist or communion; matrimony; penance; extreme unction, last rites, or annointing of the sick; holy orders) as outward signs of inner grace. Luther rejected all but baptism and communion. Luther also rejected the Roman Catholic doctrine of *Transubstantiation* (the belief that while the bread and wine of the Mass maintain their appearance, they are transformed into the Body and Blood of Christ). In its place he offered the doctrine of *Consubstantiation* (the doctrine that the transformation of the bread and wine was not literal but that God was somehow actually present in more than a symbolic way).

5. *The clergy is not superior to the laity:* Marriage is permitted; Christianity is a "priesthood of all believers"; monasticism should be abolished.

6. *The church should be subordinate to the state:* In all matters other than the theological—the appointment of church officials, the matter of taxing church lands, the organization of the church—the state is supreme. This appealed to the monarchs and to the German princes who resented papal authority and who coveted the vast landholdings and wealth of the Roman Catholic Church. It would have ramifications for Lutheranism in Germany well into the 20th century.

1520   Luther burned a *papal bull*, an official proclamation that demanded his recantation, and he was excommunicated by Pope Leo X. Holy Roman Emperor *Charles V*, instead of arresting Luther and suppressing Lutheranism, which had a growing appeal in Germany and Scandinavia, honored a political debt to Frederick the Wise, Elector of Saxony, by refusing to outlaw Luther without a hearing.

1521   Luther was called to the Rhineland in Germany to appear before *The Diet of Worms*, a tribunal of the Holy Roman Empire with the power to outlaw—to condemn to be burned at the stake. Confronted by the sharpest theological debaters of the Roman Catholic Church, Luther contended that only the Bible or reason would convince him. "I neither can nor will I recant anything, since it is neither right nor safe to act against conscience."

The empire outlawed him. Brought to safety in Wittenberg by Frederick the Wise, he organized his reformed church and translated the Bible into the vernacular, profoundly influencing the development of the modern German language.

1520s   Lutheranism spreads. Preoccupied with wars against the Ottoman Turks and the French, Charles V, Holy Roman Emperor, was unable to suppress the growth of Protestantism in Northern Europe. In addition to Northern Germany, Denmark and its province of Norway, Sweden and its holdings in Finland, and the Eastern Baltic all embraced Lutheranism.

1522   A league of Lutheran knights, under the leadership of *Franz Von Sickengen* converted to Lutheranism, attacked the Catholic princes of the Rhineland, was suppressed, but encouraged most of the Northern German princes to convert. One motive was the financial gain brought by confiscating Roman Catholic lands.

1524–1526   Luther's theological dissent inspired a variety of radical religious sects to form and to demand social reform based on the early Christian model. Demanding abolition of manorialism—the economic and social order of medieval feudalism—German peasants used force against the landowners, and Germany was wracked by the *Peasant's War*. Luther was appalled by these extremists and others who he believed took his ideas too far, such as the Anabaptists who preached adult total-immersion baptism, and the Millennarians, who expected the imminent return of Christ. He condemned the revolutionaries as "filthy swine" and encouraged the princes to exterminate them.

The radical revolt influenced Luther to demand that his followers obey constituted authority and that, while they read the Bible themselves, they leave its interpretation to knowledgeable ministers. His social and economic conservatism helped check the spread of Lutheranism in Southern Germany and elsewhere in Europe.

1525   *Albert of Brandenburg-Prussia*, ruler of the dynamic East German state, converted to Lutheranism and provided the lesser German states with a powerful ally.

1529   *The Diet of Speyer* refused to recognize the right of the German princes to determine the religion of their subjects.

1531   The *League of Schmalkalden* was formed by newly Protestant princes to defend themselves against the emperor. Charles appealed to the Pope to call a church council that could compromise with the Lutherans and regain their allegiance to the Roman Catholic Church. The Pope, fearing the papacy's loss of power, refused and lost all opportunity to reunite Western Christendom.

1530s   The Reformation spreads beyond Germany.

1531   In *Switzerland, Huldreich Zwingli,* who established Protestantism in Switzerland, was killed in a nationwide religious civil war. Although his followers accepted most of Luther's reforms, they argued that God's presence during communion is only symbolic.

The Peace of Cappel allowed each Swiss canton to determine its own religion.

1534   *Pope Paul III* (1534–1549) assumed office as the first of the "reform popes."

1534

In *England;* Parliament passed the *Act of Supremacy,* which made *Henry VIII* (1509–1547) and his successors the heads of the Anglican Church and its clergy. In 1521, when Luther was banned by the empire, Henry had been awarded the title "Defender of the Faith" by the Pope for his tract "Defense of the Seven Sacraments." By 1529, Parliament, partly because of Henry's influence, declared the English Church independent of Rome, cutting off revenues to the papacy. Henry, eager to divorce *Catherine of Aragon* in order to marry *Anne Boleyn,* had been denied an annulment for political reasons (Catherine was the aunt of Charles V, Holy Roman Emperor). Henry appointed *Thomas Cranmer* as Archbishop of Canterbury in 1533, was granted a divorce by him, and was excommunicated by the Pope.

1534–1539

The English Parliament abolished Roman Catholic monasteries, confiscated their lands, and redistributed them to nobles and gentry who supported the newly formed Anglican church.

1536

In *Switzerland; John Calvin* (1509–1564) published his *Institutes of the Christian Religion* in the Swiss city of Basel. Like Zwingli, he accepted most of Luther's ideas but differed on the role of the state in church affairs.

1. *Predestination:* Calvin argued (from an idea of St. Augustine) that since God knows even before birth whether a person is saved or damned, there is nothing anyone can do to win salvation. *The Elect* or *Saints* are a select few saved only by God's love from corrupt humanity and given indications of their status by *Conversion* (a mystical encounter with God) or by material prosperity. The latter gave rise to the *Puritan* or *Protestant Ethic,* an incentive to avoid poverty as a sign of damnation, and served to justify the rise of capitalism.
2. *Church government:* Calvin replaced the Catholic hierarchy with a democratic system whereby each individual congregation elected its minister and governed its policies. He disagreed with Luther's claim that the church should be subordinate to the state, and argued that it should actually be a moral force in the affairs of secular government. This stand encouraged *theocracy,* whereby Calvinism became the official religion and intolerant of dissent not only in parts of Switzerland but later in England and the Massachusetts Bay Colony in North America.

1539

In *England,* Parliament approved the *Statute of the Six Articles.*

1. The seven sacraments were upheld.
2. Catholic theology was maintained against the tenets of both Lutheranism and Calvinism.
3. The authority of the monarch replaced the authority of the Pope.

Despite attempts by *Mary Tudor* (Henry's daughter by Catherine) to reinstitute Catholicism and the *Puritan Revolution* of the following century, the Six Articles helped define the Anglican Church through modern times.

1540s

Calvinism spread.

1541   Calvin set up a model theocracy in the Swiss city of Geneva.

The Scottish Calvinists *(Presbyterians)* established a national church.

The French Calvinists *(Huguenots)* made dramatic gains but were brutally suppressed by the Catholic majority.

The English Calvinists (Puritans and Pilgrims—a separatist minority) failed in their revolution in the 1600s but established a colony in New England.

1540s   The Catholic and Counter Reformations began.

1540   *Ignatius Loyola* established the *Jesuits (Society of Jesus)*, a holy order that was organized in a military fashion, requiring of its members blind obedience and absolute faith.

The Jesuits swore to suppress Protestantism:

1. They served as advisors to Catholic kings.
2. They supressed heresy through the Inquisition (clerical courts that tried and convicted religious dissenters who were subject to deportation, torture, or death).
3. They established schools in Catholic nations to indoctrinate the young.
4. They sent missionaries to far corners of the earth to convert "the heathen."

The Society of Jesus became the militant arm of the Catholic and Counter Reformations.

1542   The Jesuits were given control of the Spanish and Italian *Inquisitions.* Perhaps tens of thousands were executed on even the suspicion of heresy.

The *Index of Prohibited Books* was instituted in Catholic countries to keep heretical reading material out of the hands of the faithful.

1545–1563   *The Council of Trent* responded to the challenge of Protestanism by defining Catholic dogma. Its main pronouncements:

1. Salvation is by both *good works* (such as the veneration of saints and fasts) and *faith.*
2. The seven sacraments are valid, and transubstantiation was reaffirmed.
3. The sources of religious authority are the Bible, the traditions of the Church, and the writings of the Church Fathers. Individuals cannot interpret the Bible without the guidance of the Church, and the only valid version of the Bible is the Vulgate, St. Jerome's Latin translation.
4. Monasticism, with celibacy of the clergy, and the existence of purgatory were reaffirmed.

   Attempts were made to reform abuses: the principle of indulgences was upheld while its abuses were corrected; bishops were given greater power over clergy in their dioceses; and seminaries were established in each diocese for the training of priests.

1555   The Peace of Augsburg, after over two decades of religious strife, allowed the German princes to choose the religion of their subjects, although the choice was limited to either Lutheranism or Catholicism. *Cuius regio, eius religio*— "whose the region, his the religion."

Results of the Protestant Reformation

1. Northern Europe (Scandinavia, England, much of Germany, parts of France, Switzerland, Scotland) adopted Protestantism.
2. The unity of Western Christianity was shattered.
3. Religious wars broke out in Europe for well over a century.
4. The Protestant spirit of individualism encouraged democracy, science, and capitalism.
5. Protestantism, specifically Lutheranism, justified nationalism by making the church subordinate to the state in all but theological matters.

The Thirty Years' War (1618–1648)

1. The first continent-wide war in modern history, fought mostly in Germany, it involved the major European powers.
2. It was the culmination of the religious wars of the 16th century between Catholics and Protestants.
3. Politically, German princes sought autonomy from the Holy Roman Empire; France sought to limit the power of the Hapsburgs; Spain sought to extend Hapsburg power in Germany; Sweden and Denmark hoped to strengthen their hold over the Baltic region.

THE FOUR PHASES OF THE WAR

1. *The Bohemian Phase (1618–1625):* The Czechs, also called Bohemians, who, together with the Slovaks, formed the modern nation of Czechoslovakia after World War I, were largely Calvinist. Fearful that their Catholic king, *Matthias,* would deny their religious preferences, they *defenestrated* (used the old custom of registering dissent by throwing officials out a window) his representatives and installed, as king, a Calvinist, *Frederick V from the Palatinate*. After Matthias's death, *Ferdinand II* became Holy Roman Emperor and King of Bohemia. Supported by troops of the Spanish Hapsburgs, he defeated the Bohemians at the *Battle of White Mountain* in 1620, gave away the lands of the Protestant nobles, and enabled the Spanish to consolidate along the Rhine River.
2. *The Danish Phase (1625–1630): Christian IV of Denmark,* a Lutheran, entered the war to bolster the weakened Protestant position in Germany and to annex German lands for his son.
   Holy Roman Emperor Ferdinand II countered by commissioning Albert of Wallenstein to raise a mercenary army, which pillaged and plundered Germany and defeated the Danes in 1626. In 1629, the emperor issued The *Edict of Restitution*, which restored all the Catholic states in Germany that had been secularized before the Peace of Augsburg (1555). When Wallenstein disapproved, Ferdinand dismissed him.

3. *The Swedish Phase (1625–1630): Cardinal Richelieu*, Roman Catholic regent of France, was concerned with the gains made by the Hapsburg emperor in Germany. He offered subsidies to encourage the capable Swedish king *Gustavus Adolphus* to enter the war.

Adolphus, a Lutheran, was eager to help the Protestant cause. After decisive victories over the Hapsburg forces, Adolphus was killed; Wallenstein was assassinated for contemplating disloyalty to the emperor, and the Protestant states of Germany made a separate peace with the emperor.

The Peace of Prague revokes the Edict of Restitution. The Swedes were defeated, but Richelieu was determined to undermine Hapsburg power in Germany.

4. *The French-Swedish Phase (1635–1648):* France, Holland, and Savoy entered the war in 1635 on the Swedish side. Spain continued to support the Austrian Hapsburgs. After a series of victories and reversals on both sides, *Henri Turenne*, a French general, defeated the Spanish at Rocroi, and in 1644 peace talks began in Westphalia in Germany.

The Peace of Westphalia, 1648

1. The Peace of Augsburg was reinstated *(cuius regio, eius religio),* but Calvinism was added as acceptable for Germany.
2. The Edict of Restitution was revoked, guaranteeing the possession of former Church states to their Protestant holders.
3. Switzerland and Holland were made independent states, freed from the Hapsburg dominions.
4. France, Sweden, and Brandenburg (the future Prussia) received various territories.
5. The German princes were made sovereign rulers, severely limiting the power of the Holy Roman Emperor and the influence of the Austrian and Spanish Hapsburgs. With over three hundred separate rulers in Germany, national unification was delayed until well into the 19th century.

Effects of the Thirty Years' War

1. Germany was devastated, its population reduced in some parts by well over a third. Once a cultural and political leader in Europe, it stagnated, postponing its entrance as a sovereign, united nation for more than two centuries and complicating its relations with the rest of the world into the 20th century.
2. The age of religious wars ended; the modern age of sovereign states began in Europe, and *"Balance of Power"* politics prevailed in Europe, whereby nation-states and dynasties went to war to prevent any one power from dominating the continent.
3. The Hapsburgs were weakened. The Austrian monarchy lost most of its influence over Germany, ending the possibility of a Europe united under the family. Hapsburg Spain was left a second-rate power.
4. The Catholic and Counter Reformations were slowed; Protestantism was safely established in its European strongholds.

Sample Essay Question

The sample and practice thematic essay questions presented in this chapter are types found in the Advanced Placement European History Exam, and they require knowledge of causes, effects, personalities, ideas, and events.

Sample Question

> "Luther began the Reformation as a religious reformer and ended it as a religious revolutionary." *Assess the validity of this statement.*

Comments on the Sample Question

Follow the "Simple Procedures" for writing an essay. (See page 24.)

First, *What does the question want to know?* Analyze the statement by determining the meaning of "reformer" and of "revolutionary." In this context, the role of a "reformer" is to point out the abuses or failings of an institution and the role of a "revolutionary" is to bring about extreme and immediate change. The reformer tends to seek improvement within the existing system; the revolutionary tends to abandon the system or the institution. In Luther's case, theology was his weapon in both possible roles.

Second, *What do you know about it?* The *statement,* whose *validity* must be *assessed,* suggests that Luther's original intent in posting the *95 Theses* was to reform the existing Roman Catholic Church but that his ultimate role was to create a revolutionary organization by formulating a new dogma.

Third, *How would you put it into words?* To *assess* is to judge the value, to determine whether this statement is *valid*—true, false, or partly both. Did Luther start out to improve the existing church? Did he end up creating another institution? If so, what events, personal motivations, political influences, or other factors effected this change in role? If not, how was his original intent reflective of his final role?

Sample Answer

Before he nailed the *95 Theses* on the door of the Wittenburg church in 1517, Martin Luther—a German by birth—was a Roman Catholic monk, an ordained priest, and a university theologian. Since his position as a priest was one respected by a Christian society and since his function as a teacher and theologian was eminent within the Church, he must have had a stake in the Roman Catholic Church. Therefore, he started his career as a reformer—a critic of the existing institution—and was driven by personal concerns, religious convictions, and political considerations to become a religious revolutionary who established a new sect of Christianity.

While he was a priest, Luther was plagued by a sense of damnation. Psychohistorians, such as Erik Erikson, attribute this exaggerated guilt and sense of sin to childhood influences and physical ailments (he was chronically constipated). Whatever the cause, Luther believed that he was doomed to hell despite living the life of a dedicated man of God.

He came to believe that the sacraments, fasts, prayers, and other "good works" of the church would not save him from eternal damnation. So he searched the Bible for an answer to his anguish. He found it in a passage from the New Testament: "The just shall live by faith. . . ." Using this as inspiration, he was convinced that Christians did not earn the rewards of Heaven by doing good deeds, but that they did these good things because they possessed the Grace of God. This conviction, which he arrived at after searching his soul for years, seemed to soothe his troubled spirit until 1517.

When Johann Tetzel, a priest authorized by the Pope to sell indulgences for the rebuilding of St. Peter's Church in Rome, came to Germany during that year, Luther was righteously indignant. He thought that the faithful were being bilked into believing that they could buy "tickets to Heaven." Whether his anger was based on principle or was a convenient outlet for his spiritual confusion, he acted by inviting a debate within the Church on the issue of the indulgences. Posting his ideas on the door of the local church was equivalent to calling a press conference today.

When the Pope and other Church authorities ignored his concerns, he was frustrated. Luther-the-reformer was driven to become Luther-the-revolutionary. In a series of pamphlets, written between 1517 and 1520, he formulated what were to become the basic tenets of his new sect. "Salvation is by faith alone and not good works, such as prayers and the sacraments." "The Bible, not the pope, is the final authority for Christians." "The only valid sacraments of the original seven are: Baptism and Communion."

When he was threatened with excommunication in 1520, he publically burned the Papal Bull (decree), was excommunicated, and charged with heresy. (Heretics, such as John Huss, were often burned at the stake.) All of these threats seemed to harden his resolve.

In 1521, he was brought before the Imperial Diet at Worms (a religious tribunal), and he refused to change his theological stand unless he could be proven wrong by direct reference to the Bible. His obstinate courage caused him to be outlawed by the Holy Roman Emperor. A German prince, Frederick the Wise of Saxony, offered him protection from the arresting officers of Charles V.

Secure and with time to think and write, Luther spread his ideas and organized his new sect. It is a hypothesis-contrary-to-fact to say that if the Pope had listened to Luther's criticisms of the sale of indulgences, Luther might not have formed a new branch of Christianity. But it is clear that because he was frustrated by being ignored, he moved to a more radical role than that of critic.

Luther began the Reformation as a religious reformer who hoped for a hearing and who seemed to want to improve the existing Christian Church. Ignored and frustrated, he put his doubts and new ideas on paper. Threatened, he solidified his stand on theological issues and developed a revolutionary dogma. Protected by his prince (who stood to gain power if papal authority was weakened in Germany), he spread his ideas and organized his new church.

Evaluate the Sample Answer

1. Did it have a clear introductory statement?
2. Did it reflect an understanding of the terms and the intent of the question?
3. Did it "assess the validity" of the statement by making a clear case for its truth or falsity?
4. Did it offer factual support for its argument?

5. Were the facts accurate? Abundant? Interesting?
6. Was the argument one-sided, leaving out evidence to support another interpretation?
7. Did its concluding paragraph sum up the "assessment"?
8. Was the essay long enough? Clearly written? Easily understood?

Rater's Comments on the Sample Answer

4—Well qualified

Clear and definitive assessment of the validity of the statement: From a religious man who "must have had a stake in the Roman Catholic Church" to a reformer who was "righteously indignant" at the sale of indulgences and frustrated at being ignored. His theological assertions about the importance of faith over "good works" were starting points for revolutionary change after he was excommunicated and finally outlawed.

Essay structure was logical and convincing: clear introduction, adequate summary, accurate facts to support the assessment.

Weaknesses: Although the writer referred to "political considerations" in Luther's passage from reformer to revolutionary, there is no mention of the political climate in Germany during this period. Angry over the abuses of the papacy and the authority of the Holy Roman Emperor, both the princes and the population of Germany welcomed a leader who could rally them against Pope and emperor, even if he attacked the basic tenets of the Church. The peasant rebellions of the mid-1520s attest to the seething discontent of the people; the easy conversion of many princes to Lutheranism attests to their avarice (they confiscated church lands).

The writer also fails to mention that Luther translated the Bible from Latin into the vernacular. This was a revolutionary act since it effectively diminished the power of priests by putting the "Word of God" into the hands of the people.

Finally, the writer does not mention one of Luther's most revolutionary concepts: The church should be subordinate to the state in all but theological matters. This not only destroyed the universal power of the Roman Catholic Church, but it weakened the moral restraints against a powerful nation-state.

Practice Essay Questions

The questions that follow are samples of the various types of thematic essay questions that appear on the Advanced Placement Examination in European History. The review chapters in this section (Part Two) will have samples of the major types of thematic essays: Defend or refute, Analyze, Evaluate, To what extent and in what ways, Assess the validity, Contrast and compare, Explain. (See pages 17–18 for a detailed explanation of each type and an example of each.)

> **1.** "Calvin's doctrines were a radical departure from those of both the Roman Catholic Church and Lutheranism." Evaluate this statement.

Comments on Question 1

This question leaves some room for choice. In evaluating the statement, one may choose to compare the doctrines on *salvation* of each of these Christian sects. In his stand against the indulgences, Luther departed from Roman Catholic doctrine and from Church tradition. Calvin argued still another view. The question could be approached through this issue alone.

Another way to attack the question would be through the differing relations of each of these sects to the issues of religion and the state and of church government. A clear contrast can be shown among the three.

> 2. "The reformation was caused by long-term political, social, and economic developments." Discuss this statement.

Comments on Question 2

The "discuss" essay is, by nature, less focused than the other variations. Like the others, it requires that the student take a stand on the statement; unlike the others, it does not narrow the possible approaches. Choices bring opportunities and dangers. *This type requires strict organization.*

In this particular question, the crucial term is "caused." Any great historical event is brought about by multiple and complex developments. These are the *long-term causes.* For instance, corruption among Church officials and the influence of Renaissance ideas are long-term causes of the Reformation. But people—personalities—are often at the center of immediate causation. *Immediate causes* are actions that precipitate great events. Tetzel's sale of indulgences provoked Luther to issue his *95 Theses.*

> 3. "The Catholic and Counter Reformations attempted not only to reform the Church but to suppress heresy." Defend or refute this statement.

Comments on Question 3

In a "Defend or refute" essay, it is still possible to present a mixed argument— partly for, partly against. After all, there are few human endeavors that do not encompass the whole range of moral possibility.

To "reform" implies a noble goal for a noble institution; to "suppress" implies the application of power for the denial of freedom. The point to remember with this question is not to make moral judgments but rather to consider the varying roles of individuals and organizations during the Catholic response to Protestantism.

> 4. "The Protestant emphasis on one's personal relationship with God was a logical outgrowth of the Renaissance." Assess the validity of this statement.

Comments on Question 4

A reminder: To "assess validity" is to determine whether a statement is true, false, or partly both. The pivotal concept in this statement is "logical outgrowth." Consider its implications before choosing an approach. Does it mean a necessary effect? Or the result of one influence among many?

In order to answer this, the student must be familiar with the Renaissance ideas that emphasized individuality as well as how they differed with notions of the preceding age (the medieval period). These ideas must then be linked as influences for various Protestant theological or social concepts that differed from Roman Catholic views.

This is a tough question! It would be easy to fall into the trap of over-simplifying by jumping to conclusions based on a superficial knowledge of complex ideas and doctrines.

> **5.** "Protestantism spread with the growth of nationalism." Discuss this statement.

Comments on Question 5

This question implies a link between what would appear, at first glance, to be two diametrically opposed forces: the spiritual and the political. Of course, religion has influenced politics throughout the ages; it continues to in our own country. It is less common or at least appears to be for politics to influence the growth of a new religion or, more accurately, a new dogma.

The key to answering this question is an understanding of the changed attitudes and political relationships in the 16th century and of the way Protestanism fostered nationalism.

Practice Multiple-Choice Questions

Refer to Part One, Section C of this book for advice on taking the multiple-choice section of the Advanced Placement Examination in European History. The practice questions that follow are representative of the various types that appear on the Advanced Placement European History Exam.

1. Which of the following is NOT considered a long-term cause of the Protestant Reformation?
    (A) The declining prestige of the papacy
    (B) The German mystics who emphasized individual communion with God
    (C) The activities of the Jesuits
    (D) The humanist accusation that the Church was losing the substance of Christ's message
    (E) The corruption of the Roman Catholic Church during the Renaissance

2. "Salvation by faith and by faith alone" is a major tenet first adopted by
    (A) Calvinism
    (B) Lutheranism
    (C) Catholicism
    (D) Anglicanism
    (E) Anabaptism

3. According to Luther, the ultimate authority for the interpretation of Christian doctrine is
   (A)   the Pope
   (B)   Christian tradition
   (C)   the clergy
   (D)   the Bible
   (E)   the church hierarchy

4. Luther's political conservatism is revealed in which of the following?
   (A)   His preference for political order over social justice.
   (B)   His willing acceptance of the support of the German princes
   (C)   His condemnation of the Peasants' War
   (D)   His support for the extermination of the Munster Commune
   (E)   All of these.

5. Which of the following was NOT a reason for the rapid spread of Lutheranism in the 1520s and 1530s?
   (A)   The rise of dissenting sects
   (B)   The conversion of the princes of Northern Germany
   (C)   Charles V's involvement in foreign wars
   (D)   The failure of the Pope to call a church council
   (E)   Popular resentment in Germany against Rome

6. Calvin differed from Luther by stressing which theological doctrine?
   (A)   The right of the clergy to marry
   (B)   The Bible as the ultimate authority for Christian doctrine
   (C)   The concept of predestination
   (D)   The effect of "good works" in winning personal salvation
   (E)   The rejection of all but two of the sacraments

7. According to Calvin's doctrine, salvation could be attained by
   (A)   good works
   (B)   faith alone
   (C)   the unexplainable love of God for humanity
   (D)   accumulating material wealth and achieving social standing
   (E)   faith and good works, each equal in value

8. "Poverty, considered a virtue by the Catholic Church, became shameful to the Calvinists. The middle class found in Calvinism a justification for the pursuit of wealth."
   This passage implies that Calvinism may have been a powerful influence in the development of which of the following?
   (A)   Communism
   (B)   Capitalism
   (C)   Nationalism
   (D)   Democracy
   (E)   Science

9. Which of the following was NOT a goal of the Catholic and Counter Reformations?
    (A)   The conversion of the populations of southern Europe
    (B)   The reform of abuses within the Roman Catholic Church
    (C)   The confirmation of the Church's basic dogma
    (D)   The stemming of the spread of Protestantism
    (E)   The suppression of heresy

10. Which of the following accurately depicts a doctrine defined by the Council of Trent?
    (A)   Salvation is attained by "good works" alone.
    (B)   The ultimate authority for Christian doctrine is the Bible, Church traditions, and the writings of the Church Fathers.
    (C)   Monasticism and clerical celibacy are forbidden.
    (D)   Only Holy Communion and Baptism, of the seven sacraments, are necessary to the attainment of salvation.
    (E)   The Church is subordinate to the state in all but theological matters.

11. "Like an army, it was ruled by a general who was responsible directly to the pope. Its holy soldiers practiced blind obedience, maintained absolute faith, and willingly suffered extreme hardship." This passage best describes
    (A)   the Inquisition
    (B)   the Diet of Worms
    (C)   the Society of Jesus
    (D)   the Index of Prohibited Books
    (E)   the papacy

12. The Jesuits
    (A)   became involved in the education of Catholic children
    (B)   served as advisors to Catholic kings
    (C)   rooted out heresy through press censorship
    (D)   converted "heathens" through missionary work
    (E)   All of these

13. "It began with attempts to reform the Roman Catholic Church, and it ended by shattering the religious unity of Europe." This best describes
    (A)   the Catholic and Counter Reformations
    (B)   the Spanish Inquisition
    (C)   the Council of Trent
    (D)   the Protestant Reformation
    (E)   the Italian Inquisition

14. Protestant values, sometimes differing from one sect to another, helped in the development of which of the following?
    (A)   Capitalism, nationalism, monasticism
    (B)   Science, capitalism, nationalism
    (C)   The conciliar movement, science, democracy
    (D)   Nationalism, individualism, clerical celibacy
    (E)   Science, nationalism, monasticism

15.   The Thirty Years' War
      (A)   was a religious struggle between Catholics and Protestants
      (B)   was an attempt by the princes of Germany to diminish the influence of the Holy Roman Empire
      (C)   was an attempt by France to limit Hapsburg power
      (D)   involved most of the major states of Europe
      (E)   All of these

Answers and Answer Explanations

1. C	**2.** B	**3.** D	**4.** E	**5.** A
6. C	**7.** C	**8.** B	**9.** A	**10.** B
11. C	**12.** E	**13.** D	**14.** B	**15.** E

1.   (C)   The Jesuits did not receive a papal charter until 1540; the Reformation began in 1517.

2.   (B)   This is the crux of Luther's theological divergence from indulgences and "good works."

3.   (D)   This is Luther's tenet that neither the Pope nor Church tradition serve as the ultimate source of Christian doctrine. He was outlawed by the Diet of Worms for his stand on this and other theological issues.

4.   (E)   A religious radical, Luther still prized social stability above social justice.

5.   (A)   The dissenting sects competed for converts with the Lutherans. The conversion to Lutheranism of the German princes led to the conversion of their populations. Charles's wars against the French and the Turks prevented him from using force to suppress the Lutherans. Various popes' concerns over losing power to the church councils postponed a reforming council that might have checked or accommodated Protestantism.

6.   (C)   Calvin borrowed the concept of predestination from St. Augustine, who argued that God, being omniscient, knew before their births who would be saved and who would be damned. Calvin regarded both faith and good works as signs of salvation rather than means for attaining it.

7.   (C)   According to Calvin, since neither good works or faith guarantee Heaven, it is God's unexplainable love for man that allows salvation.

8.   (B)   This is the so-called Protestant Ethic, which developed from the Calvinist tenet that material prosperity is a good indication that an individual is one of the "elect."

9.   (A)   They were already strongholds of Catholicism.

10.   (B)   This statement of dogma countered Luther's assertion of "salvation by faith alone" and Calvin's concept of predestination.

11.   (C)   The Jesuits (Society of Jesus), organized by Ignatius Loyola, were an arm of the Catholic and Counter Reformations.

12.   (E)   The Jesuits used various methods to root out heresy, to maintain orthodoxy in Catholic nations, and to spread the faith.

13.   **(D)**   This was the original intent and the ultimate effect of the Reformation. Many historical developments take on a life of their own beyond the goals of their initiators.

14.   **(B)**   Science was fostered by the Protestant spirit of inquiry. Capitalism benefited from the Puritan work ethic, which saw material success as indicative of being one of the "elect." Nationalism was fostered by Luther's assertion that the church is subordinate to the state in all but theological matters.

15.   **(E)**   These complex rivalries culminated in the Thirty Years' War (1618–1648), which devastated Germany, weakened the Hapsburgs, and brought the religious conflicts of the previous hundred years to a bloody climax.

3 The Growth of European Nation-States in the 1500s and 1600s

Overview

Centralization of governments led to the rise of powerful nation-states and concomitant European exploration of the globe and regional wars on the continent. Spain, following the Portuguese lead, explored the Atlantic and soon surpassed its Iberian neighbor in colonies, wealth, and military power. Gold and silver from the New World helped shift the balance of power from the Mediterranean basin to the Atlantic coast of Europe. The wealth from mines in the Spanish colonies created a financial and commercial center in the Netherlands, brought about rampant inflation in Europe, and eventually led to the decline of Spain as a major power.

Feudalism died gradually. The Hundred Years' War (1337–1453), which devastated France and exhausted its nobility, indirectly led to a strong monarchy. Peace encouraged commerce, which gave rise to a taxable middle class that could support a national army independent of the nobility. From the midddle of the 15th century to the second decade of the 16th, the monarchs of France centralized the state, recruited bourgeois administrators into government, and strengthened the army. Through most of the 16th century, the foreign adventures of two strong kings and the upheaval caused by the Reformation weakened the monarchy. Under the intelligent guidance of Cardinal Richelieu, prime minster to Louis XIII, the central government brought peace, prosperity, and stability to the realm during the first half of the 17th century. The Golden Age of France was during the reign of the Sun King, Louis XIV (1643–1715), whose absolutist monarchy dominated all classes in Europe's wealthiest and most populous country, upset the balance of power on the continent, and claimed the "divine right" of rule.

The strong government that developed in France contrasted with the constitutional system that evolved in England. The powers of the English kings had been checked by the nobility as far back as the 13th century, with the Magna Carta. The Tudors took the English throne in the 15th century as a compromise among the claimants who battled over it in the War of the Roses. Having only a tenuous hereditary right to the monarchy, they were forced to work through Parliament, which gradually represented a greater and greater portion of English society and therefore avoided the class distinctions that divided France. The Reformation had its effects on English government: The independence of the Anglican Church from the papacy strengthened the monarchy and Parliament; the Puritan Revolution established the supremacy of Parliament over the king and nurtured the tradition of constitutionalism.

A strong tradition of absolutism developed in Eastern Europe especially in the rising states of Russia, Prussia, and Austria. Social reform was sporadic and largely ineffectual and serfdom was widespread in the region. The baroque style of architecture was favored by the absolute monarchs of these states as a manifestation of their power and glory.

Exploration and Colonization: 1400s to 1600s

The Portuguese, from the middle to the end of the 15th century, supported by their able leader, *Prince Henry the Navigator*, explored the South Atlantic. Expeditions led by *Diaz*, *da Gama*, and *Cabral* explored the coast of Africa and eventually established trading posts in India.

Spurred by missionary zeal, personal gain, and national pride, and aided by the development of the magnetic compass, the astrolabe, and more seaworthy craft, explorers from several states on the Atlantic set out on their journeys of discovery.

Christopher Columbus, seeking a direct route to Asia for the Spanish crown, discovered the Western Hemisphere, and despite opening the "New World," laid the foundations for Europeans' oppression and exploitation of native peoples. *Ferdinand Magellan* circumnavigated the globe for Spain, and *Cortés* and *Pizarro*, respectively, conquered the great American empires of the Aztecs and Incas. Gold and silver flowed from the New World mines into the coffers of the Spanish monarchs and to the merchants and manufacturers of the Netherlands.

Chafing under the oppressive rule of the Spanish Catholic *King Philip II*, the prosperous Low Countries whose leaders were Calvinist, revolted against the Spanish from 1556–1587. The bitter and bloody conflict led to the division of the Low Countries into the Spanish Netherlands in the south (which eventually became Belgium) and the United Provinces of the Netherlands in the north (eventually Holland). The defeat in 1588 of the attempt of Philip II's armada to invade England, an ally of the Netherlands, marked the beginning of the decline of Spain's hegemony in Western Europe.

The *Thirty Years' War* (1618–1648) began as a religious conflict, evolved into a national struggle for dominance of Central Europe, and led to the destruction of vast areas in Germany and the decline of the regional hegemony of the Holy Roman Empire. The Austrian Hapsburgs confronted the powerful Muslim Ottoman Turks in an attempt to expand their control of Eastern Europe. The 1683 attack on Austria by the forces of *Suleiman the Magnificient* was beaten back, and the Austrians eventually gained control of Bohemia, Hungary, and Transylvania.

Russia and Western Europe experienced radically different paths of development until the 18th century. For centuries, the princes of Moscow had been retainers of the Mongol conquerors, and the czars were able to use their influence with the Mongols to consolidate their power over the Russian people and to establish the hereditary role of czar. *Ivan the Terrible* was an autocratic, expansionist who limited the power of the nobles (boyars), expanded the realm, and solidified the role of czar. A *Time of Troubles* ensued after his death, marked by civil war and the lack of an heir. The Romanov dynasty was established by the nobles in 1613, and the family ruled with an iron hand, reinstituting serfdom and gaining virtual control over the Russian Orthodox Christian Church.

Peter the Great expanded the power of the state and of the czars by establishing a powerful standing army, a civil service, and an educational system to train technicians in the skills developed by western science and technology. He imposed economic burdens and social restrictions on the peasants to further his power, erected the planned city of St. Petersburg on the Baltic, and built magnificent, ornate baroque palaces, churches, and public buildings to glorify his reign. Russia became one of the major powers of Europe during this period.

Brandenburg, an electorate of the Holy Roman Empire, was able to gain a degree of independence as a result of the weakening of the Hapsburg rule during the Thirty Years' War. The *Hohenzollern*, *Frederick William*, solidified autocratic rule over Brandenburg, Prussia, and the Rhine territories with a strong army and an efficient bureaucracy, and with a policy of weakening the nobles (Junkers) and suppressing the peasants. The Junkers served as elite officers in the army and absolutist rule was established in Prussia.

The Development of Absolutism in France

Francis I (1515–1547), a Valois rival of Holy Roman Emperor Charles V, battled unsuccessfully to weaken the Hapsburgs as Europe's most powerful family but managed to consolidate absolutism in France by instituting the taille (a direct tax on land and property). With the *Concordat of Bologna,* he granted the Pope the right to collect *annates* (the first year's revenue from Church offices) in return for the power to nominate high officials in the French church, effectively nationalizing the church in France and increasing the power of the monarchy.

Opposed to any reform of the Church that might weaken his influence over it, he and his successor, *Henry II* (1547–1559), actively persecuted the *Huguenots* (French Calvinists). Continued persecution under *Francis II* and *Charles IX* provoked civil war, which was halted by an *edict of toleration* issued by *Catherine de Medici*, mother of, and regent for, Charles IX.

The *Massacre of St. Bartholomew's Day* renewed the brutal civil war when Catholic mobs slaughtered Huguenot leaders who had gathered in Paris to celebrate a royal wedding. Although the Huguenots were never more than 10 percent of the French population, they wielded great influence since they came from the nobility and the bourgeoisie.

Persecution, civil war, and dynastic rivalry left *Henry of Navarre*, a Huguenot, as the only legitimate claimant to the French throne, and he ascended, after an expedient conversion to Catholicism, as *Henry IV* (1589–1610). He issued the *Edict of Nantes*, a remarkable expression of religious tolerance that guaranteed civil and religious freedom to the Huguenot minority. His finance minister, the *Duke of Sully*, reformed the tax collection system to make it more equitable and efficient, improved transportation, stimulated trade and industry, and fostered prosperity. All of this led to an increase in the prestige and power of the monarchy.

After the death of Henry IV, the government suffered from corruption and mismanagement during the regency of *Louis XIII*. In 1624, Louis appointed *Cardinal Richelieu* (1624–1642) as prime minister. It was not uncommon in this religious era for churchmen to serve as advisors to the monarchs of Europe. Richelieu centralized the government further by encouraging the commerce and industry that increased the tax base, by strengthening the military, and by instituting the *intendant system*, in which bourgeois officials, answerable only to the king, supervised the provinces and diminished the power of the nobility. Richelieu's domestic polices strengthened absolutism in France and prepared the way for its supreme embodiment in the *Sun King, Louis XIV*.

Louis XIV (1643–1715) was four when he ascended the throne of France. His mother was his regent, and she chose Italian Cardinal Mazarin as prime minister. Like Richelieu, Mazarin was a capable administrator, and he protected Louis's claim to the throne during the tumultuous *Wars of the Fronde*, which reached their height from 1650 to 1652. The *Frondeurs* were nobles who sought to limit the powers of the monarch and to decentralize the government in order to extend their own influence. With the support of the bourgeoisie and the peasants, who had little to gain in a return to the feudal order, Mazarin was able to subdue the *Frondeurs* and their ally, Spain.

When Mazarin died in 1661, Louis declared himself as his own prime minister. *L'Etat, c'est moi* ("I am the state") became the credo of this most absolutist monarch during the age of absolutism. *Bishop Jacques Bossuet* provided the philosophical justification for the *divine right theory of rule* by claiming that Louis—like any absolutist monarch—was placed on the throne by God, and therefore owed his authority to no person or group.

According to feudal tradition, French society was divided into three *Estates,* made up of the various classes. The *First Estate* was the clergy; the *Second Estate*, the nobility; these comprised respectively 1 percent and 3 to 4 percent of the population. The *Third Estate* included the great bulk of the population: the bourgeoisie or middle classes, the *artisans* and *urban workers*, and the *peasants.* Since France was, as were all European nations at this time, predominantly *agrarian,* 90 percent of its population lived on farms in the countryside. Louis XIV reigned over the Golden Age of French culture and influence: With a population of 17 million (about 20 percent of Europe's total), France was the strongest nation on the continent.

Its industry and agriculture surpassed that of any other European country. *Jean Baptiste Colbert*, "The Father of French Mercantilism," revitalized trade as Louis' finance minister by abolishing internal tariffs and creating a free trade zone in most of France. He stimulated industry by subsidizing vital manufacturing and by building up the military. He hoped to make France self-sufficient by building a large fleet that would rival that of the English and Dutch and enable the French to acquire an overseas empire. Since even France could not afford both a powerful army and navy, Louis opted for the army; the end result was the global supremacy of the British.

France developed Europe's first modern army. Artillery—usually supplied by civilian private contractors—was made a part of the army. The government—instead of officers—recruited, trained, equipped, and garrisoned troops. A chain of command was established, and the army was increased from 100,000 to 400,000, the largest in Europe.

War was an instrument of Louis's foreign policy. For two thirds of his reign, France was at war.

The War of the Devolution (1667–1668): France's unsuccessful attempt to seize the Spanish Netherlands (Belgium) as part of a feudal claim.

Invasion of the Dutch Rhineland (1672–1678): Revenge for the Dutch role in defeating France in the War of Devolution and an attempt to seek France's "natural boundary in the west," the Rhine River. Largely unsuccessful.

Seizure of Luxembourg and attempt to annex Alsace-Lorraine (1681–1697): Although France retained Luxembourg, most of Louis's ambitions were frustrated by The League of Augsburg, an alliance of Holland, Spain, the Holy Roman Emperor, and England.

The War of the Spanish Succession (1702–1714): Louis threatened to upset the Balance of Power (the theory that no single state should be predominant on the continent) in Europe by laying claim to the Spanish throne for his grandson. The Grand Alliance, which included the major states of western Europe, fought to prevent this union of the French and Spanish thrones.

The Treaty of Utrecht (1713–1714): Restored the balance of power by allowing Philip V, Louis's grandson, to remain on the Spanish throne so long as France and Spain were never ruled by the same monarch. It also awarded to the victors various European and overseas possessions of the Spanish Empire.

France enjoyed a Golden Age of culture and cultural influence during Louis XIV's reign:

French became the "universal tongue," spoken by diplomats and in the royal courts of all Europe.

Louis patronized artists and especially writers such as *Corneille, Racine, Molière, de Sévigné, de Saint-Simon, La Fontaine, De La Rochefoucauld.*

French literature and style—in dress, furniture, architecture—became standards by which all Europeans measured their sophistication.

Although his reign solidified central government and marked the high point of absolutism in France, his many wars exhausted the treasury. This left the bourgeoisie and the peasantry with an enormous tax burden since the clergy and nobility were exempted from most taxes. His personal extravagances aggravated the situation: The Royal Palace at *Versailles* cost over $100 million to build, and added to that was the money spent on his elaborate entertainments for the "captive nobility" at court. (He defanged the nobles by making participation in court life a social requirement.) He suppressed religious dissent, outlawing *Jansenism,* a form of Catholic Calvinism, revoking the *Edict of Nantes*, which had guaranteed toleration for the Huguenots, and making Catholicism mandatory.

The central government that developed in France from the era of the religious wars to Louis's reign was efficient: The power of the nobles was weakened; tax collection was systematized; royal edicts were enforced; the bourgeoisie was given a role in administration. The economic system was successful: Agriculture and trade were stimulated. The seeds for revolution were sown in the national debt that had to be paid off by the Third Estate, which bore many responsibilities and enjoyed few privileges.

The Development of Constitutionalism in England

Henry VII (d. 1509), the first of the *Tudor* monarchs, established a strong central government even though many regarded the family as usurpers invited to the throne as an expedient compromise to end the *War of the Roses.* By regulating trade and internal commerce through monopolies, charters, and licenses, Henry raised revenues from the prosperous middle class. This money enabled him to finance a standing army and keep the nobility in check. The *Court of the Star Chamber* administered central justice and further subdued rebellious nobles. Since the Tudors were beholden to Parliament for inviting them to the throne, Henry and his successors, including his son *Henry VIII* (1509–1547), consulted Parliament on significant issues.

Unlike his father, who was levelheaded and tightfisted, Henry VIII was an impetuous, extravagant, passionate man whose temper, ambitions, and appetites were legendary. The need to maintain legitimacy by having a male heir led Henry VIII to make those decisions, with Parliament's support, that led to the *English Reformation.* (See page 50.)

Edward VI (1547–1553) assumed the throne upon the death of his father, Henry VIII, and since he was only ten and of fragile health, the government was run by a regent, the *Duke of Somerset.* A devout Calvinist, Somerset imposed his religion on the people, and, as a result, was ousted in 1550. Under another regent, the basic tenets of the Anglican Reformation were restated, and the *Anglican Book of Common Prayer* was made the basis for all church services.

Mary Tudor (1553–1558), who was Henry VIII's daughter by his first wife, the Catholic Catherine of Aragon, became queen when Edward died at the age of sixteen. Unpopular, not only because she was Roman Catholic but because she was married to *Philip II* of Spain, she had to suppress a rebellion against her rule and her marriage alliance with Spain. *Bloody Mary* earned her name when she burned hundreds of Protestants at the stake for dissenting against her attempt to reinstitute Catholicism in England. When she died, she was succeeded by her half sister, *Elizabeth,* Henry's daughter by his second wife, Anne Boleyn.

Elizabeth I (1558–1603), last and greatest of the Tudor monarchs, reigned when the population of England and Wales was between 3 and 4 million, while that of France was over 16 million and that of Spain nearly 9 million. Enriched by its conquests and colonies in the New World, Spain was the predominant power of Europe; its geographic destiny determined by its island nature, England was at the fringe of the religious upheaval and political change on the continent. Its church was independent from Rome but closer to

Latin theology than any other Protestant sect. Its government balanced power between the monarchy and Parliament. Its wealth came from rich arable land and an energetic populace that excelled in commerce and trade. Its social system was unique: a *gentry,* lesser nobles whose original wealth came from ownership of land, expanded by entering the world of commerce and by intermarrying with the middle class. There were no glaring distinctions between the upper and middle classes as there were on the continent, and the interests of nobles, gentry, and bourgeoisie were represented in Parliament.

Since the Tudors had been invited to the throne of England to settle the rival claims of the Houses of York and Lancaster during the War of the Roses, Elizabeth, her charismatic father, and her capable grandfather had lived under the shadow of "dynastic pretender." The child of Anne Boleyn, whose marriage to Henry was scandalous if not outright illegal, The *Virgin Queen* (a euphemism for her never marrying, considering her notorious love affairs) had to prove her mettle in the face of the prejudices against her line, her parentage, and her gender. Her natural intelligence had been honed by substantial education; her powerful personality had been toughened by living as a family "outcast" at her father's, her half brother's, and her half sister's court. Adored by her people and feared by her enemies—at home and abroad—she reigned for nearly a half-century as one of Europe's greatest monarchs and one of the world's greatest women.

The Elizabethan Age

Religion

Upon assuming the throne, Elizabeth repealed Mary's pro-Catholic legislation and reinstated the Acts of Supremacy and Uniformity that established the English Reformation during her father's reign.

The Thirty-Nine Articles (1563) followed Protestant doctrine and was vague enough to accommodate most of the English except the *Puritans* (English Calvinists). They believed that the *liturgy* (prescribed ritual) and the *hierarchy* (the order of rank within the organization) needed "purification" from Catholic influence. Militant Puritans challenged royal authority, and while they were suppressed for the time, they grew stronger during the reigns of Elizabeth's successors and would influence the development of constitutionalism.

Diplomacy

When the Netherlands, a Hapsburg possession that had adopted Protestantism, revolted against Spanish rule, Elizabeth entered into an alliance with the Dutch in 1577 for fear that Holland would provide a base from which Spain could invade England. Both England and Holland sent *privateers* (pirates commissioned by the state) to prey on the treasure ships from the Spanish colonies in the new world. Outraged, *Philip II*, Spanish king and Holy Roman Emperor, conspired with English Catholics to overthrow Elizabeth and put her cousin, the Catholic Mary Stuart, queen of the Scots, on the throne. In 1587, Elizabeth ordered the execution of Mary for treason, and Philip declared war on England. The *Invincible Armada,* 132 mammoth ships, was defeated in August 1588 by a smaller but more maneuverable English force in the waters of the English Channel.

Culture

This was the Golden Age of English literature—the era of Shakespeare, Spenser, Donne, Marlowe, Francis Bacon—when a brilliant national literature was developed that instilled pride in the uniqueness of English culture.

The Stuart Kings and Parliament (1603–1688)

James I (1603–1625), king of Scotland and son of Mary Queen of Scots, took the throne upon Elizabeth's death since she had no direct heirs. A believer in the divine right of kings, he failed to understand the importance of Parliament in governing England. A conference at *Hampton Court*, 1604, failed to reconcile the Puritans, who opposed Anglican hierarchy, with the church of England. The *Gunpowder Plot*, 1605, was uncovered before disgruntled Catholics, led by Guy Fawkes and objecting to James's enforcement of laws that required participation in Anglican services, could blow up the king and Parliament. The years 1610 to 1611 saw the session of Parliament enmeshed in the issue of Parliament's role in financing government.

The *"Addled" Parliament* met in 1614 and was so-called by James because it spent its entire session arguing that taxes could be levied only with its consent and that rule was by king and Parliament in conjunction. Dissolving Parliament, James tried to rule without it until England's involvement in the Thirty Years' War necessitated his reconvening it. After a rancorous session in which Parliament criticized James's foreign policy, in 1621 Parliament passed the *Great Protestation*, claiming free speech and authority in conducting governmental affairs. James dissolved the body and arrested its leaders.

Charles I (1625–1649) was, like his father, devoted to the divine right theory and woefully inept at dealing with Parliament. Embroiled in wars on the continent, he called for Parliament to vote funds, which it refused to do until he signed the *Petition of Right* in 1628: Parliament alone can levy taxes; martial law cannot be declared in peacetime; soldiers may not be quartered in private homes; imprisonment requires a specific charge. The Bishops' War of 1639–1640, after Archbishop Laud persecuted Puritans and tried to force Anglican worship upon the Presbyterian Scots, led Charles to reconvene Parliament in order to pay indemnities upon defeat of his forces.

The *Long Parliament* (1640–1660) demanded, in return for paying for Charles's defeat, that he impeach his top advisors; allow Parliament to meet every three years without his summons, and promise not to dissolve Parliament without its consent. When Charles attempted, in early 1642, to arrest opposition members, Parliament seized control of the army. Charles gathered his forces, and the *English Civil War* (1642–1649) began.

The Course of the War

The middle class, the merchants, the major cities, and a small segment of the nobility supported Parliament and were called *Roundheads.* The Anglican clergy, the majority of the nobility, and the peasants backed the king and were referred to as *Royalists* or *Cavaliers.*

1643   The Roundheads allied with Presbyterian Scotland, promising to impose Presbyterianism on England in exchange for military assistance. Charles called on Irish Catholics for help.

1644   *Oliver Cromwell*, a Puritan leader of Parliament, led his *New Model Army* of Puritans against the Cavaliers at *Marston Moor* and defeated them decisively.

1645   Charles surrendered to the Scots.

1647   The Scots turned Charles over to Parliament, which was led by Cromwell's *Independents,* who favored religious toleration. The Scots turned about and allied with Charles, who promised that he would impose Presbyterianism on the English.

1648   Cromwell defeated the Scots at the *Battle of Preston* and helped purge the Presbyterians from Parliament, thereby creating the *Rump Parliament,* which voted to behead Charles for treason.

1649   With the death of Charles, England became a republic, the *Commonwealth,* and Cromwell and his army wielded the power. In suppressing Irish supporters of the crown, the Puritans committed terrible atrocities and imposed injustices that would acerbate the *"Irish Question"* for centuries.

1653–1660   Cromwell was designated *Lord Protector* by a puppet Parliament and ruled with the support of Parliament until his death in 1658. His son Richard, a far less capable ruler, was deposed in 1660, and *Charles II* was proclaimed king.

The Stuart Restoration (1660–1688)

The *Cavalier Parliament* (1660–1679) marked the development of the Tory and Whig parties. The *Tories,* made up of the nobles, the gentry, and the Anglicans, were conservatives who supported the monarchy over Parliament and who wanted Anglicanism to be the state religion. The *Whigs,* mainly middle class and Puritan, favored Parliament and religious toleration. Since the Tories prevailed in the Cavalier Parliament, Anglicanism was restored by a series of laws that forbade dissenters to worship publically, required government officials and military personnel to practice Anglicanism, and discriminated against other sects.

The *Whig Parliament*, elected in 1679, was suspicious of Charles II's absolutist and pro-Catholic tendencies, and enacted the *Habeas Corpus Act*, which limited royal power by

Enabling judges to demand that prisoners be in court

Requiring just cause for continued imprisonment

Providing for speedy trials

Forbidding *double jeopardy* (being charged for a crime that one had already been acquitted of)

The Glorious Revolution

James II (1685–1688) was unpopular the moment he took the throne. A devout Roman Catholic, he appointed Catholic ministers to important posts and gave the appearance of trying to impose Catholicism upon the English. In 1688, important nobles invited *William of Orange*, a Hollander and wife of James's oldest child, Mary, to take the English throne. When *William and Mary* arrived in England, James fled to exile in France, and the new monarchs accepted from Parliament, as a condition of their reign, the *Declaration of Rights* (enacted into law as the *Bill of Rights* in 1689). The *Habeas Corpus Act*, the *Petition of Right*, and the Bill of Right are all part of the *English Constitution*.

THE DECLARATION OF RIGHTS

1. Only Parliament can impose taxes.
2. Laws can be made only with the consent of Parliament.
3. A standing army can be maintained only through the consent of Parliament.
4. The people have the right of petition.
5. Parliament has the right of free speech.
6. The people have the right to bear arms.
7. People have the right to due process, trial by peers, and reasonable bail.
8. Parliament is to be freely elected and dissolved only by its own consent.

The *Glorious Revolution* was actually the culmination of an evolutionary process over centuries which, through historical accident, outright conflict, and painstaking design, increased the power of Parliament over the monarchy. In the centuries that followed, monarchs in England came to reign while Parliament came to rule. Although Parliament, at the time of the Glorious Revolution, served the interests of the wellborn or the wealthy, it came to represent "the people" as government came to be viewed as existing and functioning according to *John Locke's* Enlightenment concept of *"consent of the governed."* The English and those who inherited their political traditions would guarantee individual rights and would create modern democracy.

Sample Essay Question

The sample thematic essay question and the practice essays presented in this chapter are types found in the Advanced Placement Examination in European History, and they require knowledge of causes, effects, personalities, ideas, and events.

Sample Question

> *Evaluate* the reign of "The Sun King."

Comments on the Sample Question

Follow the "Simple Procedures" for writing an essay. (See page 24.)

First, *What does the question want to know?* "Judge the worth of" and discuss the "pluses and minuses" of the reign of the personification of absolutism in Europe, Louis XIV.

Second, *What do you know about it?* He was called the Sun King because he was at the center of the political life of the state *(L'état, c'est moi)*, and France was the dominant power in Europe during his nearly three quarters of a century reign.

Third, *How would you put it into words?* The abuses of political power in the 20th century may bias your evaluation of Louis, but realize that the Golden Age of French culture was during his reign. The diffusion of language, literature, and furniture styles may not be worth the ravages of military expansionism, but don't underestimate the accomplishments of one of the world's most powerful men over the course of one of the world's longest reigns.

Sample Answer

"I am the state," said Louis in 1661 when Cardinal Mazarin, his chief minister during his minority, died. Louis became more than his own prime minister; he was the embodiment of absolutism, the form of government in which a monarch ruled by Divine Right and was answerable only to God. His reign is one of the longest in history—72 years from the age of 5 in 1643 to his death at 77 in 1715. It is marked by great accomplishments and dismal failures. Any evaluation of his reign will have to consider that both his accomplishments and his failures outlived him.

His greatest accomplishments were to extend the royal authority that had been established by his predecessors and to help establish France as culturally dominant in Europe.

Cardinals Richelieu and Mazarin had left a centralized government for Louis to inherit. The *intendant system,* royal agents set up by Richelieu and strengthened by Mazarin to govern the provinces, collected royal taxes and enforced royal decrees. In this way, the king was able to blunt the power of ambitious nobles who threatened central authority. The nobility, powerful and restless over the centuries, was defanged not only by the *intendants* but by Louis's elaborate system of court ritual and favor granting. To be at the center of the high society or to gain the king's favor, the nobles had to play the roles of fawning courtiers, spending their days as virtual prisoners of court ceremony and their energies in petty intrigues. It was considered a profound honor to be able to help dress the Sun King upon his rising.

If Louis was a man of limited intellect, he was a genius at consolidating personal power. He knew how to neutralize potential enemies and how to pick talented underlings. His finance minister, Jean Baptiste Colbert (the father of French mercantilism), fostered prosperity through mercantilist policies by subsidizing industry, improving transportation, encouraging trade, and supporting overseas exploration and colonization. It was during Louis's reign that Canada and Louisiana became French colonies, that France became economically self-sufficient.

France's commercial successes enriched the royal treasury and enabled Louis to indulge in the two vices that would lead to his decline: extravagance and war.

His extravagant patronage of French writers and artists helped create the Golden Age of French culture. French became the universal language of Europe, spoken not only by diplomats but in virtually all the courts. French style was the measure of good taste in clothes, furniture, manners. His extravagant egotism led him to build Versailles Palace for over $100 million in 1682. It remains as one of the world's most magnificent edifices, more than the personal residence of the greatest absolutist in European history, but also a symbol of the power and majesty of France in his day.

France was Europe's most populous nation in Louis's day, with about 17 million inhabitants, and its richest, with fertile farmlands, productive industries, vital cities, and towns. This allowed Louis to indulge in war. Under Luvois, his war minister, he created the first modern standing army. It was well trained and equipped, massive for the times—400,000 men—and supported by integral units of artillery. He used it to carry out his basic foreign policy of expanding French influence and of extending France to its "natural boundaries" along the Rhine River. This brought France in conflict with most of the major powers in Europe and involved the nation in four separate wars fought from 1667 to 1714. French troops were called "The Huns" during this period.

When Louis died in 1714, the treasury was drained, commerce was diminished, French political influence in Europe in decline. His personal extravagances and his penchant for costly wars would lead to disaster for his successors. They may have had the pretense of absolutism, but they hadn't the resources. Louis XIV's reign was a mix of glittering achievements and dismal decline. He put on a great show and left the unpaid bills to his successors and his nation.

Evaluate the Sample Answer

1. Did it have a good introduction?
2. Did it reflect an understanding of terms and the intent of the question?
3. Did it overstate one position, fudge a decision, or make an attempt to balance the *pluses and minuses* while decisively drawing a conclusion?
4. Did it demonstrate a command of the facts? Were they relevant, accurate, interesting?
5. Was the essay long enough, well-written, easily understood?
6. Did it make its case?
7. What would you have added?
8. Did it have a conclusion that summed up effectively?

Rater's Comments on the Sample Answer

4—Well qualified

This is a well-balanced attempt to evaluate the reign of one of the world's greatest kings. It displays an understanding of the broad issues of centralized authority and the abuses of power. It lays out its intentions in a crisp introduction, sums them up in its conclusion. It is well written and clear in making its case.

Weaknesses: It makes no reference to the decline of Louis's reign due to the narcissistic twists of his substantial egotism. The descriptions of this process by Saint-Simon complete the development of this degeneracy first described by Louis in his memoirs. The death of Colbert, Louis's most gifted and trusted advisor, marks the start of the decline.

The essay also fails to consider very serious "minuses" of the reign: Louis's religious intolerance (he revoked the Edict of Nantes and made Catholicism mandatory); his deliberate failure to convene the Estates General, the only body representative of the three Estates, and therefore to offer no outlet against royal absolutism; the complexity of the wars of Louis XIV; and the humiliation of the Treaty of Utrecht, which redrew the boundaries of France to where they had been before Louis's decades of war and that diminished France's continental and international clout.

Practice Essay Questions

These questions are samples of the various types of thematic essays on the Advanced Placement Examination in European History. (See pages 17–18 for a detailed explanation of each type.)

---

1. *Contrast and compare* the development of the nation-state in France and in England from the early 16th to the end of the 17th centuries.

Comments on Question 1

This is a very general question on a very complex development. The *contrast* is glaring in that during this period the French developed *absolutism* to its pinnacle and the England continued the evolution of *constitutionalism*. "Who did what, when, and how" is a convenient formula for tracing the separate developments. Be careful not to get lost in detail. The large scope of the question requires a big-picture perspective.

The comparison of the development of these two very different styles of government is more difficult. "To compare" is to measure for similarities and differences. Were there similarities? Did the monarchs of these two diverse nations have similar traits of personality, similar methods for consolidating power? Were there similar obstacles to overcome, such as the vested interests of the nobility or the need for revenue? Despite the differences between absolutism and constitutionalism, were there common goals—consolidation, centralization of authority, and modernization?

> **2.** *Analyze* the development of absolutism in France.

**Comments on
Question 2**

Here you must "examine in detail" as well as "determine relationships." You should take the long view by starting with the end of the Hundred Years War, glancing at the roles of the early Valois monarchs in centralizing authority, considering the religious wars of the 16th century and the role of Henry IV in restoring national order and royal esteem, examining the profound accomplishments of Richelieu (one of Hollywood's favorite villains), then touring the reign of Louis XIV.

> **3.** *To what extent and in what ways* did the Puritan Revolution contribute to the supremacy of Parliament in 1689?

**Comments on
Question 3**

This is a difficult question because it requires that you demonstrate how and how much a complex set of events contributed to a complex development. An effective approach would be to divide the bigger issue into smaller questions: What was the Puritan Revolution? How did it increase the power of Parliament? How did the Restoration affect Parliament's role? How was the monarchy weakened by the Puritan Revolution? How and why did the Glorious Revolution occur?

> **4.** "The Tudors brought England into the modern world." *Assess the validity of this statement.*

**Comments on
Question 4**

To "determine the truth or value" of this assertion, you must clarify what is meant by "the modern world," examine the Tudor reign—specifically Henry VII, Henry VIII, and Elizabeth I—and demonstrate whether or not the Tudors accomplished a transformation. Be careful about dismissing Henry VIII because of "bad press." Despite his glaring personal failings—abused wives and gluttony outstanding among them—he strengthened the monarchy and intitated the English Reformation. Elizabeth may be famous for standing up to the superpower of her day—Spain—but the Golden Age of English culture was also during her reign.

> **5.** *Explain* how the Glorious Revolution of 1688 established consitutional government in England.

**Comments on
Question 5**

While this requires specific knowledge of events, laws, and effects, your answer should make clear how the abdication of James II, the invitation to the throne for William and Mary, and the conditions set for this by Parliament laid the foundation for a modern democratic state. How was Parliament's power solidified? How did the Bill of Rights establish a rule of law? How did the supremacy of Parliament and these basic rights limit the monarchy?

> 6. *Describe* the process of exploration, discovery, and colonization in the 1400s and 1500s among the European states bordering the Atlantic.

Comments on Question 6

The best approach to this question would involve a chronological account beginning with the Portuguese and Spanish, contrasting their routes of exploration and their modes of colonization, and then outlining the roles of the other Western European states involved in the issue. The question is broad in scope, but needs specific factual references to illustrate the main points.

> 7. *Contrast and compare* the development of absolutism in 17th century Prussia and Russia.

Comments on Question 7

Contrast (show differences), *compare* (show similarities) in the development of centralized monarchy under the Hohenzollerns of Prussia and the Romanovs of Russia. Compare methods; contrast unique historical backgrounds of the two nations.

> 8. *Explain* how Spain became Europe's richest and most powerful nation-state during the 16th century and then fell into an equally dramatic decline during the 17th century.

Comments on Question 8

Spain's ascendancy is attributable to the same broad factors as is its decline: a crusading zeal to explore, conquer, and colonize; a religious mission to suppress heresy and convert the nonbeliever; the acquisition of gold and silver in lieu of a vibrant commercial and manufacturing economy.

Practice Multiple-Choice Questions

(These represent the different types of questions that appear on the exam.)

1. The end of the Hundred Years' War encouraged the growth of centralized government in France for all of the following reasons EXCEPT
    (A) the nobility had been weakened by the war
    (B) the monarchy had led the fight against the English
    (C) the revival of commerce increased the taxable revenues of the bourgeoisie
    (D) nobles were recruited to serve as government administrators
    (E) the king was able to keep a strong standing army

2.   Francis I further consolidated centralized power by levying the taille, a tax on
   (A)   all land and property
   (B)   on peasant crops
   (C)   on the Gallic Church's income
   (D)   on the landholdings of the nobility
   (E)   on imports

3.   When Henry IV remarked, "Paris is well worth a Mass," he was referring to
   (A)   his prayers for the fall of the city during his seige of it
   (B)   his expected visit during the Easter season
   (C)   his conversion to Catholicism to gain popular favor
   (D)   his conversion to Calvinism to gain support of the Huguenots
   (E)   his visit with the Pope to gain absolution

4.   The Edict of Nantes, issued by Henry IV in 1598, was one of the most significant acts of his reign because of all the following reasons EXCEPT
   (A)   it was one of the first governmental guarantees of religious freedom in Europe
   (B)   it granted Huguenots civil and political equality with Catholics
   (C)   it continued the bitter civil war between Catholic and Protestant
   (D)   it brought peace to France
   (E)   it granted Huguenots political control of many towns in France

5.   Probably the most important step Cardinal Richelieu took to strengthen centralized government and an absolutist monarchy in France was
   (A)   to involve France in the Thirty Years' War
   (B)   to institute the intendant system to oversee the provinces
   (C)   to levy taxes on the clergy and nobility
   (D)   to suppress the musketeers
   (E)   to ban private duels within the realm

6.   When Louis XIV said "L'état, c'est moi," he was referring to
   (A)   his role as an enlightened despot with the peoples' best interests in mind
   (B)   his assumption of the role of his own prime minister upon the death of Mazarin
   (C)   his title as Sun King
   (D)   his resistance to the *Frondeurs*
   (E)   his belief in the divine right of kings

7.   All of the following accurately describe the reign of Louis XIV EXCEPT
   (A)   he dominated the French or Gallican Church
   (B)   he took away the independent authority of the nobility
   (C)   he filled his government with bourgeois advisors
   (D)   he impoverished the national treasury by building the Palace at Versailles
   (E)   the Golden Age of French culture coincided with his reign

8. Why, if during the reign of Louis French was the "universal language" and French styles were the measure of good taste, was the French army called the Huns of the 17th century?
    (A) It relied primarily on cavalry tactics.
    (B) It recruited troops from the Russian steppes.
    (C) Large, modern, and aggressive, it upset the continent's balance of power.
    (D) Its top commanders—Turenne, Vauban, and Conde—had trained under Attila.
    (E) It was the first European army to include integral artillery.

9. During the 16th and 17th centuries, while France developed absolutism, the English monarchy was checked by
    (A) a strong peasantry
    (B) a few powerful and independent noble families
    (C) a Bill of Rights guaranteeing individual freedoms
    (D) the Anglican Church
    (E) a strong Parliament

10. That England developed a constitutional government can be explained by all of the following EXCEPT
    (A) the English kings rejected the divine right theory
    (B) the Tudor monarchs, lacking a legitimate claim to the throne, had to cooperate with Parliament
    (C) the English gentry blurred the sharp class distinctions between the nobility and middle classes that existed elsewhere in Europe
    (D) revolution strengthened the role of Parliament
    (E) a tradition of individual rights served as a basis for constitutionalism

11. That the Anglican Church broke from Rome before altering Roman Catholic dogma indicates that
    (A) Henry started the English Reformation because he couldn't get a divorce sanctioned by the Pope
    (B) Henry's lust for Anne Boleyn motivated him to reject his devout Catholicism
    (C) because Henry was eager to have a male heir, he urged Parliament to pass the Act of Supremacy
    (D) Thomas Cranmer issued the divorce that precipitated the Reformation in return for his appointment as Archbishop of Canterbury
    (E) many factors, including resentment of papal abuses, contributed to the English Reformation

12. Which of the following was NOT a significant accomplishment during the reign of Elizabeth I?
    (A)   The Thirty-Nine Articles completed the English Reformation
    (B)   Her foreign policy encouraged the independence of the Netherlands, a commercial and colonial rival of Spain.
    (C)   She weakened the power of Spain, bastion of Catholic orthodoxy.
    (D)   She satisfied the Puritans who had criticized the Anglican lithurgy as too close to Catholicism.
    (E)   She encouraged nationalism and the development of a unique culture.

13. Probably the most significant long-term result of the Puritan Revolution (1643–1660) was
    (A)   the restoration of the Stuarts to the throne
    (B)   the issuance of the Petition of Right
    (C)   the increased authority of Parliament
    (D)   the vindication of the divine right of the monarchy
    (E)   the recognition of Calvinism as England's official religion

14. Which of the following was NOT a provision of the Declaration of Rights, 1689?
    (A)   Only Parliament can levy taxes.
    (B)   The king may maintain a standing army without the consent of Parliament.
    (C)   All laws must be made with the consent of Parliament.
    (D)   The right of trial by jury is guaranteed.
    (E)   Due process of law is guaranteed.

15. William and Mary's ascension to the English throne in 1689
    (A)   restricted the right of Parliament to raise taxes
    (B)   nullified the Declaration of Rights
    (C)   was founded on the divine-right theory
    (D)   indicated the supremacy of Parliament
    (E)   restored the Tudor dynasty

16. European exploration of the globe was motivated by
    (A)   government support for the undertakings
    (B)   religious fervor
    (C)   personal profit
    (D)   national rivalries
    (E)   all of the above

17. Which was a result of the Thirty Years' War?
    (A)   Germany replaced Austria as the predominant power in Central Europe.
    (B)   The Hapsburg reign ended Austria.
    (C)   Germany was economically devastated and its population decimated.
    (D)   The French lost all influence over German affairs.
    (E)   Sweden was victorious in all phases of the conflict.

18. Serfdom was consolidated during the 1500s and 1600s in which of the following countries?
    (A) England and France
    (B) Russia and France
    (C) Prussia and the Netherlands
    (D) Austria and Spain
    (E) Russia and Prussia

Answers and Answer Explanations

1. D	**2.** A	**3.** C	**4.** C	**5.** B
6. E	**7.** D	**8.** C	**9.** E	**10.** A
11. E	**12.** D	**13.** C	**14.** B	**15.** D
16. E	**17.** C	**18.** E		

1. (D) This is an analytical question. The growth of centralized government occurred with the weakening of the nobility and the institutions of feudalism.

2. (A) This is analysis. If you did not know that the taille was a direct tax on land and property, it helps to know that the clergy and nobility were exempt from all taxes.

3. (C) Henry IV converted from Calvinism—the Huguenots were French Calvinists—in order to placate the fears of the French majority of Catholics.

4. (C) The Edict provided rights for the Huguenot minority and so ended the bitter civil war.

5. (B) This is analytical. Choice C is out because only the French Revolution ended the exemption of these two estates; choice D is frivolous; choice E was true but not significant in itself; choice A was costly to the realm.

6. (E) When Louis said "I am the state," he was proclaiming his belief in the divine right theory.

7. (D) Despite its cost, over $100 million, and his lavish entertaining there, Versailles represented only a tiny fraction of the cost of Louis's many wars.

8. (C) Europe's largest standing army, it ravaged the countrysides of the lands it attacked and earned the epithet "Huns," referring to the Asiatic invaders who were the scourge of Europe near the end of the Roman Empire.

9. (E) Constitutionalism developed because of the struggle between the monarchy and Parliament for control of the English government.

10. (A) This is an analytical question in that an examination of the first choice reveals that it makes little sense in explaining the development of constitutional government.

11. (E) The simplistic interpretation of Henry's personal motivations as the prime cause for the English Reformation ignores other important factors.

12. (D) The Puritans continued to oppose Anglican liturgy and dogma, and this opposition was a precipitating factor for the Puritan Revolution.

13.   (C)   This is analytical in that the Stuarts were on the throne for only a few decades after the restoration, the Petition of Right was issued well before the Revolution, the theory was disgraced in England, and while Calvinism was tolerated, it was not the official religion.

14.   (B)   It is the only answer that contradicts the tone of the others.

15.   (D)   Parliament invited William and Mary, whose acceptence of the Bill of Rights established Parliament's dominance of the governing process.

16.   (E)   The impetus for exploration was multifaceted and varied among the explorers of the different Atlantic states.

17.   (C)   This confused conflict had many losers, no clear winners. France gained an influence in Germany after the treaty; Sweden fell into decline as a result of its involvement; Hapsburg Austria was frustrated in its aim to unite Germany; Germany, the battleground, was devastated and fell behind Western Europe for two centuries.

18.   (E)   Serfdom was abolished in Western European states during or even before this period; the unique political situation in Eastern Europe led to its re-establishment there.

CHAPTER 4 The 18th Century: The Expansion of Europe and the Enlightenment

Overview

An agricultural revolution took place during the later years of the 17th century and through the 18th century. The traditional "open field" system, an utterly inefficient method of agricultural production was replaced by "enclosure," and despite the social cost, productivity increased dramatically. New foods and a disappearance of the plague fostered rapid population growth. An Atlantic economy, built on trade between Europe—primarily England, France, and Holland—and the Americas benefited both Europe and the colonies, economically and socially. A series of conflicts over imperial possessions broke out among the leading European competitors during the 18th century, culminating in the French and Indian War in North America (The Seven Years' War on the continent) and the American Revolution.

The impact of science on the modern world is immeasurable. If the "Greeks had said it all" two thousand years earlier, the Renaissance Europeans rediscovered, evaluated, and elaborated or contradicted the ideas of Aristotle, Ptolemy, and other thinkers. Observation took precedence over tradition. To find out how many teeth a horse had, medieval academics scoured ancient texts to appeal to authority; modern thinkers opened the horse's mouth.

The 16th and 17th centuries saw the fruition of Renaissance individualism in religion and thought. Luther and the Protestants questioned the traditions of the Church and rebelled; Copernicus, Galileo, and Newton subjected the theories of Aristotle and Ptolemy to the inductive method and redefined the natural world. The habit of skepticism, which the Renaissance introduced and the Reformation strengthened, was science's driving force.

This skepticism gave rise to rationalism, the concept that human reason could uncover the natural laws that govern the universe and humankind itself. Inspired by the revolutionary theories of 16th and 17th century astronomy and physics, European thinkers ceased to be swayed by medieval superstition, by a belief in miracles, by a blind acceptance of tradition. Rationalism gave rise to the 18th century Enlightenment, whose philosophers argued that if humans could discover the immutable laws of the universe through the light of reason, human progress was inevitable. Critics of the status quo, they commented on the political, economic, and social ills of society and offered designs for the betterment of humanity. Their optimism and impatience aroused the forces for change and contributed to the French Revolution.

The Expansion of Europe

The *open field system*, used during the Middle Ages, divided the arable land available to a farming community into narrow strips, which were designated to the individual families of the community. Due to a lack of chemical fertilizers and ignorance about nitrogen-fixing crops, a large portion of the community's land lay fallow.

The *enclosure movement* in England, during the late 17th and the 18th centuries, fenced off the open fields to enable large landowners to employ crop rotation. By planting nitrogen-fixing crops, such as beans and certain grasses, in soil that had been used for other crops, the soil remained fertile and little land lay fallow. Many small or inefficient farmers were displaced to the towns and cities, but ultimately, food production rose dramatically.

A greater variety of foods and the introduction of foods from the New World, specifically the potato, improved general nutrition and contributed, along with the disappearance of the plague, to a dramatic increase in population. Better sanitation, introduction of quarantine methods, and the elimination of the brown rat, whose fleas carried the plague microorganisms, eliminated the plague. Except for the development of the smallpox vaccine in the late 18th century, the crude and often dangerous medical practices of the day contributed little to the health and longevity of the people.

Mercantilism was a system developed by various European states to guarantee a favorable balance of trade with other European nations or with their American colonies. By creating an imbalance of exports over imports, the difference was made up in gold or silver payments, a policy pursued to get precious metals from trading partners to pay for the costs of maintaining standing armies and government bureaucracies. Competition for colonies and for hegemony on the continent culminated in the Seven Years' War (1756–1763) fought by England and its allies against France. It resulted in the loss of France's North American possessions and in the growing independence of the British North American colonies.

Mercantilism was largely discredited by the economic liberalism of *Adam Smith* who argued that free competition, limited government regulation, and individual self-interest expressed through a supply and demand market system would foster economic growth.

The Enlightenment's Roots in the Development of Science

The Philosophers of Modern Science

Francis Bacon (1561–1626) was an English thinker who advocated the *inductive or experimental method:* observation of natural phenomena; accumulating data; experimenting to refine the data; drawing conclusions; formulating principles that are subject to continuing observation and experimentation.

Rene Descartes (1596–1650) was a French philosopher whose *Discourse on Method* (1637) argued that everything that is not validated by observation should be doubted, but that his own existence is proven by the proposition that "I think, therefore I am" *(cogito ergo sum)*. God exists, he argued, because a perfect being would have existence as part of its nature. *Cartesian Dualism* divided all existence into the spiritual and the material—the former can be examined only through deductive reasoning; the latter is subject to the experimental method. His goal to reconcile religion with science was short-circuited by the very method of skepticism that subsequent philosophers inherited from his writings.

The Revolutionary Thinkers of Science

Nicolaus Copernicus (1473–1543), a Polish astronomer, upset the comfortable assumptions of the *geocentric* (earth-centered) universe of *Ptolemy* (the 2nd century A.D. Egyptian) with his *heliocentric* (sun-centered) conception of the universe. Although his work, *Concerning the Revolutions of the Heavenly Bodies*, was not published until after his death, his theories were proven by *Johann Kepler* (1571–1630), a German who plotted the elliptic orbits of the planets, thereby predicting their movements, and by the great *Galileo Galilei* (1564–1642) whose telescopic observations validated Copernican theory and whose spirited advocacy earned him condemnation by the Inquisition. The Copernican heliocentric view seemed to contradict the primacy of humanity in God's creation and therefore to deny the teachings of the Church. Supported in Protestant Northern Europe, where the Reformation had questioned all orthodoxy, the theory and the scientific method that had formulated it symbolized Europe's new intellectual freedom. When the Roman Catholic Church tried to suppress the Copernican revolution by banning writings and by trying the charismatic Galileo, it earned a lasting reputation for rigidity. It took nearly 350 years for the papacy to exonerate Galileo.

If Copernicus shook the medieval conception of Christianity to its foundations, the work of *Isaac Newton* (1642–1727) not only tested the notion of God's intervention in human affairs but established the ascendancy of science in the modern world. Newton, an Englishman, demonstrated that *natural laws* of motion—gravitation—account for the movement of heavenly bodies and earthly objects. Since these laws are unchangeable and predictable, God's active participation is not needed to explain the operations of the forces of nature, a repudiation of medieval belief.

Deism—God as a kind of cosmic clockmaker who created a perfect universe that he does not have to intervene in—grew out of Newton's natural law theories. *Rationalism*—the conviction that the laws of nature are fathomable by human reason and that humanity is perfectable—was an assumption and a goal of the Enlightenment.

The *scientific revolution* of the 16th and 17th centuries redefined astronomy and physics. Less dramatic but still significant advances took place in *mathematics,* especially with the development of probability and calculus, in *medicine* through advances in surgery, anatomy, drug therapy, and with the discovery of microorganisms, and with the establishment of *learned societies*, dedicated to the advance of science, such as the *French Academy of Sciences* and the *Royal Society of London*.

The development of science transformed the intellectual life of Europe by convincing people that human reason could understand the secrets of the universe and transform life without the help of organized religion. The 18th century marked the end of the *Age of Religion*, which had governed European thought for over a millennium. Skepticism and rationalism—offshoots of the development of science—encouraged the growth of secularism. These modes of thought guided the Enlightenment and defined modern life.

The Enlightenment

An Englishman, Newton, inspired the Enlightenment; a group of Frenchmen, the philosophes, shaped it. Newton's work in astronomy and physics convinced European thinkers that human reason, unaided by the tenets and rituals of religion, could uncover the immutable laws of nature. The philosophes, who were actually literary figures more than academic philosophers, argued that once the natural laws that governed nature and human existence were discovered, society could be organized in accordance with them and progress was inevitable. Leaders of French culture, which dominated Europe, they lauded Newton, borrowed from Locke, and flooded Europe with radically optimistic notions about how people should live and govern themselves, ideas that were to shake the old order to pieces and build in its place the democratic, humanistic Western World.

If Newton's theories served as the inspiration for the natural law philosophy of the Enlightenment, *John Locke's* political writings translated the natural law assumption into a conception of government. Locke (1632–1704), an Englishman, provided a philosophical apology for the supremacy of Parliament during the Glorious Revolution with his *Two Treatises on Civil Government:*

> In the *state of nature*, before governments existed, humans lacked protection. Although governments, once institututed, replace individual action with the rule of law, they rest upon the *consent of the governed*. The *social contract*—the agreement between a fair government and responsible individuals—is not unconditional. If government oversteps its role in protecting the life, liberty, and property of its citizens, the people have the right to abolish and replace it.

These conceptions of the *consent of the governed*, the *social contract*, and the *right of revolution* spearheaded the philosophes' criticism of the absolutist ancien régime or old order.

The *Philosophes*

Voltaire personified the Age of Reason. Born *François Marie Arouet* in 1694 in Paris at the height of Louis XIV's reign, he lived until 1778, two years after the American Declaration of Independence. Although he was more writer than philosopher—poet, essayist, dramatist, satirist—his genius for social criticism helped inflame desire for change and set the stage for the Age of Revolution. He preached against injustice and bigotry and for human rights and science. *"Ecrasez l'infame"* ("Crush the infamous") was his rallying cry against rigid religion, governmental abuse, and vestiges of medievalism. Imprisoned briefly in the Bastille, he visited England, lived in the court of *Frederick the Great*, *Enlightened Despot* of Prussia, and earned an international reputation. Like most of the Enlightenment thinkers, he was raised as a Christian but came to reject organized religion as corrupt in its leadership and remote from the urgent message of Jesus. He was a staunch advocate of *Deism,* the theological offshoot of natural law theory. As a Deist, he believed that prayer and miracles violated the perfect natural order God had created and that the world's evils are caused by man's straying from the natural law. The social reform that he called for fit the Deist notion that human reason alone could uncover the natural law and guide humans to comply with it.

Jean Jacques Rousseau (1712–1778) is considered a philosophe, a man of the Enlightenment, but he is more accurately the founder of the Romantic movement. After the excesses of the French Revolution, the Enlightenment's emphasis on the *rule of reason* gave way to a glorification of emotion. Despising—intellectually and personally—the rigid and inequitable class structure of the ancien régime, he developed the idea of the *noble savage:* that civilization corrupted humankind and that life in the *state of nature* was purer, freer, more virtuous. The goal of the individual, he argued in his many writings, was to attain full expression of natural instincts by stripping away the artificial restraints of society and returning as far as possible to nature. The goal of a people was to achieve self-determination, a clarion call to the nationalism that the French Revolution awakened all over Europe. In *The Social Contract*, he said, "Man is born free, but everywhere he is in chains," meaning that property, when regarded as more important than people, causes social injustice. The *general will*, a kind of consensus of the majority, he thought should control a nation. This was intended to support a democratic view of government, but because it does not recognize minority viewpoints and since it has no clear way to show itself, it could be used to rationalize extreme nationalism and repression. Whatever the flaws in his philosophy, Rousseau is considered one the most influential thinkers of his day. His distrust of *civilization* and its institutions led him to criticize rigid educational practices and the strict discipline of children. In his treatise *Emile*, he argued that children have to be understood as individuals and that they need caring from their teachers as well as from their parents. He and other *Enlightenment* critics helped to change the educational and child-rearing practices of 18th-century Europe.

Baron de Montesquieu (1689–1755) in his work, *Spirit of the Laws*, argued that the powers of government—legislative, executive, and judicial—must be separated in order to avoid depotism. When these functions are divided among various groups or individuals, each *checks and balances* the powers of the others. His theories served as a blueprint for the governmental structure outlined in the U.S. Constitution.

Denis Diderot (1713–1784) published the writings and popularized the ideas of many of the philosophes in his *Encyclopedia,* a collection of political and social critiques rather than a compilation of facts.

Francois Quesnay (1694–1774) led the *physiocrats* whose motto was laissez-faire and who believed that government should remove all restraints to free trade—such as tariffs—so that the natural laws of economics were free to operate for the good of society.

Adam Smith (1727–1790), an Englishman, refined and expanded the laissez-faire philosophy of the *physiocrats* in his *Wealth of Nations.* Published in 1776, the year of the Declaration of Independence, it is considered the "Bible of capitalism": the economy is governed by natural laws, such as *supply and demand;* in a free economy, competition will induce producers to manufacture most efficiently in order to sell higher quality, lower cost goods than competitors; government regulation only interferes with this natural self-governing operation.

Enlightened Despotism

The ideal Enlightened Despot was a ruler who aimed for the advancement of society by fostering education, aiding the economy, and promoting social justice. Since Voltaire and most of the philosophers, and certainly most of Europe's monarchs, believed that the mass of people were incapable of self-government, Enlightened Despots stayed in power while promoting the good of their people.

In the 17th century, *Russia* and *Prussia* rose as powerful states, challenging Poland, the ancient *Hapsburg state of Austria*, and the declining empire of the Ottomans. In Prussia and, ironically, in Russia—whose culture often lagged decades, even centuries, behind that of the West—Enlightened Despotism held sway during important periods of the 18th century. Such rule helped slow the decline of Austria, whose monarchs still held the title of Holy Roman Emperor. In Western Europe, Enlightened Despotism manifested itself in Sweden, Spain, and Portugal, but it shone most brilliantly in the East.

Prussia

"Prussia was an army before it was a nation," it has been said, because its origin was as an outpost of the Holy Roman Empire and its *Hohenzollern* rulers cultivated a superbly trained and well-equipped army drawn from all areas of their domain. Local loyalties were transferred to the army, which then served as the focal point for Prussian nationalism. *Frederick William* (1640–1688) and his son and grandson, *Frederick I* (1688–1713) and *Frederick William I* (1713–1740), centralized the government and encouraged industry in order to support the state's relatively large standing army. Their Enlightened Despotism reached fruition during the rule of Frederick I's grandson, *Frederick II* or *Frederick the Great* (1740–1786). "First servant of the state," as he called himself, Frederick the Great was a military genius who made Prussia a major power in Europe, an urbane and educated man who patronized the great Voltaire, a domestic reformer who improved education, codified laws, fostered industry, invited immigration, and extended religious toleration. Twenty years after he died, his modernized and expanded nation was subdued by Napoleon, and the army—led by officers recruited from the Junkers (landowning aristocrats)—remained as the only viable institution to lead Prussia's resurgence in the mid-19th century and to define German nationalism well into the 20th.

Russia

Russia became a state in the 15th century when the *Duchy of Muscovy*, under *Ivan the Great* (1462–1505) overcame subjugation by the Central Asian *Tartars.* After the *Fall of Constantinople* to the Ottoman Turks in 1453, Russia became not only the inheritor of Byzantine culture and the center of the Orthodox Church, but an empire with Moscow as "the third Rome" and a czar (Caesar) on the throne. Under *Basil III* (1505–1533) and the much maligned but very capable *Ivan the Terrible* (1533–1584), expansion and consolidation of the new empire continued—with reverses, however. In order to get troops, the empire gave aristocractic landowners, the *Boyars,* control over their peasants, who gradually fell into *serfdom,* a condition of being bound to the land that had ended in virtually all of Western Europe. The Boyars influenced government policy through a council, the *Duma,* and, a theme common in most nations with a monarchy, there was a continuing battle for supremacy between a strong central government and a powerful aristocracy.

Peter the Great (1689–1725), a Romanov and a contemporary of Louis XIV of France, gained vast territories to the Baltic Sea in the north, to the Black Sea in the south, and to the Far East. Probably his greatest contribution was the *Westernization of Russia.* Although he could not be considered an Enlightened Despot, he recruited hundreds of Western artisans, built a new capital on the Gulf of Finland, *St. Petersburg*, his "window to the West," reformed the government bureaucracy and the Russian Orthodox Church, reorganized and equipped the army with modern weapons, and encouraged commerce and industry.

Catherine the Great (1762–1796), a German who succeeded to the throne after the murder of her husband, *Czar Peter III*, was a patron of many of the French philosophes and considered herself an Enlightened Despot. Inaction and panic over a social revolution, *Pugachev's Rebellion*, diluted her domestic reforms. She did continue Peter the Great's work of territorial expansion by annexing both Polish and Ottoman land.

Austria

In Austria, during the 18th century, *Maria Theresa* (1740–1780) and her son, *Joseph II* (1780–1790), qualify as genuine Enlightened Despots. The *Hapsburg Dynasty* had been weakened by the time Maria Theresa inherited the throne under a cloud of counterclaims, and she was determined to strengthen the realm by centralizing the government, promoting commerce, and limiting the power of the nobles. Joseph furthered his mother's reforms by guaranteeing freedom of the press and of religion, reforming the judicial system toward greater equality for all classes, making German the official language for the empire's many ethnic minorities in order to foster centralization, and especially *abolishing serfdom.*

Sample Essay Question

The sample and practice thematic essay questions presented in this chapter are types found in the Advanced Placement Examination in European History, and they require a knowledge of causes, effects, personalities, ideas, and events.

Sample Question

> *Analyze* the relationship between the Newtonian Revolution and the Enlightenment.

Comments on the Sample Question

Follow the "Simple Procedures" for writing an essay. (See page 24.)

First, *What does the question want to know?* The wording of the question implies a direct relationship between Newton's discoveries and the philosophical underpining of the Enlightenment.

Second, *What do you know about it?* The task is twofold: Determine the relationship; examine it in detail.

Third, *How would you put it into words?* You have to clarify the issues. What was the Newtonian Revolution? How did its discoveries influence ideas beyond the realm of the physical sciences? Who were the proponents of these ideas? How did the ideas and personalities set the tone for the so-called Age of Reason?

Sample Answer

Copernicus's heliocentric universe had shaken conventional religion's smug assumptions of humanity's importance as much if not more than the Reformation had upset orthodoxy. Since the earth was no longer the center of all creation, perhaps humankind was not the focus of God's attention. To 16th century Europe, this idea was immeasurably more traumatic than the landing of space aliens of superior intelligence would be to late 20th century earthlings. Copernicus turned the easy biases of an age upside down. Newton's discoveries, published a century and half after the death of Copernicus, established the intellectual foundations for an age: the Enlightenment.

Newton demonstrated that unchangeable natural laws governed the motion of all bodies in the universe—from the movement of the stars to the rotation of the earth to the motion of physical things on the earth's surface. Gravity and all the other natural laws were not only unchangeable, but they were predictable.

A deeply religious man who believed he would be remembered to history because of his biblical studies, Newton had no conception that his findings would lead other thinkers to discount the need for God to explain the functioning of the universe and would argue that God never intervened in a universe that he had created to function according to perfect and precise laws. "God as clockmaker," watching his creations function according to his perfectly designed mechanism, was called *Deism,* and it was the religious persuasion of many of the thinkers of the Enlightenment.

The Enlightenment, the 18th century Age of Reason before the outbreak of the French Revolution, was an outgrowth of Newton's "natural law" explanations. Commentators on Newton's findings insisted that if natural law governs the motions of physical objects, it also controls the functioning of human society. Once human intellect could uncover these laws, it could design a world in harmony with them. Progress was the faith of this Age of Reason. What these natural laws were and how human society should be designed in accordance with them was open to interpretation. That was the role of philosophes, mostly French writers and social commentators who were more literary men than academic philosophers.

Since French was the language of high culture in the 18th century, these gifted individuals influenced intellectuals and ordinary people all across Europe. Voltaire, the personification of the Enlightenment man of reason, rejected traditional Christianity as corrupted and out of touch with the natural laws that are so perfect in their workings that God would not interfere with them even to answer prayers. Rousseau argued that humans in a state of nature were purer and better than in society, which distorted their "noble savagery." They, and thinkers who shared their basic assumptions about natural law, sought to improve the lot of the mass of people who lived under the political repression and economic deprivation of the Old Regime.

Newton's laws of physics and astronomy served as models for a rational universe whose mysteries were discoverable by human reason, whose natural laws would make this "the best of all possible worlds."

Evaluate the Sample Answer

1. Did the introduction show the direction of the argument?
2. Did the analysis "determine the relationship" between the Newtonian Revolution and the Enlightenment, "examine in detail" the concepts and personalities involved, and "explain" clearly?
3. Did it miss any relevant facts or relationships?
4. Was the essay long enough, easily understood, well organized?
5. Did you disagree with any part of the argument?
6. Did the conclusion clarify and sum up the argument?

Rater's Comments on the Sample Answer

4—Well qualified

While this is a concise and general essay, it delivers the substance of a good answer. It is well reasoned, nicely organized, and convincing. It "determines the relationship" between the discoveries of Newton and the Age of Enlightenment.

Where it is lacking is in "examining that relationship in detail." What exactly was the Newtonian Revolution? What was the Enlightenment? The answers are implied, but they should have been spelled out. Were Voltaire and Rousseau the only contributors to Enlightenment thinking? What part did "natural law" play in theirs and the writings of others such as Locke, Montesquieu, Adam Smith?

Practice Essay Questions

The questions that follow are samples of the various types of thematic essays that appear on the Advanced Placement Examination in European History. (See pages 17–18 for a detailed explanation of each type.)

> **1.**   *Contrast and compare* the contributions to the development of modern science of Bacon and Descartes with those of Copernicus and Galileo.

Comments on Question 1

"Show the differences; examine similarities." This task appears to be straight-forward since, as the questions implies, the roles of Bacon and Descartes in the rise of modern science are similar, and they contrast with those of Copernicus and Galileo. Bacon and Descartes are "philosophers of science" whose writings helped establish the methodology of science: skepticism, observation, generalization, experimentation. Copernicus and Galileo, on the other hand, were "genuine" scientists whose theories or experimentation furthered the store of scientific knowledge.

The tricky part of this question is to apply the "contrast and comparison" rule to Bacon and Descartes then to Copernicus and Galileo as well as to the two pairs. Did Bacon's writings contribute differently than Descartes's to the "scientific mind"? Were Copernicus's methods and findings different from those of Galileo?

> **2.**   "Newton inspired the Enlightenment, Locke provided the blueprint; the philosophes shaped it." *Assess the validity* of this statement.

Comments on Question 2

The goal here is to "determine the truth" of this statement by ascertaining how Newtonian physics and astronomy gave rise to "natural law" theory, how Locke applied that theory to the relations between the individual and government, then how the philosophes used Newtonian "natural law" and Lockian political theory to shape the Age of Reason.

Be careful to define "natural law," to spell out Locke's applications of it in his theory of government, to characterize the Enlightenment that dominated the intellectual life of 18th-century Europe, and to show how important philosophes—Voltaire, Montesquieu, Rousseau, Quesnay—influenced the movement.

> **3.**   *Contrast and compare* Locke and Rousseau's concept of the social contract.

Comments on Question 3

Locke, who lived before the Enlightenment, influenced Rousseau. Rousseau, who dominated the Enlightenment's push for social reform, has been called more of a Romantic than a philosophe insofar as he departed from Locke's political theory. The way to "show differences" would be first to "examine similarities" in their concepts of the state of nature and the social contract, then, to show how Locke's ideas influenced Rousseau's, and finally to examine how Rousseau departed from Locke. Although this question is straightforward, it requires a thorough understanding of the abstract theories involved.

> **4.** "The Enlightened Despots were more despotic than enlightened."
> *Defend or refute* this statement.

Comments on Question 4

According to the democratic biases of our age, an Enlightened Despot is a contradiction in terms. For the world of the 18th century, mired in the excesses of anachronistic absolutism, the "Enlightened Despots" were products of the Age of Reason. They were monarchs who maintained a firm hold on the reins of power but who made decisions for the good of the masses, whom they did not trust to be self-governing.

This requires specific references and evaluations of the various monarchs who claimed to be—or are labeled by history as—Enlightened Despots. Who are some? Frederick the Great of Prussia? Peter the Great and Catherine the Great of Russia? Maria Theresa and Joseph II of Austria? Make reference to three or four. Measure their reigns for genuine reform: Did the reforms change the life of the people? Did they last? Decide whether to defend or refute.

> **5.** *To what extent and in what ways* is Deism a logical offshoot of the theory of "natural law?"

Comments on Question 5

How and how much did the concept of natural laws give rise to the "religion of the Enlightenment"? The key term in the question is "logical offshoot." The task is to demonstrate how Deism—the belief in God's nonintervention in a perfectly created universe—follows logically from the concept of a universe guided by unchangeable natural laws. The question does not require a logician's reasoning; it requires that you trace the historical development of Deism from the applications of Newtonian natural law. How did Voltaire, for instance, use natural law and the concept of the Prime Mover to argue against traditional Christianity? Why would he have argued against prayer and miracles?

> **6.** *Explain* how the replacement of the open field system by the enclosure movement increased agricultural productivity in 18th century Europe.

Comments on Question 6

Describe the open field system and its limitations, specifically, the amount of fallow land. Explain how the enclosure movement used crop rotation to expand the use of arable land and to increase food production.

> **7.** *Why* did the population of Europe increase dramatically in the 1700s?

Comments on Question 7

Explain the roles of food production, new foods, and the disappearance of the plague; emphasize that the medical practices of the day played little part in the increase.

Practice Multiple-Choice Questions

(These are representative of the types of questions found on the Advanced Placement Examination.)

1. Which was NOT a significant factor in the development of science during the 15th and 16th centuries?
   (A) The Renaissance
   (B) Scientific writings of the ancient Greeks
   (C) The Protestant Reformation
   (D) The Roman Catholic emphasis on an appeal to authority in intellectual matters
   (E) The experiences of direct observation

2. The experimental or inductive method was championed in the 16th century by
   (A) Francis Bacon
   (B) Girolamo Cardano
   (C) Wilhelm Leibniz
   (D) Aristotle
   (E) Christian Huygens

3. The Copernican Revolution was so named because
   (A) it reconciled the Ptolemaic conception of the universe with observation
   (B) it eliminated Ptolemy's cumbersome mathematics
   (C) it upset the comfortable assumptions of humanity's central place in the universe
   (D) it was suppressed by the Inquisition
   (E) its elegant simplicity reflected godliness

4. At first ignored, the work of Copernicus was validated by
   (A) Tycho Brahe
   (B) Blaise Pascal
   (C) Kepler and Galileo
   (D) Descartes
   (E) Gilbert

5. In his *Principia Mathematica,* 1687, Isaac Newton demonstrated all EXCEPT
   (A) that gravity and centripetal and centrifugal forces account for the motion of heavenly bodies
   (B) that gravity and centripetal and centrifugal forces move earthly objects
   (C) that the natural laws that govern these forces allow the prediction of all natural movement
   (D) that the natural laws explain how the universe is held together
   (E) that God created the universe but does not intervene in it

6.   The famous phrase "Cogito ergo sum," "I think, therefore I am," was the logical foundation upon which the systematic doubt of 17th century thinker René Descartes builds a proof of reality. His philosophy was significant because
   (A)   it repudiated Christianity
   (B)   it defined many of the significant issues of modern philosophy
   (C)   it proved Deism
   (D)   it established Cartesian duality as the basis for modern science
   (E)   it relegated God to the role of Prime Mover

7.   Which of the following CANNOT be said of the 18th-century Enlightenment?
   (A)   The Newtonian Revolution of the previous century set it in motion.
   (B)   It was based on the belief that unchangeable natural laws governed human society as well as the physical universe.
   (C)   It supported the assumption that human reason could fathom the natural laws.
   (D)   It reflected acceptance of social inequities and injustice as inevitable effects of the natural law.
   (E)   It was optimistic and progress oriented.

8.   What has been called the "religion of the Enlightenment"?
   (A)   Protestantism
   (B)   Agnosticism
   (C)   Atheism
   (D)   Rationalism
   (E)   Deism

"When popes and priests define their dogmas and discipline their followers, corruption is the rule and abuse is the result. 'Crush the infamous thing!' The simple beauty of Christ's message has been lost in ignorance and encrusted with superstition."

9.   To the above speaker, "the infamous thing" probably referred to
   (A)   Organized religion
   (B)   The papacy
   (C)   The Catholic priesthood
   (D)   The Roman Catholic Church
   (E)   All of the above

10.   The speaker would probably adhere to the views of
   (A)   Bishop Bossuet
   (B)   Voltaire
   (C)   Montesquieu
   (D)   Baron Holbach
   (E)   Diderot

11. Whose *Spirit of the Laws*, 1748, served as a basis for the American Constitution's "separation of powers"?
    - (A) Montesquieu
    - (B) Voltaire
    - (C) Rousseau
    - (D) Diderot
    - (E) Quesnay

12. Rousseau can be called an advocate of democracy and an apologist for dictatorship because
    - (A) many of his closest friends were of the nobility
    - (B) he argued that property is the root of social evil
    - (C) he introduced the concept of the "Noble Savage"
    - (D) his vague concept of the general will could be misinterpreted
    - (E) he believed that civilization corrupts people

13. The philosophes shared the following characteristics EXCEPT
    - (A) most were Deists
    - (B) most rejected organized religion
    - (C) most believed that this was "the best of all possible worlds"
    - (D) most sought to foster human progress according to the principles of natural law
    - (E) most accepted the philosophical principles of John Locke

14. Which best characterized Enlightened Despotism?
    - (A) The monarch is an educated person who exercises absolute authority.
    - (B) The monarch encourages the spread of Deism and rationalism.
    - (C) The monarch supports and fosters the growth of democracy.
    - (D) The monarch rules with absolute authority for the good of the people.
    - (E) The monarch believes in the people's ultimate right to, and capability for, self-rule.

15. Which of the following was generally not considered an Enlightened Despot?
    - (A) Frederick the Great of Prussia
    - (B) Peter the Great of Russia
    - (C) Catherine the Great of Russia
    - (D) Maria Theresa of Austria
    - (E) Alexander the Great of Russia

Answers and Answer Explanations

1. D	2. A	3. C	4. C	5. E
6. B	7. D	8. E	9. E	10. B
11. A	12. D	13. C	14. D	15. E

1. (D) The traditions of the Roman Catholic Church discouraged scholarly pursuits that relied on the inductive method of inquiry. Reverence for authority was a key to study.

2. (A)   Aristotle was the ancient Greek philosopher whose work on logic served the medieval philosophers. Although he analyzed the inductive method, the medievals did not stress it. The others are mathematicians of the early modern period whose work aided the advance of science.

3. (C)   An earth-centered universe supported the medieval world's conception of the utter importance of humankind as expressed by biblical creation.

4. (C)   Kepler's demonstration of the elliptic orbits of the planets and Galileo's direct observation of the heavenly bodies supported Copernicus's theories years after his death.

5. (E)   That God created but does not intervene in the universe is a precept of Deism, a religious view that was influenced by Newton's theories but not part of them. Newton was a biblical scholar who believed he would be remembered for this rather than his scientific work.

6. (B)   A religious man in a religious age, Descartes hoped to provide a logical foundation for the existence of the supernatural while he stressed the importance of observation in studying the natural world.

7. (D)   The philosophes argued for progress and social justice as reflective of the natural law.

8. (E)   It was a philosophical offshoot of Newton's natural law explanation for the motions of the universe.

9. (E)   Many of the philosophes regarded the supersitions and narrowness of religion as enemies of progress.

10. (B)   Voltaire coined the phrase "Crush the infamous thing," referring primarily to bigotry.

11. (A)   It is the most familiar concept of his complex political theory.

12. (D)   He never defined "general will" clearly. If it is equivalent in a democracy to the majority what are the rights of the minority? In dictatorship, a despot can claim to be the embodiment of the general will.

13. (C)   This concept was contrary to their belief in the perfectability of humanity.

14. (D)   The monarch, who might rule by divine right, still has the obligation to do good for his people, who are incapable of self-rule.

15. (E)   Czar during the Napoleonic Wars and after, his reforms were short-lived and halfhearted.

5 The French Revolution, Napoleon, and the Congress of Vienna

Overview

In 1789, France had a population of about 25 million, a productive economy, rich farmlands, and a culture that dominated the continent. French was not only the language of diplomacy, but it was the tongue spoken in most of the courts of Europe. France was the center of the 18th century Enlightenment. Despite its wealth and influence, its government was corrupt, inefficient, and in debt, its class structure archiac and unjust, its institutions encrusted with medieval traditionalism. Stoked by the ideals and illusions of the Enlightenment, smoldering class resentments erupted in revolution. The revolution began as a moderate attempt at reform, degenerated into radical blood-letting, then swung back to authoritarianism in search of order. Impelled by the ideals of "liberty, equality, fraternity" and by military power, the French Revolution became an international movement that overthrew the feudal structures of the Old Regime in France and shook the political and social order in all of Europe.

Napoleon defined an age, 1799 to 1815. A capable person in the right place at the right time becomes great. His genius for military success created in less than a decade a French empire that stretched across the continent. His gift for administration and reform implemented the ideals of the Revolution. Ambition and the unexpected led to his downfall. He lost the cream of his magnificent army in the wasteland of the Russian winter; he arrayed most of Europe against him when his victories in the field awakened nationalism in the rest of Europe. After his fall, the old order tried to restore itself at the Congress of Vienna. A balance of power maintained relative peace for a century, but Europe had entered the Age of "Isms," and powerful new social, economic, and political forces would define the Western World.

The French Revolution

The Old Regime

A class structure left over from the Middle Ages determined the political and social order of France:

> *The First Estate*, the clergy, made up considerably less than 1 percent of the population, but the Roman Catholic Church of France (Gallican Church) owned 20 percent of the land. The clergy and the Church were exempt from taxes.

The Second Estate, the nobles, numbered between 2 and 4 percent of the population and also owned about 20 percent of the land. They were also exempt from taxes.

The Third Estate, the middle class, urban artisans, and peasants, made up over 95 percent of the population. Although France had developed a significant commercial or middle class, the bourgeoisie, the mass of the people were peasants who lived on the land.

The Third Estate, especially the peasantry, was subjected to a variety of oppressive taxes: taille, a land tax; tithe, a church tax equivalent to 10 percent of annual income, income tax, poll tax, salt tax, and local duties paid to the feudal lord. Personal freedom was jeopardized by the lettre de cachet, by which the government could imprison anyone without charges or trial. The bourgeoisie was disenchanted by its lack of influence in a system that it disproportionately supported.

Burdened by debts run up by Louis XIV's wars and extravagances, by the corruption and inefficiency of the administration of his successors, and by France's support of the American Revolution, the government of *Louis XVI* (1774–1792) attempted to tax the previously exempt clergy and nobility. A high court of France, the *Parlement of Paris*, ruled that new taxes could not be levied unless approved by the *Estates-General*, the legislative body equivalent to a parliament and representative of the three classes.

The First or Moderate Stage of the Revolution (1789–1792)

May 5, 1789: The Estates-General met in Versailles.

June 13, 1789: Supported by a few members of the First Estate, the Third Estate broke a voting deadlock in the Estates-General by declaring itself the *National Assembly*.

June 20, 1789: After being locked out of their meeting place by the king's troops, members of the National Assembly swore the *Tennis Court Oath* not to disband until they had written a new constitution for France.

July 14, 1789: After food riots in the cities, peasant rebellions in the countryside, and the inaction of Louis and his ministers, a Parisian mob stormed the *Bastille*, a fortress that symbolized royal injustice.

August 4, 1789: The Decrees of this date mark when the National Assembly *abolished feudalism and manorialism*.

August 26, 1789: Declaration of the Rights of Man and the Citizen was passed. Freedom of speech, thought, and religion were guaranteed; due process of law was guaranteed; taxes could be imposed only by consent of the governed; the right to rule was said to be not just the king's but the whole nation's.

September, 1789: The National Assembly was also named the *Constituent Assembly* because it was drafting a constitution. October 1789: A Paris mob, mostly of women, was incited by Jean Paul Marat to *march on Versailles* and force the king to relocate to the *Tuileries*, the royal residence in Paris. The assembly also went to Paris and was intimidated by the Parisians.

November 2, 1789: The assembly *seized Church and monastery lands* for revenue.

1790: The Civil Constitution of the Clergy was drafted. Convents and monasteries were abolished; all clergyman were to be paid by the state and elected by all citizens; the clergy was forbidden to accept the authority of the pope. Alienated by this decree, half of the priests of the Gallican Church refused to accept it.

1791: The National (Constituent) Assembly drafted a new constitution that instituted an *elected Legislative Assembly*, which made the king chief executive officer, largely responsible to the assembly; the latter established voting qualifications for male citizens.

June 21, 1791: The *Flight to Varennes* of the royal family, in order to raise a counterrevolutionary army, was stopped, and the king and queen became prisoners of the Parisian mobs.

August, 1791: The *Declaration of Pillnitz* by the king of Austria threatened military action to restore order in France and encouraged the radical revolutionaries who wanted to overthrow the monarchy.

The Second or Radical Stage of the Revolution (1792–1795)

April 20, 1792: The *Legislative Assembly*, the legislature under the new constitution, *declared war on Austria* in response to an ultimatum. The *"Wars of the Revolution"* began.

July 25, 1792: The commander of a Prussian army, about to invade France, issued the *Brunswick Manifesto*, threatening the people of Paris if harm came to the king. *Jacobin* (radical republican) leaders aroused the Paris mobs.

August 10, 1792: The *Tuileries were stormed* and the king was taken prisoner; the mobs slaughtered over a thousand priests, bourgeois, and aristocrats who opposed their program.

September 21, 1792: France was proclaimed a republic, the First.

1793: An appeal to nationalism inspired the French people to drive back their invaders, and the *First Coalition*, an alliance of Austria, England, Netherlands, Prussia, and Spain, was organized to combat the French advance.

The *Jacobins*, supported by the Paris mobs, and the *Girondists*, supported by the peasants in the rural areas, battled for control of the *National Convention*, which was the new assembly under the republic.

Maximilien Robespierre, leader of the Jacobins, pushed for the execution of the king—tried for treason—and both *Louis XVI* and his queen, *Marie Antoinette*, were guillotined in January 1793.

May 1793: Enragés—radical working-class leaders of Paris—seized and arrested Girondist members of the *National Convention* and left the Jacobins in control under the leadership of Robespierre.

Summer 1793: A dictatorial *Committee of Public Safety* launched the Reign of Terror. Over 40,000 people—nearly 75 percent of them working class and peasants—were executed from the summer of 1793 to that of 1794.

Late 1793: The *Republic of Virtue* was proclaimed by the Committee of Public Safety in an attempt to de-Christianize France; it largely alienated the Catholic majority of the nation.

1794: Both *Danton*, an original Jacobin, and Robespierre, leader of the Republic of Virtue, were executed by the National Convention when public opinion turned against the excesses of the Reign of Terror.

The Final or Reactionary Stage of the Revolution (1795–1799)

The *Thermidorian Reaction*, which took place during the month of *Thermidor* (August 18–September 16) on the new non-Christian calendar, returned the moderate bourgeois reformers to power.

1795–1799: The *Directory*, a five-member executive, was established by the National Convention to run the government. When a Paris mob threatened the new government, *Napoleon Bonaparte*, a young general who by chance was in Paris at the time, put down the riot and was rewarded with the command of the French armies fighting the Austrians in Italy.

Napoleon

In 1799, Napoleon, after spectacular victories against the Austrians and later against English armies in Egypt, overthrew the Directory in a coup d'état and formed a new government, the *Consulate*, made up of three consuls with Napoleon as head consul.

Napoleon's Domestic Reforms

Even as emperor, Napoleon Bonaparte was committed to many of the ideals of the French Revolution. Son of an impoverished minor aristocrat and a virtual foreigner—Corsica, the island of his birth, had been owned by Italy for centuries until its annexation by the French shortly before his birth—Napoleon reached the heights he did because the Revolution opened society to men of ability. His reforms assured the dissolution of the Old Regime by establishing egalitarianism in government, before the law, and in educational opportunity.

Napoleon signed *The Concordat* of 1801 with the Pope whereby the papacy renounced claims over church property seized during the Revolution and was allowed to nominate bishops. In return, those priests who had resisted the Civil Constitutions of the clergy would replace those who had sworn an oath to the state. Since the pope gave up claim to church lands, those citizens who had acquired them pledged loyalty to Napoleon's government.

With the *Code Napoleon*, 1804, Napoleon replaced varied and inequitable medieval law with a uniform legal system. It was a model for codes of law in many European countries. In 1808, he instituted a *state-supported educational system* with rigorous standards and available to the masses.

He created a *merit system* to recruit and reward those in government, despite the fact that he practiced flagrant *nepotism* by placing his relatives on the thrones of nations he conquered.

He lowered the taxes on farmers, and guaranteed that the redistributed church lands remained in the hands of their new owners, who were mostly peasant farmers. This created an *independent peasantry* that would be the backbone of French democracy.

Napoleon's Conquests and Defeats

His aim was to unite Europe under France's leadership. In a decade, he was able to conquer vastly more territory and to influence the destinies of more nations than the Sun King, Louis XIV, had in his sixty and more years' reign. His very success convinced the peoples he conquered or battled that the future lay in national unity, and the force of nationalism led to his downfall and shaped the destiny of Europe well into the 20th century.

Italy: In 1797, his victories led to a Northern Italian Republic, the *Cisalpine*, and several satellites in Central and Southern Italy under French control. By 1809, he controlled virtually all of Italy, abolishing feudalism and reforming the social, political, and economic structures. He decided against national unity for the Italians, who had been divided into competing city-states and kingdoms during the Middle Ages, because unity might pose a threat to French dominance of the region.

Germany: After soundly defeating the two most powerful and influential German states—Austria and Prussia—Napoleon reorganized Germany. He consolidated many of the nearly 300 independent political entities (among these creations was the *Confederation of the Rhine*), and he abolished feudalism and carried out reforms. He awakened German nationalism.

The Continental System: Through a series of shifting alliances, the English had consistently opposed the upset of the European balance of power brought about by French victories on the continent. Unable to destroy British supremacy at sea and invade Britain, Napoleon decided to starve Britain out by closing the ports of the continent to British commerce. He coerced Russia, a temporary ally of the French, his defeated enemy Prussia, neutral Denmark and Portugal, and French satellite Spain all to adhere to the boycott.

Spain: When Napoleon tried to tighten his control over Spain by replacing the Spanish king with one of his own brothers, the Spanish people waged a costly *guerrilla war* that was aided by the British under one of their ablest commanders, the *Duke of Wellington*.

Russia: Napoleon *invaded Russia* in June of 1812, when the Russians withdrew from the Continental System because of the economic hardships it caused. Despite spectacular victories, Napoleon's *Grand Army* was forced to retreat from Moscow during the brutal Russian winter by the "*scorched earth*" tactic of the Russians.

The Collapse of the Napoleonic Empire

Having lost 500,000 of his 600,000-man Grand Army, facing riots in Italy and a British invasion of Southern France by Wellington's army, Napoleon was defeated by the combined forces of Russia, Prussia, and Austria in October 1813 at the *Battle of Leipzig*, also known as the *Battle of Nations*.

Napoleon abdicated as emperor on April 4, 1814 after he had rejected the *Frankfurt Proposals* to keep him on the throne but to withdraw French troops from Germany and after allied armies entered Paris. The *Bourbons* were restored to the throne of France in the person of *Louis XVIII*, and Napoleon was exiled to the island of *Elba* in the Mediterranean.

France surrendered all territory gained since the Wars of the Revolution had begun in 1792, and King Louis created a legislature that represented only the upper classes. The restoration, though, maintained most of Napoleon's reforms such as the Code Napoleon, the concordat with the Pope, and the abolition of feudalism.

The Congress of Vienna (September 1814–June 1815)

Representatives of the major powers of Europe, including France, met to redraw territorial lines and to restore, as far as was possible, the social and political order that existed before the Revolution and Napoleon. The *rule of legitimacy* was one primary goal: to return the "rightful" rulers of Europe to their thrones. A return to a balance of power that would guarantee peace was the other.

The august assemblage consisted of Clemens Von *Metternich*, chancellor *of Austria*; Viscount *Castlereagh*, foreign minister *of England*; *Czar Alexander of Russia*; *Prince Hardenberg of Prussia*; and Foreign Minister *Tallyrand of France*.

THE SETTLEMENT

To prevent future expansion, France was surrounded by a number of strong states—a newly united Holland and Belgium called the Kingdom of the Netherlands, a Prussian satellite area on the Rhine, and Austrian buffer states in Northern Italy.

In Germany, Napoleon's reorganization remained, and the 300 originally independent states were reduced to 39.

The Hapsburg Holy Roman Empire was not reestablished.

The Hundred Days began on March 1, 1815, when Napoleon landed in the south of France from his exile in Elba and marched, to popular acclaim, into Paris. He raised an army, defeated a Prussian army in Belgium on June 16, 1815 but was defeated by the Duke of Wellington at *Waterloo*, in Belgium, on June 18. He was imprisoned on the island of *St. Helena* in the South Atlantic and died on May 5, 1821.

The Concert of Europe was an alliance, also known as the *Quadruple Alliance*, signed by England, Prussia, Russia, and Austria in November 1815. Its aim was to maintain the status quo that the Congress of Vienna had established, upholding the territorial boundaries and shoring up the monarchies of Europe against the spread of revolutionary ideas, such as *republicanism* (that the people should elect their rulers).

Even though the alliance did not last for long, the balance of power created by the Congress of Vienna prevented a general war for a hundred years.

Sample Essay Question

The sample thematic essay questions presented in this chapter are types found in the Advanced Placement Examination in European History, and they require knowledge of causes, effects, personalities, ideas, and events.

Sample Question

> *Explain* how, although he was an autocrat, Napoleon helped put into practice many of the ideals of the French Revolution.

Comments on the Sample Question

Follow the "Simple Procedures" for writing an essay. (See page 24.)

First, *What does the question want to know?* In this question, "to explain" requires that you make clear and detail how Napoleon could be an autocrat and still fulfill many of the promises of the French Revolution. This is not a choice question where you might take the opposite position.

Second, *What do you know about it?* An "autocrat" is a ruler with absolute power; Napoleon was first a dictator and then an emperor. The ideals of the Revolution can be summed up by the phrase "Liberty, equality, fraternity," and these ideals would appear to contradict Napoleon's roles.

Third, *How would you put it into words?* The task is to "make clear" and "detail" what the ideals of the Revolution were and how Napoleon's domestic and foreign policies helped realize them both in France and beyond its borders.

Sample Answer

Even an autocrat can be a reformer. Napoleon, with all the power of a modern state in his grasp, with all the trappings of an empire, could be considered "a son of the French Revolution." Maybe the ideals of the Enlightenment—"liberty" from cruel and arbitrary government; "equality" before the law and based on merit, "fraternity," a modern sense of the unity of a whole people—could have been imposed upon the old order only by a strong ruler.

Old habits die hard, and the first or moderate stage of the French Revolution may have drafted the Declaration of the Rights of Man and the Citizen, but it was not able to put its lofty goals into practice. Neither was the second or radical stage since excess and instability, even in a republic, breed disorder rather than reform. The third or reactionary stage set the tone for Napoleon; the nation was weary of terror and turmoil and it welcomed order, a strong man's if need be.

In the coup d'état of Brumaire, November of 1799, Napoleon returned from his ill-fated Egyptian campaign and overthrew the Directory. He formed the Consulate, making himself first consul among three, and within a month he had pushed through a new constitution, engineered a landslide of popular approval, and filled the legislature with his supporters. He was dictator of France, an autocrat with virtually absolute power. By 1804, his toady Senate had named him emperor.

Napoleon's motives for putting into practice many of the ideals of the Revolution are varied. A foreigner, a Corsican, and man of less than exalted birth and of little means, he, personally, was rewarded by the Revolution for his abilities, which, in the Old Regime would have destined him to tertiary commands as a minor career officer. Reform, not simply raw power, was an instrument for maintaining his position. By rewarding those who had supported him, he earned their loyalty; by improving the lot of whole segments of society, he won popularity. Not the least of his motives was to contribute to the sense of human progress that glowed in the Age of Enlightenment. He was probably more "enlightened despot" than "modern dictator."

Some of the ideals of the French Revolution are found in the Declaration of the Rights of Man, which was meant to apply to all people, not just the French. It was proclaimed on August 26, 1789, to back up the Decrees of August 4, which ended feudalism and the privileges of manorialism. The declaration guaranteed freedom of religion and speech, due process of the law, and equality before the law—whatever one's origins. It also stated that sovereignty, the right to rule, was not the king's alone but rested with the whole nation. It did not offer the ultimate implementation of this concept, though, by seeking to set up a republic to replace the monarchy. That came in the radical stage of the Revolution after Louis XVI was beheaded.

If freedom of religion was one of the ideals of the Revolution, Napoleon's Concordat of 1801 satisfied the Catholic majority of France by revoking the Civil Constitution of the Clergy, which had allowed the state to unduly influence religious matters. If equality was another ideal, the Concordat also fostered this when the Pope renounced all claims to confiscated church lands, thereby creating independent landholders among the bourgeoisie and peasantry. When Napoleon lowered the old feudal taxes for the peasants, he guaranteed liberty from the old order by enabling them to prosper under the new.

The Code Napoleon, 1804, replaced the mishmosh of medieval laws that favored the nobility with a uniform set of laws that applied to all French men and women equally. Napoleon's state support of education for all classes of citizens and his merit system in government, rewarding ability rather than birth, both furthered the goal of equality.

Napoleon was able to spread the ideals of the Revolution to many of the nations of Europe through his conquests. In Italy and Germany, he abolished feudalism and manorialism and he reformed social, political, and economic institutions. His consolidation of the separate and often squabbling political entities in Italy and especially Germany offered a sense of national unity to these people: fraternity. The successes of his armies taught other peoples that national unity meant national power, and that sense of fraternity, ironically, led to Napoleon's defeat at their hands.

Despite his dictatorial tendencies, his imperial ambitions, his megalomania, Napoleon put into practice many of the ideals of the French Revolution. His legal, educational, and governmental reforms engendered equality. His peacemaking with the papacy encouraged a freer expression of religion, a powerful liberty, and strengthened independent landowners among the peasants and middle classes, a foundation for democracy. His conquests helped spread and put into practice the universal principles of the Declaration of the Rights of Man and the ideals of "liberty, equality, fraternity."

Evaluate the Sample Answer

1. Did it have a clear introduction?
2. Did it reflect an understanding of the terms and intent of the question?
3. Did it "explain" by making clear and detailing?
4. Did it offer abundant, relevant, and interesting facts?
5. Was it long enough, interestingly written, easy to follow?
6. Did its concluding paragraph sum up its argument?

Rater's Comments on the Sample Answer

5—Extremely well qualified

This a clearly argued, factually supported, and well-written essay. Its introduction not only lays out the body of its argument, but it ties together the two significant developments of that period, the French Revolution and the rule of Napoleon. It makes specific factual references that are relevant, accurate, and concise. It explains how Napoleon became an autocrat, what the ideals of the French Revolution involved, what his motives may have been for including them in his domestic and foreign policies, and how he put them into practice. It sums up the argument in a lucid conclusion.

Practice Essay Questions

The questions that follow are samples of the various types of thematic essays that appear on the Advanced Placement Examination in European History. (See pages 17–18 for a detailed explanation of each type.)

> 1.   *Contrast and compare* the stages of the French Revolution.

Comments on Question 1

The "contrast" part of this question is easy since the various stages of the Revolution have significant differences: the groups, personalities, and methods are glaringly different in each. The tough part of this question is to detail what they had in common, what their similarities were. Each had a form of government, a type of leadership, a constitution, a legislative body, goals. Sort them out and stress their similarities.

> 2.   *Analyze* the way Louis XVI's attempt to raise taxes to pay off his government's debts precipitated the French Revolution.

Comments on Question 2

To answer this question, you must apply all the meanings of the term "analyze." You must "determine the relationship" between Louis's attempt to raise taxes and the Revolution. The calling of the Estates General for the first time in over 150 years started the chain of events. You must "examine" the sequence of events "in detail." Class factionalism in the Estates General led to the creation of the National Assembly. And you must "explain" why this particular attempt to raise taxes was significantly different from previous attempts. Louis wanted to tax the First and Second Estates, which had been exempt since the Middle Ages.

> **3.** "Napoleon's very successes in battle awakened the nationalistic forces that defeated him." *Assess the validity* of this statement.

Comments on Question 3

In this case "assess the validity" means to "determine the truth" of the statement. Almost inevitably, the statement itself is the easiest to argue for in "assess" questions. The strategy is simple: Show how his victories over a specific state led to the awakening of nationalism there. Remember that Napoleon deliberately consolidated parts of Italy and Germany, and this had the same effect.

> **4.** *To what extent and in what ways* did the Congress of Vienna restore the Old Order in Europe?

Comments on Question 4

"How and how much" did the Congress restore the Old Order. What had the Old Order been? How had the Revolution and Napoleon changed it? What provisions of the Congress dealt with it? What was the overall result—immediately and in the long term?

> **5.** "The accomplishments of the French Revolution were not worth the violence, instability, and war it led to." *Defend or refute* this statement.

Comments on Question 5

Argue for or against or a little of each. What were the accomplishments—an end to the Old Regime, the spread of democratic ideals? What were the costs—the Terror, the Wars of the Revolution, the rise of Napoleon? Beware of simplistic moralizing. Great developments in human history are riddled with rights and wrongs on all sides.

Practice Multiple-Choice Questions

(These questions are representative of the various types that appear on the Advanced Placement Examination in European History.)

1. On the eve of the French Revolution, France was the wealthiest, most influential, and most populous nation in Europe. Its population was approximately
   - (A) 100 million
   - (B) 50 million
   - (C) 25 million
   - (D) 15 million
   - (E) 10 million

2. The immediate cause of the outbreak of revolution in 1789 was
   - (A) grinding poverty among all classes of society
   - (B) government oppression
   - (C) the ideas of the philosophes
   - (D) the insensitivity of Marie Antoinette
   - (E) the government's financial crisis

3. Although the Storming of the Bastille on July 14, 1789 is celebrated as the "start of the French Revolution," the first act of revolution may have been the resolve of the Third Estate to write a constitution. It is of
   - (A) the first session of the Estates General
   - (B) the swearing of the Tennis Court Oath
   - (C) the storming of the Tuileries
   - (D) the forming of the National Assembly
   - (E) the public proclamation of the Declaration of the Rights of Man

4. Choose the correct chronological order:
   - I. convening of the Estates General
   - II. the Declaration of the Rights of Man and the Citizen
   - III. formation of the National Assembly
   - IV. the Tennis Court Oath
   - (A) I, II, III, IV
   - (B) III, I, II, IV
   - (C) III, IV, II, I
   - (D) II, IV, I, III
   - (E) I, III, IV, II

5. Many historians divide the French Revolution into these three distinct stages:
   - (A) "The Great Fear," "The Reign of Terror," and "The Directory"
   - (B) The Monarchy, the Republic, the Empire
   - (C) The radical, the moderate, and the reactionary stages
   - (D) The moderate, the radical, and the reactionary stages
   - (E) The storming of the Bastille, of the Tuileries, of the National Convention

6. Which of the following alienated the most French Catholic clerics and believers?
    (A) The provision of freedom of religion in the Declaration of the Rights of Man
    (B) The determination of the various revolutionary governments to collect taxes from the First Estate
    (C) The seizure of church lands
    (D) The Civil Constitution of the Clergy
    (E) The abolition of monasteries

7. Arrange the following governments during the Revolution in correct chronological order:
    I.   Consulate
    II. National Assembly
    III. Directory
    IV. National Convention
    (A) I, IV, II, III
    (B) II, III, IV, I
    (C) IV, III, II, I
    (D) II, IV, III, I
    (E) IV, II, I, III

8. By the standards of the 20th century, the slaughter of French citizens during the Reign of Terror was relatively small in number. It claimed approximately how many victims?
    (A) 4 million
    (B) 1 million
    (C) 400,000
    (D) 40,000
    (E) 4,000

9. All of the following are accurate EXCEPT
    (A) France had a nonrepresentative government before the French Revolution as well as afterward
    (B) the Revolution destroyed the vestiges of manorialism
    (C) the Revolution failed to end the legal inequities between the classes
    (D) the Revolution influenced French society to measure status by ability rather than birth
    (E) the ideals of the French Revolution spread throughout Europe

10. Which of the following was NOT considered a positive accomplishment of Napoleon?
    (A) The Concordat of 1801
    (B) His use of nepotism in government
    (C) His use of the merit system in government
    (D) His Code Napoleon
    (E) His restructuring of the educational system

11.   Napoleon's purpose in instituting the Continental System was to
    (A)   defeat England through economic war
    (B)   consolidate the separate states of Germany
    (C)   unify Italy
    (D)   create a united Europe under the leadership of France
    (E)   punish Russia for his ill-fated invasion

12.   Napoleon helped make the French Revolution an international movement in the areas he conquered
    (A)   by imposing a universal currency based on the French franc
    (B)   by the brutal suppression of guerrilla resistance
    (C)   by abolishing feudalism and manorialism
    (D)   by encouraging French as the universal language
    (E)   by placing his relatives on the thrones

13.   The Congress of Vienna hoped to restore the European balance of power after the Wars of the Revolution and the Napoleonic Wars by
    (A)   surrounding France with strong states
    (B)   unifying all of Germany
    (C)   reestablishing the Holy Roman Empire
    (D)   unifying Italy
    (E)   giving Russia the left bank of the Rhine

14.   Who was the man whose ideas and aims dominated the Congress of Vienna and after whom the age of reaction, from the fall of Napoleon to the Revolutions of 1848, is named?
    (A)   Castlereagh   (D)   Talleyrand
    (B)   Metternich   (E)   Hardenburg
    (C)   Alexander I

15. What is the most likely year of the map below?

(A) 1789
(B) 1792
(C) 1800
(D) 1815
(E) 1862

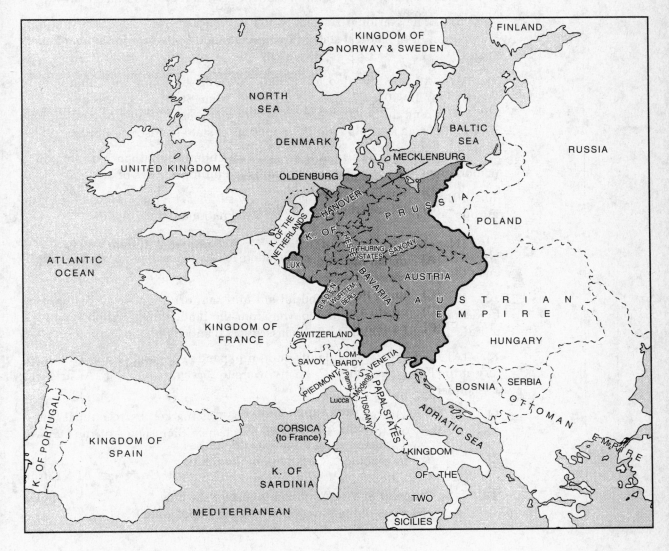

Answers and Answer Explanations

1. C	2. E	3. B	4. E	5. D
6. D	7. D	8. D	9. C	10. B
11. A	12. C	13. A	14. B	15. D

1. (C) Only about 500,000 of these belonged to the nobility and clergy.

2. (E) The convening of the Estates General in response to the financial crisis precipitated the Revolution.

3. (B) The Tennis Court Oath marks the beginning of the Moderate Stage, before the Paris mobs intervened.

4. (E) The Declaration of the Rights of Man impelled the resistance forward and gave the Revolution an idealistic model.

5.   (D)   This is the prevailing view of historians of the French Revolution.

6.   (D)   That the government would appoint Church officials, non-Catholics could vote for parish priests, and the clergy had to swear allegiance to the state angered many Catholics and at least half of the French clergy.

7.   (D)   The National Assembly fits in the moderate stage; the National convention in the radical stage; the Directory and Consulate in the reactionary stage.

8.   (D)   12 million died as a result of Nazis extermination methods in World War II; 30 million or more died from Stalinist repression in the U.S.S.R. Some authorities claim that as many as 170 million individuals perished during the 20th century as victims of state-sponsored murder.

9.   (C)   The Decrees of August 4, 1789 ended feudalism and abolished manorialism; the Code Napoleon established uniform codes of justice.

10.   (B)   By putting his relatives, mainly siblings, on the thrones of states of Europe he had conquered, he often inspired nationalistic uprisings.

11.   (A)   The Continental System proved a greater burden to many of his allies—including Russia that he invaded for its refusal to continue compliance—than to Britain.

12.   (C)   The Old Order—feudalism and manorialism—was dismantled by decree, inspiring a shift of power from the landowning aristocracy to the middle classes and promising all classes social and economic justice.

13.   (A)   A United Netherlands and an expanded Prussia (it received territory at the French border in Germany) were to serve this function. Austria was a secondary barrier.

14.   (B)   The *Age of Metternich*, 1815–1848, is marked by reactionary policies by nearly all the states of Europe to cleanse themselves of the stain of French Revolutionary idealism.

15.   (D)   This was Europe as designated by the Congress of Vienna (1814–1815). By 1861, Italy had unified.

6 Mercantilism and the Rise of Capitalism; The Industrial Revolution

Overview

From the end of the 15th century to the beginning of the 18th, the discovery of the New World and the opening of the Atlantic to exploration and colonization changed the economy of Europe. Mercantilism—medieval manorial self-sufficiency on a national scale—became the prevailing economic system of the growing nation-states. Inflation, brought about by the stores of gold and silver imported from the New World, led to an increase in trade and manufacture that encouraged the growth of early capitalism. As economic activity shifted from the Mediterranean to the Atlantic, the Italian city-states declined as trading middlemen between Europe and the Near and Far East. Portugal and Spain became the major powers of the 16th century; the Netherlands, France, and England of the 17th.

An Industrial Revolution—given birth by the growth of commerce, the development of capitalism, the introduction of improved technology, and the unique political climate in Britain during the 18th century—changed life in Western Europe in the 1800s more profoundly than the French Revolution had. The landowning aristocracy, which had its origins in the early Middle Ages and whose decline had begun with the growth of a commercial and professional middle class, lost more wealth and political power with the inception of a spectacularly wealthy capitalist class. The lives of the mass of Europeans shifted from the farm to the factory, from the predictable rhythms of a rural existence to the grinding and impersonal poverty of the industrial cities. Along with the capitalists, a new proletariat, or working class, was created, and a whole new set of social and economic doctrines sought to explain their rights and better their lives. Added to the "isms" that grew out of the French Revolution, such as republicanism, conservatism, and nationalism, were socialism and Marxism. By the last third of the 19th century—"The Age of Progress"—a technological revolution had altered the Western world and was to lead the way into the woes and wonders of the 20th century.

Mercantilism and the Rise of Capitalism

The Commercial Revolution

For over 150 years after Columbus discovered the Americas for the Europeans, thousands of tons of silver and nearly two hundred tons of gold came to Spain from the riches of the conquered Native Americans and from the mines established by the Spanish colonials. *Inflation*—"too much money chasing too few goods"—resulted because while the money supply had vastly increased, productivity had remained stable.

The *inflation stimulated production*, though, because craftsmen, merchants, and manufacturers could get good prices for their products. The middle class, the bourgeoisie, acquired much of this wealth by trading and manufacturing, and their political influence and social status increased. Peasant farmers benefited when their surplus yields could be turned into *cash crops*. The nobility, whose income was based on feudal rents and fees, actually suffered a diminishing standard of living in this inflationary economy.

The Rise of Capitalism

"Capital" is another term for *surplus money*; instead of investing labor, an individual invests capital in some venture in order to make a profit. The bourgeoisie, having accumulated more money than was needed to maintain a decent standard of living in 16th and 17th century society, used money to make money. They invested in *chartered companies* that were given a monopoly of trading rights by the state within a certain area; in *joint-stock companies* (forerunners of modern corporations), which sold shares of stock publically in order to raise large amounts for various ventures, provided *limited liability* to the shareholders, and offered a profitable return for the original investment; and in the *bourse*, a kind of stock exchange. Profit made from investment enabled more investment. The expansion of money created prosperity, advanced science and technology, and supported the growth of the nation-state.

Mercantilism

The monarchs of the early modern period needed money to maintain the standing armies that would dominate the powerful nobles of the realm and protect the state against foreign enemies. The commercial revolution and the growth of capitalism enriched a sizable segment of the population; personal riches translated into good tax revenues.

Mercantilism prevailed in the 17th and well into the 18th century as an economic policy because it seemed to offer a way for the monarchs of Europe to consolidate their centralized authority.

THE THEORY

A nation's wealth is measured by the amount of precious metals it has accumulated *(bullionism)* rather than by its productivity.

A *favorable balance of trade*—exports exceed imports—is made up of gold and silver and therefore increases the store of precious metals.

Overseas colonies supply the *mother country* with essential raw materials for manufacture and trade.

Essential industries—manufacturing for the national defense or making a product unique to the nation and valuable in trade—were encouraged through subsidies and tax credits.

The goal of mercantilism is national economic self-sufficiency.

Overseas colonization (Old Imperialism) was encouraged by the policy of mercantilism. Spain and Portugal, following up on the momentum of their early explorations to Asia around the African continent and to the Americas across the Atlantic, monopolized colonization in the 16th century. By the 17th century, the balance had shifted to the Dutch, French, and English, whose internal disorders of the previous century had stabilized and whose inroads in Asia and North America overcame the supremacy of the Spanish and Portuguese. The English colonial empire far surpassed that of any other European nation because its colonies attracted proportionately more of its subjects for settlement and because a number of them became powerful independent states: the United States, India, Canada, Australia, and a number of other nations in Asia and Africa.

The Industrial Revolution

There never was an industrial "revolution"—a violent, drastic change. Industrialization has been a continuous and usually gradual process throughout human existence, from the use of the first stone tools to the development of high technology. The so-called *Industrial Revolution* was a period of rapid development, roughly between *1780 and 1830,* during which *machine production replaced hand manufacturing and the work force was concentrated in factories.*

It began in Britain in the second half of the 18th century; moved to France, Holland, Belgium, and the United States in the second decade of the 19th; to Germany, Austria, Italy in the middle of the 19th; to Eastern Europe and Russia at the end of the 19th; to parts of Asia and Africa well into the 20th; and it continues.

The Agricultural Revolution in England

After the Glorious Revolution of 1688, English landowning aristocrats dominated Parliament and passed the *Enclosure Acts,* which fenced off the *medieval common lands.*

RESULTS OF THE ENCLOSURE MOVEMENT

Large landowners became prosperous; they invested in technology—machinery, breeding, improved planting methods. Crop yields and livestock production soared.

Surplus production enabled agriculture to support a larger population in the cities.

The population of Britain doubled during the 18th century.

Small farmers who were displaced by the Enclosure movement moved to the cities and made up the growing force of factory workers (the *industrial proletariat*).

Technological Advances

Inventions of new machines and improvement of production processes throughout the 18th century made large-scale production possible in *textile manufacturing* and *coal mining*. The *steam engine* revolutionized transportation.

THE SCARCITY OF ENERGY

By the 18th century, most of England's forests were denuded and its supply of wood for fuel nearly depleted. *Coal*, plentiful, but traditionally shunned as a fuel because of its polluting effects, gradually replaced wood as both a fuel and for industrial processes. The early *steam engines*—such as Newcomen's clumsy contraption that employed a maze of rods and leather straps—converted heat from burning coal into motion and were employed as pumps in mines, and eventually they were used to drive textile machinery.

TEXTILES

The *fly shuttle* (John Kay, 1733) cut manpower needs on the looms in half.

The *spinning jenny* (James Hargreaves, 1764) mechanized the spinning wheel.

The *water frame* (Richard Arkwright, 1769) improved thread spinning.

Use of the *steam engine* (Arkwright, 1780s) powered the looms and required factory production of textiles.

The *cotton gin* (Eli Whitney, American, 1793) separated seed from raw cotton fiber and increased supply of the raw material.

COAL

Steam pump (Thomas Newcomen, 1702) rid coal mines of water seepage.

Improved pump (James Watt, 1763).

Plentiful coal boosted iron production and gave rise to *heavy industry* (the manufacture of machinery and materials used in production).

TRANSPORTATION

The *steamship* (Robert Fulton, American, 1807) and the *railroad steam engine* (George Stephenson, 1829) enhanced an already efficient system of river transportation that had been expanded in the 18th century by a network of canals. Together they opened new sources of raw materials and new markets for manufactured goods, and they made it possible to locate factories in population centers.

The railroad building boom from 1830–1850, brought about massive social and economic changes in the largely agrarian economy in England. The ease of transport encouraged rural workers to move to the cities; the lower costs of shipping goods in bulk fostered expanding markets.

OIL

By the end of the 19th century, the refinement of petroleum allowed its use as a fuel for the newly developed *internal combustion engines* that propelled automobiles, locomotives, and even ships, and for heating and industrial processes.

Results of the Industrial Revolution

The most significant result was the *increased production and availability of manufactured goods.* Material prosperity increased because there were cheaper high-quality goods and because increased consumption led to more jobs.

Factory workers lived in poverty on subsistence wages, in dismal tenements, entire families—including children from age five up—working fourteen hours a day under unsafe and unhealthy conditions. Crowded slums were worsened by the absence of services in cities that had expanded too rapidly. Although these living conditions did not differ much from those under which people had lived for centuries on farms, the concentration of the population made them appear worse. This visibility led thinkers to ponder the causes of poverty and prompted the institutions of society to push for its alleviation. The *Sadler Commission* helped initiate legislation to improve working conditions in factories.

Effects on Class and Gender

Two new classes developed as a result of the Industrial Revolution—*industrialist/capitalists* and *factory workers*. The competitive nature of the markets led many of the factory owners to offer low wages for long hours, create poor and unsafe working conditions, and to employ child labor. The rigid discipline of factory work contrasted with the rural pace of the farm work most of the laborers had been accustomed to; and not until the mid-19th century did the standard of living improve for the average industrial worker.

Child labor laws were enacted after the first three decades of the 19th century to limit the number of hours children could be required to work, and a sexual division of labor emerged. Men became the main breadwinners while married women tended to stay home to raise the children. Jobs available to women were "dead-end" and poorly paid. The early attempts of workers to organize were met with hostility from industrialists, anti-union regulations from governments, and very limited success.

The rapid growth of cities during the Industrial Revolution necessitated urban reform to improve conditions that had existed for centuries: poor sanitation and other services, overcrowded housing, inadequate transportation. Influenced by *Jeremy Bentham*, whose philosophy of *utilitarianism* emphasized "the greatest good for the greatest number," city planners and urban reformers redesigned the many European cities and initiated a public health movement to improve urban life for all classes.

The standard of living improved for most Europeans from the middle of the 19th century and into the early 20th. Disparities in wealth between the classes led to conflict between the classes and encouraged the growth of political radicalism. Hierarchies of wealth and status existed among both the middle and working classes, and the relegation of women to menial jobs or to child-raising fostered a women's rights movement, the first wave of *feminism*, whose goals included gender equality in opportunity, legal rights, and voting.

Theories of Economics   *Adam Smith* (see page 88) can be considered the first modern economist. His *Wealth of Nations* has been called the "Bible of capitalism" and is the foundation for *classical* or laissez-faire economics, which opposed the regulations imposed by mercantilism by arguing that certain natural laws, such as *supply and demand,* govern an economy and should be free to operate. If people follow their own "enlightened self-interest," without the interference of government in the economy, this private initiative will result in benefits to all in society.

Thomas Malthus (1766–1834) was the first of the classical economists to try to explain why the mass of people did not benefit from the operation of the "natural laws" of economics. Poverty existed, he said, because the *population increased at a geometric rate while the food supply increased arithmetically.* He believed that poverty was a divine punishment for humankind's lust.

David Ricardo (1772–1823) introduced the *Iron Law of Wages:* the natural wage is that which maintains a worker's subsistence. When labor is in demand, though, the wage will increase, the worker will prosper, the size of families will increase, and the general population will grow. The result will be more workers competing for fewer jobs and inevitable starvation. Government attempts to change this, he contended, only lead to greater suffering.

Utopian Socialists rejected the *"dismal science"* of the classical economists and sought solutions to the plight of the masses. *Robert Owen* (1771–1858) was a Scottish textile manufacturer whose humane working conditions—shorter workday, decent housing, free education—served as a model for capitalists who wanted to make a profit without exploiting workers. The *Comte de Saint-Simon* (1760–1825) was one of the early French founders of *socialism.* He helped define the movement by advocating *public ownership of factories* and a professional managerial corps to run them, the *technocrats.* He coined the slogan, "From each according to his ability, to each according to his need," an idealistic but vague proposal for a *planned economy.*

Karl Marx (1818–1883) is in a class of his own. His *Communist Manifesto,* written with *Friedrich Engels* during the Revolution of 1848, calls for radical solutions to the dilemma of mass poverty in the industrialized world. *Das Kapital,* the first volume of which was published in 1867, offers a complete analysis of capitalism.

MARX'S THEORIES

Hegelian dialectic (so named after the German philosopher Georg Hegel): In every historical period a prevailing ideal, *thesis*, conflicts with an opposing ideal, *antithesis*, and results in a new ideal, *synthesis*. This becomes the thesis of the next period and the process continues.

Dialectical materialism: Marx adapted the Hegelian dialectic to argue that society is a reflection of economics. History progresses from agrarian communalism, to slaveholding, to feudalism, to bourgeois commercialism, to capitalism, to socialism, and finally to *Communism* (a classless society in which the workers own the means of production and government is unnecessary).

Class Struggle: The *dominant class* in every society—slaveholders, feudal lords, capitalists—is a thesis with an antithesis—slaves, serfs, workers—that will overthrow the old order.

Inevitable Revolution: This is the result of the capitalists' increasing profits by lowering the workers' wages for labor to the point that the proletariat cannot afford to consume the products of manufacture *(surplus-value theory)*. Economic depression occurs and lays hardship on the working class until it carries out a revolution. A *dictatorship of the proletariat* will establish a socialist government to wipe out capitalism.

Communism: The *"withering away of the state"* will follow, whereby private property will cease to exist and economic exploitation will stop, ending crime, vice, and injustice; democracy will prevail on local level; *Utopia* (a perfect society) will result.

The Technological Revolution

Around the last third of the 19th century, the applications of science to industry brought about a radical change in the way Europeans lived. *Mass production* lowered the cost of goods and made them available to the general public; consumer goods became part of the mass market. Smaller companies merged and consolidated until whole industries were dominated by *big business*. High wages in the cities caused a *population shift* from the countryside. Electricity and the internal combustion engine not only increased productivity but improved the quality of life.

Sample Essay Question

The sample thematic essay and the practice essays that follow are of types found on the Advanced Placement Examination in European History, and they require knowledge of causes, effects, personalities, ideas, and events.

Sample Question

> *To what extent and in what ways* was the light of Adam Smith's economic optimism dimmed by the "dismal science" of Thomas Malthus and David Ricardo?

Comments on the Sample Question

Follow the "Simple Procedures" for writing an essay. (See page 24.)

First, *What does the question want to know?* How and how much was Smith's "natural law" theory of the operation of an economy altered by the pessimistic views of Malthus and Ricardo? This is the crux of the question.

Second, *What do you know about it?* Smith was considered an Enlightenment philosopher, a theoretician for the inevitable human progress that age had projected. Malthus and Ricardo observed the mass misery that the Industrial Revolution and laissez-faire economics had created, and, while accepting Smith's basic theory, they sought explanations for its failure in practice.

Third, *How would you put it into words?* Show how and how much Malthus and Ricardo created the "dismal science" of economics while still accepting the basic principles of Smith's "natural law" economy.

Sample Answer

In 1776, at the peak of the Enlightenment and during the heyday of governmental mercantilistic regulation of European economies, Adam Smith published his *Wealth of Nations*. Describing the small business economy of the British "nation of shopkeepers," Smith applied the prevailing natural law theory to the operation of economies. An individual's "enlightened self-interest," if left alone (borrowing the laissez-faire economics of the French physiocrats), will allow the operation of the natural laws of economics.

Whenever a government interferes with one of these laws, such as that of "supply and demand," it creates more problems than are solved. In a free and unregulated economy, each producer will try to lower the cost of production by using the most advanced technology, by making the best use of materials, and by using efficient labor. In that way, the product can be sold cheaper than a competitor's and the profit will be higher. Also, producers will turn out high-quality goods to try to surpass those of their competitors.

Smith's natural laws of economics fit the progressive, optimistic view of human society that saturated the thinking of the Age of Enlightenment. Following Isaac Newton's momentous discoveries that universal and unchangeable laws govern the planets and all earthly motion, Enlightenment philosophes sought "natural laws" to govern everything from political morality to economics.

By the time the Industrial Revolution had taken hold of the British economy—in the first two decades of the 19th century—Smith's laissez-faire economics had not delivered the general prosperity he had promised. Poverty blighted the new industrial cities of England and Scotland. Men, women, and young children labored long hours for subsistence wages at tedious, dangerous, unhealthy work. Poverty had been the rule among the rural population of small farmers, but it was now unavoidably visible in the crowded, dirty slums of the cities.

Since both Thomas Malthus and David Ricardo were believers in Smith's classical or laissez-faire economics, they felt compelled to explain why the free operation of economic natural laws did not lead to general prosperity. Their pessimistic views were to earn economics the label of the "dismal science."

Malthus, a clergyman, argued that people were poor because the population had outrun food production. Food increased at an arithmetic rate while population increased at a geometric rate. He thought that war, famine, and disease were divine punishments for humankind's lust.

Ricardo offered a less cosmic but equally despairing view of why poverty is inevitable. His Iron Law of Wages stated that while workers are usually paid a subsistence wage (enough to keep them and their family alive), when labor is in great demand, the wages will exceed the "natural wage." Workers prosper; prosperity leads to bigger families; a larger population causes an overabundance of workers; wages drop; workers and their families starve.

During the Age of Reason, Smith's natural laws of economics promised general prosperity. He was reacting against the arbitrary regulation of economics by modern monarchs seduced by the bullionism of mercantilist theory, and he was following the optimistic assumptions of the Enlightenment. Observing the abuses of industrialization, Malthus and Ricardo tried to salvage classical economics by explaining how poverty could exist in an unregulated economy. Their appeal to inevitable laws of God or the Iron Law of Wages definitely dimmed Smith's optimistic predictions. Once they had offered their theories, they felt no obligation to alleviate the economic and social ills that they had pronounced unavoidable. That they left to the socialists and Marxists who would follow them.

Evaluate the Sample Answer

1. Did it have a good introduction?
2. Did it reflect an understanding of the terms and intent of the question?
3. Did it show "to what extent and what ways"?
4. Did it reflect a thorough understanding of the economic theories?
5. Did it answer the question clearly, completely, convincingly?
6. Was it long enough, well written, easy to understand?
7. Did its concluding paragraph sum up the argument?

Rater's Comments on the Sample Answer

5—Extremely well qualified

Not only does this answer demonstrate a thorough command of the economic theories involved, but it shows an understanding of the historical context of each. It is clear, to the point, well-written, and complete. It answers "to what extent and in what ways" the economic and philosophical optimism of Adam Smith was altered by the real-life observations and "dismal science" of Malthus and Ricardo. It is factually accurate and shows an understanding of the effect of an age on human attitudes and ideas.

Practice Essay Questions

The questions that follow are samples of the various types of thematic essays that appear on the Advanced Placement Examination in European History. (See pages 17–18 for a detailed explanation of each type.)

---

1. *Analyze* the way the opening of the Atlantic sparked the rise of capitalism.

Comments on Question 1

This question requires all the applications of analysis: examining in detail, determining relationships, explaining. A special emphasis should be on determining the relationships between what appears to be remotely connected events. How could the Atlantic discoveries and colonization of the New World have encouraged the growth of capitalism in Europe? The relationships are complex but strong: Precious metals from the New World colonies of Spain, mainly, led to runaway inflation in Europe; that inflation influenced productivity and commerce, which, in turn, created wealth and the possibilities of its investment. Be sure to show the causal relationships, to describe the effects, and to define terms such as "inflation," "surplus wealth," "capitalism."

> 2.   *Explain* why the monarchs of Europe favored mercantilism.

Comments on Question 2

In this and any "explanation" essay, the task is to offer reasons for your answer. The monarchs of Europe, the question is saying, DID favor mercantilism.

Approach this first by considering what mercantilism was and what it accomplished, and then by examining how that would benefit the growing nation-states and their monarchs in the 15th and 16th centuries. Money is the clue.

> 3.   "It is no accident that the Industrial Revolution occurred in late 18th century England." *Assess the validity* of this statement.

Comments on Question 3

"To determine the truth" of this assertion, it is necessary to examine what fertile fields nurtured the development of industrialization in England from 1780 to 1830. You must identify the links in the causal chain: the supremacy of Parliament after 1688, the Enclosure movement, the Agricultural Revolution, the growth of towns, the improvement of technology.

> 4.   "The Industrial Revolution diminished the quality of life of the common person in Europe." *Defend or refute* this statement.

Comments on Question 4

Use facts to argue for or against. In this case, the prevailing bias of our times—that industrialization subjected the masses to miserable labor and grinding poverty—may not be either accurate or easily defended. In deciding whether to *defend or refute,* consider: What was the quality of life for peasant farmers before industrialization? Did life in manufacturing towns offer advantages? Did the increase in productivity benefit the common person?

> 5.   *Explain* how Marx's theories offer both a reason for, and a solution to, mass poverty in the industrialized world.

**Comments on
Question 5**

In order to "make clear" and "detail," you must understand Marx's critique of capitalism and his theory of revolution, the social, economic, and political environment of his day (mid-19th century), and the failure of classical economics to alleviate poverty. This is a *very tough* question. The core of the answer lies in Marx's theories: the dialectic, the class struggle, surplus-value theory, inevitable revolution, socialism, and Communism.

Practice Multiple-Choice Questions

(These questions are representative of the various types that appear on the Advanced Placement Examination in European History.)

1. Mercantilism, the prevailing economic theory of 17th century Europe, was based on all of the following ideas EXCEPT
    (A) that a nation's wealth was measured by its accumulation of precious metals
    (B) that a nation's wealth would be increased by a "favorable balance of trade"
    (C) that war was a natural state of affairs between nations
    (D) that a nation's accumulated gold and silver was needed to build a navy and to equip a standing army
    (E) that government should not regulate or interfere with the nation's economy

2. Which nation dominated overseas colonization in the 16th century?
    (A) England
    (B) Spain
    (C) France
    (D) Austria
    (E) Holland

3. Encouraged by the mercantilist theory that stressed the need for overseas colonization to obtain the essential raw materials to provide economic self-sufficiency, these three European nations established colonial empires during the 17th century:
    (A) Portugal, Spain, Italy
    (B) Portugal, England, France
    (C) England, France, Prussia
    (D) England, France, Holland
    (E) Portugal, France, Holland

4. Which was NOT one of the results of the opening of the Atlantic to commerce with Europe during the 16th and 17th centuries?
    (A) Tons of precious metals from the New World came to Spain.
    (B) The money supply expanded but productivity remained stable.
    (C) Runaway inflation occurred.
    (D) Inflation encouraged productivity.
    (E) The nobility increased its wealth.

5. An immediate result of the commercial revolution that occurred with the increased productivity stimulated by the precious metals coming from the Americas was
    (A) the formation of an urban working class
    (B) a dramatic shift of population from the countryside to the cities
    (C) a drastic increase in the manorial fees due from the peasants
    (D) the rise of capitalism
    (E) the abolition of the bourse

6. All of the following are characteristics of the Industrial Revolution (1780–1830) EXCEPT
    (A) that it replaced hand manufacture with machine production
    (B) that it concentrated the working force in factories
    (C) that it was a period of dramatic advancement
    (D) that it took place first in France
    (E) that it transformed European society

7. Which of the following was NOT a factor in the development of the Industrial Revolution in Britain?
    (A) The dominance of the commercial middle class in Parliament
    (B) The Enclosure movement
    (C) The Agricultural Revolution
    (D) The shift of the population from rural to urban areas
    (E) A series of technological advances

8. A number of technological advances throughout the 18th century made possible the large-scale production of which of the following?
    (A) Shoes
    (B) Textiles
    (C) Heavy machinery
    (D) Ships
    (E) Precision tools

9. The Industrial Revolution created two new social classes:
    (A) the bourgeoisie and the landowning peasantry
    (B) the proletariat and the merchant class
    (C) middle-class professionals and landowning aristocrats
    (D) capitalists and the proletariat
    (E) capitalists and urban aristocrats

10. The Industrial Revolution demonstrated significant advances in all of the following EXCEPT
    (A) the uses of the internal combustion engine
    (B) the mining of coal
    (C) the powering of ships
    (D) the development of railroads
    (E) the manufacture of textiles

11. Both the French and Industrial Revolutions gave rise to a number of conflicting doctrines, or "isms." Which of the following was expounded and popularized decades after the others?
    (A) Marxism
    (B) Liberalism
    (C) Radicalism
    (D) Conservatism
    (E) Socialism

12. Thomas Newcomen's pumping machine, invented in the early 1700s, was considered a radical innovation because
    (A) it generated electricity
    (B) it was powered by electricity
    (C) it was powered by steam
    (D) it used fine-kilned brick as a heat insulator
    (E) it was the world's first perpetual motion machine

13. Which is NOT a feature of Marxist theory?
    (A) Hegelian Dialectic
    (B) Dialectical Materialism
    (C) The Class Struggle
    (D) Natural Selection
    (E) Inevitable Revolution

POPULATION ESTIMATES IN THE MILLIONS

Selected Nations in Europe	1800	1900
ENGLAND	9	33
GERMANY	25	56
ITALY	17	34
FRANCE	27	39

14. The chart above provides population estimates for selected European countries in the years 1800 and 1900. Which of the following is the most valid interpretation of the statistics?
    (A) The population doubled in each of the countries identified.
    (B) The population of Italy and Germany doubled because of national unification.
    (C) The population growth reflects the degree to which each of the nations industrialized.
    (D) The population of England grew at a faster rate than any of the nations identified.
    (E) Colonialism caused the indigenous population of England to increase fourfold.

15. Which of the following economists accepted Adam Smith's classical economics and tried to explain why his prediction of general prosperity under laissez-faire capitalism was not coming to fruition?
    (A) Utopian Socialists
    (B) Karl Marx
    (C) Proudhon
    (D) Robert Owen
    (E) Malthus and Ricardo

Answers and Answer Explanations

1. E	**2.** B	**3.** D	**4.** E	**5.** D
6. D	**7.** A	**8.** B	**9.** D	**10.** A
11. A	**12.** C	**13.** D	**14.** D	**15.** E

1. (E)   Most mercantilist economies were "command economies," controlled by government regulation and incentives.

2. (B)   Spain's colonies in the New World brought untold wealth to Europe in the 16th century. Internal problems in the other Atlantic nations—England, France, Holland—prevented their entrance onto the colonial scene until the following century.

3. (D)   See question 2.

4. (E)   The commercial middle class accumulated the wealth; the landed nobility maintained itself on feudal fees that rarely rose.

5. (D)   Inflation made productivity profitable; surplus wealth encouraged investment in economic ventures.

6. (D)   Britain, by a fortunate set of circumstances, gave birth to the Industrial Revolution.

7. (A)   The dominance of the landowning aristocracy as a result of the Glorious Revolution enabled passage of the Enclosure Acts, which in turn encouraged the Agricultural Revolution and the shift in population from the farm to the city.

8. (B)   A rash of innovation during the 18th century dramatically increased productivity in textiles.

9. (D)   Factory owners and factory workers were created by the Industrial Revolution.

10. (A)   The internal combustion engine—both diesel and gasoline—was a late-19th-century invention.

11. (A)   Marx expounded his theories after the Revolutions of 1848. The others were ideologies that flowed from the experience of the French Revolution and the Age of Metternich.

12. (C)   Animal and human muscle, wind and water, provided power before that.

13. (D)   "Natural selection" applies to Darwin's theory of evolution.

14. (D)   The other answers are misinterpretations of the chart.

15. (E)   The term "dismal science" comes from their dire predictions.

7 The Growth and Suppression of Democracy from the Age of Metternich to the First World War (1815–1914)

Overview

The period from the fall of Napoleon in 1815 to the Revolutions of 1848 is called the Age of Metternich. Klemens von Metternich personified the spirit of reaction that followed a quarter-century of revolution and war. Chancellor of Hapsburg Austria and one of the chief participants at the Congress of Vienna, he and others like him all over Europe designed a Continental balance of power that would keep the peace for a century (until the First World War) and imposed a reconstructed Old Order that would burst at the seams in 1848.

Two great nations, during the Age of Metternich, developed the bases for modern constitutional democracy: one—England—through a continuation of the unique and stabilizing evolutionary process that represented the interests in government of more and more of its populace, the other—France—through unstabilizing seesaw battles between reaction and radicalism. For both nations the processes continued through the 19th century and into the early 20th until they had established the foundations for modern welfare states.

Three nations that played important roles in the 19th and early 20th centuries—Germany, Austria, and Russia—suppressed the democratic urges of significant elements of their populations. In Germany, the move toward unification of the varied and independent states fell out of the hands of the constitutionalists and into those of Prussian militarists. In Austria, the Germanic Hapsburg rulers continued to suppress the move toward autonomy of the polyglot nationalities that made up the empire. In Russia, sporadic attempts at reform and modernization were consumed by the ruling class's obsession with "Autocracy, Orthodoxy, and Nationalism."

The Growth of Democracy

England

The ideals and promises of the French Revolution and a growing and poverty-stricken working class vibrated the stability of Europe's greatest emerging democracy. Parliament, after the end of the Napoleonic Wars in 1815, represented the interests of aristocrats and the wealthy. In 1815, food riots and general unrest in the industrial cities led to repressive measures by the government. By the 1820s, though, new and younger leaders of the *Tories* (the conservative party) implemented reforms such as restructuring the penal code, providing for a modern police force, allowing membership in labor unions, and granting Catholics basic civil rights.

By 1830, when abortive revolutions had broken out all over the continent, the *House of Commons,* the lower chamber of Parliament, had not been reapportioned since 1688. Many of the boroughs that had representatives no longer existed, while large and growing industrial cities had none at all. *The Great Reform Bill,* 1832, abolished the *rotten boroughs,* expanded the electorate, and enpowered the industrial middle class.

The *Chartist movement,* representing demands by radical working-class activists, sought an array of reforms from 1838 into the late 1840s. It advocated universal male suffrage, a secret voting ballot, "one man, one vote" representation in Parliament, abolition of property qualifications for public office, and public education for all classes. Although its program failed during the decade of its existence, all of its features were eventually incorporated into English society.

When the discontent of the working class on the continent exploded during the *Revolutions of 1848,* the English proletariat was able to trust in its government's capacity to make gradual reforms.

In 1866, *Whig* (liberal party) prime minister *William E. Gladstone* (1807–1898) attempted to expand voter eligibility but was defeated. A new government under Tory (conservative) *Benjamin Disraeli* turned the tables on the Whig reformers by getting the *Second Reform Bill,* 1867, through Parliament. It not only doubled the size of the electorate, but it gave the vote to many industrial workers. When Disraeli's party lost the general election in 1868—the head of the party that wins the most seats in a parliamentary election forms a government and becomes prime minister—Gladstone returned to power and enacted sweeping reforms. *Labor unions were legalized;* the *secret ballot* was introduced; *free public education* was offered to working-class children. The Third Reform Bill of 1885, largely granted universal male suffrage.

In the decade immediately before the start of World War I, Britain laid the foundations for its *social welfare state:* government institutions and laws that guarantee all citizens a decent standard of living. The right of unions to strike was put into law; government insurance was provided for those injured on the job; unemployment insurance and old-age pensions were enacted; and a compulsory school attendance law went into effect.

France

During the *Age of Metternich*—the period of reaction after the Congress of Vienna, 1815, that ended with the continent-wide Revolutions of 1848—France was ruled by Bourbon reactionaries and a "bourgeois" king whose watered down constitutions excluded the expanding proletariat from representation. After the upheavals of 1848, a self-styled emperor, a relative of Napoleon, was on the French throne.

When Bourbon *Louis XVIII,* a brother of the guillotined Louis XVI, was restored to the throne in 1814, he issued a constitution but gave power to only a small class of landowners and rich bourgeois. Absolutist pretenses were continued with his successor and younger brother, *Charles X* (1824–1830), whose repressive measures led to rioting in Paris in the summer of 1830, a year when abortive insurrections broke out all over Europe.

Charles's abdication caused a rift between radicals who wanted to establish a republic and bourgeoisie who wanted the stability of a monarchy. Through the intercession of the *Marquis de Lafayette,* hero of the American Revolution, *Louis Phillipe,* an aristocrat, became the *"bourgeoisie king"* by agreeing to honor the Constitution of 1814. His reign, from 1830 to 1848, empowered the bourgeoisie but left the proletariat unrepresented.

Rampant corruption in his government incited republican and socialist protests, which erupted in violence and led to his abdication in February 1848. The *Chamber of Deputies,* the lower house of the two-chamber French legislature that was created in 1814 by Louis XVIII's constitution, was pressured by Parisian mobs to *proclaim a republic* and to name a provisional goverment that would rule temporarily until a Constituent Assembly could be elected to draft a new constitution. When the provinces—the countryside outside the large cities—elected a largely conservative Constituent Assembly, conflicts between the government and socialist and radical workers erupted into bloody class battles on the streets of Paris by early summer 1848.

Frightened by the threat of a radical takeover, the Constituent Assembly brutally suppressed the riots, then established the *single-chambered Legislative Assembly* and *a strong president,* both to be elected by *universal male suffrage.*

Louis Napoleon Bonaparte, Napoleon's nephew, was elected President of the *Second Republic.* (The First Republic had been established in 1792 during the French Revolution.) He dedicated his presidency to law and order, the eradication of socialism and radicalism, and the interests of the conservative classes—the Church, the army, property-owners, and business. Through a political ploy, he was able to discredit many members of the Legislative Assembly, win a landslide re-election, and proclaim himself in 1852 as Emperor *Napoleon III* of the *Second French Empire.* (His uncle, Napoleon Bonaparte, had crowned himself emperor in 1804.)

While the Second Empire was not an absolutist government, it was an autocracy. Napoleon III controlled finances and initiated legislation. He was immensely popular in the early years of his reign because of his internal improvements—highway, canal, and railroad construction—and because of his subsidies to industry and his stimulation of the economy. The bourgeoisie was grateful for the general prosperity; the proletariat was appreciative of employment and the right to organize unions. During the *Liberal Empire* (1860–1870), he eased censorship and granted amnesty to political prisoners.

Foreign affairs were his downfall. The *Crimean War* (1854–1856), in which the French and English went to war to prevent the Russians from establishing dominance over the Black Sea possessions of the Ottomans, was costly on all sides. The French backdown in the 1860s, when confronted by the United States over establishment of a *French satellite in Mexico,* humiliated France. The disastrous *Franco-Prussian War* (1870) led to the collapse of the Second Empire and the establishment of the *Third Republic* in February of 1871. Controlled by monarchists and the bourgeoisie, the new National Assembly brutally suppressed a radical socialist countergovernment, the *Paris Commune.*

In 1875, the assembly voted to set up a *Chamber of Deputies,* elected by universal male suffrage, a *Senate,* indirectly elected, a ceremonial president, elected by the whole legislature, and a premier, directly responsible to the

Chamber of Deputies. From the establishment of the Third Republic in 1871 to the beginning of World War I in 1914, *the French government fell dozens of times.* The governments were inherently unstable because there were so many political parties—in a *multiparty system* unlike the British or American two-party systems—that none could win a clear majority in the Legislative Assembly, and the coalitions fell apart during many a crisis.

The *Dreyfus Affair* (1894–1906), in which a Jewish Army captain was falsely accused of spying by antirepublican conservatives, was one instance of the political infighting that often paralyzed the government.

The multiparty system of France seemed to carry democracy to excess, but by the First World War France had universal male suffrage and had instituted a *social welfare system* similar to that in Britain.

Britain and France by the early part of the 20th century had evolved into two of the world's three most powerful democracies, the United States being the third. The *old liberalism* of laissez-faire government had been replaced by a *new liberalism* that supported the extension of suffrage and the improvement of living conditions for all citizens.

The Suppression of Democracy

Germany through the Age of Metternich (1815–1848)

The Congress of Vienna had set up a *Germanic Confederation* of the thirty-nine independent German states that existed after the fall of Napoleon in order to deal with problems common to all. Radical student organizations, *Burschenschafts,* which were dedicated to the creation of a unified Germany that would be governed by constitutional principles, organized a national convention in 1817 and, in 1819, attempted the assassination of reactionary politicians. Metternich sponsored the *Carlsbad Decrees* in 1819 by which the various states forbade the *Burschenschafts,* censored materials that advocated unification, and set up secret police in the universities.

Although the reactionary forces in Germany quickly put down the *Revolutions of 1830,* Prussia set up an economic union of seventeen German states, the *Zollverein,* which eliminated internal tariffs and set the tone for greater union.

The Prussian king *Frederick William IV* reacted to the *Revolutions of 1848* by calling a nominal legislative assembly rather than using military force. In 1850, he granted a constitution that established a *House of Representatives* elected by universal male suffrage but controlled by the wealthiest classes.

The *Frankfurt Assembly,* an extralegal convention not to be confused with the king's Legislative Assembly, met from May 1848 to May 1849 and *established the nature of the future union of Germany.* Advocates of a *Greater Germany* wanted to include Austria and to have a Hapsburg emperor rule over the union. Supporters of a *Lesser Germany* wanted to exclude Austria and to have Prussia lead the union. The debate was resolved when Austria backed away from the proposed union. When the Frankfurt Assembly offered Frederick William the crown of a united Germany—Austria excluded—he declined by saying that he would accept it only from the German princes themselves.

The failure of the Frankfurt Assembly to implement its design for a democratic union (it had framed a kind of bill of rights) left the job of German unification to Prussian militarism and *Bismarck's policy of "Blood and Iron."* (German politics until World War I will be considered in a later chapter.)

Austria from the Age of Metternich to World War I (1815–1914)

The Revolutions of 1830 hardly touched the reactionary government of Austria under Metternich. However, the ethnic mix that made up the Austrian Empire—Germans, Hungarians, Slavs, Czechs, Italians, Serbs, Croats, and others—helped bring about revolution in 1848. When Paris erupted in rebellion in March of 1848, *Louis Kossuth,* a Hungarian nationalist, aroused separatist sentiment in the *Hungarian Diet* (a national assembly legal in the empire). Rioting broke out in Vienna. Prince Metternich, then chancellor, fled the country, and the Hungarians, the Czechs, and three Northern Italian provinces of the empire declared autonomy. The empire collapsed.

The *Prague Conference,* called by the Czechs in response to the all-German Frankfurt Conference, developed the notion of *Austroslavism,* by which the Slavic groups within the empire would remain part of the empire but also set up autonomous national governments. Before the idea could be adopted, a series of victories by Austrian armies restored Hapsburg authority over the various nationalities that had declared independence.

Franz Joseph (1848–1916) replaced *Emperor Ferdinand I,* and conservative forces within the government centralized power and suppressed all opposition. The Revolutions of 1848 failed in Austria largely because the empire's ethnic minorities squabbled among themselves rather than make a united front against imperial forces.

The defeat of Austria in the Austro-Prussian War of 1866 (to be considered in a subsequent chapter) led to some governmental reform. The *Compromise of 1867* set up a constitutional government with limited suffrage, granted the Hungarians internal autonomy, and created a *dual monarchy,* the *Austro-Hungarian Empire.* Exclusion of the Slavic minorities from a voice in government encouraged the *Pan-Slavic movement* to seek independence for ethnic minorities. It was an important cause for World War I.

Russia from the End of the Napoleonic Wars to World War I (1815–1914)

Alexander I (1801–1825) began his reign by extending the reforms of Catherine the Great, by modernizing the functioning of his government, and by offering greater freedom to Jews within his empire. Napoleon's invasion of Russia in 1812 turned this disposition about, until, by 1820, Alexander had ordered statewide censorship and the adherence of all his subjects to the Russian Orthodox Church.

When Alexander died, a confusion of succession—his two brothers, *Constantine* and *Nicholas,* were in line—led to the *Decembrist Revolt* in December 1825 of army officers in the capital of St. Petersburg. They supported the candidacy of Constantine, who they believed would modernize the nation and offer a constitution. *Nicholas I* (1825–1855) attained the throne after crushing the revolt, and his reign continued Alexander's autocratic policies. He was creator of the infamous *Third Section,* the secret police who prevented the spread of revolutionary or Western ideas. "Orthodoxy, Autocracy, Nationality" was the rallying cry of his reaction. Intellectuals in Russia developed two opposing camps during this period: *Slavophiles,* who believed that Russian village (the mir) culture was superior to that of the West; and *Westernizers,* who wanted to extend the "genius of Russian culture" by industrializing and setting up a constitutional government.

Alexander II (1855–1881) began his reign as a reformer and ended it as a conservative. His *Emancipation Proclamation* of 1861 *ended serfdom*—the medieval institution largely abolished in the rest of Europe—under which peasants were bound to the land and virtually owned by the aristocratic landowners. His murder at the hands of a militant faction of the *Narodniks,* a socialist group who wanted Russia to return to some mythical ideal of village life, increased repression under his successors, who turned to "Autocracy, Orthodoxy, and Nationalism."

By the 1890s, Russia had undertaken *industrialization* in order to remain a world power. At the beginning of World War I, 25 million of its population of 140 million were city dwellers, the *Trans-Siberian Railroad* linked European and Asiatic Russia, and the members of the growing proletariat were largely employed in state-owned factories that exploited and abused them.

(Political developments of the early 20th century are dealt with in a subsequent chapter.)

Sample Essay Question

The sample thematic essay question and the practice questions that follow are types found in the Advanced Placement Examination in European History, and they require knowledge of causes, effects, personalities, ideas, and events.

Sample Question

> *Explain* how, from the Age of Metternich to the beginning of World War I, democracy in England and France reached much the same place over decidedly different routes.

Comments on the Sample Question

Follow the "Simple Procedures" for writing an essay. (See page 24.)

First, *What does the question want to know?* In order to answer this question, determine the meaning of the terms "the same place" and "decidedly different routes." The implication is that both nations achieved a comparable level of democracy before the First World War but that the processes varied.

Second, *What do you know about it?* Consider what type of government each had at the start of the Age of Metternich (1815); second, trace the changes in each country during the following century; finally, spell out the degree and type of democracy that each had developed by 1914.

Third, *How would you put it into words?* The key term, "explain," requires that the answer makes clear the different political processes that led each nation to the same basic form of democratic government.

Sample Answer

Early in the Age of Metternich, conservative or reactionary governments had been set up in both England and France. In England, progressive Tory leadership had put through some reforms before the Revolutions of 1830 broke out in Europe. In 1832, the Great Reform Bill was passed, giving more representation in Parliament. The Chartist movement, active before the Revolutions of 1848, had a program that was a model for later reforms. The Second Reform

Bill, 1867, gave the vote to many of the working class, and many reforms were enacted in the following decade. In the ten years before World War I, Britain had established the basic structure of a modern welfare state.

In France, over the same span of time, the reactionary governments of the Bourbons had been set up by the Congress of Vienna and were overthrown during the Revolutions of 1830. A "bourgeois king" was installed under the constitution that the Bourbons had written in 1814, and he represented the interests of the upper and middle classes. When the Revolutions of 1848 broke out, a republic was proclaimed and a Constitutent Assembly was elected to write a new constitution. Socialist and radical riots were put down by the new government, and Louis Napoleon, nephew of the great Bonaparte, was elected president. In 1852, he proclaimed the Second French Empire with himself as emperor. He was popular until his foreign policy backfired, and he was ousted after the French lost the Franco-Prussian War. During the Third Republic, many coalition governments fell during crises because no one party could get a majority in the assembly. By the First World War, France had universal male suffrage and a social welfare system like Britain's.

Evaluate the Sample Answer

1. Did it have a clear introductory statement?
2. Did it reflect an understanding of the terms and the intent of the question?
3. Did it "explain" the processes and results of the growth of democracy in both nations?
4. Did it offer factual support for its argument?
5. Were the facts accurate? Abundant? Interesting?
6. Did its concluding paragraph sum up the "explanation"?
7. Was the essay long enough?
8. Was it well-written?

Rater's Comments on the Sample Answer

3—Qualified

This a "barebones" factual presentation. It presents the basic outline of the development of democracy through the 19th century and into the 20th for both England and France, but it fails to flesh out the facts. It is overly brief. It lacks both an introductory and concluding statement. It qualifies, despite these failings, because it is accurate, it answers the question, explains the development of democracy in both countries, and is reasonably clear.

Possible Improvements

The English and French experiences in developing democracy are clear contrasts. The English, despite some reactionary backsliding, followed their tradition of evolutionary empowerment: Over the decades, more and more of its populace enjoyed greater representation, more rights, a better standard of living. The French, their "old order" overthrown by violent revolution then forcibly restored, ran the gamut from virtual absolutism till 1830 under the Bourbon restoration, to bourgeois monarchy, to republicanism, to a return of empire, to unstable coalition democracy. As in the first French Revolution, the Paris mobs and the political radicals play crucial roles.

In 1815, in England at the end of the Napoleonic Wars, the ruling Tory conservative party passed the Corn Laws forbidding the importation of grain from overseas. When workers demonstrated for the repeal of these laws that raised the price of food, the government suspended civil rights and, in 1819, fired on a crowd of peaceful demonstrators in the Peterloo Massacre.

By the 1820s, a younger and less conservative Tory leadership—under George Canning and Robert Peel—freed itself from the influence of the reactionaries led by the Duke of Wellington (hero of Waterloo). Laws were reformed, civil rights expanded, and workers given the right to join unions.

The Great Reform Bill of 1832 reapportioned parliamentary representation, empowering the burgeoning industrial cities and expanding the electorate. Other reforms of this era limited the abuses in employment of children and women.

The Chartist movement advocated a broad program of reform including universal male suffrage, a secret ballot, "one man, one vote," and free public education. Although it failed to get these reforms enacted in the 1840s, it served as a model for future improvements in English society.

The Second Reform Bill, 1867, both doubled the size of the electorate and empowered many workers in the cities. Soon after, labor unions were legalized, free public education offered to working-class chidren, and a secret ballot introduced in elections.

By World War I, worker's compensation and social-security-type protection was enacted into law, and the right to strike and universal public education had laid the foundation for the modern welfare state, whereby government guarantees all of its people a decent standard of living.

After the Bourbons fell again in the face of rioting in the abortive Revolutions of 1830, Louis Phillipe reigned as the bourgeois king by honoring the nominal constitution of 1814 and representing the interests of the middle and upper classes. Corruption in his government precipitated the Revolution of 1848, resulting in a republican government and a Constituent Assembly to draw up a a new constitution. When radical riots broke out later that year, the assembly put them down and drew up a new constitution with a strong president as head of government. Drawing on the popularity of his late uncle, the great Bonaparte, Louis Napoleon got elected, dedicated his administration to protecting the interests of the conservative classes, and eventually declared himself emperor of the Second French Empire. Despite his domestic improvements that raised the standard of living and reforms that liberalized the government, his diplomatic misadventures—peaked by defeat in the Franco-Prussian War in 1870—drove him from power and replaced the empire with the Third Republic.

The governments that ruled under a new constitution and redesigned National Assembly were coalitions made up of the dozens of competing parties that ran the spectrum from extreme left to extreme right. Despite a gradual expansion of suffrage and of civil rights, economic reforms and improved standard of living, the French government up to World War I was inherently unstable.

Both the English and the French, from the Age of Metternich to the First World War, set the firm beginnings of the social welfare state, but the English did with a minimum of violence, a maximum of gradualism, and by maintaining the stability of social and governmental institutions.

Practice Essay Questions

The following are samples of the various types of thematic essays that appear on the Advanced Placement Examination in European History. (See pages 17–18 for detailed explanations of each type.)

---

1. *To what extent and in what ways* did the move toward unification in mid-19th-century Germany fall out of the hands of the constitutionalists and into the hands of the Prussian militarists?

Comments on Question 1

There is little room for choice in this question, since it requires that you show "how and how much" of German unification was the result of a failure of the forces of democracy to take the lead, thereby leaving it to the militarists in Prussia. Refer to specifics in the breakdown of the leadership of constitutional forces, in the assumption of leadership by Prussia, and in the militaristic nature of Prussian leadership.

---

2. "Attempts at reform and modernization in 19th-century Russia were inevitably diluted by the habit of reaction." *Assess the validity* of this statement by offering factual evidence.

Comments on Question 2

To "assess the validity" is to determine whether a statement is true, false, or partly both. The pivotal concept in this statement is "inevitably diluted." Does it mean that "the habit of reaction" canceled or weakened "reform and modernization"?

---

3. "Austria's suppression of Slavic autonomy within the empire created more dissolution than unity." *Defend or refute* this statement.

Comments on Question 3

"Defend or refute" usually allows the presentation of a mixed argument. In this case—because of the crucial phrase "more dissolution than unity"—the argument must show that one or the other was true.

As is often the case, the question itself shows the direction of the best possible argument: that dissolution was the result of Austria's policy toward its Slavic minorities.

---

4. *Evaluate* the achievements of Napoleon III.

Comments on Question 4

There is always room in an "evaluation" question since it requires "judging the worth" or comparing "pluses and minuses." The trick here is to give a balanced view. History's greatest villains appealed to *somebody* for *some reason*.

Napoleon III was immensely popular for a time and for specific achievements.

> 5. *Contrast and compare* the growth and suppression of democracy in 19th-century Europe.

Comments on Question 5

This is a double effort: to "show differences" and to "examine similarities." Democracy did not grow easily in the states where it was ultimately successful nor did it flounder completely in those where it was suppressed. This is a broad question that requires more than a comparison of only two states.

Practice Multiple-Choice Questions

(These questions are representative of the types found on the Advanced Placement Examination in European History.)

1. The period from the fall of Napoleon in 1815 to the Revolutions of 1848 is often referred to as the Age of Metternich for all the following reasons EXCEPT
    (A) the reactionary policies of Prince Metternich of Austria dominated continental politics
    (B) republicanism was suppressed and the nationalistic urges of most ethnic groups were denied
    (C) support of the Old Order was widespread among the political elite
    (D) the industrial middle class was increasingly denied representation in government
    (E) the liberal ideas of the French Revolution were suppressed

2. Which of the following did NOT reflect the conservative policies of the English government from 1815 to 1832?
    (A) The Corn Laws
    (B) The Peterloo Massacre
    (C) The "Rotten Borough system"
    (D) The Six Acts of 1819
    (E) The establishment of a modern police force

3. Which of the following was NOT a demand for reform of the Chartists, a radical working-class reform movement?
    (A) Universal suffrage
    (B) A secret ballot
    (C) "One man, one vote" for representation in Parliament
    (D) Expansion of public education
    (E) Abolition of property qualification for public office

4. Which would be the best description of the political situation in France from 1815 to the start of World War I?
    (A) A series of contrasting types of governments were established and removed.
    (B) There was a gradual but continual move toward reform and greater representation for all classes.
    (C) There was a disintegration of republicanism.
    (D) Imperialism replaced Bourbon despotism.
    (E) Ceaseless despotism was relieved by brief periods of revolution.

5. Elected by a landslide after the failed Revolution of 1848, he founded the Second French Empire:
    (A) Louis XVIII
    (B) Louis Philippe
    (C) Louis Napoleon
    (D) Louis Blanc
    (E) Louis Quatorze

6. The Revolutions of 1848
    (A) overthrew the governments of France, Germany, and Russia
    (B) erupted in England as well as on the continent
    (C) marked the decline of the political influence of the proletariat
    (D) gave rise to Communism and realpolitik
    (E) dissipated the nationalistic urges of the peoples of Eastern Europe

7. The original goal of the Frankfurt Assembly (1848–1849) was to
    (A) design and implement a constitutional government for a unified Germany
    (B) consolidate Germany under Austrian Hapsburg leadership
    (C) unify the northern states of Germany under Prussia
    (D) create a united Germany for Germans only
    (E) convince Prussia to unite Germany by force

8. Which is the best characterization of the status of reform in Russia from 1815 to 1914?
    (A) "Orthodoxy, Autocracy, Nationality" was the slogan of all.
    (B) Repeated attempts to Westernize and reform resulted in reaction.
    (C) Gradual democratization was effected by the "Westernized" intelligentsia.
    (D) A purge of all Western influences was effected by the "Slavophiles."
    (E) There was a total suppression of all attempts to reform and modernize.

9. Which was NOT a change in the democratic movement in Europe in the last three decades of the 19th century?
   - (A) Liberals sought to limit government authority in social and economic affairs.
   - (B) Suffrage had expanded to include most of the male population.
   - (C) Liberals argued for government regulation of industry.
   - (D) Governments became increasingly involved in alleviating poverty.
   - (E) Industrial workers demanded a higher standard of living.

10. Between the end of the Second Empire in 1871 and the start of World War I, France
    - (A) had one stable government
    - (B) had developed a two-party system
    - (C) suffered a single-party dictatorship
    - (D) had dozens of separate and unstable governments
    - (E) was ruled by socialist radicals

11. All of the following are features of the social welfare systems that had developed in France and England before World War I EXCEPT
    - (A) the right of workers to strike
    - (B) government insurance for job injuries
    - (C) old-age pensions
    - (D) compulsory school attendance
    - (E) universal suffrage

"He is guilty! Damn that Jewish officer and his rabble-rousing novelist friend! Republicans and their spies will be the ruin of us. That cursed officer has become a symbol. Let him not blind us to the truth that we need a king. May he rot on Devil's Island."

12. To whom is the speaker referring?
    - (A) Leon Gambetta
    - (B) Marshal MacMahon
    - (C) Alfred Dreyfus
    - (D) Major Esterhazy
    - (E) Georges Boulanger

13. The accused in the above passage was exonerated, partly through the efforts of Emile Zola, the writer. The conflict involved an attempt by a rival political faction to embarrass the government with trumped-up charges of espionage. Which faction was responsible for the false imprisonment of the man referred to above?
    - (A) monarchists
    - (B) liberals
    - (C) republicans
    - (D) radical workers
    - (E) socialists

14. The man whose reestablishment of a French Empire brought in the mid-1800s temporary prosperity then ruinous defeat to the nation was
    (A)   Cavour
    (B)   Louis Napoleon
    (C)   Louis Kossuth
    (D)   Leon Gambetta
    (E)   Georges Boulanger

15. During the dramatic growth of scientific experimentation in the later half of the 19th century, which two physicians helped develop the science of bacteriology?
    (A)   Lister and Koch
    (B)   Marie and Pierre Curie
    (C)   Boyle and Lavoisier
    (D)   Dalton and Mendeleev
    (E)   Roentgen and Rutherford

Answers and Answer Explanations

1. D	2. E	3. A	4. A	5. C
6. D	7. A	8. B	9. A	10. D
11. E	12. C	13. A	14. B	15. A

1. (D)   The wealth of the industrial middle class gave it leverage with the government.

2. (E)   This was a reform since crime was on the rise in the rapidly expanded cities.

3. (A)   They did not support women's suffrage.

4. (A)   Instability of individual governments and change of types of government prevailed.

5. (C)   A nephew of the great and first Napoleon, he capitalized on his uncle's fame to get elected and to establish an empire.

6. (D)   The failure of the revolutions inspired new methods of getting power for the "have-nots."

7. (A)   The other issues came up during the conference and helped wreck the chances for a democratic Germany.

8. (B)   For every step forward, a step back.

9. (A)   This was the liberal program in the earlier part of the century. Abuses of industrialization changed it.

10. (D)   The coalition governments often fell at the hint of a major crisis.

11. (E)   Women did not get the vote until after World War I in Britain, after World War II in France.

12. (C)   The infamous Dreyfus Case pitted supporters of a republican government against the conservative classes. Strong evidence indicates that Major Esterhazy was the guilty party who passed military secrets to the Germans.

13. (A) Although a court-martial never found him innocent, the president of France pardoned him and public opinion turned against the monarchists and other conservative factions.

14. (B) It is Louis Napoleon, also known as Napoleon III. Cavour was the unifier of Italy; Gambetta and Boulanger were French politicians; Louis Kossuth was the Hungarian nationalist hero.

15. (A) They discovered the role of germs in causing infection and the use of antiseptics in treatment. The Curies were pioneers in the study of radioactivity; Boyle and Lavoisier were chemists; Dalton and Mendeleev formulated atomic theory; Roentgen discovered X-rays; Rutherford was a physicist who worked on atomic theory.

CHAPTER 8 19th Century "-ISMs": Nationalism, Ideologies, and Culture

Overview

The period following the French Revolution and the Napoleonic Wars, known as the *Age of Metternich* (see Chapter 7), saw the rise of powerful ideologies— "-isms"—some of which were legacies of the French Revolution, and some of which were responses to the political, economic, and social upheavals of the previous decades. *Nationalism* was the most promising and the most pernicious of these. It was the prime motive for the unification of Italy and of Germany; it was a force that redefined political boundaries and loyalties and that encouraged claims of national or racial superiority.

Liberalism, socialism, and romanticism profoundly influenced the politics, economics, and culture of the first half of the 19th century. *Realism* defined the literature of the later half of the century, *impressionism* brought the artist's personal visual experience to painting, and *Social Darwinism* and *positivism* provided scientific models for politics and the arts.

One decade, 1861 to 1871, saw the triumph of the large nation-state as Europe's primary political unit. Italy and Germany consolidated; Austria and Hungary formed autonomous but united states; Russia centralized government control.

The nation-state is founded upon a sense of nationalism: a common identity; a specific geographic area; a common language, history, destiny, culture, ethnicity, or religion. It is a consciousness of belonging and of the differences between one's own people and all others on this planet.

The French Revolution and Napoleon's successes inspired the drive to unity. Nationalism promised power, the mystical connection that the Romantic movement glorified, and autonomy from the remote leadership of amorphous multinational empires. France and England were the two most powerful nation-states before 1861; Italy became a united kingdom in 1861; Germany formed a new empire in 1871. War played the crucial role in both processes.

The idealism of the Revolutions of 1848 had failed to realize the nationalist aspirations of the Italians or the Germans. If the Italian and German peoples, separated into traditionally small independent states, were ready for unification, it still took the "power politics" (realpolitik) of two determined men to bring about unity. Camillo di Cavour, Sardinian prime minister, and Otto von Bismarck, Prussian chancellor, used the might and prestige of their states to bring smaller independent entities together to create the modern nation-states of Italy and Germany. After 1871, the balance of power in Europe was changed well into the 20th century.

The Age of Nationalism

After the Revolutions of 1848, Europe, as well as other regions of the globe, adopted *nationalism* (the supremacy of the nation-state in organizing the political, social, economic, and cultural activities of a people).

Louis Napoleon was the nephew of *the Napoleon* (Napoleon I) who despite defeat, exile, and death was considered by the French to be one of their greatest leaders. Louis Napoleon was elected president of France by a landslide in 1848, largely because of his illustrious name. Between 1852, when he had proclaimed a Second Empire, and 1870, after France's ignominious defeat in the Franco-Prussian War, he had restored the economy, laid the foundations for democratic reforms, and renewed the national pride of the French people.

The Civil War (1861–1865) in the United States resulted in a more solid union and in a more powerful federal government.

After defeat at the hands of the French and English in *The Crimean War* (1853), Russia modernized, industrialized, and initiated a program of limited reforms to solidify Czarist control over the multinational peoples of Russia's vast reaches.

Japan, in response to Western incursions in the 1850s and '60s, developed a modern military, an industrial economy, and a centralized government under Emperor Mejii, whose ancestors had been figureheads.

The Unification of Italy

Italy Before Unification

THE SEPARATE STATES

The Kingdom of Naples (Two Sicilies) was made up of Sicily and the southern half of the Italian boot.

The *Papal states* were in the middle of the peninsula.

Lombardy-Venetia were industrialized provinces in the north, and they were ruled by Austria as were Tuscany, Lucca, Modena, and Parma.

The Kingdom of Sardinia (Piedmont-Sardinia), was made up of the island of Sardinia and the northwestern provinces of Nice, Savoy, and Piedmont.

Sardinia was a constitutional monarchy ruled by *Victor Emmanuel II* (1849–1878), and it was the only independent state in Italy. In 1854, *Camillo di Cavour* became prime minister of the parliament instituted during the Revolutions of 1848. He rejected the romantic nationalism of *Giuseppe Mazzini* (1805–1872), who had argued in his *Duties of Man* that the nation was a divine device and an extended family, and decided that Italy could be unified only through force and that Sardinia would have to lead the battle.

In order to gain the support of liberals throughout Italy, Cavour reformed the government of his state by weakening the influence of the papacy, by investing in public works such as railroads and harbor improvements, by abolishing internal tariffs, by encouraging the growth of industry, by emancipating the peasantry from the vestiges of manorialism, and by making the Sardinian government a model of progressive constitutionalism.

Cavour's "Power Politics"

After the Crimean War ended in 1856, Cavour, who had brought Sardinia into the war on the side of France, petitioned Emperor Napoleon III to support Sardinia in a projected war with Austria, which controlled many Italian provinces. At *Plombieres* in 1858, Cavour got Napoleon to agree to send a supporting army into Italy in the event that Sardinia could trick Austria into a war. Napoleon, who wanted to weaken the Austrians, was promised the French-speaking provinces of Nice and Savoy in return for allowing the Sardinians to annex Northern Italy.

In April 1859, *Austria declared war on Sardinia* and the French came to Cavour's aid. After a series of victories by the combined Sardinian-French forces, Napoleon suddenly pulled out of the war because of criticisms at home and threats from the Prussians. The Austrians were left with Venetia, and only Lombardy went to the Sardinians. Several of the northern duchies under Austrian domination declared independence and carried out plebiscites for union with Sardinia by 1860.

Giuseppe Garibaldi, an ardent nationalist, invaded Sicily in 1860 with the encouragement of Cavour. His thousand-man *Red Shirts* used popular support to defeat a Bourbon rulers' force that was ten times that number. Within months, Garibaldi had subdued Sicily and Naples. The *Two Sicilies* (Kingdom of Naples) joined Sardinia, and in *March 1861 the Kingdom of Italy was proclaimed* with Victor Emmanuel II on the throne.

Final Unification

By 1870, Venetia and the Papal states—despite opposition from the Pope—had been incorporated into the union. *Italia Irredenta* ("Italy unredeemed"—Italian areas still under Austrian control) remained unliberated, but Italy had been united and was a constitutional monarchy. Democracy was diluted by the small percentage of the male population that had suffrage and by the dominance, in Southern Italy, of the landowners.

The Unification of Germany

Germany Before Unification

In the two or so decades before German unification took place, the population, productivity, and wealth of the German states increased many times over. The *Zollverein* (customs union) had opened most of the states to a mutually advantageous trade, and Germany became a single economic unit. Prussia, with its booming industry, powerful army, militaristic Junkers (land-owning aristocrats), and expansionist ambitions led the states of Northern Germany and faced off against Austria. The Hapsburgs of Austria—rulers of a multinational empire held together by tradition and raw power and the prime influence among the divided states of Germany—had long feared a Germany united by the Hohenzollerns of Prussia. After the Frankfurt Assembly failed to unify the independent German states in 1848, though, the Prussian *Hohenzollern* kings determined to achieve it by force.

Bismarck's Realpolitik

When the Prussian Parliament refused to approve military expenditures in 1862, *King Wilhelm I* appointed Otto von Bismarck (1815–1898), a prominent and conservative Junker, as chancellor. He trampled the Parliament by collecting illegal taxes, ignoring its protests, enlarging the army, and, in the process, killing democracy in Prussia.

"Blood and Iron," he insisted, would unite Germany, and after involving Prussia in three wars, he achieved unification under Prussian leadership.

The War against Denmark, 1864, allied Prussia, Austria, and the other German states in an *all-German war* against Denmark, which had hoped to annex the neighboring province of *Schleswig.* Denmark was quickly defeated, and, after some prodding by Bismarck, Prussia and Austria fell out over who should get what.

The *Austro-Prussian War (Seven Weeks' War),* 1866, broke out when the issues of the war with Denmark remained unresolved. Although the Austrians enlisted the help of most of the other German states, the superior arms, training, and leadership of the Prussian Army defeated them in seven weeks. Hoping to gain Austria's support in the inevitable struggle with France, which had become alarmed by Prussia's swift victories, Bismarck made the surrender terms lenient.

Bismarck established the *North German Confederation*—in 1867 to replace the *German Confederation*—that loose union that Napoleon had set up and that the Congress of Vienna had confirmed. Twenty-one states of North Germany were united under the leadership of the Prussian king, with a two-house legislature, the *Reichstag* or lower house to represent all the people and to be elected by universal male suffrage, and the *Bundesrat* or upper house to represent the princes.

The *Franco-Prussian War,* 1870, broke out after a dynastic dispute over the Spanish throne led to a flurry of diplomatic exchanges between Prussia and France. Bismarck deliberately altered the wording of the *Ems Dispatch,* an account of the German king's meeting with the French ambassador over the issue, and made the inflammatory revision public. Napoleon III, bowing to public opinion and bad advice, declared war on Prussia in July 1870. In less than four months, the Prussian army had defeated the French and taken the emperor prisoner. *The Treaty of Frankfurt,* May 1871, gave *Alsace-Lorraine* to Germany and imposed a punishing *indemnity,* both of which the French people were to resent for generations to come.

Unification

Four South German states—Baden, Bavaria, Hesse, and Württemberg—that did not belong to the North German Confederation joined after the flush of victory, and *the German empire was born* in January 1871. The Prussian king became emperor or *kaiser.*

The Empire with Bismarck as Chancellor

Although the lower house of the imperial legislature, the *Reichstag,* was elected by universal male suffrage, it had little real power because the chancellor and his ministers were responsible to the kaiser rather than to the legislature. Democracy in Germany took a backseat to autocracy.

Bismarck's *Kulturkampf* (cultural conflicts) was his repression of the so-called subversive elements in the empire—Catholics and socialists. Reversing his original attacks on the *Catholic Center party* by the late 1870s, he turned to the socialist "menace" represented by the growing *Social Democratic party.* When his official measures backfired and the party grew even more popular, he pulled the rug out from under it by sponsoring a series of social reforms himself. Workmen's compensation, old-age pensions, and medical protection created one of the world's most advanced social welfare systems.

Bismarck's Fall   When *Wilhelm II* assumed the throne in 1888, he brought with him the archaic notion of *divine right* of rule and a deep resentment of Bismarck's personal power. In 1890, he *dismissed Bismarck* and up until his abdication at the close of World War I, 1918, he dominated his chancellors. Arrogant and limited, his ambitions and aggressiveness in the late 1800s and early 1900s upset the balance of power and drove Europe closer to world war.

Ideology and Culture

Liberalism   Classical *Liberalism,* an offshoot of the ideals of liberty and equality of the French Revolution, set as its political goals legal equality, freedom of the press, freedom of assembly and of speech, and above all, representative government. Reacting to monarchial absolutism and to the reactionary repression (as represented by the policies of Austria's Prince Metternich, whose conservative attempt to roll back the ideals of the French Revolution amounted to a crusade against liberalism), the liberalism of the early 19th century generally opposed government intervention.

Laissez-faire, a form of economic liberalism and a principle espoused most convincingly by Adam Smith, argued for a free market system unfettered by government regulations. While this concept fostered economic growth, the theories of economists Thomas Malthus and David Ricardo (see Chapter 6) were often used to back up the predatory business practices of early capitalists and industrialists.

After the first few decades of the 19th century, liberalism was espoused mostly by the middle class and tended to ignore the rights and aspirations of the working class.

Socialism   Early *socialism* was a reaction to the gross inequities created by the Industrial Revolution. The exploitation of workers by the early capitalists convinced the *utopian socialists* (see Chapter 6) that one of the best remedies for this was to have governments intervene in the economy. Their program included government control of property, economic equality for all, and government economic planning. *Charles Fourier*, a Frenchman, described a scheme for a utopian community based on a socialist idea. His countryman, *Louis Blanc,* pushed a program for the democratic takeover of the state by workers to guarantee full employment.

The impracticality of their programs relegated the early *utopian socialists* to a minor political role, and modern socialism was largely founded by the theories of Karl Marx. (See Chapter 6.)

Romanticism   *Romanticism*, a glorification of the emotional component of human nature, was a reaction to the rationalism and restraint of the Enlightenment. The excesses of the French Revolution and the destructiveness of the Napoleonic Wars eroded faith in the "inevitable perfectability" of humankind through reason.

Romantic artists, composers, and writers shared a worldview: a willingness to express the deepest and most turbulent emotions, a fervent belief in personal freedom, awe of nature, reverence for history.

SOME REPRESENTATIVE FIGURES

William Wordsworth (1770–1850): English, a poet who glorified the beauty and solemnity of nature.

Victor Hugo (1802–1885): French, a poet and dramatist best remembered for his vibrant novels, such as *The Hunchback of Notre Dame,* which explored the darker side of the human experience.

George Sand (1804–1876): French, a countess who took a man's name as her pen name. She wrote modern, autobiographical, emotionally revealing novels about unconventional love.

Ludwig van Beethoven (1770–1827): German, his musical genius is expressed in virtually every musical form of his day, from songs to symphonies, and his evolution as a romantic is evident in the course of his composing. The symphonic music of his later period makes full use of the expanded orchestra, a romantic innovation that added three times as many instruments as the classical orchestra known to Mozart, and that expressed the profound emotionality of romantic music.

Realism

Realism, the literary movement that had replaced literary *romanticism* by the middle of the 19th century, portrayed a kind of *determinism,* the belief that human nature and human destiny are formed by heredity and environment and that human behavior is governed by natural laws that preclude free will.

Writers, such as the Frenchmen *Emile Zola*, *Honoré de Balzac*, and *Gustave Flaubert*, the English woman *George Eliot* (Mary Ann Evans), and the Russian *Leo Tolstoy* devoted their works to a depiction of everyday life, especially of the working class and especially of its more unsavory aspects. Spurning the romantic obsession with distant times and distant places, they focused on the here and now, often shocking readers with their objective depictions of life in the cities, the slums, and the factories.

Impressionism

The advent of photography in the 19th century encouraged a group of artists, *Impressionists,* to avoid realistic depiction (better served by photography) and to capture, instead, the transitory feeling of a scene, the personal "impression." Frenchmen *Pierre-Auguste Renoir* (1841–1919) and *Claude Monet* (1840–1926) were major practitioners of the style.

Science

After the first few decades of the 19th century, and directly as a result of the technological requirements of the Industrial Revolution, "pure" scientific discoveries found application in explaining how the machinery and techniques of industrial processes worked. Physicists were able to formulate principles of *thermodynamics* applicable to a variety of technological systems, such as the operation of engines, which converted heat into motion.

The theories of biology were used by researchers, such as *Louis Pasteur* (1822–1895), to preserve food and to improve medical procedures. A burgeoning chemical industry provided a variety of new products from medicines to synthetic dyes, and the generation of electricity created whole new industries in transportation and lighting.

Charles Darwin (1809–1882) was not the first theorist to formulate the concept of evolution, but his meticulous research and voluminous specimens added weight to his idea that life evolved in its myriad forms from a common ancestor, through the process of a *struggle for survival*. The mechanism that aided this was the development of anomalies in a given species, which would actually aid in the survival of that species. His insight predates the development of the science of *genetics*. For instance, when the only foliage available for grazing was on high trees, the mutant long-neck giraffe would outlive and out-propagate his short-neck cousins. Thus, his characteristics would be more successfully passed on to later generations.

Darwin's theory had a powerful effect on the intellectual life of Europe. It was used by skeptics to attack the Biblical account of creation and religion itself. *Friedrich Nietzsche* (1844–1900), a German philosopher and contemporary of Darwin, argued that Christianity presented a "slave morality" that fettered the creativity of great individuals, the *ubermench* (superman), who must free himself from conventionality and redefine life and morality.

Herbert Spencer (1820–1903) used Darwin's theories to argue that history and human society reflect a struggle for supremacy resulting in the *survival of the fittest*: the rich, the rulers, the powerful nations are "fit"; the poor, the downtrodden masses, the world's colonies are "weak." This *Social Darwinism* appealed to those in power and to racists and imperialists of every stripe.

Sample Essay Question

The sample thematic essay and the practice essays presented in this chapter are types found in the Advanced Placement European History Exam and they require a knowledge of causes, effects, personalities, ideas, and events.

Sample Question

> *Contrast and compare* the methods of Cavour and Bismarck in unifying their respective nations.

Comments on the Sample Question

Follow the "Simple Procedures" for writing an essay. (See page 24.)

First, *What does the question want to know?* The "compare" part of this question is relatively easy; the "contrast" part is more subtle.

Second, *What do you know about it?* Both men headed the dominant states of the respective unions; both men used "power politics"—diplomacy, Machiavellian manipulations, war—to gain their ends; both viewed their roles with the kind of hardheaded realism that avoided romantic illusions about the processes and results of unification. Their contrasts: Their domestic policies differed; their methods of "power politics" differed because of the different degrees of independent strength of their states. Bismarck could rely on "Blood and Iron"; Cavour maneuvered among the giants, pitting one against the other.

Third, *How would you put it into words?* Use the question's basic structure—"contrast" and "compare"—to develop your essay. Be sure to offer specifics to back up your generalizations.

The failure of the Revolutions of 1848 created a new diplomacy: "Power Politics," a very ungentlemanly and often ruthless application of the Machiavellian misinterpretation that "the end justifies the means." Camillo di Cavour and Otto von Bismarck became masters of the game and won the unification of two of Europe's traditionally disunited regions.

Before 1861, Italy had been a well-defined geographic area—the "Boot"—made up of separate entities, one of which was independent, most of which were dominated by the Austrian Empire, all of which had long been battlegrounds in the struggle for hegemony by the larger nation-states of Europe. Before 1871, Germany was a conglomeration of nearly forty fiercely independent states, and Prussia and Austria competed for economic and political dominance.

Napoleon's battlefield successes in the early 1800s and his attempts at consolidation in both regions passed on the passion of nationalism to both the Italians and the Germans. It took the right timing, the gifted leadership of the heads of the two outstanding states of each region, and war to achieve national unification. The methods in achieving unification that both Cavour of Italy and Bismarck of Germany used can be contrasted: One built up democracy at home while the other suppressed it; one relied on the help of stronger nation-states while the other conquered all opposition without outside help. Their methods can be compared in that they used deceit and war to achieve their ends.

The Kingdom of Sardinia (Piedmont-Sardinia) consisted of the island of Sardinia, off the west coast of Italy in the Mediterranean, and the region in the northwest corner of Italy that bordered on Switzerland and France. In the decade before unification, it was the only independent state of Italy. Under Cavour, made its prime minister in 1852 by King Victor Emmanuel II, the state became a constitutional monarchy. It was modernized by a system of roads and railroads; it was industrialized; it was reformed by the abolition of all forms of manorialism, by the reduction of the influence of the Roman Catholic Church, and by the establishment of a strong parliament. It served as a model for liberal reform and was a leader in the movement for unification.

In 1858 at Plombieres, after years of quiet diplomacy, Cavour got Napoleon III, the grandiose emperor of the Second French Empire, to back him up if he could trick Austria into declaring war. The idea was for Piedmont to annex Austrian territory in the north of Italy. The trick worked; Austria was provoked into a declaration of war in 1859; Napoleon III kept his promise; the Austrians were defeated. This was "power politics" at its most ruthless and effective.

Then the bottom dropped out of the plan. Napoleon III made a separate peace with the Austrians because of opposition to the war at home and because of fear of the Prussians, who opposed French dominance in Italy. Cavour was alone. Negotiations won only one northern province for Cavour. But revolutions in a number of other Northern Italian states created governments whose electorates voted for union with Piedmont.

Despite opposition from the Austrians and the Pope, who lost territory in those revolutions, the Kingdom of Piedmont was recognized by a number of powerful European states.

Unification was completed when Giuseppe Garibaldi's Red Shirts conquered Sicily from its Bourbon rulers and then Naples. Cavour, careful not to alienate the Pope or the French, received permission for his troops to pass through the Papal states and to take over from Garibaldi. The former Kingdom of the Two Sicilies was joined with the expanded Kingdom of Piedmont-Sardinia, and in March 1861 Victor Emmanuel II became king of Italy.

Prussia was the most modern and powerful of the German states. Referred to as "an army before it was a state," its efficient and fast-growing industry supported its influential military establishment. Conservative aristocratic landowners, the Junkers, had the strongest voice in a weak constitutional monarchy. In 1862, Parliament voted down military appropriations, and King Wilhelm I appointed the tough-minded Junker Bismarck to deal with the crisis. Over the next several years, Bismarck virtually wiped out parliamentary democracy in the country. He collected taxes over the protests of Parliament, enlarged the army, and ignored the opposition. He and Prussia were ready to lead the battle for unification.

His "realpolitik" was similar to Cavour's power politics: He used deceit, intimidation, and insult to precipitate war with national unification the goal. The all-German war against Denmark allied Hohenzollern Prussia and its traditional Hapsburg rival, Austria. They quickly defeated Denmark and divided two German-speaking duchies, Schleswig and Holstein, between them. Bismarck nurtured a dispute between his state and Austria, and then isolated Austria from potential allies with promises of territory. Austria managed to get the support of the German Confederation (most of the other independent states of the region), and in 1866 they went to war against Prussia, which was without allies.

In seven weeks, the well-led, well-equipped, and well-trained Prussian army defeated Austria and her allies. Deliberately moderating the terms of the peace treaty to gain German support for his next venture, Bismarck dissolved the old German Confederation (originally set up by Napoleon) and replaced it with the North German Confederation, a watered-down constitutional monarchy, made up of the bulk of the German states and ruled by the Prussian king.

Waiting for a pretext to draw France into a war that would draw the Southern German states into a union with Prussia's new confederation, he found the perfect issue in the succession of a German to the Spanish throne. By doctoring an account—the Ems Despatch—about the meeting between the Prussian king and the French ambassador to resolve the issue, Bismarck provoked popular opinion in both Germany and France. In July 1870, France declared war on Prussia.

Less than six months later, France was defeated, Napoleon was humiliated, and the remaining German states had joined the North German Confederation to form the German empire. Cavour's and Bismarck's methods in unifying their countries can be contrasted.

Cavour carried out reforms that strengthened parliamentary democracy in Piedmont and in newly united Italy while Bismarck rolled over the Prussian Parliament and imposed a militaristic autocracy on Prussia and later all of Germany. When Cavour brought Piedmont into war with a stronger Austria, he managed to win most of his goals by manipulating an alliance with an even stronger France. Bismarck, on the other hand, used Prussian military and industrial might—*Blut und Eisen*—to stand alone against all of the enemies his realpolitik set up for the kill.

Both men's methods can be compared in that they led their strongly independent states in the movement for national consolidation and that they used deception, intrigue, and war to gain their goals. Single-minded and hardheaded, they rejected the romantic appeal of mystical national bonds and hammered out unification with hardball politics, diplomatic deceit, battlefield victories.

Evaluate the Sample Answer

1. Did the introduction point out the direction the essay would take?
2. Did the essay "contrast and compare" the methods of both men?
3. Was it generalized or oversimplified, or did it employ relevant, accurate facts?
4. Did it miss any important differences or similarities between the men?
5. Was the essay long enough, well written, convincing?
6. Did the conclusion sum up the argument?

Rater's Comments on the Sample Answer

5—Extremely well qualified

Not only does this essay contrast the methods of Cavour and Bismarck in unifying Italy and Germany by "showing differences" but it clearly compares their styles and means by "examining similarities." The introductory paragraphs lay out the structure of the argument. The essay then provides relevant historical background. The body of the essay demonstrates a scholarly, fact-based account of the methods of each man in operation. The conclusion sums up admirably.

Practice Essay Questions

The questions that follow are samples of the various types of thematic essays that appear on the Advanced Placement Examination in European History. (See pages 17–18 for a detailed explanation of each.)

---

1. *To what extent and in what ways* did Mazzini break new ground for Cavour's program of unification? Did Garibaldi help complete it?

Comments on Question 1

Mazzini has been called the "poet" of Italian unification, Cavour the "architect," and Garibaldi the "cavalier." How and how much did Mazzini's proselytizing of the glories of mystical union prepare the Italian people and the world for the realpolitik of Cavour? How and how much did Garibaldi's flamboyant appeal and adventures in the two Sicilies enable Cavour to complete unification?

> 2. *Explain* why the political situation in Italy in the decade before unification prompted Piedmont-Sardinia to take the lead in the movement.

Comments on Question 2

The Revolutions of 1848 were the kind of failures that whet the appetite for greater success and that pointed the way. Power politics grew out of the frustrations of the erstwhile reformers. Piedmont was the logical leader of unification because it was the only independent state in Italy. Most of the north was under the yoke of Austria, central Italy was controlled by the traditionalistic politics of the papacy; the south was underdeveloped and under the sway of anachronistic manorialism. When Cavour reformed and strengthened Piedmont, he was making the most of its opportunities.

> 3. *Analyze* Bismarck's use of war to achieve unification.

Comments on Question 3

"Examine in detail" how the All-German War, the Seven Weeks' War, and the Franco-Prussian War were used by Bismarck to effect unification. It was a process of distinct stages: War with Denmark aroused a sense of German nationalism and set Austria up for the fall; the Seven Weeks' War aligned most of Germany with the loser, Austria, and against the winner, Prussia, but generous terms achieved the North German Confederation; finally, victory over France inspired a patriotic yearning for union that created the empire.

> 4. "Germany did not unite itself; rather, it was conquered by Prussia." *Assess the validity* of this statement.

Comments on Question 4

To "determine the truth" of this statement, consider that Prussia stood alone against the rest of Germany in the Seven Weeks' War, that Bismarck's realpolitik united Germany by "Blood and Iron," that even the Franco-Prussian War served to draw the remaining German states into union.

> 5. *Evaluate* Bismarck as chancellor of the new German Empire.

Comments on Question 5

Don't confuse this question of his role as chancellor of the united Germany with his role as uniter. What happened under Bismarck after 1871?

His "pluses"—his diplomacy, his mediation of the colonial rivalries in Africa, his masterful ability to maintain the delicate balance of peace despite Germany's upsetting the balance of power by its stunning victory over France, his social welfare reforms.

His "minuses"—his continued repression of democracy in Germany, *Kulturkampf* against the Catholic influence, anti-Socialist crusade.

Practice Multiple-Choice Questions

(These questions are representative of the types that appear on the Advanced Placement Examination in European History.)

1. Which state took the lead in the process of Italian unification?
   - (A) The Kingdom of Naples
   - (B) The Papal States
   - (C) Lombardy-Venetia
   - (D) Piedmont-Sardinia
   - (E) Tuscany

2. Who was called "the architect of Italian unification"?
   - (A) Mazzini
   - (B) Garibaldi
   - (C) Victor Emmanuel II
   - (D) Cavour
   - (E) Napoleon III

3. During Cavour's administration as prime minister of Piedmont-Sardinia, which of the following was NOT true?
   - (A) The influence of the Church diminished.
   - (B) There was industrialization.
   - (C) Manorialism was strengthened.
   - (D) Constitutionalism was established.
   - (E) Commerce was encouraged.

4. Cavour's "deal" with Napoleon III at Plombieres was significant because
   - (A) it was a manifestation of his "power politics"
   - (B) it brought peace with Austria
   - (C) it guaranteed French nonintervention in the war with Austria
   - (D) it freed Napoleon III to fight Prussia
   - (E) it alienated Garibaldi's "Red Shirts"

5. *Italia Irredenta* was the name given to
   - (A) the process of unification
   - (B) the newly united Italian constitutional monarchy
   - (C) the rural south of Italy
   - (D) the split between the new government and the papacy
   - (E) the Italian enclaves remaining under Austrian control

6. Victor Emmanuel II was proclaimed king of Italy in
   - (A) 1850
   - (B) 1860
   - (C) 1861
   - (D) 1870
   - (E) 1871

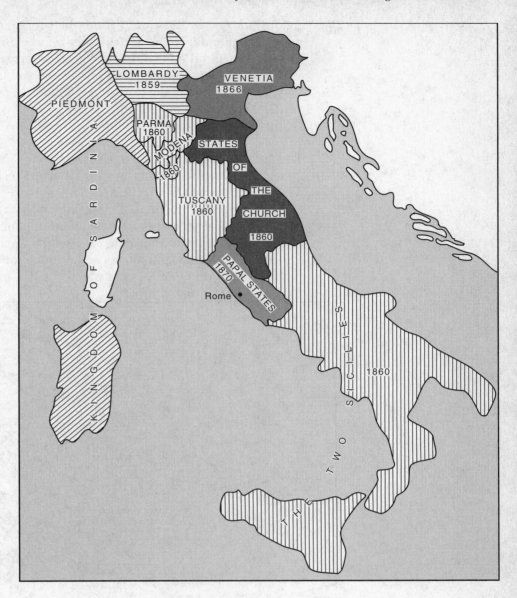

7. Which province shown on the map above was gained by the Kingdom of Italy in return for its support of Prussia in the Seven Weeks' War against Austria?

   (A) Parma
   (B) The states of the Church
   (C) The Papal states
   (D) Modena
   (E) Venetia

8. The two decades following the Revolutions of 1848 saw all of the following changes in the German states EXCEPT

   (A) the German Confederation, created at the Congress of Vienna to replace the Holy Roman Empire, was revived
   (B) repression of republicans, nationalists, and liberals was common
   (C) the German population shrank due to the immigration to America of refugees from political persecution
   (D) the separate states were economically interdependent
   (E) industrial productivity rose dramatically

9.   Before German unification, Prussia had instituted a series of govern-
      mental, economic, social, and military reforms in response to
      (A)   the humiliating defeats by France during the Napoleonic Wars
      (B)   the insurrection of peasants against landowning aristocrats
      (C)   the urging of the Frankfurt Assembly
      (D)   pleas from the Junkers
      (E)   the threat of a unified Italy

10.   The term realpolitik applies to Bismarck's
      (A)   realistic support of the liberal factions in the Prussian
            Parliament
      (B)   use of subterfuge, deceit, and military force to accomplish
            unification and to implement other policies
      (C)   opposition to Hapsburg leadership in a united Germany
      (D)   admiration of Cavour's constitutional reforms in Italy
      (E)   support of Pan-Germanism

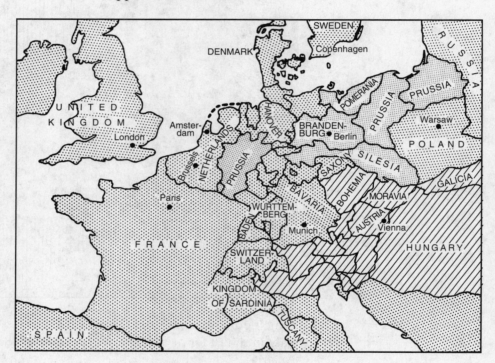

11.   The map above shows the German states before unification. Which of
      the following was NOT part of Prussia?
      (A)   Brandenburg
      (B)   Pomerania
      (C)   Hanover
      (D)   Silesia
      (E)   East Prussia

12. All of the following were wars fought by Prussia as part of Bismarck's realpolitik to unify Germany EXCEPT
    (A) the war against Denmark, 1864
    (B) the All-German War
    (C) the Crimean War
    (D) the Seven Weeks' War
    (E) the Franco-Prussian War

13. In 1867, the Germanic Confederation, dissolved by the Treaty of Prague, was replaced by
    (A) the North German Confederation under Prussian leadership
    (B) a resurrected Holy Roman Empire under Hapsburg rule
    (C) the Austro-Hungarian Dual Monarchy
    (D) the new German Empire
    (E) the Hanseatic League

14. After unification in 1871, the king of Prussia, Wilhelm I, became kaiser of the German Empire. He belonged to what dynasty?
    (A) Hapsburg
    (B) Battenburg
    (C) Bundesrat
    (D) Hohenzollern
    (E) Württemberg

15. The failure of Germany to develop democracy from 1871 to 1914 was due to all of the following EXCEPT
    (A) the chancellor was responsible to the kaiser rather than to the Reichstag
    (B) there was limited male suffrage
    (C) the Bundesrat represented the German states rather than the people
    (D) Bismarck's *Kulturkampf* suppressed the political activities of the influential Catholic minority
    (E) the social welfare programs created by state paternalism fostered autocracy

16. The ideology, an inheritor of the ideals of the French Revolution, that set as its political goals in the first half of the 19th century, freedom of press, assembly and speech, and the establishment of representative governments is
    (A) socialism
    (B) conservatism
    (C) liberalism
    (D) positivism
    (E) realism

17. *Laissez-faire* economic liberalism is most compatible with the theories of
    (A) Karl Marx
    (B) Adam Smith
    (C) Charles Fourier
    (D) Louis Blanc
    (E) Friedrich Engels

18. The artistic and literary movement that reacted to the rationalism of the Enlightenment by emphasizing the emotional component of humanity along with individual freedom was
    (A) Impressionism
    (B) Expressionism
    (C) Realism
    (D) Social Darwinism
    (E) Romanticism

Answers and Answer Explanations

1. D	2. D	3. C	4. A	5. E
6. C	7. E	8. C	9. A	10. B
11. C	12. C	13. A	14. D	15. B
16. C	17. B	18. D		

1. (D) It was the only independent state in Italy at the time.

2. (D) Mazzini is called "the poet of unification"; Garibaldi led the Red Shirts in seizing Sicily and Southern Italy; Victor Emmanuel was king of Piedmont-Sardinia; Napoleon III was emperor of France.

3. (C) Manorialism was abolished in order to strengthen constitutional government and make Piedmont a model for all of Italy.

4. (A) He got Napoleon to back him when he provoked Austria into war.

5. (E) It was a bone of contention that these areas remained out of Italy's hands even after World War I.

6. (C) Unification was completed, except for the Austrian enclaves, by 1871.

7. (E) The Seven Weeks' War was fought in 1866.

8. (C) It grew due to rapid industrialization.

9. (A) The militarists in Prussia pushed reform in order to strengthen the army.

10. (B) "Blood and Iron" was the method chosen by the Iron Chancellor.

11. (C) Hanover was an independent state.

12. (C) The Crimean War was fought from 1854 to 1856 by England and France against Russian encroachments in the Black Sea area of the Ottoman Empire.

13.   (A)   The German Confederation had been a creation of Napoleon, who had consolidated the three hundred independent German states, and it was kept by the Congress of Vienna. The Treaty of Prague, which ended the Seven Weeks' War, dissolved it.

14.   (D)   Hapsburgs were the legendary rulers of the Holy Roman Empire and the Austrian Empire as well as various other states of Europe; Battenburg was the family name of the British monarchs until they changed it to Mountbatten during World War I; the Bundesrat was the upper house of the German Parliament; Württemberg is a state in Germany.

15.   (B)   There was universal suffrage, but Parliament was dominated by Prussian conservatives.

16.   (C)   *Classical Liberalism* evolved from the revolutionary goals of Liberty, Equality, Fraternity, and representative government at the core of its program.

17.   (B)   Smith's *Wealth of Nations* supported this "hands off" view of government interference in the economy. All the others were socialists.

18.   (E)   The Romantic Movement was a direct and immediate reaction to the belief in reason espoused by the Enlightenment.

9 Imperialism (1870–1914)

Overview

Imperialism is the control of one people by another. The colonial power may rule the colony politically or exploit it economically or impose its culture upon it. During the so-called old imperialism of the 16th through 18th centuries, the Europeans did not acquire overseas territories—except in the Americas, where the sparse native population allowed establishment of colonies—as much as they set up trading stations. They largely respected and frequently cooperated with the local rulers in India, China, Japan, the Spice Islands (Indonesia), and the other geographic areas where a flourishing trade developed between locals and European coastal trading centers.

The new imperialism that began in 1870s colonized Asia and Africa by using military force to take control of local governments, by exploiting the local economies for the raw materials required by Europe's growing industry, and by imposing Western values to benefit the "backward" colonies. Most of Asia's rich and ancient cultures were either carved up into economic "spheres of influence" or colonized outright; virtually all of Africa was taken over by only six European nations; and Latin America was dominated by the United States.

Causes of Imperialism

1. The search for *markets* and for raw *materials*
    The rapidly industrializing and competing nations of Europe produced more manufactured goods than their own populations could consume and since favorable balance of trade was not possible for all, colonies promised potential markets. In the long run, since the non-Europeans lacked purchasing power, the promise of markets far outweighed the reality. Studies of foreign trade from 1870 to 1914 show that the best consumers of manufactured goods were other industrialized nations rather than undeveloped colonies. As the income level of Western workers rose, so did the profitablity of investing *surplus capital* into domestic ventures.
    Since many raw materials essential to the manufacturing process—from minerals to fibers—were native to the non-Western world, the Europeans were driven to acquiring the lands that produced these

materials as a guarantee of a sufficient supply. They argued that unless their more advanced technologies and business methods were applied to the mining and processing of these materials, not enough would be supplied to the voracious factories of the West. Also, they claimed that they had to set up colonies in order to maintain the stability that would protect their investments.

2. Missionaries

   A burst of religious revivalism during the mid-19th century in Western Europe and the United States led to development of *worldwide missions* to convert the people of Asia and Africa to Christianity. On those rare occasions when missionaries were attacked or endangered by locals, the public sentiment in the home country was so powerful that governments often had to send military help that was the first step—sometimes a reluctant one, sometimes a pretext—in setting up a colonial administration.

3. Military and naval bases

   Once trade developed, the *home country* felt compelled to establish a chain of naval bases to protect its overseas interests, and military outposts to stake its claim and to maintain order. This process tended to feed on itself since a *competition to acquire colonies* developed among the industrialized nations to maintain the international *balance of power* and for unvarnished *prestige*. This led to increased tensions when the "haves"—like the British Empire, which had acquired colonies for two or more centuries—clashed with the "have-nots"—like the Germans and Italians, whose late-blooming national unity gave them a slow start in the race.

4. Ideology

   The so-called "white man's burden" was a form of racist patronizing that preached that the "superior" Westerners had an obligation to bring their culture to "uncivilized" peoples in other parts of the world. *Social Darwinism*, a half-baked philosophical application of Darwin's theory of natural selection, bolstered the idea that some races or peoples were more fit for survival than others and therefore designed by nature for rule.

   Imperial adventures and adventurers appealed to the masses in the industrialized countries who felt part of some great crusade to improve people whose lot was even worse than theirs. Imperialism won votes; politicians coddled the voters.

Regions

Africa

Egypt, after winning autonomy within the Ottoman Empire in the mid-19th century, became a British protectorate in the 1880s. The British had invested in the *Suez Canal*, a vital link to India and Asia, and to maintain stability in the area, they helped Egypt take control of the Sudan and set up an *Anglo-Egyptian Administration* for both areas.

Algeria, *Tunisia*, and most of *Morocco* had fallen into French hands right before World War I. *Libya*, once part of the decrepit Ottoman Empire, was taken by the Italians.

Africa South of the Sahara was terra incognita until the 1870s, when Belgian, German, and French explorers began to lay claims. The *Berlin Conference of 1885*, sponsored by Bismarck to prevent disputes among the imperialists, set up rules that diminished squabbles and encouraged the partition of the entire continent among the major European powers.

Asia

In 1857, the *Sepoy Mutiny*, of native troops against their Indian overlords and the *British East India Company* brought British administration to the *Indian subcontinent*. By the mid-1880s the British also took control of Burma, the Malay Peninsula, and North Borneo. Although the British did not interfere with the basic social structure of these colonies, they introduced educational reforms and technological advances, especially to India, that smoothed the way for eventual independence. Of all the colonial powers, the British proved to be most enlightened.

The Dutch expanded their hold over the *Dutch East Indies* (the islands of Indonesia); the French seized Indochina (Vietnam, Cambodia, Laos); the Germans occupied islands in the Pacific; the Russians set up a *sphere of influence* (an area under the economic and military control of one imperial power) in Persia (Iran).

China—with its teeming population, vast land area, and incredibly rich and ancient culture—was carved up into spheres of influence by the Western powers. *Extraterritoriality* subjected Westerners to their home country's laws rather than China's; *leaseholds*, exclusive trading rights and limited governmental powers, were given to the Western nations; the Chinese were forced to cede outlying territories, such as Manchuria and Korea, to the Europeans. The *Open Door Policy*, sponsored by the United States in 1899 in order to open commerce to imperial latecomers like itself, urged the Europeans to allow free trade within China while respecting its territorial integrity. The *Boxer Rebellion*, a patriotic uprising by Chinese nationalists against Western encroachment, was put down by the imperial powers in 1900. Since the *Dowager Empress*, who had seized control of the government, had supported the Boxers, the *Manchu dynasty* fell into decline until it was overthrown in 1911. *Sun Yat-sen* set up a republic dedicated to modernizing China through *three principles*: *nationalism, democracy, livelihood*.

Japan was the only major Asian power to resist being swallowed up by the imperialists. In the mid-16th century, Portuguese traders had opened the insular Japanese to commerce and Christianity, both of which were suppressed by the *shogun*, medieval military ruler. U.S. warships, under the command of Commodore Perry, reopened the islands in 1853, and, unlike China and India, the Japanese modernized. The rule of the shogun was replaced by that of a powerful emperor, *Meiji*; feudalism was abolished; industry fostered; a central government installed; and education and the military reformed. Japan became so Westernized, while maintaining its basic social structure, that it jumped on the imperialist bandwagon by going to war with China in 1898 and winning Korea, then shocking the West by decisively defeating the Russians, in 1905, during the *Russo-Japanese War*.

The End of Colonialism

Imperialist acquisitions ended before World War I when virtually the entire non-Western world was divided among the Western powers. *Colonialism*—the control of overseas colonies by imperialist powers—was shaken by World War I and collapsed in the decades following World War II.

Long-term causes for its fall were *Westernized educational systems* that preached the ideals of democracy and awakened nationalistic yearnings among the colonials; the concept of *self-determination* espoused by the Allies after World War I; the example and ideals of the *Russian Revolution* and the anti-imperialist *dogma of Communism*; the *decline of Europe* in the decades after World War II; the *example of Japan's resistance* to Western domination.

The British Empire

India, "crown jewel of the British Empire," attained independence in 1948. Decades of *nonviolent resistance*, led by *Mahatma Gandhi*, helped prepare the populace for self-rule, but bloody clashes between Hindu and Moslem factions marred the move to independence. The subcontinent was partitioned by the British into Hindu India and Moslem Pakistan. Britain's other colonies in Asia—Ceylon (Sri Lanka), Burma, Malaya—and its colonies in Africa attained independence in the two decades after World War II, and most joined the British *Commonwealth of Nations*, a loose political grouping that offered economic advantages.

When the former British mandate, Palestine, was voted independence by the United Nations in 1948 to become a Jewish State, ancient rivalries between Westernized Jewish settlers and Moslem Arabs developed into a volatile and long-term conflict. Wars broke out in 1948, 1956, 1967, and 1973. Nationalization of the Suez Canal, a vital waterway to British trade, by charismatic Egyptian leader Gamal Abdel Nasser provoked war in 1956 between Egypt and allies Britain, France, and Israel. The area continues to be one of the world's most unstable.

The Dutch Empire

Early in World War II, the Japanese drove the Dutch out of the *Dutch East Indies* (originally called by the Europeans the *Spice Islands*, called *Indonesia* after independence). When the Dutch tried to resume control after the war, nationalists under the leadership of *Sukarno*—an eventual dictator until his overthrow in 1966—fought a bloody war of resistance and attained total independence in 1954.

The French Empire

After World War II, the French in Indochina (Vietnam, Cambodia, Laos) tried, like the Dutch in Indonesia, to take back the possessions that they had been driven from by the Japanese. After a costly seven-year guerrilla war, nationalists under Communist *Ho Chi Minh* attained independence in 1954. The Geneva Accords recognized the independence of Vietnam, Laos, and Cambodia, and provisionally partitioned Vietnam into a northern and southern sector until nationwide elections would determine leadership. The agreement broke down into full-scale civil war between the Communist-led north and the pro-western south. By the mid-1960s the United States had sent massive military forces to aid the south. In North Africa, *Morocco* and *Tunisia* were granted independence by the French in 1956, but Algeria, considered by many French to be an integral part of France, was not. The bitter *French-Algerian War* led to independence and the mass exodus of French settlers in 1962.

African Independence

In sub-Saharan Africa independence came suddenly from the late 1950s through the 1960s. The process was painful and costly in some places—such as the former Belgian Congo (Zaire)—and because the Europeans had ignored tribal loyalties when drawing up imperial boundaries, the newly independent states often lacked a unified heritage. The former British colonies were best prepared for self-rule, since the British had gradually transferred administration to locals.

Impact of Imperialism

The collapse of the European colonial empires was one of the modern world's most revolutionary and sudden developments. Within two decades after World War II, the European colonies, governing more than 25 percent of the earth's population, had disappeared. Most of the newly independent states, though, do not enjoy genuine freedom and democratic rule. While they often started out with democratic constitutions, poverty, ethnic conflicts, and inexperience in self-rule often led to military dictatorship or one-party rule. Freedom from foreign rule did not guarantee political freedom.

Although imperialism exploited and abused its colonial peoples, it provided them with the technological, industrial, and cultural achievements of the West and linked all the world's peoples.

Sample Essay Question

The sample thematic essay and the practice essays in this chapter are types found in the Advanced Placement Examination in European History and they require knowledge of causes, effects, personalities, ideas, and events.

Sample Question

> *Analyze* the various motives for the "New Imperialism" and their relative importance.

Comments on the Sample Question

Follow the "Simple Procedures" for writing an essay. (See page 24.)

First, *What does the question want to know?* Why did the European world impose its economic, social, and political institutions on virtually the entire non-Western world from the last three decades of the 19th century to the beginning of World War I?

Second, *What do you know about it?* Was it the search for new markets or religious missionary fervor? Was it ethnocentrism or the need for military and naval bases? Was it to "keep up with the Joneses"? If it was all of these and more, which had the greatest pull and why?

Third, *How would you put it into words?* Remember that "to analyze" is "to examine in detail" and "to determine relationships."

Sample Answer

From 1870 to 1914, European nations used their superior military technology to colonize Africa, Asia, and the islands of the Pacific. The New Imperialism differed from the Old Imperialism, which was basically a trade relationship between the Europeans and local rulers, in that it took over the native governments, created often artificial markets for manufactured goods, exploited natural resources, converted the native peoples to Christianity, and measured the behavior of the locals by Western moral and social standards. Even great democracies like Britain and France denied native peoples the rights and representation of constitutional government. Why did the Europeans launch this New Imperialism?

The motives were diverse; some were more powerful than others; they often fed on each other.

It is often said that economics was the driving force. Industrialization demanded a limitless supply of raw materials for the factories and an ever-increasing market for the products. Tin, rubber, petroleum, and other natural resources abundant outside of Europe fueled the voracious appetite of industry. Billions of people, hungering for the manufactured goods of the West, promised profits. According to the "surplus capital" theory, the industrialists needed new investments outside of Europe—in mines and plantations—because there were few good ones in overdeveloped Europe.

Missionaries soon followed the traders and other profit seekers. A revival of evangelical Christianity in the latter half of the 19th century created the zeal to convert "the heathens." When missionaries got in trouble with the locals, who sometimes resorted to violence to protect their native customs or religions, the army was often sent in to protect the missionaries.

Military units required an expanded navy to get them to far-off lands; navies necessitated bases; bases had to be secured through treaties with local rulers or by takeovers of territory. Once one nation had bases in a region, other European rivals felt it was "in the interests of national security" to establish their own. The scramble became a competition between nations, and prestige was often measured in the size, riches, and numbers of colonies. The masses in the "mother countries" reveled in the contrived dramas of "heroic conquests" of "ignorant savages," the Christianization of "godless" natives, and the supremacy of Western culture. The so-called white man's burden became a rationalization for what was already being done.

The motives for the New Imperialism varied, but they were tied to one another. The push for profits started a chain of causation that led to the Europeans dividing the non-Western world among themselves.

Evaluate the Sample Answer

1. Did its introduction make the design of its argument clear?
2. Did it identify the New Imperialism?
3. Did it "examine in detail" and "determine the relationships" of the various motives?
4. Was it overly general or did it offer specific factual references to support its argument?

5. Was its consideration of the various motives balanced, complete?
6. Was the essay long enough? What should have been added?
7. Did the conclusion sum up the argument of the essay?

Rater's Comments on the Sample Answer

3—Qualified

This is a well-organized examination of the various motives for the New Imperialism. It analyzes the importance and the relationships of each. The essay's structure is based upon a judgment that economic motives were primary and that every other motive followed the profit motive. This is a commonsensical, if somewhat conventional, analysis.

While the essay stresses the importance of seeking new markets and better investments for "surplus capital," it omits the very convincing critique of this view. In the first place, the non-Europeans simply lacked the purchasing power to buy most of the manufactured goods that the Europeans produced. In the second place, most of the surplus capital of Western Europe was actually invested in other industrialized countries: British capitalists invested heavily in North America, French capitalists in the development of Russia, and German capitalists in the Ottoman Empire.

The elegant logical clarity of the essay's structure is also one of its shortcomings. It oversimplifies the process, and there is little reference to actual instances of the operation of the New Imperialism. Was profit-seeking always the prime motive? Did missionary activity sometimes precede commercial ventures, as in equatorial Africa? If this is the exception that proves the rule, specific factual support should be given: the British policies in India, the Dutch ventures in the East Indies, the French in Indochina. Strategic considerations often came before missionary activity as when: Pacific island bases were set up to protect shipping lanes. Military intervention was used to secure a vital region, as when the British took over Egypt to protect the Suez Canal.

Practice Essay Questions

The questions that follow are samples of the various types of thematic essays that appear on the Advanced Placement Examination in European History. (See pages 17–18 for a detailed explanation of each type.)

---

1. *Contrast and compare* the Old Imperialism with the New Imperialism.

Comments on Question 1

Sometimes called colonialism, the Old Imperialism follows the Age of Exploration of the mid-15th to the early 17th century. It was characterized by commercial ventures, coastal enclaves for the seagoing trade, and trade with the local peoples. There was little attempt, except in the New World, to encourage immigration to the colonies; there was very little attempt to impose the European social, political, or economic structures on the local population.

In contrast, the New Imperialism of the late-19th century took over the governing of its colonies; it exploited native labor and natural resources; it judged local behavior according to European mores; and it forced religious conversion.

The two forms of imperialism were similar in that the Europeans rarely attempted to absorb the culture of their colonies, nor did they encourage immigration to the mother country.

> **2.** "By the end of the 19th century, European nations had divided the rest of world among themselves." *Assess the validity* of this statement.

Comments on Question 2

To "determine the truth" of this statement, consider the various regions that were targets of imperialism in the 19th century. The scramble for Africa left only two nations independent: Liberia and Ethiopia. In Asia, China was divided into spheres of influence that left a disintegrating monarchy, but one that was Chinese. Japan maintained its independence even though it was forced to open up to Western trade. In the Western Hemisphere, the United States regarded Latin America as its sphere of influence.

> **3.** *Contrast and compare* the responses of China and Japan to Western encroachment.

Comments on Question 3

The contrast was glaring because China resisted Westernization and was carved up into spheres of influence while Japan modernized and kept its autonomy. Why and how? Detail the Chinese response to Western militarism from the Opium War to the Boxer Rebellion to the establishment of Sun Yat Sen's republic. Trace the Japanese response from the "opening" by Commodore Perry to the Russo-Japanese War.

The comparison of similarities can be made in that both nations managed to hold onto their rich and ancient cultures, one by a stubborn adherence to tradition, the other by blending the best of the West with its own unique ways.

> **4.** *Evaluate* the New Imperialism.

Comments on Question 4

Imperialism was rampant with injustice: exploitation of people, natural resources, markets; ethnocentrism; religious and cultural intolerance; poverty and repression during and after the period of rule; two world wars caused in part by the competition for colonies.

Imperialism did introduce the non-Western world to the educational, political, economic, and social institutions of the West, many of which have been adopted by emerging nations.

This question has a broad scope, but it can be answered effectively by picking out particular peoples or regions and detailing some of their experiences under and after imperialism.

> **5.** *Explain* why the colonial empires of Britain and France ended after World War II.

Comments on Question 5

To "offer the reasons for" the disintegration of these great empires, consider the exhaustion of Europe after the devastation of the war; the promise of self-rule, India, for example; the humiliation of the "white peoples" at the hands of the Japanese in the early days of the war; the theories of self-determination and nationalistic aspirations aroused by World War I; the ideals of the Russian Revolution; the anti-imperialist dogma of Communism; the example of democratic institutions offered by many of the imperialist nations; the awakenings provided by a Western-style education.

Again, this is a question whose broad scope could be managed with specific examples of newly independent nations.

Practice Multiple-Choice Questions

(These questions are representative of the types found on the Advanced Placement Examination in European History.)

1. Imperialism of the 1870 to 1914 period can best be described as
    (A) overseas mercantilism
    (B) development of a profitable trade with non-Western regions
    (C) establishment of coastal trading posts in the non-European world
    (D) the imposition by Europeans of their social, economic, and political systems upon non-Europeans
    (E) the establishment of European democratic government in the non-European world

2. The imperialism of the 1870 to 1914 period was directed by the Europeans primarily in which regions?
    (A) the Americas
    (B) Africa and East Asia
    (C) Eastern Europe
    (D) Australia and Oceania
    (E) Africa and the Middle East

3. Which of the following European nations was NOT a major imperial power from 1870 to 1914?
    (A) France
    (B) Britain
    (C) Germany
    (D) Belgium
    (E) Austria

4. All of these could be considered major causes of imperialism EXCEPT
   (A) the search for new markets for industrial products
   (B) the acquisition of raw materials
   (C) missionary activities
   (D) the desire to absorb the culture of non-Europeans
   (E) the race for colonies

5. The Berlin Conference of 1885, sponsored by Germany's Bismarck,
   (A) determined the "rules" for the partition of Africa
   (B) set up spheres of influence in China
   (C) divided Ottoman possessions in the Middle East among six European powers
   (D) Recognized the United States' dominance in Latin America
   (E) internationalized the former Belgian Congo

6. Which was NOT a British colony or protectorate by 1914?
   (A) India
   (B) Egypt
   (C) Burma
   (D) The Malay Penninsula
   (E) Morocco

7. The European partition of Africa began in
   (A) 1850   (D) 1919
   (B) the 1870s   (E) 1939
   (C) 1880

8. British colonial administration of India from 1857 to 1948 was comparatively enlightened because
   (A) they supported the landlords
   (B) they completely ended the caste system
   (C) they left the entire subcontinent under local control
   (D) Indians were encouraged to serve in the colonial government
   (E) British colonial administrators adopted local customs and language

9. Which of the following avoided European colonialization by rapidly modernizing and industrializing?
   (A) China
   (B) Japan
   (C) Persia (Iran)
   (D) Siam (Thailand)
   (E) Ethiopia

10. All of the following are valid generalizations about European imperialism in China EXCEPT
     (A) China was not directly colonized
     (B) China lost its outlying territories
     (C) Europeans residing in China were not subject to Chinese law
     (D) after the failure of a nationalist uprising, China was forced to pay indemnities to the imperialists
     (E) China was partitioned by both Europeans and Japan

11. Rudyard Kipling's stirring poems for the English to take up "the white man's burden" are compatible with which of the following?
     (A) Social Darwinism
     (B) The obligation of the West to enlighten the "benighted races" of the non-Western world
     (C) The urgings of Jules Ferry in France and Josiah Strong in the United States to "spread the culture"
     (D) None of these
     (E) All of these

12. The Suez Canal induced British imperialism in which of the following?
     (A) Egypt   (D) Libya
     (B) Ghana   (E) South Africa
     (C) Nigeria

13. All of these helped bring about the collapse of colonialism EXCEPT
     (A) Western-style education in the colonies
     (B) Japanese successes in World War II
     (C) the principle of self-determination espoused at the peace conferences that ended World War II
     (D) the exhaustion of Europe after World War II
     (E) the idealism of the Russian Revolution

14. On the whole, the colonies of which European nation made the smoothest transition to independence?
     (A) the Netherlands   (D) Portugal
     (B) Britain   (E) Belgium
     (C) France

15. Europe's world hegemony lasted roughly
     (A) from 1870 to 1914   (D) from 1900 to 1945
     (B) from 1900 to 1914   (E) from 1870 to 1900
     (C) from 1870 to 1945

Answers and Answer Explanations

1. D	2. B	3. E	4. D	5. A
6. E	7. C	8. D	9. B	10. E
11. E	12. A	13. C	14. B	15. C

1. (D)   The other descriptions apply more aptly to the Old Imperialism, from the 16th to 18th centuries.

2. (B) The Americas were the sphere of influence of the United States; the Middle East was largely part of the Ottoman Empire; Australia was a British Dominion; Eastern Europe was mostly part of the Austrian or the Russian empires.

3. (E) Austria was neither a great seapower nor, with its nationalities problem, was it interested in overseas expansion.

4. (D) The ethnocentrism of the Europeans ruled this out.

5. (A) It began the scramble for Africa by setting up guidelines acceptable to everybody but the Africans.

6. (E) Morocco belonged to France.

7. (C) Africa was largely terra incognita in 1870; the Union of South Africa, Italian Somaliland and Eritrea, German East Africa, and so on did not exist in 1880; the German colonies did not exist after the Paris Peace Conferences in 1919.

8. (D) Their support of the landlords against the peasants, their dismissal of the ancient and rich Indian native culture, and their failure to abolish the caste system were less than enlightened; they did not leave the entire subcontinent but only part of it to local control.

9. (B) Japan managed to industrialize and modernize its institutions in about fifty years by borrowing the best from the Europeans and maintaining the best of their own traditions.

10. (E) It was never partitioned but rather divided into spheres of influence, in which a given imperialist nation monopolized trade, set up military bases, and influenced local government.

11. (E) The "fittest" should rule the planet, claimed Social Darwinists; the Europeans were the most enlightened and owed the "darker races" education and religion; Jules Ferry and Josiah Ferry were imperialist birds of a feather.

12. (A) Control of Egypt guaranteed domination of the Canal. The other states are in different regions of Africa.

13. (C) The principle of self-determination was espoused after World War I.

14. (B) The British prepared the subject peoples with education and a degree of self-government; it fit their constitutional nature.

15. (C) It began roughly around the time of German unification; it ended not long after World War II.

CHAPTER 10 World War I (1914–1918)

Overview

The beginning of the First World War marks the height of European power on this planet; its ending marks the beginning of the decline. Great empires fell: the Russian, Austro-Hungarian, German, and Ottoman. Others declined in power and influence: Britain and France, which had reached the zenith of imperialist expansion by 1914, saw their economies in shambles by 1918. A generation of young European men was decimated in the trenches of France, on the plains of Eastern Europe, and on global battlefronts.

It was the first "total war," involving mass civilian populations in a war effort that required rationing, employed both sexes in war plants, and pumped up popular fervor with distorted propaganda.

Narrow nationalism flourished with the fall of the old ethnically diverse empires when dominant ethnic groups formed the basis for smaller nation-states such as Yugoslavia, Czechoslovakia, Austria, and Hungary. The triumph of Communism in Russia was a direct result of the war; fascism in Italy and Nazism in Germany indirect results. The drain of Europe's resources made the United States the world's leading creditor and greatest producer, and the unresolved issues of the vindictive and haphazard peace process led inevitably to World War II.

Long-term Causes of World War I

Rival Alliances:
Triple Alliance **and**
Triple Entente

1870: The balance of power of Europe was upset by the decisive Prussian victory in the Franco-Prussian War.

1871: Germany was unified under the leadership of militant Prussia.

German Chancellor Bismarck feared French revenge and negotiated treaties to isolate France:

1873: Three Emperors' League (Germany, Austria, and Russia in a mutual defense pact).

1879: Dual Alliance (Germany and Austria after Russia pulled out).

1881: Triple Alliance (Germany, Austria, Italy).

1894: France, eager to check German power, invested in Russian internal improvements. Russia, anxious for support for its ambitions in the Balkans, allied with France.

1904: Britain, facing serious competition from Germany for naval supremacy, for overseas markets, and for colonies, agreed to a "close understanding" with France over common interests, the *Entente Cordial.*

1907: The Triple Entente to check the Triple Alliance was agreed to by Britain, France, Russia. (Not a formal alliance.)

Anglo-German Rivalries

1880: Germany became a serious rival to Britain in manufacturing and in overseas trade. Although the Industrial Revolution began in Britain, Germany's industries were more modern and efficient; German products were often better and cheaper.

Arms Race: Traditional British policy was to have their fleet—which was the guardian of their vital shipping lanes—larger than the combined fleets of any two rival nations.

1898: Kaiser Wilhelm II of Germany initiated an expansion of the German navy to protect a growing international trade and colonialism.

A naval race between Britain and Germany began, requiring enormous expenditures, reflecting national pride, and fostering insecurity in Britain that drove it closer to the French and Russian camp.

Imperialism

Late to national unity (1871), Germany also came late to imperialism. While the West gobbled up most of what is now the Third World, Germany was busy consolidating. By the turn of the century, it sought colonies to bolster its world image with the fervor of a nation seeking to compensate for its sense of inferiority.

1902: Germany won the right to build the Berlin to Baghdad Railroad. Britain sought to check German influence in the Middle East, which could menace the Suez Canal and the sea routes to India.

1905: The kaiser, on a visit to French Morocco, advocated Moroccan independence.

1906: After the First Moroccan Crisis, the Algeciras Conference was called in Spain. Britain and Italy supported French hegemony in Morocco and Tunisia; only Austria supported Germany.

1907: Britain, shaken by German assertiveness on the world stage, settled its differences with Russia over Persia (they divided it between them) and convinced Russia to join the Triple Entente.

1911: The Second Moroccan Crisis occurred when a German gunboat, the *Panther*, was sent to Morocco in protest of the French occupation of the city of Fez. When Britain supported France once again, the Germans backed down for minor concessions in equatorial Africa.

Although none of these crises precipitated war between the Triple Alliance and Triple Entente, the two camps were armed to the teeth and stood eyeball to eyeball.

Nationalism

At the turn of the 20th century, Slavic nationalism disrupted the unity of two great but decaying empires. The Ottoman Empire—in an advanced state of dissolution—held onto a strip of territory in Europe north of Greece, south of Bulgaria and Rumania, stretching from Istanbul to the Adriatic. The *Dual Monarchy* of Austria-Hungary failed to appease the Slavic separatist movement within the weakened ancient Hapsburg Empire. *Pan-Slavism*, a nationalistic movement to unite all the Slavic peoples, encouraged the Serbs, Bosnians, Slovenes, and Croats to seek a single political entity in Southern Europe. Nationalistic ambitions fomented unrest. Russia—the southern Slavs' "big brother" to the east—added fuel to the fire by turning its territorial ambitions to those regions in the Austro-Hungarian and Ottoman empires after a humiliating loss in the Russo-Japanese War. This dangerous chemistry of volatile nationalism and power politics brought the Triple Entente and Triple Alliance closer to armed conflict.

1908: The First Balkan Crisis broke out when the *Young Turks* set up a parliamentary government in the Ottoman Empire, and Austria and Serbia vied for control of Turkish Bosnia. A secret agreement with Russia guaranteed Austria annexation of Bosnia in return for its support of Russian naval access to the Mediterranean through the Dardanelles (straits controlled by the Ottomans). Clever maneuvering enabled Austria to annex Bosnia while Russia failed to gain access, and Serbia was frustrated in its nationalistic aims. The crisis passed, but tempers were inflamed.

1911–1912: The *Turkish-Italian War* pitted empire-ambitious Italy against the weakened Ottomans. Not only did Italy gain Libya on the North African coast, but it revealed how decrepit the Ottoman Empire had become.

1912–1913: Their appetites whetted by Italy's easy victory, Serbia, Greece, and Bulgaria allied to drive the Turks out of their last European possessions in the Balkan "strip" during the First Balkan War.

1913: The Second Balkan War broke out between Bulgaria and its former allies when the Bulgarians claimed the bulk of Macedonia as spoils of the previous conflict. To avoid a general war, after Bulgaria was defeated and Serbia seized most of Albania, the great powers enforced a peace. Austria, with German support against Russia, which had backed Serbian claims, was able to prevent Serbia from holding Albania and from gaining access to the Adriatic Sea. Once again Serbia was frustrated and Russia humiliated.

The volatile chemistry of *rival alliances*, *imperialistic* ambitions, arms races, and fervent *nationalism* awaited a spark; it came in the form of the murder of one man and his wife.

Immediate Cause for World War I

June 28, 1914: Archduke Francis Ferdinand, heir to the Austrian throne, was assassinated along with his wife in Sarajevo, capital of the Austrian province of Bosnia. When evidence was uncovered that high Serbian officials had plotted the murder, Austria sought German support to crush Serbia. Kaiser Wilhelm issued the infamous *blank check*, promising backing for any action Austria might take. Serbia turned to "big brother" Slav Russia, which in turn got a guarantee of French support against Germany and Austria in a similar *blank check*.

July 23, 1914: Austria presented an ultimatum to Serbia that would make Serbia a virtual protectorate of Austria.

July 28, 1914: Austria declared war on Serbia after pronouncing the Serbian response inadequate. Russia mobilized.

August 1, 1914: Germany declared war on Russia.

August 3, 1914: France declared war on Germany.

August 4, 1914: Britain declared war on Germany after German forces violated Belgium's neutrality in their attempt to invade France.

The First World War had begun.

The War

The Sides

The Allies: Britain, France, and Russia (1914)
    Italy (1915)
    United States (1917)
    Russia out (1918)
The Central Powers: Germany, Austria-Hungary, Turkey, and Bulgaria

The Western Front

August–September 1914: The *Schlieffen Plan* failed. Since a *war of attrition* (wearing down of the resources and morale of the enemy) was to Germany's disadvantage because of the superior land mass, resources, and population of its enemies, Germany aimed for a quick victory.

THE STRATEGY OF THE SCHLIEFFEN PLAN

1. Defeat France in six weeks as in the Franco-Prussian War.
2. Hold off Russia, which the high command assumed would take six months to fully mobilize.
3. Invade France through neutral Belgium, by being granted access, in order to outflank the French armies and seize Paris.

WHY THE SCHLIEFFEN PLAN FAILED

1. The Belgians protested and put up unexpectedly stiff resistance.
2. The Russians mobilized with great speed, drawing German reserves to the Eastern Front to bolster the Austrians.
3. The French counterattacked heroically at the Battle of the Marne River (September 5, 1914) to stop the German drive to Paris.

THE WESTERN FRONT STALEMATED INTO TRENCH WARFARE

1. The trench lines extended from the North Sea to Switzerland in the south.
2. The bloody, costly fighting, after the Battle of the Marne, caused no significant breakthrough for either side.
3. Technological developments in weaponry—machine guns, poison gas, massed artillery, tanks, strafing, and bombing aircraft—were far in advance of the pitifully archaic tactics. The result was the slaughter of a generation of young Western Europeans in the trenches of France and Flanders (region of Northern France, Belgium, and the Netherlands).

The Eastern Front Remained a Mobile War

1914: German forces, under *Paul von Hindenburg* (later a president of the postwar Weimar Republic) and Erich Ludendorff won important victories over the Russians; the Russians pushed the Austrians out of Galacia (Western Poland).

1915: Combined German-Austrian forces pushed the Russians out of Poland and inflicted awesome casualties. Bulgaria entered the war on Germany's side (Germany and its Allies become known as the Central Powers), and the Germans overan the Balkans. The British launched the *Gallipoli Campaign* to knock Turkey, which had joined the Central Powers, out of the war by landing at the Dardanelles, a vital control point for access between the Aegean and Black Seas.

1916: The Germans pushed deep into Russian territory. The Gallipoli Campaign failed, and its planner, Winston Churchill, future British prime minister, resigned his post as first lord of the admiralty.

1917: The Russian czar fell in March; the provincial government under Alexander Kerensky continued the war. The Bolsheviks seized power in November and eventually pulled Russia out of the war.

Waging the War

World War I was the 20th century's first *total war*, whereby the entire civilian populations of the belligerent nations were mobilized for winning the war. Propaganda lionized the men at the front and dehumanized the enemy. News was censored. Economic production was focused on the war effort: Women replaced factory workers in uniform; rationing of food and scarce commodities was instituted; people financed the war by buying bonds. Each side aimed at "starving out" the enemy by cutting off vital supplies to the civilian population.

Naval Blockades

1. Britain used its superior fleet and sea mines to cut the Central Powers off from overseas trade.

2. Germany employed *unrestricted submarine warfare* to prevent the British from getting vital materials from their colonies. The sinking of the passenger ship *Lusitania* in May 1915 helped turn American public opinion against Germany. (Note: There is strong evidence to suggest that the *Lusitania* was carrying contraband munitions, as the Germans claimed.)

3. After promising to refrain from unrestricted submarine warfare, the Germans took a calculated risk to hasten victory against Britain and began it again in February 1917.

4. President Woodrow Wilson asked for a declaration of war against Germany on April 6, 1917. (Note: Although more neutral U.S. ships were sunk by British mines than by German U-boats, the massive debt the Allies owed the United States, the skillful British propaganda, and a variety of other factors led the United States to war against Germany).

Diplomacy

1915—Neutral Italy entered the war against the Central Powers (its former Allies) with the promise of *Italia Irredenta* (unredeemed Italy) and some German colonies and Turkish territories.

1917—The infamous *Zimmerman Note* promised Mexico some of its former American holdings if it entered the war on Germany's side against the United States.

Arabs and Jews in Palestine were promised autonomy if they joined the Allies.

Eastern Europeans were promised ethnic control in return for support of the Allies.

The War Ends

Although the United States had only a small standing army, it was able to field nine divisions in France by the summer of 1918, in time to help halt the last major offensive of the exhausted German Army.

By the fall of 1918, Bulgaria and Turkey had sued for peace, Austria-Hungary had collapsed, and Germany was wracked with revolution. The kaiser abdicated, fled to neutral Holland, and a provisional German government requested negotiations on the basis of President Wilson's Fourteen Points peace plan.

On the eleventh hour of the eleventh day of the eleventh month of 1918, an *armistice* ended World War I.

(NOTE: More people died in the influenza epidemic that followed the war than died in the war itself—10 million died in combat, nearly 20 million from the disease.)

The Peace Settlements

The Fourteen Points (Wilson's peace plan that was never implemented because of the secret treaties and diplomatic maneuvering that had taken place among the Allies before the entrance of the United States in the war.)

1. End to secret treaties
2. Freedom of the seas
3. Free trade
4. Arms reduction
5. Just settlement of colonial claims
6–13. Evacuation of occupied territories *and* national self-determination
14. Establishment of a League of Nations: an international political organization to settle disputes

(NOTE: Ironically, even though it was Wilson's creation, the United States never joined the league. It was largely ineffectual, for this and other reasons, in dealing with the aggressive dictatorships of the 1930s).

The Paris Peace Conference, January 1919

The Big Four—Wilson of the United States, David Lloyd George of Britain, Georges Clemenceau of France, and Vittorio Orlando of Italy—made all the decisions. The Central Powers were excluded; the Fourteen Points were compromised; nationality lines in Central and Eastern Europe were blurred.

The *Treaty of Versailles* ended the war with Germany but never settled the explosive issues that had led to war in the first place. Many of its provisions provided grist for Nazi propaganda mills in the 1920s and 1930s.

PROVISIONS OF THE TREATY OF VERSAILLES

1. Certain German territories were ceded to the Allies (such as Alsace to France, Schleswig to Denmark, West Prussia to Poland, control of mineral-rich Saar to France), and German overseas colonies were distributed to the Allies.
2. Germany was blamed for starting the war in the infamous "war guilt" clause.
3. The German army and navy were severely cut back.
4. The Rhineland (the vital strip between France and Germany) was to be demilitarized and occupied.
5. Germany had to pay *indemnities* for the civilian damage done in the war.

Results of the War

1. Ten million battle dead and countless civilians; $300 billion war costs and in property destroyed.
2. An end to the Russian, German, Austrian, and Ottoman empires.
3. The creation of a patchwork of ethnically arbitrary, weak, and poor states in Eastern Europe, such as Yugoslavia and Czechoslovakia.
4. The establishment of Communism in Russia.
5. The enmity of the German people, who were blamed for the war and saddled with enormous reparations.

World War II broke out in Europe twenty years after the signing of the Treaty of Versailles.

Sample Essay Question

The sample thematic essay question and the practice essays presented in this chapter are types found in the Advanced Placement Examination in European History, and they require knowledge of causes, effects, personalities, ideas, and events.

Sample Question

> *Analyze* the long-term causes of World War I.

Comments

Follow the "Simple Procedures" for writing an essay. (See page 24.)

First, *What does the question want to know?* "Examine in detail" "determine relationships," and "explain" what brought about World War I. Be sure to consider the difference between a long-term cause and an immediate cause. Be sure to measure the degrees of importance of the various causes, to determine how they were related, and to explain how they are all tied together.

Second, *What do you know about it?* What was the arms race, and did it affect all the nations that eventually went to war? What was the rivalry behind the arms race? How did nationalism increase tensions and ambitions? What instabilities were caused by Pan-Slavism, by Pan-Germanism, by Italian ambition for *Italia Irredenta*? What role did imperialism play? How did the rival alliances form, and how did they set the stage for war?

Third, *How would you put it into words?* With an essay like this, that demands analysis and detailed explanation, you should organize your answer logically: rival alliances, arms race, imperialism, nationalism. Relate them and offer specifics. You are writing a short history here. There's lots to tell, and coherence can be overwhelmed up by detail. Don't lose the forest for trees!

Sample Answer

A complex event like the First World War is really a long-term development made up of myriad lesser events—decisions, made in response to situations, that heightened tensions, increased conflict, then exploded in a chain reaction. History is the sorting out and telling of these events and their culminations. At best, it generalizes to get at the big picture and the elements that created it. At worst, it establishes artificial categories that oversimplify the complexities and neatly trim the ragged edges of human drama. In the broadest terms, a group of developments, distinct yet interrelated, served as long-term causes for World War I.

First, two rival alliances, armed to the teeth and continually testing each other's strength and resolve, formed and faced off while waiting for a reason, maybe an excuse, to go at each other. France, Russia, and England were thrown into each other's arms by a common distrust of Germany and Austria, and by turns of events that submerged their tradional rivalries with each other under new needs and fears.

Second, economic competition for overseas markets between Britain, whose aged factories had grown up with the Industrial Revolution, and Germany, whose modern industry used the latest technology, degenerated into a naval arms race. British policy was to keep a navy more powerful than the combined fleets of the next two greatest powers. Their dependence on their far-flung empire seemed to necessitate this. Germany policy was a reflection of Kaiser Wilhelm II's bellicose insistence on overcoming his own inferiority complex by proving German superiority. The need for a powerful German navy was less for the protection of its growing world trade or its newly acquired colonies than for the aggrandisement of its newfound power.

The race for colonies aggravated the tensions and enmities between the rivals. Germany and Italy came late to the imperialism game and they wanted to catch up by sometimes muscling in. Britain and France had a head start on the others, and they wanted to hold onto their acquisitions. The result was a series of crises in Africa and confrontations over China.

The nationalistic urges for autonomy that had disrupted Europe since the French Revolution had awakened the idea of the uniqueness of a "people" and since the time of Napoleon had been effective in making war. The Slavs of Austria-Hungary wanted recognition and a share of power if not necessarily independence. The captive nations of the Ottoman Empire pushed and pulled and proved its weakness, adding to the overall instability. The rival nationalites of the Balkans warred with each other over ancient causes and new dominance, sucking Austria and Russia into the morass. The Italians wanted *Italia Irredenta*, enclaves still controlled by Austria, as well as territories belonging to the Turks. The Germans believed in the uniqueness of their *Kultur*, the desirability of expanding German influence, the necessity of uniting all "Germans" in Europe.

Volatile nationalism, colonial jealousies, trade wars and arms races, and a neatly arranged alignment of competitors just waited for a spark to set the whole mixture off. The assassination of the archduke could have been dealt with using rational diplomacy and good sense if conditions had been different. Smug predictions of inevitable progress for Europe and the world hid the swarming tensions underlying the relations of nations.

Evaluate the Sample Answer

1. Did it have a clear introduction?
2. Did it "examine in detail" the long-term causes, "determine their relationships," and "explain" their connections?
3. Did it offer factual support, or was it too general?
4. Was it accurate, well-balanced, objective?
5. Did its concluding paragraph sum up the argument of the essay?
6. Was it long enough, clearly written, easily understood, convincing?
7. What would you have added?
8. Was it a "big picture" or a narrow view?

Rater's Comments on the Sample Answer

4—Well qualified

This was a sophisticated, well-written essay that answered the question from a broad perspective. It lacks, however, sufficient factual reference to make a totally convincing analysis of a very complex issue: What long-term developments led to World War I?

It definitely rose above the usual pat answer by connecting the events and offering insights into human behavior, the relations between nations, and the writing of history. The introductory paragraph grabs the reader's attention as well as making some philosophical observations. The body of the essay lays out the argument clearly but does fail to flesh it out with pertinent facts.

Some unanswered questions:

How and why did the rival alliances develop? Did they change, and why? Why was Britain brought out of its "splendid isolation" from the affairs of the continent?

Were there reasons other than the kaiser's mental state that encouraged the naval arms race? What were the crises and confrontations brought on by colonial rivalry? What were the Balkan crises that "sucked" the great powers into the morass? What were some of the specifics about the nationalistic urges that created conflict?

Practice Essay Questions

The questions that follow are samples of the various types of thematic essays that appear on the Advanced Placement Examination in European History. (See pages 17–18 for a detailed explanation of each type.)

> **1.** "Each of the belligerents in Europe was responsible for the outbreak of World War I." *Defend or refute* this statement.

Comments on Question 1

Many Americans, influenced to this day by creative Allied propaganda and by German aggression in World War II, believe that Germany was responsible for starting the First World War. Certainly the kaiser's prewar arrogance was one of the friction points, but England, France, and Russia each carried out policies that aggravated the tension. In framing your answer, consider the network of alliances that France and Germany engineered after the Franco-Prussian War; economic rivalry between Germany and Britain; the roles of Britain as well as Germany in the naval arms race; the mentalities of both "have" and "have-not" nations in the race for colonies; Russian support for Pan-Slavism in Austria-Hungary; the volatile Balkan situation.

> **2.** "After the first few months of war, the combat on the Western Front was very different from anything the strategists on either side had envisioned." *Assess the validity* of this statement.

Comments on Question 2

Each of the belligerents anticipated a quick, decisive victory at the outbreak of war. The end result was a war of attrition—a gradual and inexorable wearing down of the manpower, resources, and will to fight. In "determing the truth" of the assertion, consider the German Schlieffen Plan, the unexpected speed of Russian mobilization, the Battle of the Marne, the attempts at outflanking, the resulting line of trenches from Switzerland to the North Sea. Be aware of the development of new tactics and weaponry: sea blockades, unrestricted submarine warfare, massed artillery, poison gas, aircraft, and tanks.

> 3.   *Explain* why the war ended the Russian, Austro-Hungarian, and German empires.

Comments on Question 3

"Explain" in this context means to "offer the causes and reasons for" the collapse of those great empires. The scope of the issue is very broad, so a detailed accounting of each is not practical. Look for causes common to all three: the strains of a war of attrition—shortages, casualties; political instabilities; defeats in battle. Emphasize the different characters of their problems: the Bolshevik movement in Russia; ethnic rivalries in Austro-Hungary; democratic and socialist opposition movements in Germany.

> 4.   *Contrast and compare* the Fourteen Points with the peace settlements in Paris.

Comments on Question 4

Had President Woodrow Wilson's idealistic plan for peace been implemented, the grievances that led to World War II might have been settled. The main provisions of the Fourteen Points: no secret treaties; freedom of the seas; free trade; arms reduction; settlement of colonial claims; national autonomy and adjustment of borders; establishment of a League of Nations. The Big Four Allied leaders met in Paris and drew up three treaties, without representatives of any of the Central Powers, to end the war. It is not necessary to show the differences or ascertain similarities between the Fourteen Points and each of these treaties. In general terms, show what Wilson gave up during the negotiations in order to attain his prime goal, the League of Nations.

> 5.   *Evaluate* the Treaty of Versailles.

Comments on Question 5

To "judge the worth of," "discuss the advantages and disadvantages, the pluses and minuses," examine the main provisions—border adjustments, occupation, colonial adjustments, war guilt, indemnities, German disarmament—and consider the significance and consequences. How did the reparation payments by Germany affect its economy? How did Hitler use the war guilt clause in his propaganda? How did the Polish Corridor create conflict between Germany and newly independent Poland? What were the implications of Japan's receiving German Pacific colonies? How did Hitler use the remilitarization of the Rhineland and German rearmament to increase his popularity and power?

Practice Multiple-Choice Questions

(These questions are representative of the types found on the Advanced Placement Examination in European History.)

1. World War I had been called a "total war" for all of the following reasons EXCEPT
   (A) campaigns were fought on every continent
   (B) it involved the whole civilian population of the belligerents
   (C) the entire resources of the nations at war were marshaled for the war effort
   (D) those not serving in the military, including women, were expected to work in war plants, buy bonds to support the war, and morally back the nation's aims
   (E) there were more civilian than military casualties

2. Which of the following did NOT contribute to the outbreak of World War I?
   (A) Rival alliances
   (B) Conflicting colonial claims
   (C) Slavic nationalism
   (D) A naval arms race
   (E) Japanese militarism

3. An important cause of the Anglo-German rivalry from the last decades of the 19th century to 1914 was
   (A) competition in world trade and territorial expansion
   (B) the declining strength of the German navy
   (C) the conflict over the Berlin to Baghdad railway
   (D) Britain's *Entente Cordial* with France
   (E) traditional enmities between the nations

4. The significance of the Algeciras Conference of 1906 was that
   (A) it granted Morocco independence from France
   (B) it gave Germany a foothold in North Africa
   (C) it demonstrated the resolve of the Triple Alliance
   (D) it solidified the rivalry of the two camps, the Triple Alliance and the *Triple Entente*
   (E) it embarrassed Kaiser Wilhelm II

5. The series of Balkan crises, from 1908 to 1913, helped precipitate the First World War by
   (A) pitting Austria and Russia against each other
   (B) arousing Slavic nationalism
   (C) revealing the weakness of the Ottoman Empire
   (D) None of the above
   (E) All of the above

6. After the assasssination of Archduke Ferdinand in June of 1914, the infamous "blank check" issued by Germany to Austria
    (A)   promised support in whatever action Austria took against Russia
    (B)   was matched by a "blank check" from Russia to Serbia
    (C)   limited Austria's response to Serbia
    (D)   created a rift between Russia and France
    (E)   brought an ultimatum from Britain to Germany

7. The German Schlieffen Plan failed for all of the following reasons EXCEPT
    (A)   it was based on the strategy of attrition in a drawn-out war
    (B)   Russian mobilization was too swift to allow the "holding action" in the east
    (C)   Belgian resistance to their violated neutrality was stiff
    (D)   German divisions were transferred from France to East Prussia
    (E)   the French counterattack at the Marne was successful

8. War on the Western Front from late 1914 through most of 1918 can best be characterized as
    (A)   a series of clashes over vast areas by mobile armies
    (B)   a stalemate during which offensive operations exacted high casualties
    (C)   a seesaw conflict in which each side repeatedly gained then lost vast areas
    (D)   spectacular cavalry operations supported by infantry attacks and aircraft bombing
    (E)   a series of tank battles followed up by infantry assaults

9. War on the Eastern Front
    (A)   quickly degenerated into static trench warfare
    (B)   was similar in character to that on the Western Front
    (C)   involved a defensive stand by the German armies against the numerically superior Russians
    (D)   was characterized by decisive German victories, horrific Russian losses, and the acquisition of vast territories
    (E)   was marked by spectacular Austrian victories against the Turks and the Russians

10. Which was an innovation first employed in World War I?
    (A)   Massed artillery
    (B)   Tank warfare
    (C)   Naval blockade
    (D)   Large-scale infantry assaults over a broad front
    (E)   Trench warfare

11. The belligerent nations directed the war effort by instituting all the following controls on their civilian populations EXCEPT
    (A) press censorship
    (B) allocation of raw materials for industry
    (C) mobilization of industrial output for war production
    (D) outlawing of labor strikes
    (E) denial of religious freedom

12. Choose the corect chronological order of the following events:
    I. Russia pulls out of World War I.
    II. Italy enters the war.
    III. The United States enters the war.
    IV. The Ottoman Empire enters the war.
    (A) I, II, III, IV
    (B) II, IV, III, I
    (C) IV, III, II, I
    (D) IV, II, III, I
    (E) III, II, IV, I

13. Which was NOT one of President Woodrow Wilson's Fourteen Points?
    (A) No secret treaties
    (B) Freedom of the seas
    (C) Free trade
    (D) Independence for all German colonies
    (E) Autonomy for the peoples of the Austrian and Ottoman empires

14. As a result of the war, all of these empires ended EXCEPT
    (A) the French
    (B) the Ottoman
    (C) the Austro-Hungarian
    (D) the Russian
    (E) the German

15. All of the following states were granted independence at the peace conferences that ended World War I EXCEPT
    (A) Poland
    (B) Czechoslovakia
    (C) Yugoslavia
    (D) Hungary
    (E) Romania

Answers and Answer Explanations

1. A	2. E	3. A	4. D	5. E
6. C	7. A	8. B	9. D	10. B
11. E	12. D	13. D	14. A	15. E

1. (A) The war was fought primarily in Europe—Western and Eastern—and in the African colonies, in parts of the Mideast, in Asia, and on both the Atlantic and the Pacific oceans. Although North Americans and Australians participated, the war did not reach the Americas or Australia.

2. (E)   Japanese militarism helped cause World War II.

3. (A)   Germany having come later to industrialization than the British, had more efficient factories, and the Germans took a bite out of the British world trade in the later part of the 19th and early part of the 20th centuries.

4. (D)   The British and French hung together; only Austria backed Germany.

5. (E)   It was the world's powder keg.

6. (C)   Germany gave Austria a free hand with Serbia; France gave Russia a free hand with Austria.

7. (A)   the Central Powers knew they hadn't the population, industry, or resources to win a drawn-out war. The Schlieffen Plan aimed for a quick victory as in the Franco-Prussian War of 1871.

8. (B)   The trench lines by fall of 1914 extended from Switzerland in the south to the North Sea.

9. (D)   In the first months of the war, the Germans fought a holding action; then they launched massive and successful offensives to back the Austrians against the Russians.

10. (B)   Massed artillery was used before the time of Napoleon; naval blockade was used by the British against the American colonies and Napoleon; infantry assaults on a broad front was a tactic introduced in the American Civil War; trench warfare was a defensive tactic used in many previous wars.

11. (E)   Since organized religion tended to back the nation's war aims, there was no need to deny religious freedom.

12. (D)   This is a chronological identification; if you don't know at least some of the dates, don't answer the question.

13. (D)   The German colonies were largely made protectorates of one or another of the Allies but not freed from domination.

14. (A)   France was a republic without an emperor but it had colonies that it maintained until after World War II.

15. (E)   Romania was already an independent state.

11 The Russian Revolution and Communism in Russia (1917–1939)

Overview

Czarist Russia was a casualty of the First World War. What began for the Russian people—peasants, middle class, nobility—as a popular crusade, quickly became the focal point of revolution. Within a year of the start of the war, devastating defeats by the Central Powers and staggering casualties demoralized the Russian people. Military incompetence, the corruption and ineptitude of the czarist government, and deprivations on the home front sparked the revolutionary spirit that had smoldered for decades.

Defeat in the the Russo-Japanese War (1904–1905) and the abortive Revolution of 1905 demonstrated the vulnerability of the czarist regime. Despite accelerated industrialization in the period between 1890 and the start of the war, Russian workers were brutally exploited, and peasants—who made up the great bulk of the population—were oppressed.

The Revolution of 1917 began as an attempt at reform by the middle class and some enlightened nobles. When the moderates maintained Russia's unpopular involvement in the war, the radical Marxist Bolsheviks seized power and established the Communist regime that would change the politics of the 20th century.

Chronology:

1881–1894

Czar Alexander III, reacting to the assassination of his predecessor by radical socialists, instituted a reactionary policy of "Russification, orthodoxy, and autocracy."

1890s

Russia industrialized, but the great mass of its population was still made up of rural peasants whose quality of life was comparable to that of farmers in the West during the Middle Ages. Since the French were eager for Russian support against the Germans, they granted loans and credits that enabled the Russians to build factories, import Western technology, and expand the railroad system. The *Trans-Siberian Railroad* linked European and Asiatic Russia.

A commercial middle class grew in influence; a proletariat of exploited workers also grew. Political parties were formed to meet the demands of these new elements. *Constitutional Democrats (Cadet)* reflected the aims of the new middle class and some liberal landowners for parliamentary government and gradual reform. Social Revolutionaries (Narodniks) stressed the glories of Slav culture (Slavophiles) and sought to keep Russia agrarian. *Marxists* urged radical revolution.

1903

A meeting of the Russian Marxist Congress resulted in a split in the party when *Vladimir Lenin* favored a party of elite revolutionaries instead of an open democratic organization. When most of the attendees walked out in protest, Lenin convinced those remaining to endorse his ideas. Although his supporters made up a minority of the party, he called them Bolsheviks (majority) and referred to the actual party majority as Mensheviks (minority).

1904–1905

The Russo-Japanese War: Competing over Manchuria—a mineral rich province of China—Russia and newly modernized Japan came to blows. What the czar hoped would be a "short, glorious war" to divert unrest in his realm was a devastating defeat, the first in modern times of a European power by a nonwhite nation. A surprise attack on the Russian fleet at Port Arthur in Manchuria, a defeat at the Battle of Mukden on Manchurian soil, and the sinking of the Russian European fleet off Tsushima Straits brought a peace mediated by President *Theodore Roosevelt*. The Treaty of Portsmouth granted Japan Russia's railroad rights in Manchuria, half of the Sakhalin Islands off Russia's Pacific coast, and guarantee of Japan's protectorate in Korea. Humiliated, Russia suffered from the Revolution of 1905 before the war was even over.

The Revolution of 1905: Faced with the growing unrest of the working class, *Czar Nicholas II* commissioned a Russian Orthodox priest, *Father Gapon*, to organize a conservative union to counteract the radical Marxists. Gapon, horrified by the conditions in St. Petersburg (the czarist capital), led a peaceful protest march of tens of thousands of workers and their families on January 22, 1905. Troops fired on the crowd, killing hundreds. "Bloody Sunday" provoked general strikes, peasant uprisings, and the formation of workers' revolutionary councils, Soviets. In the *Zemstvos* (the provincial councils elected by landowners and peasants and set up by Czar Alexander II in 1864 as part of his great reforms), the liberals demanded reforms.

The *October Manifesto*: After a general strike was called by the Soviet of Petersburg, the czar issued a promise for reform. Its major provisions were a constitution, civil liberties, and a Duma (legislature) to represent all classes.

1906

A Duma was elected, but did not include the Marxists, who boycotted the elections because they mistrusted the czar's motives. Nicholas dissolved it anyway because the Duma demanded that his ministers be responsible to it.

Reforms were instituted including the strengthening of the Zemstvos, abolishing the peasant debt for the emancipation of serfs in the 1860s, and thereby creating a wealthy peasant class, the kulaks, who worked large tracts of land and hired other peasants.

1914

With the outbreak of World War I, the government suspended the Duma so that political bickering would not compromise the war effort. A national union of Zemstvos, made up of the various local elective districts, was organized to increase productivity.

Rasputin, "the mad monk," began to influence *Czarina Alexandra* after he claimed to have cured the czar's only son of hemophilia.

1915   Horrific losses at the front provoked the national union of Zemstvos and the middle class to demand that the Duma be reconvened to initiate reforms.

1916   The Duma met for the first time since its disbanding and, with support of its dominant conservatives, criticized the czar's government.

Rasputin, whose sway over Alexandra had poisoned her advice to her easily influenced husband, was murdered by a band of young noblemen. The Czar attempted to suppress any reform.

1917   *The March Revolution*: Food riots broke out in Petrograd (St. Petersburg), and when the czar ordered the Duma to dissolve and troops to suppress the disorder, neither obeyed. Workers and soldiers in Petrograd organized radical legislative bodies called Soviets. The rebellion spread throughout the country and to the troops at the front, who deserted by tens of thousands.

On March 14, the Duma formed a provisional government under *Prince Georgii Lvov*. *Alexander Kerensky*, a moderate member of the Soviet, played a major role.

On March 15, the czar abdicated.

On March 17, Russia was proclaimed a republic.

Lenin and other *Bolshevik* leaders came back from exile to Petrograd in April. Their demands to the provincial government:

1. Russia withdraw from the war
2. The Petrograd Soviet run the government
3. Land be redistributed to the peasants, and factories be controlled by the Soviets (worker's committees)

After an abortive coup in July, Lenin and the Bolshevik leaders fled to Finland. Prince Lvov turned over the provincial government to Kerensky.

The October Revolution (November 1917 by the Western calendar).

Kerensky's government failed to win the support of the people because of continued shortages and because it stayed in the war against the Central Powers.

Lenin returned to Petrograd with the rallying cry of "Peace, Land, Bread."

Leninist Doctrine: According to orthodox Marxism, a social revolution is possible only in highly developed capitalist countries, such as those in the West during this period. Since Russia was virtually a feudal society and primarily agrarian, some Bolsheviks argued for a coalition with the middle classes until Russia had developed sufficiently. Lenin argued that since Western Europe was ripe for revolution, a Marxist seizure of Russia would precipitate such takeovers elsewhere, and these in turn would help Russia to bypass the capitalist stage. Lenin won the support of Leon Trotsky, Joseph Stalin, and most of the Bolshevik leaders.

October 6–7: The Bolsheviks stormed the *Winter Palace*, headquarters of Kerensky's government, and seized other key centers in Petrograd. Kerensky's provisional government fled; the Congress of Soviets, representing the local Soviets formed all over Russia, established a Council of People's Commissars with Lenin as head, Trotsky as foreign minister, and Stalin as nationalities minister. Within months, the government abolished the freely elected legislative assembly and established a secret police organization, the Cheka, also known later as the OGPU, NKVD, MVD, and KGB.

1918

The Dictatorship of the Proletariat was proclaimed in tune with Leninist doctrine:

The Bolsheviks renamed their party Communist.

Important industries were nationalized.

Russian Orthodox Church lands were seized.

Russia pulled out of World War I, surrendering Latvia, Lithuania, Estonia, Poland, and the Ukraine to Germany in the *Treaty of Brest-Litovsk.*

1918–1922

The Russian Civil War was fought for control of the remainder of the Russian Empire. Opposed by czarists, the middle class, many peasants, and socialist factions, the Communists were able to win because their enemies could not unite. Despite the intervention of many Allied nations, including the United States, which feared the spread of Communism, the Red Army under Trotsky conquered European Russia by the end of 1920 and Siberia and central Asia by 1922. The Communist International (Comintern), to organize Communism worldwide, was organized in 1919.

1922

Nationalities Reform: The old empire was reorganized into the Union of Soviet Socialist Republics, uniting the various nation groups into a federal entity of major republics and smaller autonomous regions. Cultural identity was encouraged and toleration of various ethnic groups became an official policy.

1924

The Constitution:

1. Only workers and peasants are allowed to vote for local Soviets.
2. Local Soviets elect provincial or district Soviets which, in turn, choose a republic Soviet for each autonomous republic. A *Congress of Soviets* represents all the republics and elects a *Council of People's Commissars* (similar to a government cabinet).

Lenin died at the age of 54, never fully recovering from an assassination attempt in 1920. Trotsky was at a disadvantage in becoming Lenin's successor both because he was a Jew in an anti-Semitic society and because he was considered an intellectual by the rank and file.

As secretary of the Communist party, Stalin garnered loyalty within the party by making many key appointments.

Their policy differences further alienated the men from each other: Trotsky pushed for a worldwide revolution; Stalin argued for a strengthening of Russia by industrialization before it undertook worldwide revolution— "Building socialism in one country."

1927

Stalin won the support of the party, and Trotsky fled the country. He was murdered in 1940 by a Stalinist agent.

1928	The first *Five-Year Plan* promoted rapid industrialization by centralized planning. Coal and steel production were accelerated, and a modern transportation system was developed, using the domestic resources of the U.S.S.R. since foreign nations were hostile to the new government.
Early 1930	*Farm Collectivization* consolidated small farms into *Communes*, modernizing agriculture but displacing many peasants, some of whom resisted the process. The kulaks, the most successful peasant farmers, were destroyed as a class, and between 5 and 12 million people, mostly in the Ukraine, perished by murder and famine.
1933	A second *Five-Year Plan* was begun that increased production of steel and heavy industry, modernized Soviet factories, created a boom when the West was in the depth of the *Great Depression,* and made Russia a leading industrial power.
1936–37	*The purge trials*: Stalin's paranoid tendencies convinced him of plots within the party and the government to unseat him. Many original Bolsheviks, instrumental in carrying out the revolution, as well as high military officers, some of the most competent, were tried on trumped-up charges. As many as 1 million were executed; 5 to 7 million were sent to the gulags (Siberian labor camps) where many eventually died. Stalin strengthened his hold over the party, the government, and the nation, and became one of the century's most powerful dictators.

Sample Essay Question

The sample thematic essay question and the practice questions in this chapter are types found in the Advanced Placement Examination in European History, and they require knowledge of causes, effects, personalities, ideas, and events.

Sample Question

> *Analyze* the stages of the 1917 Russian Revolution.

Comments on the Sample Question

Follow the "Simple Procedures" for writing an essay. (See page 24.)

First, *What does the question want to know?* This is a straightforward question that requires "an examination in detail" of the complex series of events that are called the Russian Revolution.

Second, *What do you know about it?* According to the Brinton model (*Anatomy of Revolution*), both the French and Russian revolutions manifest three stages: the moderate, the radical, and the recovery. The difference between the French and Russian revolutions is that in Russia the same power group—the Bolsheviks—carried out both the radical and recovery stages.

Third, *How would you put it into words?* Probably the best way to approach this question is to chronicle the events, from March through October, and to explain the roles of the personalities—Lvov, Kerensky, Lenin, and Trotsky.

Sample Answer

After three years of horrific losses in the First World War—hundreds of thousands of deaths, battle defeats, shortages on the home front—workers in Petrograd, the capital of the Russian Empire, rioted for food on March 8, 1917. The Russian Revolution had begun.

Czar Nicholas II, a stupid and misguided monarch who for decades had suppressed all moves toward democracy on the advice of his wife, Czarina Alexandra, and the "mad monk," Rasputin, called out the troops. He also dissolved the Duma, the national legislature that had been convened during the war. The troops refused to fire on the people. The Duma refused to disband.

Soon after, workers and military personnel in Petrograd formed *Soviets*, democratic political units to take control of the government. Together with the Duma, a coalition of Petrograd Soviets set up a provisional government to replace the czar's corrupt regime on March 14. The new government was headed by Prince Lvov, a liberal aristocrat in the Duma, and it had Alexander Kerensky, a moderate in the Petrograd Soviet, as his second in command. The czar abdicated, and Russia became a republic on March 17.

In July, Lenin and other Bolshevik leaders who had come back from exile after the fall of the czar tried to overthrow the moderate provisonal government. They failed and fled, but Kerensky replaced Prince Lvov. Despite popular opposition, he decided to keep Russia in the war.

Back in Petrograd again, Lenin and the Bolsheviks ordered a takeover of the provisional government on the night of October 6. The Winter Palace—seat of Kerensky's government—was fired upon by a ship controlled by sailors in the Soviet, and Kerensky's government fled.

Evaluate the Sample Answer

1. Did its introduction spell out its intentions clearly?
2. Did it "examine in detail" the various stages of the 1917 Revolution, the roles of the main players, the complexity and sequence of events?
3. Were there factual errors, serious omissions?
4. Was the essay long enough, clearly written, easily understood?
5. Were the "stages" clearly delineated?
6. Did the concluding paragraph sum up adequately?

Rater's Comments on the Sample Answer

2—Possibly qualified

This is a sketchy, incomplete, and uneven effort. There is a rampant tendency to oversimplify and to omit crucial events. The early or moderate stage, the March Revolution, is adequately dealt with despite some omissions. The October Revolution is glossed over as are the roles and appeal of Lenin and the Bolsheviks.

On March 14, 1917, the Petrograd Soviet urged soldiers at the front to elect their own officers. This caused utter chaos, and the army virtually collapsed. Troops left their posts in droves in order to share in the redistribution of land being spontaneously carried by peasants who had seized their landlords' estates.

In April 1917, Lenin and the Bolsheviks were sent from exile to Petrograd by the Germans, who hoped to disrupt the Russian commitment to the war. Ironically, the triumph of Communism in Russia became an eventual threat to German security and helped lead to World War II.

The Bolshevik program was in glaring contrast to the policies of the provisional government. Lenin harangued crowds with promises of "Peace, land, and bread": an end to the war against the Central Powers, redistribution of the landed estates, workers' control of the factories, and political power to the Petrograd Soviet.

Lenin's argument for the Soviet to take power was opposed by orthodox Marxists among the Bolsheviks (Kamenev and Zinoviev), who argued that Russia had not developed a capitalist system sufficient to enable a successful socialist revolution. Lenin countered with the assertion that if Communism seized Russia, Western Europe, which was ripe for revolution, would follow and would then help Russia to skip capitalism.

Once the Bolsheviks had seized power in Petrograd on the night of October 6, the Petrograd Soviet set up a Council of Commissars to govern: Lenin as chief, Trotsky in charge of foreign affairs, Stalin as ethnic commissar. The assembly that had been elected under Kerensky's government to write a constitution was forcibly dissolved. The secret police, the Cheka, suppressed opposition and the "dictatorship of the proletariat" was set up.

Practice Essay Questions

The questions that follow are samples of the various types of thematic essays that appear on the Advanced Placement Examination in European History. (See pages 17–18 for a detailed explanation.)

---

1. *To what extent and in what ways* did the failure of reform and abortive revolution lead to the Revolution of 1917?

Comments on Question 1

"How and how much" did attempts to make the government better, improve the economy, and modernize the institutions of Russia cause the open rebellion of the people against the government and society? "How and how much" did the failed Revolution of 1905 contribute?

What were the attempts at reform? When did Russia modernize its economy and how did this lead to greater discontent among the people? Why was the Duma reconvened, and how did it precipitate events? How did the Russo-Japanese War cause discontent? What was "Bloody Sunday"? What reforms were aimed at by the marchers? What was the October Manifesto? What were Stolypin's reforms? What were the implications of his death?

> **2.**   *Analyze* Lenin's Marxism and his role as leader in establishing Communism in Russia.

Comments on Question 2

"Determine the relationship" between Lenin's interpretation of Marxism and the way he defined the new Soviet government. Orthodox Marxist theory insisted that a socialist revolution can take place only under certain conditions. What were those conditions? How did that apply to the governmental shift taking place in Russia in 1917? How did Lenin disagree with the orthodox view? How did he translate that once the Bolsheviks had seized power?

> **3.**   *Contrast and compare* the methods of governing of Lenin and Stalin.

Comments on Question 3

The contrast is glaring: Lenin established the basic institutions of Soviet Communism; Stalin evolved them into a grotesque parody of their original aims. Lenin ruled for about seven years; Stalin for over thirty. Lenin believed that the end justified the means; Stalin's paranoia distorted even this precept. Lenin designed the blueprint for modernization and reform; Stalin built the edifice into one of the world's worst totalitarian regimes.

The comparison, the similarities, are in their usurpation of power to gain their ends, their use of dictatorship, their methods of suppressing dissent.

This is a difficult question that requires broad statements backed by selective facts.

> **4.**   "Despite the human cost, Russia progressed under Communism." *Defend or refute* this statement.

Comments on Question 4

The impulse, if you know the cost of Soviet totalitarianism, 30-million-plus lives to start, is to refute. It is easy to overlook the modernization and industrialization of a feudal society on the facts alone without reverting to ideological biases. The first step in this question is to define "progress." Is it economic? Social? Some indefinible movement forward? You can get lost in trying to measure the improvement of the human condition from one age to another. Do the drudgery and social stagnancy of feudalism compare to the alienation and confusion of modernity?

Stick to the tangible. The Five-Year Plans—did they improve life for the Soviet people, and what was their cost? Was there a better standard of living for the Russian people under Communism or the czar? Was Communist tyranny worse than czarist despotism?

Remember, whether you defend or refute, it is the case you make that counts.

> **5.** "The Russian Revolution of 1917 was a major force in determining the character of the 20th century." *Assess the validity* of this statement.

Comments on Question 5

"Determine the truth" of this statement by considering not only the confrontation between ideologies known as the Cold War, but also the role of Soviet Communism in disrupting the world order before World War II and after. What part did it play in dismantling colonialism, as a model for new nations, as a counter to the status quo? In what ways was it a focal point for world affairs after World War I, before World War II, after World War II?

Practice Multiple-Choice Questions

(These questions represent the various types found on the Advanced Placement Examination in European History.)

1. After the assassination of Russia's czar Alexander II in 1881, his successor, Alexander III, adopted a policy of
   - (A) constitutional reform
   - (B) industrialization
   - (C) "Orthodoxy, Russification, and Autocracy"
   - (D) Westernization
   - (E) modern scientific rationalism

2. Which was NOT a result of Russia's dramatic industrialization in the 1890s?
   - (A) The doubling of its railroad mileage
   - (B) Vastly increased exports
   - (C) The growth of the proletariat
   - (D) The growth of the commercial middle class
   - (E) Private ownership of all industry

3. Which is the best characterization of Lenin's program at the Russian Marxist Party Conference in Brussels and London, 1903?
   - (A) Democratic socialism open to all new members
   - (B) Professional revolutionaries with a small, elite leadership
   - (C) Rank and file participation in policy formulation
   - (D) Party division along the lines of autonomous national groups
   - (E) Party cooperation with liberal and socialist parties

4. All are results of the Russo-Japanese War (1904–1905) EXCEPT
   - (A) Russian forces were decisively defeated
   - (B) Japanese was given some of the Sakhalin Islands
   - (C) Russia was forced to pay Japan an indemnity
   - (D) Japan got Russia's railway concessions in Manchuria
   - (E) Japan's Korean protectorate was recognized

5. Which is the most valid statement regarding the October Manifesto issued by Czar Nicholas II in 1905?
   - (A) It precipitated a general strike that paralyzed the economy.
   - (B) It brought about significant constitutional reform of the government.
   - (C) It created a Duma (national legislature), to which the czar's ministers were directly responsible.
   - (D) It was an expedient and temporary promise of reform in response to civil unrest.
   - (E) It imposed martial law and suppressed antigovernment political activities.

6. The Russian people's support for Russian participation in World War I changed drastically
   - (A) when Rasputin took virtual control of the government
   - (B) after the Battles of Masurian Lakes and Tannenberg
   - (C) because the Duma was reconvened in 1916
   - (D) when the Germans and Austrians went on the offensive in 1915
   - (E) after the Bolshevik Revolution of 1917

7. The slogan "Peace, Land, and Bread" is most closely associated with
   - (A) the Duma liberals
   - (B) Alexander Kerensky's moderates
   - (C) Prince Lvov's coalition government
   - (D) Lenin's Bolsheviks
   - (E) Czar Nicholas's cabinet

8. Choose the correct chronology:
   - I.   the Bolshevik seizure of power
   - II. Alexander Kerensky's government
   - III. Prince Lvov's provisional government
   - IV. dissolving of the Duma during the Petrograd food riots
   - (A) IV, III, II, I
   - (B) III, IV, II, I
   - (C) III, II, IV, I
   - (D) IV, II, III, I
   - (E) II, III, IV, I

9. Within a year after the October Revolution, the Bolsheviks had accomplished all of these EXCEPT
   - (A) the abolition of the provisional government
   - (B) the establishment of the Council of Commissars to rule Russia
   - (C) the election of the National Constituent Assembly to frame a new government
   - (D) the nationalization of large industries
   - (E) the confiscation of Russian Orthodox Church lands

10. The organizer of the Red Army who lost the struggle for leadership of the Soviet Union to Stalin after Lenin's death was
    (A) Alexander Kerensky   (D) General Kornilov
    (B) Alexander Nevsky   (E) Nikita Khrushchev
    (C) Leon Trotsky

11. During the Russian Civil War, 1918–1921, which of the following did NOT oppose Bolshevik rule?
    (A) Czarists
    (B) The middle class
    (C) Peasants
    (D) Urban workers
    (E) The Allied Powers of World War I

12. In 1922, after the Civil War had ended, Lenin undertook his "nationalities reform." It accomplished all of the following EXCEPT
    (A) uniting the major ethnic groups into a federation
    (B) giving smaller ethnic groups autonomous regions within the major republics
    (C) allowing schools to teach native languages
    (D) encouraging cultural uniqueness
    (E) requiring that instruction in schools be exclusively in Russian

13. Trotsky and Stalin's interpretations of Marxism differed most significantly in which way?
    (A) Trotsky wanted to foster world revolution while Stalin wanted "to build Socialism in one country."
    (B) Stalin wanted to foster revolution in Western Europe while Trotsky wanted to develop the Soviet Union first.
    (C) Stalin was a Bolshevik; Trotsky was a Menshevik.
    (D) Trotsky was deviationist; Stalin followed the party line.
    (E) Stalin believed that Russia was too backward to support Communism; Trotsky believed the opposite.

14. Stalin supported the rapid industrialization of Russia in the 1920s and early 1930s by
    (A) purging the Soviet Communist party of "deviationists"
    (B) obtaining loans from the West
    (C) slaughtering the kulaks
    (D) collectivizing agriculture to support the First Five-Year Plan
    (E) seeking international recognition of the Soviet Union

15. The original purpose of Comintern (Communist International), a congress of socialist parties in 1919, was to
    (A) combat Fascism and Nazism
    (B) foster democratic socialism worldwide
    (C) establish Moscow's leadership in fomenting Marxist revolution around the world
    (D) improve relations with the capitalist West
    (E) encourage socialists to join in coalition governments with other parties in the West

Answers and Answer Explanations

1. C	2. E	3. B	4. C	5. D
6. B	7. D	8. A	9. C	10. C
11. D	12. E	13. A	14. D	15. C

1. (C)   Tepid reform reverted to hard repression.

2. (E)   Most industry was owned and controlled by the government, so that the government was the employer that exploited most Russian workers.

3. (B)   Lenin believed it was the only way to effect a revolution.

4. (C)   The indemnity was not imposed, but the effect of the war was catastrophic to the stability of the czar's government anyway. The Revolution of 1905 broke out.

5. (D)   The czar went back on his promises as soon as the disorder ended.

6. (B)   The terrible casualties and territorial losses turned the people against the war.

7. (D)   A masterful slogan of masterful propagandists.

8. (A)   One of those chronological identifications that is hard to analyze.

9. (C)   The elections for a constitutional convention took place during Kerensky's regime. The Bolsheviks wanted to consolidate, not share, power.

10. (C)   Leon Trotsky was the hero of the Red Army.

11. (D)   Like the French Revolution before it, the Russian Revolution was largely supported by the urban workers, the vaunted proletariat.

12. (E)   To win over the various nationalities, Lenin did the opposite of the czar's hated Russification.

13. (A)   Trotsky had many followers among the Bolsheviks who supported his ideas. Stalin may have been right to strengthen the U.S.S.R. first, though.

14. (D)   Consolidating small farms into communes made agriculture more productive and the party used the profits to industrialize. When the kulaks, wealthy peasant farmers, resisted, Stalin slaughtered them by the millions, but this did not contribute to industrialization.

15. (C)   Comintern convinced the capitalists that there was a monolithic Communist conspiracy to take over the world.

CHAPTER 12 Democracy, Depression, Dictatorship, Aggression (1919–1939)

Overview

The fall of four great empires after World War I—Russian, German, Ottoman, and Austro-Hungarian—not only created a polyglot of smaller nations but left a political vacuum among peoples without a tradition of democracy. In the two decades between the world wars, totalitarian dictatorships were established in Russia, Italy, and Germany. For the first time in history, governments of great nations were dedicated to the total control of every area of human life, and individuals were expected to subordinate themselves to the needs of the state as defined by the single party in control. Italian fascism and German Nazism shared a common ideology of racist nationalism and the glorification of war. Russian Communism—despite its idealistic goal of the withering away of the state—imposed the same brutal repression in the name of the "dictatorship of the proletariat."

The Western democracies of England, France, and the United States came out of World War I with their heritage of democracy intact. In the 1930s, their tradition of dissent and their democratic institutions were sorely tested both by economic collapse and by the aggressions of the dictatorships. Ten years after the end of World War I, the worst depression in modern history began and lasted for over a decade. The human misery brought each of these nations close to the point of collapse and encouraged extremist movements—on the left and right—to offer simple solutions that would have destroyed democracy. Wracked by weakness and dissent, the democracies were unable to respond to the aggressions of the European dictators and the Japanese militarists. The policy of appeasement, which sought to placate the aggressors with concessions, only whet their appetites and led eventually to the worst war in human history.

The Western Democracies After the First World War

1920s in England

The nation did not recover, during the 1920s, from the economic losses suffered during the war. Its merchant fleet had been decimated by German submarines and its foreign trade had declined disastrously. International

197

competition from worldwide industrialization and from rival shipping nations further eroded an economic system already saddled by war debts, defaulted loans, and war relief programs.

The Liberal party, headed by David Lloyd George, fell into decline and was replaced by the Conservatives (Tory party), who favored high tariffs and welfare payments to the growing numbers of unemployed. The Labour party, whose program included a gradual nationalization of major industries, took power briefly; by 1929 and the start of the depression, an alliance of Labourites and Conservatives led by *Ramsay MacDonald*, then *Stanley Baldwin*, and finally *Neville Chamberlain* ran the government until the start of World War II. Chamberlain's black umbrella became a symbol for the policy of *appeasement* (the willingness to give into the demands of the aggressive dictatorships).

British foreign policy during this period was occupied by the *Irish Question*, the granting of eventual independence to Southern Ireland after failure to suppress rebellion; the ending of the *British protectorate* in *Egypt*, although control of the Suez Canal was continued; and by the *Statute of Westminster*, which formally recognized the equality of the British Dominions—such as Canada and Australia—and set up a *Commonwealth of Nations*, which enjoyed special trading privileges.

1920s in France

The death, devastation, and debt of the First World War created economic chaos and political unrest. When the Germans defaulted on their reparations to France (which was to get 52 percent of the $33 billion), the economy nearly collapsed.

Through the 1920s, the government—a multiparty system requiring coalitions to operate—was dominated by the parties on the right, which supported the status quo and had the backing of business, the army, and the Church. In 1922, when Germany managed to pay only part of that year's reparation bill, *Raymond Poincaré*, prime minister, sent French troops to occupy the mineral-rich *Ruhr Valley* in Western Germany. The *Dawes Plan,* the *Young Plan*, and the *Lausanne Settlement* each, in turn, pared down German payments and diminished the ability of the French to collect. Tax and spending reforms by Poincaré's government, though, led to a temporary resurgence of prosperity until the worldwide depression hit.

French foreign policy during the decade aimed at neutralizing Germany in the event of a resurgence of militarism there. A series of alliances with buffer states such as Belgium and Poland surrounded Germany with French allies; the *Locarno Pact* of 1925 attempted to settle French-German border disputes; and the *Kellogg-Briand Pact* of 1928 aimed at outlawing war.

1920s in the United States

Disillusionment with the *Versailles Treaty* resulted in the Senate's rejection of U.S. membership in the League of Nations and the election to the presidency of *Warren G. Harding,* who promised a "return to normalcy."

Despite nostalgia for traditional *isolationism*, the United States participated in a series of naval disarmament conferences that agreed to limit the building of new battleships and fix the size of the major powers' navies.

Despite an economic boom in the United States, international trade was thwarted by a series of shortsighted *tariffs* (taxes on imports) which contributed to the *Great Depression* by diminishing foreign markets and limiting the ability of the Europeans to pay off their war debts to the United States.

Immigration quotas, which favored Northern Europeans over those from the south and east, ended the *age of immigration* that peaked at the turn of the century.

The Age of Anxiety

The carnage and disruption of World War I and the collapse of the "old order" that had defined European politics and diplomacy for nearly a century resulted in what commentators have called an *"age of anxiety."* The traditional assumption of the perfectibility of mankind through reason collapsed under the weight of events and new ideas.

Philosophy, science, the arts, and literature contributed to this crisis of confidence and conscience, but also offered new models to explain and portray humanity.

PHILOSOPHY

Friedrich Nietzsche, a German, attributed the decline of Western Civilization to the *slave morality* of Christian ethics. *Henri Bergson*, a French thinker, argued that intuition and experience are as powerful tools as science and reason for understanding the human condition. *Edmund Husserl* and *Martin Heidegger*, both Germans, extended the work of Nietzsche and *Soren Kierkegaard*, a Dane, to establish the foundations of *existentialism*, a philosophical school, popularized by *Jean-Paul Sartre* after World War II, that emphasized individual responsibility and capability for giving meaning to a meaningless universe.

PSYCHOLOGY

Sigmund Freud, an Austrian, portrayed human behavior as the interplay of powerful irrational and *unconscious* forces. The *id* was the driving force of the personality, a reservoir of sexual and aggressive drives; the superego, in the unconscious mind like the id, presented conflicting parental and social values that clashed with the selfish drives of the id. Individual lives and civilization itself were fragile balancing acts to keep these unconscious and potentially destructive forces in balance.

PHYSICS

The work of *Max Planck*, a German, demonstrated that atoms were not the basic building blocks of the universe. The theories of *relativity* of *Albert Einstein*, another German, further disrupted the comfortable assumptions of an orderly, rationally discoverable universe that Newton's 17th century physics had supported and encouraged *relativism* in ethics, politics, and worldviews.

LITERATURE

The aftermath of the war and intellectual trends, such as Freudianism, influenced writers to emphasize the irrational aspects of the human condition. *Stream of consciousness*, the portrayal of an individual's random thoughts and feelings, was a style perfected by *James Joyce*, an Irish novelist, and *Virginia Woolf*, an English fiction writer. It reflected the prevailing view of human life as alienated, irrational, and chaotic.

ART

Expressionism, abstract and nonrepresentational, replaced *impressionism* and was pioneered by *Vincent van Gogh*, *Paul Cézanne*, and *Paul Gauguin* who painted with bold colors and images to focus on emotions and imagination. *Pablo Picasso*, a Spaniard, invented *cubism,* the depiction of mood through the use of geometric angles, planes, and clashing lines. *Dadaism* and *surrealism* were among the abstract styles created by artists of many nationalities, most of whom did their experimentation in postwar France. Architecture exemplified *functionalism,* buildings designed with practicality and clean lines instead of ornamentation.

MEDIA

Film and radio became major means for entertainment, information, and propaganda in the 1920s and 1930s. National broadcasting networks were set up by every major European power, and radio was employed by Adolf Hitler and other European dictators for propaganda and indoctrination. Movies became a prime medium for mass entertainment and also were employed to produce powerful propaganda. The modern *cult of celebrity*— the ironic glorification of the personalities who portrayed people other than themselves—was born with the advent of movies.

The Great Depression (1929–1939)

United States

The *economic boom* of the "Roaring Twenties" masked a deep-seated malaise. Farm prices had dropped disastrously after the peak selling during wartime; sizable segments of the population were poor; credit buying encouraged exorbitant personal debt; a dearth of new products (once the market for radios, autos, and refrigerators had been saturated) discouraged business investment.

The *stock market crash* of October 1929 was more a symptom than a cause of the depression that seized America and most of the industrialized world for the next decade. Since the American and European economies were interdependent through extensive investments and war debts owed to the United States, the failure of the U.S. economy led to a global breakdown. (The *command economy* of the U.S.S.R. managed to maintain and even surpass earlier productivity.) By 1932, nearly 15 million Americans were unemployed, about a quarter of the work force. Herbert Hoover's stubborn insistence that the depression was a normal fluctuation of the economy and would run its course brought the Roosevelt Democrats into the White House with a New Deal.

Franklin Delano Roosevelt (FDR) and the New Deal may not have ended the depression in America, but they helped preserve capitalism and democracy in the United States by using the deficit-spending theories of *John Maynard Keynes* and by establishing profound involvement of the federal government in the economy. The *Federal Deposit Insurance Corporation* protected individual depositors against bank failures; the *Agricultural Adjustment Act* provided price supports and subsidies for farmers; the *National Recovery Act* regulated industry; the *Civilian Conservation Corps* improved the ecology while providing jobs to young people; the Public Works Administration reconstructed the infrastructure of America while offering employment. The *Wagner Act* gave organized labor the right to collective bargaining and to strike. The *Social Security Act* guaranteed benefits to seniors.

Although the depression ended in the United States only when it began to rearm (1940–1941), the New Deal created a social welfare state with the obligation to relieve economic hardship while it preserved a modified and revitalized American capitalism.

England

During the 1930s, under the *National party* (the coalition of Labourites and Conservatives) the British tried to alleviate the depression by reorganizing industry, abandoning free trade, reforming finances, and cutting government spending. Like the United States, Britain came out of the depression only through rearmament for the coming world war.

France

The depression increased class tensions and gave birth to a radical right that supported government reorganization along Fascist lines. After a financial scandal that involved high government officials in 1934, pro-Fascist riots broke out all over France. A coalition of socialists, republicans, labor unionists, and Communists responded by organizing the Popular Front, which opposed fascism, supported reform, and upheld the republic. In 1936, socialist *Leon Blum* became prime minister under the *Popular Front* banner. He instituted a *"French New Deal,"* which offered labor and agricultural reforms similar to those in the United States except that his measures were ineffective in ending the depression. Opposed by the conservative bloc in the Senate, the program failed to hold together the Popular Front coalition, and Blum resigned in 1937 to be replaced by conservative *Edouard Daladier*, who overturned the Blum reforms and practiced a policy of *appeasement* of Hitler's aggressions.

Dictatorship

Fascism in Italy

The peace settlements that ended World War I were extremely disappointing to Italian nationalists. None of the Austrian and Ottoman territories and German colonies in Africa that had been promised were received. To add to Italian discontent, a depression hit in 1919 and provoked nationwide strikes and class antagonisms. Terrified of a Communist revolution, the propertied classes looked hopefully for a strong leader to restore order.

Benito Mussolini, editor of a socialist newspaper and paradoxically an ardent nationalist, organized the Fascist party, a combination of socialism and nationalism, named after fasces (the rods carried by Imperial Roman officials as symbols of power). His *squadristi*, paramilitary *blackshirts*, attacked Communists, socialists, and other enemies of his program. Promising to protect private property, Mussolini won the support of the conservative classes and quickly abandoned his socialist programs.

The Fascist *March on Rome*, October 1922, caused the government to collapse and won Mussolini the right to organize a new government. King Victor Emmanuel III granted him dictatorial powers for one year to end the nation's social unrest.

The *corporate state* was the economic core of Italian fascism:

Labor unions manage and control industry.

Those unions then set the national political agenda.

Unlike socialist corporate states, where workers make decisions, authority flowed from the top.

The Fascists consolidated power through the 1920s by rigging elections and intimidating and terrorizing opponents. By 1928, all independent labor unions had been organized into government-controlled syndicates, the right to vote had been severely limited, and all candidates for the Italian parliament were selected by the Fascist party. Through the 1930s, an organization of corporations, headed by Mussolini, effectively replaced parliamentary government. Democracy was suppressed; the totalitarian state was created in Italy.

FASCIST ACCOMPLISHMENTS

Internal improvements such as electrification and roadbuilding

More efficient municipal governing

Suppression of the Mafia and improvement of the justice system (except for "enemies of the state")

Reconciliation with the papacy through the *Lateran Pact*, 1929, which gave the papacy $92 million for seized church lands in return for Pope Pius XII's recognition of the legitimacy of the Italian State

FASCIST FAILINGS

Italian democracy destroyed—press censorship, no right to strike, denial of all dissent, destruction of suffrage

Terrorism a state policy

Poor industrial growth due to militarism and colonialism

Attempt to recapture the imperialistic glories of ancient Rome led to disastrous involvements in war

Nazism in Germany

In November 1918, a provisional government—socialist and democratic—was organized to negotiate a peace with the Allies. Although this government had very little input to the decisions made at the Paris Peace Conference, it did sign the Versailles Treaty and would be held responsible by conservative factions for the pact's inequities.

The *Weimar Constitution*, drafted in July 1919, set up Germany's first modern democracy by providing for a directly elected president and parliament (the *Reichstag*), by setting up a senate (the *Reichsrat*) to represent the German states, and by providing for a chancellor (prime minister), who represented the majority party of the Reichstag, and a cabinet to run the government.

After the *inflation of 1923*, Germany defaulted on its reparations to France, the French seized the Ruhr Valley, and German workers there went on a general strike. To pay these workers, the Weimar government printed paper currency and the prevalent inflation in the country became runaway. When debtors rushed to pay off their creditors with this worthless currency, the middle class was financially wiped out.

The Munich Beer Hall Putsch

The disasters for the Weimar government in 1923 encouraged *Adolf Hitler* and his Nazi *Brownshirts* to seize power from the government of Bavaria, a state of Germany. Hitler, an Austrian who had fled poverty in his native land and had joined the German army at the start of World War I, helped organize the *National Socialist German Workers' Party (Nazis)* after the war. Racist, paranoid, sociopathic, and megalomaniacal, he was a brilliant orator and political strategist who played on popular discontent with the Weimar government by blaming democracy, Communism, and Jews for Germany's ills. He and *Erich Ludendorff*, a distinguished general who had led German troops to victory on the Eastern Front during the First World War, led the attempted coup in Munich at the end of 1923. It was suppressed, and Hitler was sentenced to five years in jail. He served only about a year of his already lenient term because many higher-ups in the justice system sympathized with his narrow nationalistic goals. While in prison, he wrote his blueprint for domination of Germany and eventually Europe, *Mein Kampf (My Struggle)*, which was a rambling, irrational, but convincing tract. It argued that Germany was never defeated in the First World War but was betrayed from within by Jews and socialists, that the Treaty of Versailles was a humiliation, that the Germans were a master race destined to expand into Eastern Europe to obtain lebensraum (living space) and to rule or exterminate inferior races such as Jews and Slavs.

After the *Dawes Plan* stabilized Germany's economy in 1924, the Nazi party's membership fell off so that by 1928 the Nazis won only twelve seats in the Reichstag. When the depression hit Germany in 1930, the Nazis won 107 seats and the Communists 77. Since the center parties—socialist and Christian Democrat—were unable to maintain a ruling coalition, many conservatives, including large landowners, industrialists, and army officers, threw their support to Hitler to avoid a Communist takeover. In January 1933, after a series of machinations, Hitler was invited by the aging president of the Weimar Republic, *Paul von Hindenburg*, another renowned general of the First World War, to form a government as chancellor. Hitler entered government legally, according to the constitution that he was dedicated to destroy.

The Nazi Revolution

The week before the elections of March 1933, which Hitler ordered to obtain a clear majority in the Reichstag, the *Reichstag building was destroyed by fire*. Although the Nazis almost certainly started the fire, Hitler used it as a pretext to declare emergency powers for his government. The election that followed was influenced by a suspension of freedom of the press and of speech, and by outright terrorizing of political opponents. After gaining a majority coalition in the Reichstag, the Nazis granted dictatorial powers to Hitler for four years in the Enabling Act. Within six months, all political parties but the Nazis were outlawed. When President Hindenburg died in 1934, Hitler was given a 90 percent vote of confidence by the German people to assume the presidency.

The Nazis Consolidated Power

Dachau, the first concentration camp, was opened in March 1933. Although the camps did not become death factories for mass extermination until 1941, they were brutal centers for punishing political opponents of the Nazis. During the *Night of the Long Knives*, in June 1934, Hitler purged the party by executing left-wing Nazis who had pushed for the socialist programs that Hitler had promised and leaders of the Brownshirts who had maintained autonomy within the party. The black-uniformed elite guard, the infamous *SS* (Schutzstaffel) became the party and the nation's enforcer. The *Gestapo* was the secret police force of the SS, and a rigorous selection and training process was set up for the SS, which would become the overseers of the death camps.

Labor unions were replaced, as in Fascist Italy, by a Nazi labor organization; strikes were outlawed, and factories put under the management of local Nazi officials who had dictatorial powers over the workers. Full employment resumed with arms production that thrived despite its prohibition under the terms of the Versailles Treaty.

A policy of *autarchy*, economic self-sufficiency, was developed to make Germany independent of imports and foreign markets.

The *Nuremberg Laws* of 1935 stripped Germany's half-million Jews of their rights as citizens. When Nazi mobs wrecked Jewish temples throughout Germany during *Kristallnacht* (Night of the Broken Glass) in 1938, the *Holocaust*—the systematic extermination of Jews in Germany and eventually throughout Europe—began. About 200,000 German Jews managed to escape from Germany. Of those that remained, over 90 percent were murdered.

Aggression and Appeasement

1933

Hitler pulled Germany out of the League of Nations.

1935

Hitler began rebuilding the German armed forces in open violation of the Treaty of Versailles. The Western powers, immersed in the Great Depression, objected but did not act.

Mussolini attacked the independent kingdom of Ethiopia in East Africa; the League ordered *sanctions* (an embargo on trade in arms and raw materials) but the sanctions are not enforced.

1936

Hitler's troops occupied the *Rhineland*, which the Treaty of Versailles had made into a demilitarized zone between France and Germany. France and England failed to act, giving birth to the policy of *appeasement* (the submission, by default or deliberately, to the demands of the dictators).

1936

General *Francisco Franco* and his Spanish Falangists (Fascists) began an insurrection against the democratically chosen republican government of Spain. The Fascist dictators, Mussolini and Hitler, supported Franco with men, arms, and money. Stalin backed the Republicans, a significant number of whom were Communists, but he was unable to drum up anymore than lackluster support for the republican cause among the democracies. Although individual Americans, Britons, Frenchmen, and many others joined voluntary brigades in the fight against fascism, the policy of appeasement prevailed. The brutal and destructive *Spanish Civil War*, which lasted for over three years and claimed the lives of 600,000, became a testing ground for the war machines of the dictatorships. The Fascists won, and Franco remained as the longest reigning Fascist dictator, his regime ending when he died in 1975.

1937
Germany, Italy, and Japan signed the *Anti-Comintern Pact* to oppose international Communism. It marked the beginning of their alliance, the *Axis*.

Japan invaded mainland China, quickly conquering the seacoast and driving *Chiang Kai-shek's Nationalists* deep into the interior, where they waged a guerrilla war that proved costly to the Japanese.

1938
Hitler engineered the *Anschluss* (the forced union of Germany and Austria), again in violation of the Versailles Treaty. Once again the Western powers failed to act.

Hitler prepared to annex the *Sudetenland* (a part of Czechoslovakia that had been German territory). France and England, at the urging of the U.S.S.R., issued warnings. After tensions and talks, a conference was called, at Mussolini's suggestion, in which *Chamberlain*, prime minister of Britain, and *Daladier*, prime minister of France, met with Hitler and Mussolini. The infamous *Munich Conference* ceded the Sudetenland to Germany and marked the pinnacle of appeasement.

1939
Hitler seized the rest of Czechoslovakia, abandoned by the West, and the western part of Lithuania.

Mussolini invaded Albania.

Hitler and Stalin signed a *nonaggression pact*, which cleared the way for Hitler's *invasion of Poland*.

Sample Essay Question

The sample thematic essay question and the practice questions that appear in this chapter are types found in the Advanced Placement Examination in European History, and they require a knowledge of causes, effects, personalities, ideas, and events.

Sample Question

> *Explain* how, during the Great Depression, traditionally democratic European governments maintained their democracy while some of the newer European democracies fell under dictatorship.

Comments on the Sample Question
Follow the "Simple Procedures" for writing an essay. (See page 24.)

First, *What does the question want to know?* You must "offer the reasons for" and "detail" why democracy survived in some European nations and failed in others.

Second, *What do you know about it?* In England and France, the institutions and impulses of democracy prevailed over the crisis. In England, a coalition reformed the economic system. In France, the socialist "French New Deal" matched Roosevelt's policies in the United States. In Germany, the weak Weimar Republic crumbled with the election of a plurality of Nazis. In Spain, the Republican government—lacking popular support—was crushed by Franco's Falange. In Italy, Mussolini's Fascists completed the "corporate state" in response to the depression.

Third, *How would you put it into words?* Be sure to explain why democracy prevailed or failed.

Sample Answer

The economic disaster of the Great Depression shattered international trade, resulted in unemployment rates as high as 30 percent in the capitalist world, and tested the political systems of the traditional democracies and those created after World War I. Britain and France—among the world's three great constitutional governments, which included the United States—relied on their "habits" of democratic problem-solving to deal with the crisis. Germany, Spain, and, to some degree, Italy fell under the yoke of dictatorship during the depression.

Britain's well-established parliamentary system came to the fore during the depression, when a coalition of the Labour and Conservative parties developed a program to regulate commerce and industry and to extend the social welfare system that had its foundations in the pre-World War I period. A responsiveness to the electorate had been achieved gradually through the course of British history, and it prevailed over the extremist promises of the right and left.

The strong Socialist segment in France's political life came through with a "French New Deal" patterned after the programs of America's Franklin Delano Roosevelt. Labor legislation and farm subsidies, put through the assembly by a coalition led by the Socialists, offered hope to the electorate. Although the program was largely unsuccessful, rather than falling under the sway of the growing Communist party or French Fascists, the people returned the government to conservative factions. The hard-won republican democracy of the French seemed to have ingrained a sense of moderation and mistrust of extremism.

The Weimar Republic was a creation of the peace conferences at the end of World War I. Resented by the conservatives for its part in accepting the harsh Versailles Treaty, mistrusted by the masses for its haphazard responses to the runaway inflation of the mid-1920s and to the hardships of the depression, it was destroyed from within. When his Nazis won a plurality of Reichstag seats in 1932, Hitler was appointed chancellor and within less than two years he had laid the foundations for one of the world's most terrible totalitarian regimes. Democracy had been imposed on the Germans by their enemies; their history had not developed democratic institutions. The monarchies of the separate states, the despotism of Bismarck's new empire, and the virtual absolutism of Kaiser Wilhelm II's aggressive "fatherland" were the only prelude to the messy and inefficient coalition governments of the Weimar Republic. Hard times nurtured extremists, like the Nazis, that promise simplistic solutions. The Nazis were elected by the very democracy they destroyed.

Since its unification in the late 15th century, Spain has been the bulwark of Catholic, monarchical conservatism. When a republic was set up in 1931, after the king was ousted, leftists tried to diminish the influence of the Roman Catholic Church by secularizing the schools, seizing church lands, and abolishing the Jesuits. This attempt, along with their land redistribution program, alienated the conservative faction—the military, the church, the monarchists—and Falangists (Spanish Fascists) organized a government. When the popular election in 1936 put a coalition of leftists back in power, General Francisco Franco started a civil war against the republican government. Backed by a sizable segment of the populace and by the arms and men of the Italian Fascists and the German Nazis, while the Republicans were backed by the Soviet Communists, Franco won the bloody and costly civil war and seized power in 1939. He ruled Spain as the world's longest reigning Fascist dictator until his death in 1975.

Mussolini used the Great Depression as an excuse to impose his plan for the "corporate state" on Italy. He and his party had been in power since 1922, and he completed his restructuring of the government by about 1934. In essence, labor unions managed industry and set the national political agenda. Of course, the unions were unrepresentative of the workers' real needs and they were dominated by the Fascists.

The failure of democracy during the Great Depression in Germany, Italy, and Spain resulted from the lack of adaptable democratic institutions and from the peoples' general mistrust of an unaccustomed form of government. Its success in Britain, France, and the United States came from their well-established constitutional systems.

Evaluate the Sample Answer

1. Did its introduction point the way?
2. Did it detail, make clear, and offer reasons for the successes and failures of democratic governments during the depression?
3. Were the facts accurate, sufficient, and did they provide convincing support?
4. Was the essay clear, interesting, and convincing?
5. What was missing?
6. Did the concluding paragraph sum up the thrust of the essay?

Rater's Comments on the Sample Answer

5—Extremely well qualified

The essay more than fulfills the requirements of the question. It offers the two most important examples of European democracy's resilience during the depression and three of the most important instances of its failure. The essay is supported by accurate information, although its tone is generalized. Specific mention might have been made of the personalities and parties that led the British and French governments during this crisis: Labourite Ramsey MacDonald, Conservatives Stanley Baldwin and Neville Chamberlain for Britain; rightist Raymond Poincaré, socialist Leon Blum, conservative Edouard Daladier, the Fascist-type party, *Action Francaise,* and the prorepublican coalition, *Popular Front* for France.

Practice Essay Questions

The questions that follow are samples of the various types of thematic essays that appear on the Advanced Placement Examination in European History. (See pages 17–18 for a detailed explanation.)

> **1.**   *Evaluate* the successes and failures of fascism in Italy.

Comments on Question 1

A system as heinous as fascism makes an objective evaluation difficult, but Mussolini stayed in power as long as he did—1922 to 1943—because he and his party appealed in some way to the Italian people. Even if the minuses far outweigh the pluses, consider the domestic policy of the regime. For instance, did the corporate state increase employment while it destroyed unionism? What internal improvements were made? Mussolini's aggressive foreign policy was costly to both the Italians and targets of his grandiose colonizing, but he did play the peacemaker during some of the early crises caused by Hitler.

> **2.**   "Nazi totalitarianism was a different breed from ordinary dictatorship." *Assess the validity* of this statement.

Comments on Question 2

To "determine the truth" of this statement, you have to consider the phrase "different breed." It implies that that the Third Reich was far more encompassing and repressive than the usual military dictatorship. The task is to explain how. How did the Nazis use state-sponsored terrorism to gain and hold power? How did their racist theories lead to genocide? What was the structure of their police state? How did they use propaganda and education to inculcate their program? How was war an integral part of their ideology?

> **3.**   "The Versailles Treaty gave birth to the Nazis; the Great Depression gave them power." *Defend or refute* this statement.

Comments on Question 3

A few crucial questions point the way when answered. How did the Nazis and other rightist extremists grow in membership after Germany's defeat in World War I? What part did the war guilt clause of the treaty play in their propaganda? How did the indemnity payments destabilize the German economy? What was happening to Nazi party membership during the late 1920s and how did the depression affect that trend?

> **4.**   *Explain* how, in order to gain their foreign policy goals during the 1930s, the "have-not" nations used force while the "have" nations refrained from its use.

**Comments on
Question 4**

Who were the "haves"? Britain, France, the United States. The "have-nots"? Germany, Italy, Japan. How did the peace settlements after the First World War make them that way? What acts of aggression did the "have-nots" perpetrate in the name of international justice? What was the response—or lack of it—from the "haves"? Aggression and appeasement is the story here.

> **5.**   *Contrast and compare* German Nazism and Italian fascism.

**Comments on
Question 5**

The similarities are easier to lay out: the means by which Hitler and Mussolini got into office, gained control of the state, and used propaganda, education, and force to subdue internal enemies; the ideology of war for the glorification of the state; the subversion of the institutions of society to serve the state.

The differences are of kind and degree: the Fascists never preached or practiced the poisonous racism that led to genocide; their military never achieved the kind of power that enabled the Nazis to impose their murderous policies all over the continent; their program and ideology was never digested by the Italian people with the relish with which the Germans swallowed Nazism.

Practice Multiple-Choice Questions

(These questions represent the various kinds found on the Advanced Placement Examination in European History.)

1.   Britain failed to recover economically after the First World War for all of the following reasons EXCEPT
    (A)   its merchant fleet had been decimated by German U-boats
    (B)   its Commonwealth trading partners had industrialized considerably during the war
    (C)   other maritime nations had entered the competition for overseas shipping
    (D)   German wartime bombing had devastated its cities
    (E)   its Allies defaulted on war loans

2.   In the first decade and a half after World War I, British foreign policy focused on
    (A)   the "Irish question" and problems in the Middle East
    (B)   Mussolini's overseas expansionism
    (C)   Japanese aggression in mainland Asia
    (D)   the rise of Nazism
    (E)   Communism in Russia

3. The French post-World War I economy was in chaos for all of these reasons EXCEPT
   (A) the tremendous loss of life and property damage inflicted by the war
   (B) the economic policies of Raymond Poincaré
   (C) the Russian default on prewar investments by the French
   (D) the cost of fighting the war
   (E) the failure of the Germans to pay expected reparations

4. The goal of French foreign policy in the interwar years was
   (A) a prevention of the Japanese takeover of French Indochina
   (B) a return to isolation
   (C) the containment of potential German and Russian expansion
   (D) to check aggression by Fascist Italy
   (E) to aid the republican government against Franco's Spanish Fascists

5. In 1925, Germany's democratic Weimar government signed the Locarno Pacts which
   (A) set a ten-year moratorium on naval construction
   (B) guaranteed the territorial integrity of the Chinese Republic
   (C) outlawed war
   (D) recognized the French-Belgium-German boundaries set at Versailles
   (E) allied Germany with Fascist Italy

6. How did the high tariffs set by the United States in 1922 and 1930 affect Europe?
   (A) They undermined the overseas trade
   (B) They limited the ability of the British and French to pay the United States for their war loans
   (C) They soured relations between the United States and its former allies
   (D) They contributed to the Great Depression
   (E) All of the above

7. The United States and Britain came out of the depression largely because of
   (A) social welfare programs of the American New Deal and the British National party
   (B) high tariff barriers to foreign competition
   (C) currency manipulation
   (D) raised taxes and lowered spending
   (E) rearmament for the coming war

8. American foreign policy regarding Europe in the 1930s was primarily directed toward
   - (A) maintaining U.S. neutrality
   - (B) containing the spread of Soviet Communism
   - (C) blocking Fascist aggression
   - (D) guaranteeing the safety of the democracies that had emerged after World War I
   - (E) supporting the Loyalists in the Spanish Civil War

9. Totalitarianism includes all of the following characteristics EXCEPT
   - (A) the state has the right to control the lives of its citizens from cradle to grave
   - (B) total control by the state is essential to society
   - (C) the state has an existence apart from the individuals who comprise it
   - (D) every citizen owes the state absolute obedience unless the government violates individual rights
   - (E) war brings glory and the state must arm for it while the citizen must train for it

10. Which of the following contributed to Mussolini's acquisition of power in Italy in 1922?
    - (A) Italian disillusionment with peace settlements after World War II
    - (B) Severe unemployment in Italy right after the war
    - (C) Peasant unrest in the countryside
    - (D) Communist-inspired strikes in the cities
    - (E) All of the above

11. Despite its totalitarian suppression of political freedom and human rights, fascism appealed to many Italians for all these reasons EXCEPT
    - (A) the improvement of municipal government under centralized control
    - (B) the electrification of rural Italy
    - (C) overseas colonization
    - (D) the Lateran Pact with the Pope, 1929
    - (E) the suppression of the Mafia in Southern Italy

12. In January of 1933, Adolf Hitler assumed the post of Reichschancellor
    - (A) by means of the Munich Beer Hall Putsch
    - (B) by seizing control of the government
    - (C) after his party received a plurality of votes in the democratic elections
    - (D) after he overthrew the Weimar Republic
    - (E) by staging a coup against Paul Hindenburg, president of the republic

13. The Weimar Republic (1919–1933), despite a valiant attempt to introduce democracy to Germany, failed to gain support of the German people mainly because
   (A) the Nazis maintained a wide following throughout the 1920s and 1930s
   (B) Von Hindenburg's presidency was marred by his personal corruption
   (C) monarchists, supporters of the abdicated kaiser, and militarists, humiliated by defeat in World War I, opposed it from the start
   (D) the government was unable to stabilize the economy or maintain law and order
   (E) a conspiracy of Jewish-capitalist-Communist bankers weakened the government

14. Hitler's Nazi program for Germany, as explained in his rambling autobiography *Mein Kampf,* included all of the following EXCEPT
   (A) Germany was defeated in World War I not on the battlefield but rather by traitors and revolutionaries
   (B) Germany was in the process of being destroyed from within by Jews, Communists, and democrats
   (C) the Germans were a master race destined to rule Europe
   (D) Germany must acquire lebensraum (living space) in Western Europe
   (E) "inferior races" must be enslaved or exterminated

15. This is often considered the most dramatic failure of the policy of appeasement before World War II
   (A) when Great Britain and France declared war on Germany after its invasion of Poland
   (B) when the U.S.S.R. and Germany signed the Non-aggression Pact of 1938
   (C) when the United States instituted the *Lend-Lease program*
   (D) when the Austrian chancellor announced the *Anschluss*
   (E) when the prime ministers of Britain and France met Hitler's demands at the Munich conference of 1938

Answers and Answer Explanations

1. D	2. A	3. B	4. C	5. D
6. E	7. E	8. A	9. D	10. E
11. C	12. C	13. C	14. D	15. E

1. (D) Massive bombing of British cities took place during the "Blitz" in the Battle of Britain during World War II. Lighter-than-air Zeppelins did only minimal damage during World War I.

2. (A) The independence of Ireland, the status of Northern Ireland, and issues in the Middle East, such as the Palestine Question, were major concerns.

3. (B) Poincaré's policies helped reform and stabilize the economy.

4. (C)   The traditional enemy, Germany, was an inevitable threat given the Treaty of Versailles, inequities; Russia under Communism was a renewed threat.

5. (D)   Germany signed the Locarno pacts, accepting the boundary settlements made at Versailles, in an attempt to improve its international relations.

6. (E)   all of the above.

7. (E)   War brings full employment.

8. (A)   The depression aggravated the isolationist policies that World War I had encouraged.

9. (D)   Individual rights do not exist in a totalitarian state; there is no right of revolution.

10. (E)   The Italian people wanted a strong man to solve what constitutional government seemed unable to.

11. (C)   Mussolini's ill-fated attempts to recapture the glories of ancient Rome led to his overseas debacles in Libya, Albania, Ethiopia, and Greece, and it drew Italy into World War II.

12. (C)   Von Hindenburg appointed Hitler after the Nazis won a plurality of votes in the 1932 elections and a coalition government had fallen. The Beer Hall Putsch took place in 1923; the Weimar Republic was never overthrown since Hitler took power legally.

13. (C)   The Weimar government restored order and economic stability from 1924–1929, therefore C is the best answer since these influential "interest groups" opposed the Republic from the start.

14. (D)   Eastern Europe, especially the vast spaces of the U.S.S.R., was the draw; Western Europe was already among the most densely populated areas on earth.

15. (E)   Neville Chamberlain's pathetic promise of "peace in our time" after Munich epitomized appeasement of the aggressors.

CHAPTER 13 World War II and Its Aftermath (1939–1953)

Overview

At least 55 million people perished in World War II, and for the first time in history the majority of the casualities were noncombatants. Saturation bombing of enemy cities, widespread starvation caused by war damage and displacement of people, and state-sponsored murder to exterminate a people (*genocide*) contributed to the terrible losses.

The war was fought on every continent but the Americas; it was global in scale; it was made up of separate conflicts, each with an identifiable beginning and end; it was a series of strategic improvisations rather than the result of carefully laid plans; it began at various times, as early as 1931 for the Manchurians and Japanese, as late as 1941 for the Russians and Americans.

It began over the issues never resolved after World War I: the failure of the Versailles Treaty to settle the problems of nationalistic yearnings for autonomy, of economic security, of blame for the First World War. The "have-not" nations—Germany, Italy, and Japan—under the rule of repressive dictatorships sought to redress what they saw as the inequities of the peace settlements after World War I. The "have" nations—the United States, France, and England—were absorbed in dealing with economic depression and with avoiding another costly war. When the Western democracies' policy of appeasement failed to stop the aggressions of the Axis powers, war resulted. It was officially declared in Europe in September 1939, after Germany's invasion of Poland. It ended with the unconditional surrender of Nazi Germany to the Russians, British, Americans, and French in May 1945, and with the surrender of Japan in September 1945.

It not only changed the balance of power in Europe with an international "balance of terror" created by nuclear weapons, but it gave rise to a nonmilitary conflict between the world's two superpowers, the Cold War.

Triumph of the Axis Powers (1939–1942)

Although Germany, Italy, and Japan were often referred to as Fascists, their dictatorships were significantly different. The German Nazis and to a lesser degree the Italian Fascists imposed totalitarian systems upon their people. The Japanese, whose constitutional government was loyal to the emperor—a "living god," they believed—had a military dictatorship imposed in the 1930s. The term "Axis" came from the *Rome, Berlin, Tokyo Axis*, a pledge of mutual cooperation between the three nations that led to virtually no combined military ventures between the two European powers and Japan.

1939

September 1: Hitler invaded Poland, ostensibly to get back the part of East Prussia that the Versailles Treaty had ceded to Poland for access to the Baltic Sea, the *Polish Corridor*.

September 3: England and France declared war against Germany to honor their treaty with Poland.

October: Poland fell, occupied by the Germans in the West and the Russians in the East as part of the 1938 *Nonaggression Pact* between the two dictatorships. Russia also annexed the Baltic states of *Latvia, Lithuania,* and *Estonia,* which had been granted autonomy by the Versailles Treaty. The Nazi *Gestapo* (secret police) began a systematic roundup and slaughter of Polish military officers, intellectuals, Jews, and political foes.

November: The *Russo-Finnish War* began when the Red Army invaded Finland over disputed borders. Although the superior numbers of the Russian forces eventually prevailed, the Finns' valiant resistance and the Russians' painfully slow victory convinced Hitler that the Russian army was weak.

1940

The time period from the fall of Poland to April 1940 was called the *Phony War* (sitzkrieg) because the French sat behind their supposedly impregnable *Maginot Line*, a series of fortresses on the German border, the *British Expeditionary Force* in France made no moves, and the Germans prepared secretly for a spring offensive.

April: In a matter of days, Nazi forces overran and occupied Denmark and Norway.

May–June: After seizing Holland, the *Wehrmacht* (German Army) cut through neutral Belgium and Luxembourg to outflank the Maginot Line. Within six weeks, the Nazi tactics of *blitzkreig* ("lightning war" using swift armored columns and air support in place of slow-moving heavy artillery) caused France to fall. The world was shocked because four years of trench warfare in World War I had failed to move the initial lines of battle more than a few miles. Isolated and surrounded, the 250,000 man British Expeditionary Force was evacuated from Dunkirk in Belgium to England along with about 100,000 *Free French* fighters but without most of its heavy equipment.

June 10: Mussolini invaded Southern France, an invasion that was ineffectual militarily but symbolic of Nazi-Fascist solidarity.

June 22: France surrendered. Germany occupied the north and west, and here, as in all the Nazi-occupied lands, terror and repression reigned. A puppet government, under World War I French *Marshal Philippe Petain*, controlled the south and the North African possessions.

August: The *Battle of Britain*, an air war for supremacy of the skies over England, began. The *Luftwaffe* (German Air Force) vainly attempted to knock out the *Royal Air Force* (RAF) for months in order to launch an invasion of England across the English Channel. The industrial cities of Southern England, including massive London, were subjected to nightly bombings called "the Blitz."

1941   *March–May:* Attacking from Egypt, British forces drove deep into *Libya,* the Italian possession in North Africa.

The Germans invaded *Greece* and *Yugoslavia.*

The British occupied *Iran, Iraq, and Syria.*

June–December: The Germans invaded the U.S.S.R. with a force of well over 2 million men who attacked in three directions: north toward Leningrad, east toward Moscow, and south toward the oil fields of the Caucasus. Although they occupied most of the Western Soviet Union and reached the outskirts of Moscow and Leningrad, the Germans were halted by *"General Winter,"* the harsh climatic conditions.

The United States extended *Lend-Lease* (ships for bases) to Britain becoming the *"arsenal of democracy."* (In World War II, the United States' war production would be greater than that of all the other belligerents combined.)

President Franklin Delano Roosevelt and *Prime Minister Winston Churchill,* who had replaced Neville Chamberlain during the Battle for France, signed the *Atlantic Charter* in August. It was an idealistic statement, similar to Wilson's Fourteen Points, of the war aims of the Allies. It called for freedom from want and tyranny, for freedom of religion and thought, for free trade and national sovereignty.

December 7: Japanese carrier-borne aircraft attacked the U.S. Pacific Fleet based at Pearl Harbor in Hawaii. Although it was done before an official proclamation of war, the United States and Japan had confronted each other over Japan's brutal invasion and occupation of China and over its expansion into the Southeast Asian colonies of France and Holland (Indochina and Indonesia).

December 8: The United States declared war on Japan.

December 11: Germany and Italy declared war on the United States. All the major powers on earth were now in the conflict. It was indeed a world war.

1942   By June, the Axis powers in Europe controlled virtually the entire continent from the Atlantic in the west to the gates of Moscow in the east, from Scandanavia in the north to a good part of North Africa in the south. The Nazis set up extermination camps in Poland, Austria, and Germany, and they transported millions of Jews, other minorities, Soviet prisoners of war, and political enemies there for systematic murder. Auschwitz-Birkenau was the most infamous of these new extermination camps. Well over 12 million people were slaughtered in accord with Nazi racist doctrine; 6 million of those were European Jews (about 60 percent of the prewar Jewish population). The Asian Axis partner, Japan, had seized the cities of coastal China, Indochina from the French, Indonesia from the Dutch, Malaya and Burma from the British, and the Philippines from the United States.

General *Erwin Rommel,* the Desert Fox, had managed to push the British in North Africa deep into Egypt, and the Suez Canal, lifeline of the British Empire, was threatened.

The Tide of War Turns (mid-1942–1943)

June 1942: Rommel's *Afrika Corps,* the elite mechanized force that spearheaded the Axis forces in this theater of war, was stopped at El Alamein in Egypt by British Forces under General Montgomery.

American aircraft carriers won a stunning victory against a superior Japanese naval force at the *Battle of Midway*.

August 7, 1942: U.S. Marines launched the first American offensive operation of the war by invading *Guadalcanal* in the Solomons Islands in the South Pacific. It was the start of the *island-hopping* campaign that culminated in the invasion, in 1945, of *Okinawa*, an island at the fringe of the Japanese home islands.

Summer to winter 1942: The Russia city of *Stalingrad*, controlling the lower Volga River, stood against German invaders and the fierce battle there marked the end of Nazi advances in the Soviet Union.

November 1942: A joint Anglo-American force landed on the shores of Axis-held territory in *North Africa*.

1943

The Axis was cleared from North Africa.

The Russians began the advance that would lead them ultimately into Germany itself. (About 80 percent of German casualties in World War II were inflicted by the Soviets. Between 25 and 30 million Russians died during the war.)

Allied war leaders Roosevelt, Churchill, and representatives of Stalin met at *Casablanca* in North Africa and agreed to demand *unconditional surrender* of the Axis powers.

Allied Victory (1943–1945)

1943

American, British, and Canadian forces invaded the island of Sicily off the boot of Italy. Mussolini was overthrown, and the Allies landed in Italy proper and fought against determined German resistance.

At the *Teheran Conference* the Big Three—Roosevelt, Churchill, and Stalin—agreed that after the war was won, Germany would be occupied by the Allied powers and demilitarized.

1944

The *D-Day Invasion* of the French coast at *Normandy* marked the beginning of the end of Nazi domination of the continent. Paris was liberated by August. The last German offensive took place at the *Battle of the Bulge* in Belgium during December. From that point on, the Germans were in retreat on all fronts.

1945

January–March: The Red Army smashed into East Prussia, Hungary, and Czechoslovakia while the Americans crossed the Rhine River.

April–May: Hitler committed suicide; encircled Berlin was seized by the Russians; Germany surrendered, unconditionally, on May 8.

August 6: The United States dropped the *first atomic bomb* on the Japanese city of *Hiroshima*. (70,000 people died immediately; tens of thousands suffered aftereffects.)

August 9: A second atomic bomb fell on the city of *Nagasaki*, and Japan surrendered.

September: Japan signed an official surrender and agreed to occupation by U.S. forces. Under the supervision of *General Douglas MacArthur*, commander of Allied forces in the Pacific theater, the emperor denied his own divinity, an antiwar constitution was imposed, wartime destruction was repaired, technical and financial assistance was given for further industrialization and modernization, and a democratic government was set up.

Aftermath of the War

Crucial Conferences for Postwar Europe

The *Yalta Conference*, between the Big Three—Roosevelt, Churchill, and Stalin—in February of 1945, drew up a plan for the postwar settlement in Europe. Its main provisions:

> Eastern Europe—Bulgaria, Czechoslovakia, Hungary, Poland, and Romania—would be set up with coalition governments of Communists and non-Communists until free elections could be held.

> Germany would be partitioned into four zones of occupation—American, British, French, Russian.

> Russia would enter the war against Japan in return for territories in Asia and islands north of Japan.

> A *United Nations* was set up as a successor to the defunct League of Nations, with a *General Assembly* to represent all member nations in deliberations and a *Security Council* of fifteen members dominated by five permanent members, the Great Powers—the United States, the U.S.S.R., Britain, France, and China—each of which would have veto rights over any proposal for involving the organization in preserving international peace.

The *Potsdam Conference*, July 1945, was attended by Churchill, Stalin, and Harry S. Truman, the latter who had become president after Roosevelt's sudden death in April. Already cracks showed in the alliance between the Western democracies and Communist Russia when Truman and Churchill criticized Stalin for not allowing free elections in Soviet-occupied Eastern Europe.

The Conflict for Control of Europe

At the end of World War II, only two great powers remained with the resources, land mass, population, industrial capacity, and military strength to affect world events. The United States, virtually untouched by the war, and the U.S.S.R., devastated but industrially and militarily powerful, became *superpowers*. Since the 17th century, there had been powerful single nations in Europe—Spain, France, England, Germany—but six or seven other great states had managed, through alliances, to maintain a balance of power. Soon after the war, two competing blocs would emerge: the *Soviet Bloc* with its *satellites* of puppet governments in Eastern and Central Europe and the *Western Bloc* or "Free World" made up, primarily, of the democracies. With the collapse of the colonial empires (see Chapter 9, "Imperialism"), a third bloc would emerge: the *Third World*, consisting of newly independent nations.

In a speech in Fulton, Missouri, in 1946, former prime minister Winston Churchill described Stalin's expansion of Communist totalitarianism as an *Iron Curtain* separating the captive peoples of Eastern and Central Europe from the rest of the world. A competition began between the *superpowers* to win Europe, its cities in ruins, its population decimated and displaced, but still a great industrial and population center of the world.

The *Cold War* had begun.

Sample Essay Question

The sample thematic essay question and the practice essays in this chapter are types found in the Advanced Placement Examination in European History, and they require a knowledge of causes, effects, personalities, ideas, and events.

Sample Question

> *Explain* why for the Allies—Britain, the United States, and the U.S.S.R.—1942 was the bleakest year of the war.

Comments on the Sample Question

Follow the "Simple Procedures" for writing an essay. (See page 24.)

First, *What does the question want to know?* In this context, "explain" means "give the reasons for" and "detail," the emphasis on the latter. This is primarily an informational essay that requires that you write on the events of the war during 1942, providing an accounting of the reverses for the Allied cause.

Second, *What do you know about it?* Be sure to include all theaters of war: the North Atlantic, Russia, North Africa, Asia, and the Pacific. Make reference to previous conquests by the Axis Powers.

Third, *How would you put it into words?* In this case, *explain* means primarily to detail the events that marked a turning point for Britain, the United States, and the U.S.S.R.

Sample Answer

Through most of 1942, the Western Allies—Britain and the United States—and the Soviet Union saw defeat after defeat on land, sea, and in the air at the hands of the Axis powers—Germany, Japan, and Italy. That year marked the highwater mark of Axis conquests, and to the people and even the strategists in the Allied countries, the seeming invincibility of the enemy prevented any balanced assessment of the outcome of the global war that was to last through most of 1945 and claim the lives of 55 million people.

By early summer of 1940, the German war machine had overrun Western Europe with the blitzkrieg, an innovative tactical use of fast armored divisions and close air support. France, considered to have the mightiest land army on earth, had been defeated in six weeks. Britain stood alone against the threat of invasion as it had during the heyday of Napoleon. The United States remained uncomfortably neutral behind its ocean barriers, and the Soviet Union watched nervously under the false security of its Nonaggression Pact with Germany. Italy had already occupied considerable territory in North Africa, its captive colony of Libya menacing British Egypt and the vital Suez Canal. Japan had seized the coast of China and was pushing inland; after the fall of France, it occupied Indochina.

A year later, in June of 1941, the Germans, not satisfied with the conquest of nearly the entire continent of Europe—from Scandinavia in the north to Greece and the Balkans in the south, from France and the Low countries in the west to central Poland in the east—invaded the Soviet Union. By December of 1941, as the Japanese destroyed the U.S. Pacific Fleet at Pearl Harbor in the Hawaiian Islands, the Wehrmacht had reached the gates of Moscow, had surrounded Leningrad in the north, and were on the move south toward the oil fields of the Caucasus.

The first half of 1942 saw continued Axis triumphs. The Japanese overran Western colonies in the Pacific: the Dutch East Indies (Indonesia), the U.S. possession of the Philippine Islands, and British territories in Asia, Malaya, Burma, Hong Kong, and Singapore. They were within striking distance of Australia. The Germans and Italians moved across North Africa and threatened the British held Suez Canal. The Germans continued their offensives in the vastness of the Soviet Union while their U-boats sank convoy ships sending supplies across the North Atlantic from the "arsenal of democracy," the United States, to beleaguered Britain and Russia. Doomsayers predicted a linkup between the Germans in Soviet Central Asia and the Japanese through India.

It was a bleak year for the enemies of Nazism, fascism, and Japanese militarism. The Doolittle Raid of B-52 medium bombers launched from the decks of the aircraft carrier *Hornet* to bomb Tokyo and other Japanese cities raised America's morale in April of 1942. The stubborn resistance of the Russian armies made some realize that the Wehrmacht would be bled to death in the vast spaces of Russia. But hope for victory was still scarce among the Allies.

The tide of the war began to turn with the U.S. naval victory in the Battle of Midway in June of 1942 and with the U.S. Marine invasion of Guadalcanal in the Solomons in August. With the British and American invasion of North Africa in November and the heroic stand of the Russians at Stalingrad through the winter of 1942 to 1943, the momentum had shifted from the Axis to the Allied cause.

Evaluate the Sample Answer

1. Did it have a clear introductory statement?
2. Did it reflect an understanding of the terms and the intent of the question?
3. Did it "explain" why 1942 was a "bleak year" for Britain, the United States, *and* the U.S.S.R.?
4. Were the facts used in support accurate, sufficient, relevant?
5. What would you have added?
6. Was the essay long enough, well organized, interesting?
7. Did the concluding paragraph sum up adequately?

Rater's Comments on the Sample Answer

5—Extremely well qualified

This clearly written, factually rich essay gave the "reasons for" and thoroughly "detailed" why 1942 was "a bleak year" for the Allied cause. It considered the various theaters of war affecting each of the Allies; it provided relevant background with the Axis victories in 1940 and 1941. Although the essay was necessarily general in nature, it provided interesting specifics.

One suggested improvement would be to explain how the Blitz, or bombing of English cities, affected morale, how America's "two-ocean war" was perceived by the public and the strategists, or how the Russian scorched-earth policy caused severe hardships for the Soviet people.

Practice Essay Questions

The questions that follow are samples of the various types that appear on the Advanced Placement Examination in European History. (See pages 17–18 for a detailed explanation.)

---

1. "The Berlin-Rome-Tokyo Axis was more an ideological than an actual alliance." *Assess the validity* of this statement.

Comments on Question 1

To "determine the truth" of this statement, you have to consider the ways in which the Axis partners aided each other's war efforts. Did the Italians and the Germans actually coordinate battlefield strategy? Recall Mussolini's "stabbing France in the back" in 1940; the North African campaign; the "Balkans Rescue"; the invasion of Sicily. Did the European Axis partners ever coordinate battle plans, send or receive war materials, plan overall strategy with the Japanese? How were they united in aims, ideology, political methods?

---

2. *To what extent and in what ways* did the United States, the U.S.S.R., and Britain coordinate war aims and strategies?

Comments on Question 2

"How and how much" is the issue here. In dealing with Russian and Western cooperation, consider the Big Three conferences: Teheran, Yalta, Potsdam (after the death of Roosevelt); the second-front controversy; the material aid from the United States to Russia.

The American-British alliance is more tangible: Lend-Lease; the Atlantic Charter; North Africa, Sicily, Italy, Normandy, the bombing and invasion of Germany; the Pacific War.

---

3. The Allied decision to demand "unconditional surrender" of the Axis powers lengthened the war needlessly." *Defend or refute* this statement.

Comments on Question 3

This has been an issue much argued, "a hypothesis contrary to fact." Would the war have ended sooner if the Allies had negotiated with the Axis governments or even with antigovernment military factions? In framing your answer, consider that despite the saturation bombing of Germany's cities, the Nazis maintained an iron grip until the end; despite assassination attempts, Hitler ruled until his suicide when the Russians were at the gates of Berlin; despite firebombing and the dropping of the first A-bomb, the Japanese refused to surrender.

> 4.   *Contrast and compare* the results of the war on both the United States and the U.S.S.R.

**Comments on
Question 4**

"Show differences": What was the destruction to the homelands of each? What political, social, or economic changes took place for each? What were the human losses? What were the war gains?

"Examine similarities": They were the only two powers—superpowers—with the strength left to influence European and world events; they had established parallel spheres of influence; they had simultaneously solidified their competing ideologies and launched the Cold War.

This is an abstract question that requires crisp organization and thoughtful presentation.

> 5.   *Analyze* the way the wartime cooperation of the United States and the Soviet Union degenerated, within a few years after the end of the war, into the Cold War.

**Comments on
Question 5**

The wartime alliance between the West and the Soviet Union was the cooperation of competing systems in order to defeat a common enemy. Strains showed early in the Russian push for a second front, manifested themselves in the tensions at Yalta and at Potsdam in the Russian refusal to allow free elections in Russian-occupied Eastern Europe. The geographic expansion of Communism because of the war frightened the West. The presence of massive U.S. forces in Europe frightened the Soviets.

Practice Multiple-Choice Questions

(These represent the types of questions that appear on the Advanced Placement Examination in European History.)

1.   The shaded area of the map on the following page shows
     (A)   the belligerent nations at the start of World War II in Europe
     (B)   the furthest extent of Axis conquest in Europe and Africa
     (C)   the Nazi Empire
     (D)   the gains of the Red Army at the end of World War II
     (E)   the Axis-occupied territory right before the D-Day Normandy invasion

2.   Refer to the map on the following page to determine what year it represents.
     (A)   before 1939   (D)   1942
     (B)   1939   (E)   1944
     (C)   1940

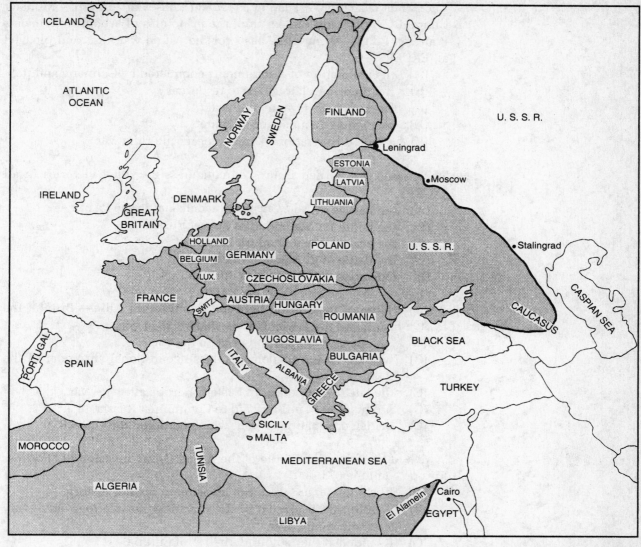

ICELAND

ATLANTIC
OCEAN

NORWAY   SWEDEN   FINLAND

U. S. S. R.

Leningrad

IRELAND

DENMARK

ESTONIA

LATVIA

Moscow

GREAT
BRITAIN

LITHUANIA

HOLLAND

BELGIUM   GERMANY   POLAND   U. S. S. R.   Stalingrad

LUX.

CZECHOSLOVAKIA

FRANCE   AUSTRIA   HUNGARY

SWITZ.

CASPIAN SEA

CAUCASUS

ROUMANIA

YUGOSLAVIA   BLACK SEA

ITALY   BULGARIA

ALBANIA

GREECE   TURKEY

PORTUGAL

SPAIN

SICILY

MALTA

MOROCCO

TUNISIA

MEDITERRANEAN SEA

Cairo

ALGERIA

El Alamein   EGYPT

LIBYA

3. The period of relative military inaction in Europe between the fall of
    Poland and the fall of France is called
    (A)   the Russo-Finnish War
    (B)   the Vichy period
    (C)   the Battle of Britain
    (D)   the Blitzkrieg
    (E)   the Sitzkrieg

4. Choose the correct chronological order.
    I.   United States enters World War II.
    II.   The Battle of Britain rages.
    III. The U.S.S.R. is invaded by the Nazis.
    IV.   The Nazis conquer Western Europe.
    (A)   II, IV, I, III
    (B)   I, II, IV, III
    (C)   III, II, I, IV
    (D)   IV, II, III, I
    (E)   IV, III, II, I

5. The Atlantic Charter—issued by President Roosevelt and Prime Minister Churchill in 1941 and drawn from the principles of Woodrow Wilson's Fourteen Points—formed the basis for the Allied war aims and pledged all EXCEPT

   (A) the restoration of governments conquered by Germany and Italy
   (B) free trade and fair access to resources
   (C) freedom from tyranny and want
   (D) freedom of thought and religion
   (E) a U.N. organization to ensure peace after the war

6. The tide of war turned from Axis conquests to Allied victories in all EXCEPT

   (A) the Battles of Midway and Guadalcanal in the Pacific
   (B) the Battle for Stalingrad in Soviet Russia
   (C) the evacuation at Dunkirk in Europe
   (D) the Battle of El Alamein in Egypt
   (E) Operation Torch in North Africa

7. A major issue of contention between the Western Allies—Britain, the United States, and the Soviet Union—before 1944 was

   (A) the opening of a second front in Europe
   (B) whether or not to demand the unconditional surrender of the Axis
   (C) the fate of democracy in Eastern Europe after the war
   (D) promised U.S. military aid to Communist Russia
   (E) British occupation of Iran, which bordered the U.S.S.R.

8. Which of the following is true of the Allied D-Day invasion of "Fortress Europe" on June 6, 1944?

   (A) It was the largest seaborne invasion in human history.
   (B) It inflicted 50 percent of the casualties the German Army suffered during the war.
   (C) It landed at the "soft underbelly" of Europe.
   (D) After the landing the Germans were unable to launch another major offensive during the course of the war.
   (E) It was a joint operation of American, British, and Russian forces.

9. The agreements of Roosevelt, Stalin, and Churchill at Yalta in 1945 are controversial for all of the following reasons EXCEPT

   (A) they gave Stalin a free hand in dominating the liberated states of Eastern Europe
   (B) they gave the Russians control of a sizable segment of Germany
   (C) they lacked provision for the de-Nazification of Germany
   (D) they gave the U.S.S.R. Japanese territories in Asia
   (E) they gave the U.S.S.R. Polish territory

10. During World War II, most of the damage to cities in Western Germany was caused by
     (A) seige cannons of the Russian army
     (B) search-and-destroy tactics of the Americans
     (C) the scorched-earth policy of the retreating Nazis
     (D) sabotage by anti-Nazi Germans
     (E) saturation bombing by American and British air forces

11. The movement of peoples for the period from 1939 to 1950 was due most likely to
     (A) voluntary immigration
     (B) forced deportation by the Nazis
     (C) deportation and resettlement because of war and its aftermath
     (D) policies of the United Nations
     (E) Stalinist policies

12. In 1945, the war left only these nations with the economic and military strength to significantly influence world affairs
     (A) United States, U.S.S.R., Great Britain, France, China
     (B) United States, U.S.S.R., Great Britain, China
     (C) United States, U.S.S.R., Great Britain, France
     (D) United States, U.S.S.R., Great Britain
     (E) United States, U.S.S.R.

13. Which was NOT a feature of the Cold War between the United States and the U.S.S.R.?
     (A) A series of confrontations short of direct military conflict
     (B) A competition of productivity between differing economic systems
     (C) A number of direct and open military clashes between U.S. and Soviet forces
     (D) An ideological conflict that involved espionage, propaganda, and military and economic support for erstwhile Allies
     (E) A division into blocs of politically and ideologically aligned nations

14. Soviet and Western wartime cooperation had already degenerated into serious tensions at the Potsdam Conference in July 1945 because
     (A) Harry S. Truman, who had succeeded to the presidency after the death of Roosevelt in April, plainly expressed his dislike of Stalin
     (B) Winston Churchill had strained relations with his claims of Soviet empire building in Eastern Europe
     (C) the Soviets had reneged on their promise to enter the war against Japan
     (D) Stalin had reneged on his promise to allow free elections in Soviet-occupied Eastern Europe
     (E) the U.S. A-bomb attacks on Japan had intimidated the Soviets

15. The phrase "iron curtain," used by Winston Churchill in his 1946 speech at Fulton, Missouri, refers to
    - (A) the security measures employed by Stalin's bodyguards
    - (B) the Berlin Wall
    - (C) Stalin's policy of holding firm in negotiations with the West
    - (D) the Kremlin's veil of secrecy
    - (E) Soviet domination of Eastern Europe

Answers and Answer Explanations

1. B	**2.** D	**3.** E	**4.** D	**5.** E
6. C	**7.** A	**8.** A	**9.** C	**10.** E
11. C	**12.** E	**13.** C	**14.** D	**15.** E

1. (B) The Mediterranean was an Italian lake; Western Europe was in Hitler's hands; the Nazis had reached the suburbs of Moscow.

2. (D) By late 1942, the tide of war was turning in favor of the Allies.

3. (E) This lull is often called the Phony War.

4. (D) A chronology identification. Know it or leave it.

5. (E) It was not part of the Atlantic Charter but was proposed during the wartime Big Power conferences.

6. (C) A tactical victory, it was still a retreat.

7. (A) The Russians, under attack by the Germans, wanted the pressure taken off.

8. (A) It was the largest seaborne invasion; over a million troops were landed within the first week or so. The largest land invasion force was the 2 million plus Nazi Operation Barbarossa, the invasion of the U.S.S.R. in June 1941.

9. (C) De-Nazification was carried out by all four of the occupying powers. The United States, especially, was rigorous in its pursuits of Nazi war criminals and in its reconstruction of the political and social institutions of Nazism.

10. (E) The bombing of these cities was indiscriminate in its choice of targets—military, industrial, civilian. The theory was that the enemy's will and capacity to make war would be destroyed. By early 1945, the Germans were producing more in the occupied countries than they had before the bombing had started, and there is evidence that bombing strengthened German resolve and German willingness to swallow the Nazi line.

11. (C) Government policies of deportation and resettlement carried out primarily by the Nazis and Soviets as well as flight from war caused a radical transformation in Central and Eastern Europe's population distribution.

12. (E) That is how they became superpowers.

13. (C) There was no direct war between the United States and the U.S.S.R.

14. (D) Truman and Churchill berated him for this, but could do little.

15. (E) The Soviet Empire was forming.

14 Postwar Europe: Recovery, Communism, and Cold War (1945–1970)

Overview

The destruction of Europe after World War II was far more extensive than that at the end of the First World War. The technology and tactics of the First World War had limited the damage to specific regions of Europe: Flanders, which consisted of Northeastern France and parts of Belgium, Poland and sections of European Russia, some provinces of Northern Italy and Southern Austria; some areas of the Balkans.

During the Second World War, the mass bombing of industrial and population centers severely damaged virtually all the cities of the European belligerents and it left Germany in ruins. The German destruction and the scorched-earth policy of the Soviets leveled tens of thousands of villages, towns, and cities in the Western Soviet Union. Ruined transport systems, factories, and housing shattered the economies of Western and Eastern Europe.

The economic recovery of Western Europe was so amazing, it was referred to as "the miracle." Within a decade, productivity had reached prewar levels; within two, unparalleled prosperity prevailed. Germany, defeated, demoralized, and divided, had been the key to recovery. The United States infused massive aid through the Marshall Plan to rebuild not only its former Allies but also its former enemies—Germany and Italy. By the end of the 1950s, Western Europe had made the first moves toward economic and, perhaps, political union. The United States also aided Japan and set up a viable democratic government.

The rebuilding of the U.S.S.R. was no less spectacular. Under Stalin's Five-Year Plans, most of the war damage had been repaired within a decade. A vastly expanded Soviet Empire, established by the successes of the Red Army against the Nazis, included most of the countries of Eastern Europe, which became satellites of the brutally repressive Stalinist Soviet Union. After the death of Stalin in 1953, new leaders redefined the role of Soviet Communism but kept an iron grip on the U.S.S.R. and Eastern Europe.

The emergence of the United States and the U.S.S.R. as superpowers at the end of the war created a new balance of power in Europe and in the world. Europe quickly became divided into the Western and Communist blocs, the West dedicated to the containment of Soviet expansionism, the Communists intent on both spreading their philosophy and defending their gains against the "capitalist conspiracy." The Cold War—the ideological, economic, and, at times, military rivalry between the two blocs—was all the more dangerous for the development of nuclear weapons. The peaks of tension, during which the superpower confrontations almost led to war or even nuclear holocaust, alternated with "thaws" until a policy of "peaceful coexistence" emerged.

Western European Recovery (1945–1957)

1945   Since Germany's *Ruhr Basin* was the industrial center of a devastated Europe, the Western Allies decided that Germany would have to be rebuilt. The Soviets had hoped to use German reparations for reconstruction of their own massive war damage, and the *Morgenthau Plan* had been developed by the U.S. secretary of the treasury to transform Germany back into an exclusively agricultural society. Led by the Americans, the British and French agreed that in order for Western Europe to recover, Germany would have to be rebuilt.

1946   Joint administration of the *four occupation zones* broke down. The American, British, and French sectors would eventually became West Germany; the Russian sector, East Germany.

1947   Agitation by Communist parties in France and Italy worsened relations between the democracies and the Soviet Union.

1948   The Czech Communists seized power in Prague, seat of the government.
     The Marshall Plan—developed by Secretary of State and former military chief of staff *George Marshall*—was put into operation. Billions of dollars in grants went to Western Europe and Germany to rebuild housing, transportation systems, and industrial plants.

1949   The United States and eleven other nations formed the *North Atlantic Treaty Organization* (NATO) to rearm non-Communist Europe and safeguard it against invasion. Soon after, West Germany (the *Federal Republic of Germany*), Greece, and Turkey joined. Eventually Germany was encouraged to organize a national army under NATO command.

1950   Productivity in those countries that were aided had exceeded prewar rates, and the United States urged the Europeans to develop a European free-trade zone similar to that among the various American states. The Marshall Plan combined self-interest—Communism in Europe would be contained and markets for U.S. goods opened—with altruism.

1952   Under the French-sponsored *Schuman and Monnet Plan*, six industrial countries on the continent—Belgium, France, Holland, Italy, Luxembourg, and West Germany—formed the *European Coal and Steel Community* to pool their resources.

1955   The U.S.S.R. formed military alliances—the *Warsaw Pact*—with its satellites in Eastern Europe to counter NATO.

1957   The *European Economic Community*, the *Common Market*, was created by the same six nations that formed the European Coal and Steel Community. It aimed at an end to internal tariffs and the free exchange of money and workers between members. By 1968, its plan would be in full effect. By 1973, Britain, previously denied membership by France, joined as a full partner along with Ireland and Denmark.

Communism: The Soviet Union and Its Satellites (1945–1968)

1945

Backed by the Red Army, local Communist parties in Eastern Europe—Bulgaria, Czechoslovakia, Poland, and Romania—took over the coalition governments and fell into the Soviet orbit. East Germany, under occupation, also became a satellite. *Albania* and *Yugoslavia,* under Communist party rule, managed to maintain independence from Moscow since they had not been liberated from the Nazis by Soviet troops.

1945–1953

Communist governments in the satellite nations carried out land distribution reforms and nationalization of industry. Forced *collectivization* of agriculture was only moderately successful. Soviet-type five-year plans helped reconstruction and built up heavy industry at the expense of consumer goods. Police state methods were used—domestic spying, arbitrary imprisonment, censorship, torture—to silence opposition parties and to remove the influence of the Roman Catholic Church.

Repression was tightened to the breaking point in the U.S.S.R. itself during the last years of Stalin. His achievements—industrialization of Europe's backward giant, victory in the *Great Patriotic War* against the Nazis, postwar reconstruction accomplished in a decade, and the spread of a Soviet Communist empire to Eastern Europe—had to be measured against the brutal repression he imposed on the Russian people. Over the course of his totalitarian regime he was responsible for the slaughter of perhaps 30 million of his citizens, for denying basic civil rights, for establishing forced labor camps (gulags), for repressing any and every form of free expression.

1953

Stalin died, and there was a power struggle in the Soviet Union. The party leadership executed *Lavrenti Beria*, head of the secret police, to prevent a coup, and it set up a figurehead premier.

Riots against Soviet domination broke out in East Berlin, a precursor of greater resistance from the satellites.

1956

Nikita S. Khrushchev, a former deputy of Stalin and by 1954 head of the Soviet Communist party, made a speech to the Central Committee on the *crimes of Stalin*. Stalin, he said, had built a *cult of personality*, created terror among citizens and party leaders alike, and had even been responsible for the dismal failure of Soviet troops to stop the initial advances of the Nazi invaders in 1941.

De-Stalinization encouraged resistance in the satellites; *revolts* broke out *in Poland and Hungary.* In Poland, *Wladysaw Gomulka* managed to win concessions from Soviet leaders and to liberalize the government. In Hungary, armed revolt in Budapest and other cities threatened the existence of the Communist regime, and the Soviets brutally crushed all resistance.

1957   The launching of the first artificial earth satellite, *Sputnik,* pointed out the considerable technological achievements of the Soviets. In 1949, they had tested *their first atomic bomb*; in 1953, they had developed their first *hydrogen bomb.* Their work on rocketry, aided by German scientists captured after the war, enabled them to eventually develop *intercontinental missiles* capable of striking the United States.

1964   Khrushchev was ousted. *Centralized economic planning (Gosplan)* had developed the five-year plans that reconstructed the U.S.S.R. after World War II and had raised the Soviet gross national product from 30 percent of the American in 1950 to about 50 percent in the mid-1960s. Agriculture performed badly, though, partly because of the failure of collectivized farms to provide incentives for production and partly because of bad decisions by Khrushchev. Party rivals resented his personal power, and they found an excuse to oust him.

1968   In August, Soviet leaders sent a massive military force to end the *liberalization of Czechoslovakia*, a threat to both the Warsaw Pact and Soviet domination. The *Brezhnev Doctrine,* formulated by the head of the Soviet Communist party and future premier, stated that the *U.S.S.R. had the right to intervene* in the internal affairs of any satellite nation if Communism was threatened. This doctrine and the intervention in Czechoslovakia ended Soviet leadership of the Communist world and its role as a model for Communist governments.

Cold War

The *Cold War* was the economic, cultural, ideological, political, diplomatic, and, under certain circumstances, military struggle between the Western and Communist blocs. It took place, in varying degrees of severity, over decades after the end of World War II. The two superpowers that led the opposing blocs—the United States and the U.S.S.R.—allocated great portions of their military might toward defeating each other in a projected war but never did directly confront each other militarily.

The initial phase of the Cold War involved a struggle for the control of war-devastated Europe. By the late 1940s, U.S. aid had shored up the exhausted democracies of Western Europe against Soviet encroachments, and the Red Army had installed Communist governments in Eastern Europe under Moscow's domination.

The next phase involved the containment of Communism by the West in the Third World, those regions that had emerged from colonialism after World War II. Wars involving the European democracies or the United States against Marxist nationalists broke out in Asia, Africa, and Latin America. Foreign aid and regional alliances, primarily provided and engineered by the United States, countered the influence of Moscow. A nuclear arms race created a "balance of terror" between the two superpowers while cracks in their systems of alliances aggravated the overall conflict. The role of the United Nations, however controversial, expanded as more newly independent nations joined and the superpowers realized the limitations of their might.

With the collapse of the Soviet Union in the 1990s, the Cold War is said to have ended. The "new world order" has yet to emerge from the vacuums of power created by shifting leadership and loyalties. The Cold War gave a focus to the amorphous conflicts and competitions among the earth's peoples, and decades of waging it seemed to establish some rational limitations to winning it. (The two main protagonists managed to keep the peace between themselves for nearly a half century.) Despite its repressiveness and creaky inefficiencies, Soviet Communism helped to restrain the uglier expressions of narrow nationalism and ethnic rivalry. The world may be a more dangerous place until people settle into new definitions.

1945–1947

Communist-agitated strikes in Western Europe and takeovers of governments in Eastern Europe worsened relations between former World War II Allies, the United States and the U.S.S.R.

The *Truman Doctrine* was announced, pledging military aid to Greece, Turkey, and any other nation threatened with Communist aggression.

1948

A Soviet *blockade of Berlin*—the former capital city administered by the four occupying powers but deep within the Russian zone—was countered by the *Berlin Airlift*. The Soviets had initiated the blockade to retaliate for the unification of the American, British, and French zones into West Germany.

The *European Recovery Plan* (Marshall Plan) went into effect, and the Soviets, although invited, decline to participate and forbade their satellites to.

1949

NATO was established along with regional military alliances in the Middle East, Southeast Asia, and the Southwest Pacific.

After nearly two decades of civil war, the Chinese Communists led by *Mao Zedong* and aided by the U.S.S.R. defeated the corrupt regime of *Chiang Kai-shek's Nationalists*, despite massive U.S. military aid, and drove them from the Chinese mainland to the Island of *Formosa (Taiwan)*. The United States opposed the recognition of the Communist regime in the United Nations.

1950

The *Korean War* (1950–1953) was the first major military conflict between the West and the Communists. After the Japanese had been driven from the peninsula, south of Manchuria, the country had been occupied in the north by the Soviets and south of the 38th parallel by the United States. The Soviets rejected free elections in a unified Korea and, instead, supported a satellite regime under *Kim Il Sung*. Elections in South Korea in 1948 brought *Syngman Rhee* into power. In June 1950, a powerful North Korean army, supported by Soviet aid, invaded south of the 38th parallel and expected quick victory.

President Truman, fearful of repeating the pre-World War II policy of appeasement, convinced the United Nations' Security Council to condemn North Korean aggression and oppose it militarily. Since the Russians were boycotting the United Nations for failing to recognize Communist China, they could not veto the proposal, and a U.N. force led by *General Douglas*

MacArthur—freed from his occupation duties in Japan—and made up of mostly U.S. troops landed in South Korea. A brilliant amphibious landing at *Inchon* routed the North Koreans, and U.N. forces—fifteen nations provided mostly token contingents—drove close to the *Yalu River*, the border between North Korea and Communist Manchuria.

Hundreds of thousands of Chinese Communist troops attacked the U.N. force in November 1950, driving them back to the 38th parallel. When General MacArthur insisted on attacking China, President Truman, fearful of involving the United States in an Asian land war, removed him from command.

A cease-fire ended serious fighting in July 1951; an armistice, returning the Koreas to the situation before the war, was signed in 1953.

The war pitted United States forces against a Communist foe supported and aided by the Soviet Union, and despite the losses—54,000 U.S. dead, 2.5 million Koreans and Chinese—it convinced the United States that military might could contain the spread of Communism. Neither the European democracies, preoccupied with rebuilding their shattered nations, nor the large, non-Communist Asian nations of India, Burma, and Indonesia, mistrustful of a new kind of Western imperialism, shared the U.S. enthusiasm.

1953   The death of Stalin *thawed* the Cold War. Tensions rose and relaxed and then returned again, but *peaceful coexistence* seemed possible.

1955   *The Geneva Summit* between President *Dwight Eisenhower* of World War II fame, the British and French prime ministers, and Soviet leaders led to a conciliatory atmosphere.

1956   War in the Middle East, between Israel and its Arab neighbors, renewed tensions between the Soviets, who aided the Arab states, and the West, which supported Israel. (France and Britain made military moves against Egypt for nationalizing the Suez Canal.) The Geneva Accords divided Vietnam into the Communist North and the Non-Communist South.

1959   U.S. and Soviet relations soured further when *Fidel Castro*, an avowed Marxist, was openly aided by Soviet and Chinese Communists in his overthrow of Cuban dictator *Fulgencio Batista*.

1960   The *Paris Summit* ended when Khrushchev proved that the United States had been making spy flights over the U.S.S.R. after a *U-2* high-altitude reconaissance plane had been shot down over Soviet territory.

The U.S.S.R. became capable of launching direct nuclear attacks against the United States.

1961   The *Bay of Pigs invasion* of Cuba by anti-Castro Cuban refugees was a total disaster and a humiliation for newly elected president *John F. Kennedy*, whose administration had supported it.

The infamous *Berlin Wall*, as powerful a symbol of Soviet tyranny as the Bastille had been of royal abuses, was erected to keep East Berliners from fleeing to the West.

1962   The first U.S. troops, "military advisers," arrived in South Vietnam to shore up its anti-Communist government against attacks by Communist North Vietnamese infiltrators and *Vietcong* guerrillas.

The *Cuban Missile Crisis* brought the world to the brink of nuclear war when President Kennedy demanded that Premier Khrushchev remove nuclear missiles that the Soviets had installed in Cuba. The "eyeball-to-eyeball" confrontation ended when the bases were dismantled.

1963   A *nuclear test ban treaty* to stop atmospheric explosions was signed by three of the world's four nuclear powers: the United States, the U.S.S.R., and Britain. France refused.

A *hotline* or direct communication phone was installed between the Kremlin and the White House to prevent accidental nuclear war.

A *rift between the Soviets and Chinese Communists* led to growing tensions and a parting of the ways between the two giants.

1964   Communist China became the fifth member of the "nuclear bomb club."

1965   *Lyndon Johnson*, who succeeded to the presidency after the assassination of Kennedy, bolstered American involvement in the Vietnam conflict by continuing bombing raids against North Vietnam and by sending a massive ground force. The Soviets and Chinese Communists supplied great quantities of arms and other aid to help the northerners maintain the fight against an eventual U.S. force of well over a half-million troops.

Despite more U.S. battle deaths than in Korea, nearly 2 million Vietnamese dead, and waves of bitter demonstrations against the war in the United States, the U.S. troops did not withdraw from the undeclared war until 1973. The support that the U.S.S.R. and the *Chinese People's Republic* (Communist China) gave to the North Vietnamese all through the war was a sore spot in the relations between the Soviets and the United States.

1969   During the administration of President *Richard Nixon*, an avowed anti-Communist in his early political career, he and his secretary of state, Henry Kissinger, pursued a policy of détente, peaceful coexistence between the Western and the Communist blocs. Leaders exchanged visits, and the *SALT* negotiations (Strategic Arms Limitations Talks) began. The United States landed a manned expedition on the moon.

1970   A *nonproliferation treaty* to limit the spread of nuclear weapons was signed by the United States and the U.S.S.R. Unfortunately, nations with nuclear power plants proved it was possible to reprocess spent fuel in order to make nuclear bombs. (India became the sixth member of the "nuclear bomb club" this way in 1974.)

1972   *Nixon's dramatic visit to Communist China*—followed by scientific and cultural exchanges—resumed relations between the two former enemies.

Détente prevailed in the years that followed. Splits in the ranks of both the Western and Communist blocs had changed relations between the two superpowers, which in the late 1940s and through the 1950s had faced off with the support of allies or satellites. DeGaulle's France had questioned the leadership of the United States in European affairs just as Mao's China had questioned that of the Soviet Union in the Communist world. The suppression of Czechoslovakia had tarnished the Soviet image just as the Vietnam War had the American. A prosperous and independent Western Europe took more and more charge of its own affairs, and nationalist resistance in Eastern Europe diminished Soviet influence. The Cold War between the United States and the U.S.S.R. began to "thaw."

Sample Essay Question

The sample thematic essay question and the practice questions presented in this chapter are types found in the Advanced Placement Examination in European History, and they require a knowledge of causes, effects, personalities, ideas, and events.

Sample Question

> *Explain* the significance of the Marshall Plan.

Comments on the Sample Question

Follow the "Simple Procedures" for writing an essay. (See page 24.)

First, *What does the question want to know?* What did the Marshall Plan do? What intended and unintended consequences did it have?

Second, *What do you know about it?* The significance of the Marshall Plan (European Recovery Program) is in three areas: it marked the commitment of the United States to European affairs, a turnabout from its traditional policy of postwar isolationism; it was the keystone to the rebuilding of war-devastated Western Europe; it was the first economic weapon used in the containment of Soviet Communism.

Third, *How would you put it into words?* The task here is to "make clear" and to "detail" how. Why was the United States willing to commit billions of dollars to the restoration of Europe? Why did it help even its former enemies, Germany and Italy? What prompted fear of the spread of Soviet Communism?

Sample Answer

"Get the boys home in time for Christmas." It seems to be the habitual response of America after its foreign wars are won. After World War I, the United States participated in the partial and very temporary occupation of Germany and in an ill-fated expedition against the Red Army during the civil wars that followed the Russian Revolution of 1917. The troops—well over a million who served in Europe during the First World War—soon went home. The U.S. Congress—following a tradition established by Washington—slipped back into isolation, and the Senate refused to join Wilson's League of Nations. Twenty years later, 12 million Americans were back in uniform to fight the Axis.

The policies of isolation, neutrality, and appeasement had not worked against the Fascist dictators, and the United States had learned. Not only did the U.S. military occupy Germany in 1945—along with British, French, and Russian forces—but the United States realized that only it and Stalin's Soviet Union were strong enough to make a difference in European affairs. In 1947, at an address at Harvard University, George Marshall, U.S. secretary of state and, during the war, chief of staff of the military, proposed the European Recovery Plan to rebuild wartorn Europe.

By 1948, eighteen European nations, excluding Fascist Spain, which was not invited to join, and Russia and its East European allies, which refused to participate, formed the Organization for European Economic Cooperation. It was designed to first rebuild the cities, factories, energy sources, housing, and transport systems of Europe and then to increase productivity and reduce trade barriers.

From 1948 to 1952, the United States spent about $14 billion on the Marshall Plan, most of it in the form of U.S.-produced nonmilitary machinery, raw materials, and food. The aim of the United States in spending this money was more than altruistic. There seemed to be no precedent in modern history for the victor-nation to build not only an enemy country but those that would be potential economic competitors. But the United States understood that if the non-Communist nations of Western Europe remained weak, they would be vulnerable to Soviet expansionism. Already Eastern Europe was part of the satellite empire. Also, the United States had another realistic motive: to create potential markets in a prosperous and free Western Europe.

The significance of the Marshall Plan was threefold. It marked the commitment of the United States to "winning the peace as well as the war." It helped to rebuild the shattered states of Western Europe and to keep them from falling under Communism. It also marked the beginning of European economic cooperation that has evolved into the Common Market's attempts to foster political consolidation as well as economic.

Evaluate the Sample Answer

1. Was the introduction a clear statement of the essay's intentions?
2. Did the essay "make clear" and "detail" the significance of the Marshall Plan?
3. Were the facts used in support accurate, abundant, relevant?
4. Did it look at the "big picture," the large issues?
5. What was missing?
6. Was the essay long enough, clearly written, convincing?
7. Did the conclusion sum up the argument?

Rater's Comments on the Sample Answer

4—Well qualified

This is a good compact summary of the significance of the Marshall Plan. In general terms, it explores the plan's importance to U.S. foreign policy in marking the departure from traditional isolationism by helping to rebuild shattered Western Europe and "contain" Communism in Europe.

Suggestions for improvement:

Reference could have been made to other U.S. economic and military assistance programs like Point Four technical assistance to underdeveloped nations and the Truman Doctrine to help Greece and Turkey to fight Communist insurgents. A brief discussion of the enormity of U.S. involvement in world affairs would have been useful. A consideration of why the U.S.S.R. and its satellites did not avail themselves of the plan would have been relevant: they saw it as a form of "American imperialism." A further exploration of the role of the Organization for European Economic Cooperation in the movement for consolidation was called for.

Practice Essay Questions

The questions that follow are samples of the various types of thematic essays that appear on the Advanced Placement Examination in European History.

---

1. *Explain* the major confrontations of the Cold War before the death of Stalin.

Comments on Question 1

To "detail" is the task. First, determine what is meant by "confrontation." The very essence of the Cold War was that the superpowers never directly confronted each other militarily.

Before 1953 and the death of Stalin, one of the most serious confrontations involved the United States and the U.S.S.R. over the Berlin Blockade. Through the winter of 1948–1949, mostly American aircraft flew over Soviet-held East Germany to supply West Berlin. The forces of each of the superpowers were within easy shooting distance, but moderation prevailed on both sides.

The Korean War (1950–1953) brought the United States and other U.N. forces into a shooting war with the new Communist China, which was considered a close ally of the Soviets and was supplied with Russian arms and aided by Russian "volunteers." President Truman's sacking of General MacArthur limited the scope of the war.

The Truman Doctrine and NATO, the West's responses to the Communist threat in Europe, could be considered elements of the overall confrontation.

---

2. *Evaluate* the role of NATO in the defense of Western Europe.

Comments on Question 2

"What minuses?" you ask. Did its establishment in 1949 increase tensions between the West and the Soviets? Should West Germany have been rearmed by 1950? Should it have been authorized to create a "national army" by 1954? Did its role in NATO exaggerate the importance of the United States in Europe? Would the Warsaw Pact have been consummated if not for the existence of NATO? Were there alternatives?

The pluses? It seems to have averted an invasion of Western Europe after its inception. The stationing of hundreds of thousands of American troops on European soil not only aided the Western Europeans in their defense, but it enabled them to invest in their economies the huge sums needed for defense. The United States also gave billions of dollars to other NATO powers to build up their military forces, and U.S. bases boosted their local economies.

> **3.** *Analyze* the movement toward economic union in Western Europe.

**Comments on
Question 3**

Recall that the Marshall Plan inspired the Organization for European Economic Cooperation. Did this set the tone for the Schumann and Monnet Plan? What was the European Coal and Steel Community? How did it evolve into the Common Market? Who were the Common Market's first members? Why wasn't Britain one of them? What was the role of the French in delaying British membership? How has European consolidation gone beyond the economic?

> **4.** *Contrast and compare* the status of the Eastern European satellites before and in the two decades after the death of Stalin.

**Comments on
Question 4**

Eastern Europe before the Soviet takeover after World War II was an agricultural, not an industrial, region. How did land redistribution and Soviet-type Five Year Plans change this? What was the political situation for the satellites? How did the East Berlin riots of 1953 set a new precedent in the relations between the Soviets and their satellites?

How did "de-Stalinization" help precipitate revolts in Poland and Hungary in 1956? How did these revolts affect the political and economic reform of Eastern Europe? How did the suppression of Czechoslovakia in 1968 diminish the Soviet reputation as anti-imperialistic in the Third World? What changed, what remained the same after Stalin's death?

> **5.** *Analyze* how and why the Cold War gradually thawed.

**Comments on
Question 5**

Again, the death of Stalin cannot be underestimated as an influence. Be aware, though, that while the "cult of personality" disappeared from Soviet political life, the edifices of the totalitarian state remained. The so-called thaw involved a number of "quick-freeze" crises.

The summit meetings played an invaluable role in decreasing superpower tensions. The Cuban Missile Crisis may have alerted the United States and the U.S.S.R. to the ultimate disaster that "brinksmanship" could lead to. The year 1963 was significant in that the Test Ban Treaty was signed and the monolithic Communist Bloc cracked with the Soviet-Chinese rift. Nixon's policy of détente, despite the Vietnam War, was a giant step. The Nonproliferation Treaty and the SALT treaties were significant.

Practice Multiple-Choice Questions

(These questions represent the various types found in the Advanced Placement Examination in European History.)

1. By late 1945, the Western Allies had decided that in order for Western
    Europe to recover from the devastation of war, Germany would have to
    be rebuilt because this area of Germany was still the industrial center of
    Europe.
    (A)   Berlin
    (B)   the Rhineland
    (C)   the Ruhr Basin
    (D)   East Prussia
    (E)   Bavaria

2. Tensions between the West and the Soviets manifested themselves in
    1946 when the joint administration of which of the following broke
    down?
    (A)   The de-Nazification program
    (B)   The four zones of occupied Germany
    (C)   Berlin
    (D)   The trials of Nazi war criminals
    (E)   The reconstruction of German industry

3. A definitive break from the United States' traditional policy of isola-
    tionism was marked by its
    (A)   criticism of Stalin's establishment of repressive governments in
          Eastern Europe
    (B)   participation in the Nuremberg War Crimes trials
    (C)   growing anti-Communism at home
    (D)   commitment to the reconstruction and defense of Western Europe
    (E)   generosity to its former enemies

4. The U.S. Marshall Plan combined altruism with self-interest because the
    sheer generosity of the United States was rewarded by
    (A)   high interest on the loans
    (B)   the unquestioning support of Western Europe nations for
          American foreign policy
    (C)   the approval of the American people who elected Democrats to
          the presidency for the following decade
    (D)   the containment of Communism and the opening of a rich
          market for U.S. industry
    (E)   the participation of the Soviet satellites in Eastern Europe

5. Under the Schuman and Monnet Plan, the first move toward economic union in Europe was made in 1952 when six industrial countries in the West pooled what resources?
   (A) Coal and steel
   (B) Hydroelectric power
   (C) Military equipment
   (D) Uranium and plutonium
   (E) Skilled labor

6. The European Economic Community or "Common Market" was created in 1957 by the same six nations that had pooled resources under the Schuman and Monnet Plan. It was made up of Belgium, Holland, Luxembourg, and
   (A) Britain, France, Italy
   (B) Britain, France, West Germany
   (C) Spain, Italy, West Germany
   (D) France, Italy, Spain
   (E) France, Italy, West Germany

7. Which two Communist nations were not considered Soviet satellites because they were able to maintain their independence from Moscow, not having been liberated from the Nazis by the Red Army?
   (A) Poland and Czechoslovakia
   (B) Bulgaria and Romania
   (C) Albania and Yugoslavia
   (D) Yugoslavia and East Germany
   (E) Albania and Austria

8. All of the following are true of the Soviet satellites in Eastern Europe from 1945 to 1953 EXCEPT
   (A) land-distribution programs were carried out
   (B) agriculture was forcibly collectivized
   (C) industrialization was discouraged
   (D) Soviet police state methods silenced opposition to the regimes
   (E) the influence of the Roman Catholic Church was removed

9. Despite his record as one of history's most brutal dictators, responsible for the death of tens of millions of his own countrymen and for the establishment of Communist totalitarianism in Russia, Stalin achieved which of the following?
   (A) The industrialization and modernization of a backward agrarian nation
   (B) Postwar reconstruction of the U.S.S.R.'s massive devastation within a decade
   (C) The expansion of Soviet hegemony
   (D) Victory in the "Great Patriotic War"
   (E) All of the above

10. After the death of Stalin in 1953, the new party leadership, headed by Nikita Khrushchev, did all of the following EXCEPT
    (A) leave intact most of the basic structure of Stalinist totalitarianism
    (B) grant the satellites of Eastern Europe greater autonomy
    (C) denounce the "crimes of Stalin" in victimizing the people and the party
    (D) accuse Stalin of failing to respond effectively against the initial advances of the Nazi invaders
    (E) accuse Stalin of creating a "cult of personality"

11. Despite the spectacular Soviet reconstruction successes of the postwar Five-Year Plans developed by centralized economic planning (Gosplan), production of which of the following lagged far behind the rest of the economy by the 1960s?
    (A) Military weaponry
    (B) Heavy machinery
    (C) Automobiles
    (D) Food
    (E) Spacecraft

12. All of the following are true of the Korean War (1950–1953) EXCEPT
    (A) it was the first major military conflict between the West and the Communists
    (B) although strong evidence points to the participation of Russian military personnel, combat was exclusively between U.N. and North Korean forces
    (C) the U.N. military presence was made possible because the Russians were boycotting the Security Council and did not veto the measure
    (D) President Truman removed General MacArthur from command to prevent a wider war
    (E) the relative success of its operations convinced the United States that military force could stop the spread of Communism

13. The Cold War "thawed" because of all of the following EXCEPT
    (A) the U-2 incident
    (B) summit diplomacy
    (C) the SALT negotiations
    (D) the Soviet-Chinese rift
    (E) Nixon's policies toward the U.S.S.R. and China

14. A serious flaw of the Nonproliferation Treaty of 1970 was
    (A) that the Soviets continued to export nuclear weapons technology
    (B) the United States provided its allies with tactical nuclear weapons
    (C) China was eager to develop nuclear weapons
    (D) Britain and France refused to honor it
    (E) many nations with nuclear power plants were able to reprocess spent fuel in order to produce bombs

15.   Which of the following did NOT contribute to the split during the 1960s and 1970s within the ranks of both the Western and Communist Blocs?
  (A)   DeGaulle's questioning of U.S. leadership of a restored Europe
  (B)   Mao Zedong's charge of "revisionism" against Soviet leaders
  (C)   nationalism in Eastern Europe
  (D)   the tarnished images of both superpowers
  (E)   the policy of détente

Answers and Answer Explanations

1.	C	2.	B	3.	D	4.	D	5.	A
6.	E	7.	C	8.	C	9.	E	10.	B
11.	D	12.	B	13.	A	14.	E	15.	E

1.   (C)   The Ruhr Valley in Western Germany was and is one of the world's most important industrial centers.

2.   (B)   The three zones administered by the United States, Britain, and France became West Germany (the Federal Republic of Germany) in 1949; the Russian sector became East Germany (the People's Democratic Republic of Germany).

3.   (D)   The Marshall Plan and NATO signaled the USA's global commitment.

4.   (D)   A rebuilt Western Europe was less prone to Communist subversion or military takeover, and it offered a populous and prosperous market for U.S. goods as well as a source of high-quality manufactured products.

5.   (A)   It all started with a sharing of these two basic raw materials of industrial production.

6.   (E)   The big six did not include Britain at first because Britain had its commonwealth trading partners.

7.   (C)   Albania was liberated by the Western Allies and Yugoslavia, under Marshal Tito, maintained a fierce independence from Moscow.

8.   (C)   The Soviets did, under Five-Year Plans, industrialize the region, which had been primarily agricultural.

9.   (E)   Even today, Stalin has his supporters.

10.   (B)   The basic structure and institutions, such as the secret police, of Stalinist totalitarianism were kept intact.

11.   (D)   A crisis in agriculture because of the failure of collectivized farming—it lacked incentives, a basic problem in Communist economies—led to the downfall of Khrushchev.

12.   (B)   The Communist Chinese entered the war in November of 1951.

13.   (A)   The downing of the U.S. U-2 high-flying spy plane derailed the Paris Summit between President Eisenhower and Premier Khrushchev in 1960.

14.   (E)   Many "have-not" nations of the Third World gained and continue to strive for more status and self-importance by belonging to the once exclusive "nuclear club."

15.   (E)   This policy was made easier by the split in the once solid ideological blocs.

CHAPTER 15 Trends in Contemporary Europe

In the 1970s, high energy prices resulting from instability in the Middle East and the disintegration of the American-dominated global monetary system brought about a worldwide recession. Western Europe suffered stagflation and huge government deficits.

During this decade, détente between East and West was furthered by West Germany's attempts to reconcile with Eastern Europe and by the Helsinki Agreements, and it was strained by the U.S. involvement in Vietnam, the Soviet involvement in Afghanistan, and a massive American arms buildup.

The most important and dramatic developments of the 1980s and early 1990s were the largely peaceful anti-Communist revolutions in Eastern Europe and the collapse of Soviet Communism that led to the dismantling of the Soviet Union. The Solidarity movement in Poland, liberalization in Hungary and Czechoslovakia, and the unification of East and West Germany marked the end of Soviet domination of Eastern Europe. The gradual decline of Soviet economic strength under Brezhnev and Andropov led Gorbachev to initiate profound political and social reform (glasnost) and economic restructuring (perestroika). In 1989, the first free elections were conducted since the 1917 revolution. A military coup against Gorbachev in the summer of 1991 faced popular opposition and failed, many Soviet republics declared independence, and with the promise of reform Boris Yeltsin was elected president of the Russian Republic.

The entrance of great numbers of women into the workplace and the feminist movement altered the lives of women in Europe and the United States. The birthrate dropped, the divorce rate rose, and sexual and social attitudes toward women changed.

Economics

Through the 1960s, Europe, led by the *Common Market*, accounted for a quarter of the world's industrial output. West Germany alone was third behind the United States and Japan in gross national product. In 1970, twenty-five years after World War II had ended, prosperity and democracy in Western Europe submerged centuries of national rivalry and promised peace and even greater economic progress and political cooperation.

The *oil embargo of 1973* helped change this rosy picture. The *Arab-Israeli War of 1973* incited Arab oil-producing nations to stop the flow of oil to those nations that had supported Israel. Since over 70 percent of Western Europe's petroleum came from the Middle East, the embargo and the resulting price rise threatened to destroy not only Europe's economy but the world's economy. *Stagflation,* a combination of slowdown and inflation that developed into a worldwide recession, had already been a problem that the oil embargo only aggravated. Western Europe's unparalleled economic growth and prosperity in the postwar period—as well as that of the United States and the rest of the industrialized world—was threatened.

Although the recession, the most severe since the Great Depression of the 1930s, improved by early 1976, and while unionism and welfare benefits enabled working people to cope with it more easily, economic growth rates slowed.

By late 1991, the twelve members of the *European Community*—the Common Market—had completed a plan to integrate economically and to consolidate politically. The *Maastricht Treaty*, if approved by all twelve nations, would create a common currency and a common citizenship, and develop a common defense and foreign policy for all member states. It would be the first step in the creation of a United States of Europe.

The economic integration of the member states of the European Community is a powerful cohesive force. Just as the *Zollverein*, customs union, bound the separate states of Germany before final unification in 1871, the Common Market may well be the first step in the political consolidation of Europe.

Science

World War II changed the way scientists did their work, how they were funded, and where their research was directed. Scientists the world over were employed by their various governments to aid the war effort and their work led to technological advances, such as the use of atomic energy, the development of radar and jet aircraft, the advent of computers. New discoveries, inventions, and industries spurred research after the war in both *pure and applied science*.

New means of funding and organization of the increasingly specialized fields of research led to the advent of *Big Science*, which stressed teamwork, the combining of theoretical research with engineering techniques, and complex research facilities with professional managers and expensive, sophisticated equipment. The United States took the lead in this area after World War II and by the mid-1960s most scientific research (which doubled the sum of human knowledge every decade) was funded by the federal government, whose principal aim was defense. A "space race" between the United States and the U.S.S.R. led to Russia's development of the first artificial satellite in 1957, *Sputnik*, and to a manned moon landing in 1969 by the United States. To stem the *brain drain* of their best scientists to the United States, European nations began funding their own research programs.

Population and Poverty

Industrialization, urbanization, attitude changes, and modern contraception had lowered the birthrate during this century in Europe and other areas with developed economies. In the *Third World*, including newly independent nations that had been colonial possessions, the population exploded in the second half of this century. Cultural and religious attitudes and economic dependence on large families maintained a high birthrate. Better food production and distribution, and modern medical and sanitation practices led to a decline in the death rate. Investments that could have been made to improve the standard of living in these areas was used instead to support the burgeoning population. Even with population control programs and a growing women's movement, the problem continues to get worse.

The gap between the rich industrialized nations and the less developed countries of the Third World widened. When the worldwide recession of the early 1970s caused the West to reduce its aid to the Third World, the less developed nations became more militant in demanding a more equitable share of the world's resources and industrial production. The result is a revolution of rising expectations that helps create worldwide political instability.

The Collapse of Communism and the End of the Cold War

In 1985, the election of *Mikhail Gorbachev* by the Soviet Communist party leadership to serve as party general secretary promised fresh blood to reform the ailing economy and to invigorate the party after the stagnation of the Brezhnev era. An intended reformer, Gorbachev became the agent of an unintended and unexpected revolution that led to the collapse of Communism and the dissolution of the world order that had reigned since the end of World War II.

In 1987, two years after he took office, Chairman Gorbachev and President Ronald Reagan signed the *INF Treaty*, which began the delicate and dangerous process of nuclear disarmament with the destruction of all short-and intermediate-range nuclear missiles. Two years after that, the U.S.S.R. withdrew from the *War in Afghanistan*, its "Vietnam." Gorbachev's perestroika or restructuring of the economy and his policy of glasnost or openness seemed to be moving Soviet Communism toward reform.

In 1989, the *collapse of Communism* began when the *Congress of People's Deputies* replaced the calcified Supreme Soviet as the nation's legislature. Freer elections had ended the monopoly of the Communist party, and the Congress demanded even greater reforms. A chain reaction of reform and independence swept through Eastern Europe, once the satellite region of the Soviet Empire.

Solidarity, the Polish trade-union movement, which had opposed the rigid Communist government and been suppressed under martial law, was swept into office by the first free elections since before World War II. Changes in the Communist governments of Hungary, Bulgaria, and Czechoslovakia took place over the next several months. In November of 1989, the *Berlin Wall*, symbol of Communist oppression, was breached. It marked the beginning of the downfall of the Communist East German government. A violent revolution in Romania overthrew the longtime Communist dictatorship. Free elections established non-Communist governments in many of the old East European satellites.

In October of 1990, *Germany reunited*. Despite fears of a resurgent and aggressive united Germany, Gorbachev had allowed the union of West and East Germany without the promise of its neutrality. Germany joined NATO, and less than a year later the Warsaw Pact, its Communist counterpart, was dissolved. *The Cold War officially ended* in November, when Soviet, U.S., and Western European leaders signed the *Charter for a New Europe*.

In mid-1991, *Boris Yeltsin*, an outspoken and charismatic political rival of Gorbachev, was elected as president of the Soviet Republic of Russia. He had run as an independent candidate on a platform of drastic economic and political reform. During that same month, June, *Croatia and Slovenia declared their independence from Yugoslavia* and a civil war, made more brutal by ancient ethnic rivalries, broke out.

START, the Strategic Arms Reduction Treaty, was signed in July of 1991 by Gorbachev and President George Bush to reduce the long-range nuclear missiles of both nations.

One month later, old-line party and military leaders launched a coup against the vacationing Gorbachev as they sent military units towards Moscow. Within days, the coup collapsed in the face of massive public demonstrations against its leaders. *Latvia, Lithuania, and Estonia* declared their independence from the Soviet Union. By late 1991, Russia, Ukraine, and Belarus formed the *Commonwealth of Independent States* and the Soviet Union effectively ceased to exist.

By 1993, ethnic rivalries among the former Soviet republics, the bloody war pitting Serbia and Croatia against their former Yugoslavian brothers Bosnia and Herzegovina, and the division of Czechoslovakia has created a dangerous and fluid political situation in Europe. Despite initial reluctance to get involved in the Balkan crisis, the United States and Western European nations have imposed a settlement on the warring factions and have prosecuted war criminals in the World Court.

The collapse of Communism in Europe created a *fluid* political situation worldwide that is similar to the disruptions of the old orders after World Wars I and II. Power has shifted; the rules have changed. The end of the Cold War has diminished the prospects of nuclear war but has created new rivalries and unleashed bloody ethnic conflicts to test the resolve of NATO. The allies of the Gulf War alliance have adopted varying policies in the Middle East that often reflect their own economic interests. The birth of a new international order will, as always, be difficult.

Society

After World War II, European class distinctions blurred due to unprecedented economic growth in the West and its accompanying opportunities in jobs and in higher education. Western Europeans enjoyed a new social mobility and a greater democratization of their governments. Education and ability outweighed family connections. Health care and other social security programs alleviated traditional class conflicts and promoted greater economic equality.

General prosperity promoted a *consumer culture*, making big businesses out of such products and services as food, leisure, entertainment, and travel.

Powerful social changes occurred after World War II. Prosperity and increased educational opportunities swelled the middle classes in both Europe and the United States. With science and technology wedded by war, *big science*, which was funded by government and industry, created new products and new career opportunities. With greater educational opportunities available to women, more females sought careers outside the home. Cities grew as agricultural workers left the farms in search of new vocations.

In the 1960s, a youth culture, which grew first in the United States from the great numbers of *baby boomers*, the unparalleled prosperity, and the increased enrollment in higher education, spread globally. Rebellion against the status quo manifested itself in rock music, widespread use of illegal drugs, and less rigid sexual attitudes. The materialism of the West encouraged a revolutionary idealism among young people who participated in the antiwar movement in the United States and in the student radicalism of Europe. Student revolts against rigid educational practices in universities broke out in France and in other European countries.

Economic setbacks in the 1970s and 1980s spurred changes in family life. In order to maintain the family's standard of living, many women in Europe and the United States went into the work force. Income independence enabled more women to get divorces; birth control allowed them to plan their families and resulted in a decreased birthrate. This newfound independence and a number of gifted female writers, such as Simone de Beauvoir in France and Betty Friedan in the United States, helped launch a new feminism that attacked gender inequalities in all aspects of society and that used political action and attitude alteration.

Recent Developments

The 1990s marked powerful political and economic changes in Europe, comparable in magnitude to those at the end of World Wars I and II. After the collapse of Communist governments in the former Soviet Union and its Cold War satellites, a new order emerged.

Western Europe, with the exception of Britain, instituted a *monetary union*, a natural evolution from the political and economic ties of the European Union.

Germany, completely and peacefully united (although with unforseen complications that came from the need to absorb the former Communist East), set up its capital in Berlin once again, and became the most powerful country in Europe, a status it had not held since the end of World War II.

Poland, Hungary, and the Czech Republic established democratic governments, instituted capitalist reforms of their economies, and joined NATO.

Independence movements from the Serb-dominated Yugoslavian government in Belgrade degenerated into bitter and bloody struggles between various ethnic groups (Serbs, Croats, Bosnians, Kosovars, Montenegrins, Albanians) and revived the specter of *genocide* in the form of "*ethnic cleansing.*" The intervention of NATO resulted in a precarious peace and in the prosecution of Slobodan Milosevic, Serbian president, and other Serbian leaders for war crimes.

Russia, the largest, richest, and most populous republic of the former Soviet Union, grappled with a faltering economy, a fitful start to democratization (widespread corruption during Boris Yeltsin's presidency tainted the effort), and a bloody ethnic war with Chechnya. The replacement of Yeltsin by Vladimir Putin as president promised reform, a renewed *détente* with the West, and a more enlightened role for Russia in regional and world affairs.

The *9/11 Terrorist Attacks* against the United States in 2001 marked the beginning of a new international era, one more dangerous to world peace and stability than at any time since the height of the Cold War. Widespread poverty in the Third World and ethnic rivalry all over the globe have fostered religious fanaticism and conflict, such as that in the Middle East between Israelis and Palestinians, and both the United States—as the world's only *superpower*—and the European states must respond to the challenge.

Sample Essay Question

The sample thematic essay question and the practice questions presented in this chapter are types found in the Advanced Placement Examination in European History, and they require a knowledge of causes, effects, personalities, ideas, and events.

Sample Question

> Assess the validity of the following statement. *The collapse of Communism in Europe has created a more dangerous world.*

Comments on the Sample Question

Follow the "simple procedures for writing an essay." (See page 24.)

First, *What does the question want to know?* Is the world safer after the fall of the Communist governments of Eastern Europe and the USSR, or have the drastic changes created hazardous instabilities?

Second, *What do you know about it?* The fall of the Communist governments in Eastern Europe and the U.S.S.R. ended the military threat to NATO and the Cold War. The possibility of nuclear war between the United States and U.S.S.R. seemed more remote than ever. But the ethnic rivalries and weak democracies that have resulted could encourage nationalistic dictatorships that might use nuclear weapons to resolve their conflicts.

Third, *How would you put it into words?* To "assess the validity" of the statement, you must evaluate whether the global situation was more or less stable before the collapse of European Communism. You could argue against the statement or agree wholly or partially.

Sample Answer

"Nature abhors a vacuum." The vacuum created by the fall of Communism in Europe has been filled by weak democracies and by ugly nationalism. Russia, the most powerful and populous autonomous republic of the former Soviet Union, is suffering economic breakdown and social dislocation. Its underpaid and poorly housed military may someday overthrow the parliamentary government that has no tradition of democracy. The Soviet Republics of Azerbaijan and Armenia gained independence and waged bitter "tribal war" against each other. The civil war between the regions of the former Yugoslavia involved atrocities and "ethnic cleansing" genocide not seen in Europe since the defeat of the Nazis. The instability in the Balkans could lead to a regional or even worldwide war as it did in 1914.

Evaluate the Sample Answer

1. Did the introduction clearly state the essay's intentions?
2. Did the essay clearly "assess the validity" of the statement?
3. Were supporting facts accurate, abundant, relevant?
4. Did it look at the "big picture"?
5. What was missing?
6. Was it long enough, clearly written, convincing?
7. Did the conclusion sum up the argument?

Rater's Comments on the Sample Answer

3—Qualified

This was a one-sided and somewhat simplistic approach to a very complex issue. The writer has overstressed remote possibilities of "danger" while ignoring the significant and tangible risks that have ended with the fall of the Eastern Bloc.

Suggestions for improvement:

The validity of the statement could be argued much more convincingly if future dangers had been weighed against past risks. Does the danger posed by a possible military takeover of the Russian government measure up to the risks of nuclear war during the Cold War? Is the suffering caused by ethnic and nationalistic rivalries equivalent to the miseries of life under Communist totalitarianism? Is the world more stable with two rival ideologies aligned against each other or with fractious states struggling to establish democracy and capitalism?

Practice Essay Questions

The questions that follow are samples of the various types of thematic essays that appear on the Advanced Placement Examination in European History. (See pages 17–18 for a detailed description.)

> **1.** To what extent and in what ways did Gorbachev's reforms bring about the dissolution of the U.S.S.R.?

Comments on Question 1

How important were his reforms in the process? Which ones affected it? Consider both perestroika and glasnost. Be sure to show how their degree of success or failure provoked the final breakdown. Consider his repudiation of the Brezhnev Doctrine.

> **2.** Analyze the causes of the economic crises in Europe during the 1970s.

Comments on Question 2

Trace the causes and determine the relationships of the world monetary crisis and the OPEC oil embargoes in bringing about the regional stagflation of the 1970s.

> **3.** Describe the Eastern European Revolutions of 1989.

Comments on Question 3

Explain the patterns of revolution in the various East European states during 1989. Consider the role of Solidarity in Poland, the liberalization policies in Hungary, the bloody uprising in Romania, the opening of the Berlin Wall in Germany.

> **4.** Discuss how the entrance of great numbers of women into the workplace has altered European society.

Comments on Question 4

Relate the "big picture" and offer specific effects of this powerful trend. How has life changed for the mass of European women? How has the trend affected family, birthrate, divorce and marriage?

> **5.** Explain how the Solidarity movement in Poland evolved from a trade union movement to a force for national democratization.

Comments on Question 5

Offer reasons for, and make clear why, a trade union was able to democratize a Communist dictatorship. Be sure to examine origins; leadership on both sides; the role of the Roman Catholic Church; the nature of Polish society; and the gains, losses, and final triumphs of the movement.

Practice Multiple-Choice Questions

(These questions represent the various types found in the Advanced Placement Examination in European History.)

1. All of the following contributed to the global economic recession of the 1970s and early 1980s EXCEPT
    (A) the collapse of the American-dominated world monetary system
    (B) the OPEC oil embargo of 1973
    (C) President Reagan's elimination of federal deficits
    (D) President Nixon's refusal to sell American gold
    (E) An end to cheap oil

2. An important reason why the widespread unemployment and inflation of the 1970s and 1980s did not lead to profound political instability in Western Europe was
    (A) the existence of welfare systems set up after World War II
    (B) the imposition of martial law
    (C) the austerity measures pioneered by Britain's Thatcher
    (D) the kind of nationalization and public investment introduced by France's Mitterand
    (E) the European-wide investment in *big science*

3. The economic setbacks of the 1970s and 1980s had what social consequences?
    (A) more married women entered or remained in the work force
    (B) young people tended toward political conservatism
    (C) the age of marriage rose sharply in Western countries
    (D) university students stressed career preparation
    (E) all of the above

4. The *second wave* of feminism began in
    (A) the later 19th century
    (B) right before World War I
    (C) during the 1920s
    (D) right after World War II
    (E) in the 1960s

5. Willy Brandt's most important contribution as a leader of West Germany was
    (A) the construction of the autobahn
    (B) the initiative for reconciliation with the Eastern Bloc
    (C) the unification of West and East Germany
    (D) the demolition of the Berlin Wall
    (E) the banning of the Communist party from all elective office

6. The U.S.S.R.'s invasion of, and stalemate in, what country has been likened to the U.S. failure in Vietnam?
    (A) Czechoslovakia
    (B) Poland
    (C) Afghanistan
    (D) Hungary
    (E) Germany

7. The world monetary system adopted at Bretton Woods in 1944 and upon which postwar recovery progressed was based on
    (A) The Japanese yen
    (B) The German mark
    (C) The French franc
    (D) The American dollar
    (E) Gold

8. When Communism fell in Eastern Europe in 1989, bloody revolution took place in
    (A) East Germany
    (B) Poland
    (C) Romania
    (D) Hungary
    (E) Czechoslovakia

9. All of the following contributed to the success of the Solidarity movement in Poland EXCEPT
    (A) a lack of Soviet-style collectivization
    (B) the independence of the Polish Roman Catholic Church
    (C) a booming economy
    (D) the leadership of Lech Walesa
    (E) the Gdansk Agreement

10. An important reason for the failure of Gorbachev's perestroika was
    (A) the continuance of rigid price setting
    (B) the refusal of the government to allow private profit seeking
    (C) failure to allow state enterprises some independence
    (D) the centrally planned economy's failure to adapt to free market mechanisms
    (E) the resentment of the Soviet people of attempts at reform

11. Gorbachev's repudiation of the Brezhnev Doctrine
    (A) accelerated the peaceful revolutions in Eastern Europe
    (B) enabled the U.S.S.R. to invade Afghanistan
    (C) caused a diplomatic confrontation with the United States
    (D) increased East-West tensions
    (E) suppressed nationalist demands in the Soviet Republics

12. Her book *The Second Sex* was the first and one of the major intellectual influences on the second wave of feminism
    (A) Betty Friedan
    (B) Olympe de Gouges
    (C) Mary Wollstonecraft
    (D) Margaret Thatcher
    (E) Simone de Beauvoir

13. The diplomatic initiative to relax Cold War tension around the globe was
    (A) the policy of détente
    (B) the Brezhnev doctrine
    (C) the Warsaw Pact
    (D) glasnost
    (E) the Pentagon Papers

14. One of the most significant trends in the life of women in Europe over the last three decades is that
    (A) Motherhood is occupying a greater part of their total life span
    (B) Many are foregoing careers in order to raise their children
    (C) Motherhood is occupying less of their total life span
    (D) Most are opting for large families
    (E) Their span of fertility has diminished

15. Glasnost is best characterized as
    (A) a form of re-Stalinization
    (B) an openness of expression
    (C) a restructuring of the economy
    (D) a form of central planning
    (E) a guarantee of human rights

Answers and Answer Explanations

1. C	2. A	3. E	4. B	5. C
6. D	7. D	8. C	9. C	10. D
11. A	12. E	13. A	14. C	15. B

1. (C) Reagan's fiscal policies tripled the U.S. deficit.

2. (A) Social welfare programs maintained the political stability in Western democracies, preventing the kind of dictatorships that grew after WWII.

3. (E) Downturns in the economy led to multiple social effects.

4. (E) Although De Beauvoir's classic, *The Second Sex*, was published in the late 1940s, the movement it helped inspire came to fruition in the 1960s.

5. (B) His peace initiative prompted Nixon and his advisors to push for global détente.

6. (C) The Soviet Union's failure in Afghanistan, like that of the United States in Vietnam, was the case of a superpower ground to a halt by a Third World, agrarian nation.

7. (D) At the time the U.S. currency was the world's most stable.

8.   (C)   A bloody repression by the Communist government led to a bloody overthrow.

9.   (C)   The lagging Polish economy gave the movement its impetus.

10.   (D)   The reforms did not go far enough to transform the moribund Soviet economy.

11.   (A)   The revolutions of 1989 in Eastern Europe were fostered by Gorbachev's pledge not to interfere in the internal affairs of those nations.

12.   (E)   It was published nearly twenty years before Friedan's work.

13.   (A)   Inspired by Brandt's peace initiatives in Europe, it was designed largely by Nixon's secretary of state, Henry Kissinger.

14.   (C)   The social implications of this are staggering; the structure of family life has changed; the role of women in society and the economy has broadened.

15.   (B)   It was the more successful of Gorbachev's reforms.

PART THREE MODEL ADVANCED
PLACEMENT
EXAMINATIONS IN
EUROPEAN HISTORY

ANSWER SHEET FOR THE MODEL
ADVANCED PLACEMENT EXAM NO. 1

Name _____

Date _____

Grade _____

FOR SECTION I — MULTIPLE CHOICE

Sample: 1.   The Reformation began in

       (A)   1450   (D)   1517

       (B)   1492   (E)   1618

       (C)   1507

1. Ⓐ Ⓑ Ⓒ ● Ⓔ

Box D is filled in since the correct answer for the sample question 1 is D.

1. Ⓐ Ⓑ Ⓒ Ⓓ Ⓔ	21. Ⓐ Ⓑ Ⓒ Ⓓ Ⓔ	41. Ⓐ Ⓑ Ⓒ Ⓓ Ⓔ	61. Ⓐ Ⓑ Ⓒ Ⓓ Ⓔ
2. Ⓐ Ⓑ Ⓒ Ⓓ Ⓔ	22. Ⓐ Ⓑ Ⓒ Ⓓ Ⓔ	42. Ⓐ Ⓑ Ⓒ Ⓓ Ⓔ	62. Ⓐ Ⓑ Ⓒ Ⓓ Ⓔ
3. Ⓐ Ⓑ Ⓒ Ⓓ Ⓔ	23. Ⓐ Ⓑ Ⓒ Ⓓ Ⓔ	43. Ⓐ Ⓑ Ⓒ Ⓓ Ⓔ	63. Ⓐ Ⓑ Ⓒ Ⓓ Ⓔ
4. Ⓐ Ⓑ Ⓒ Ⓓ Ⓔ	24. Ⓐ Ⓑ Ⓒ Ⓓ Ⓔ	44. Ⓐ Ⓑ Ⓒ Ⓓ Ⓔ	64. Ⓐ Ⓑ Ⓒ Ⓓ Ⓔ
5. Ⓐ Ⓑ Ⓒ Ⓓ Ⓔ	25. Ⓐ Ⓑ Ⓒ Ⓓ Ⓔ	45. Ⓐ Ⓑ Ⓒ Ⓓ Ⓔ	65. Ⓐ Ⓑ Ⓒ Ⓓ Ⓔ
6. Ⓐ Ⓑ Ⓒ Ⓓ Ⓔ	26. Ⓐ Ⓑ Ⓒ Ⓓ Ⓔ	46. Ⓐ Ⓑ Ⓒ Ⓓ Ⓔ	66. Ⓐ Ⓑ Ⓒ Ⓓ Ⓔ
7. Ⓐ Ⓑ Ⓒ Ⓓ Ⓔ	27. Ⓐ Ⓑ Ⓒ Ⓓ Ⓔ	47. Ⓐ Ⓑ Ⓒ Ⓓ Ⓔ	67. Ⓐ Ⓑ Ⓒ Ⓓ Ⓔ
8. Ⓐ Ⓑ Ⓒ Ⓓ Ⓔ	28. Ⓐ Ⓑ Ⓒ Ⓓ Ⓔ	48. Ⓐ Ⓑ Ⓒ Ⓓ Ⓔ	68. Ⓐ Ⓑ Ⓒ Ⓓ Ⓔ
9. Ⓐ Ⓑ Ⓒ Ⓓ Ⓔ	29. Ⓐ Ⓑ Ⓒ Ⓓ Ⓔ	49. Ⓐ Ⓑ Ⓒ Ⓓ Ⓔ	69. Ⓐ Ⓑ Ⓒ Ⓓ Ⓔ
10. Ⓐ Ⓑ Ⓒ Ⓓ Ⓔ	30. Ⓐ Ⓑ Ⓒ Ⓓ Ⓔ	50. Ⓐ Ⓑ Ⓒ Ⓓ Ⓔ	70. Ⓐ Ⓑ Ⓒ Ⓓ Ⓔ
11. Ⓐ Ⓑ Ⓒ Ⓓ Ⓔ	31. Ⓐ Ⓑ Ⓒ Ⓓ Ⓔ	51. Ⓐ Ⓑ Ⓒ Ⓓ Ⓔ	71. Ⓐ Ⓑ Ⓒ Ⓓ Ⓔ
12. Ⓐ Ⓑ Ⓒ Ⓓ Ⓔ	32. Ⓐ Ⓑ Ⓒ Ⓓ Ⓔ	52. Ⓐ Ⓑ Ⓒ Ⓓ Ⓔ	72. Ⓐ Ⓑ Ⓒ Ⓓ Ⓔ
13. Ⓐ Ⓑ Ⓒ Ⓓ Ⓔ	33. Ⓐ Ⓑ Ⓒ Ⓓ Ⓔ	53. Ⓐ Ⓑ Ⓒ Ⓓ Ⓔ	73. Ⓐ Ⓑ Ⓒ Ⓓ Ⓔ
14. Ⓐ Ⓑ Ⓒ Ⓓ Ⓔ	34. Ⓐ Ⓑ Ⓒ Ⓓ Ⓔ	54. Ⓐ Ⓑ Ⓒ Ⓓ Ⓔ	74. Ⓐ Ⓑ Ⓒ Ⓓ Ⓔ
15. Ⓐ Ⓑ Ⓒ Ⓓ Ⓔ	35. Ⓐ Ⓑ Ⓒ Ⓓ Ⓔ	55. Ⓐ Ⓑ Ⓒ Ⓓ Ⓔ	75. Ⓐ Ⓑ Ⓒ Ⓓ Ⓔ
16. Ⓐ Ⓑ Ⓒ Ⓓ Ⓔ	36. Ⓐ Ⓑ Ⓒ Ⓓ Ⓔ	56. Ⓐ Ⓑ Ⓒ Ⓓ Ⓔ	76. Ⓐ Ⓑ Ⓒ Ⓓ Ⓔ
17. Ⓐ Ⓑ Ⓒ Ⓓ Ⓔ	37. Ⓐ Ⓑ Ⓒ Ⓓ Ⓔ	57. Ⓐ Ⓑ Ⓒ Ⓓ Ⓔ	77. Ⓐ Ⓑ Ⓒ Ⓓ Ⓔ
18. Ⓐ Ⓑ Ⓒ Ⓓ Ⓔ	38. Ⓐ Ⓑ Ⓒ Ⓓ Ⓔ	58. Ⓐ Ⓑ Ⓒ Ⓓ Ⓔ	78. Ⓐ Ⓑ Ⓒ Ⓓ Ⓔ
19. Ⓐ Ⓑ Ⓒ Ⓓ Ⓔ	39. Ⓐ Ⓑ Ⓒ Ⓓ Ⓔ	59. Ⓐ Ⓑ Ⓒ Ⓓ Ⓔ	79. Ⓐ Ⓑ Ⓒ Ⓓ Ⓔ
20. Ⓐ Ⓑ Ⓒ Ⓓ Ⓔ	40. Ⓐ Ⓑ Ⓒ Ⓓ Ⓔ	60. Ⓐ Ⓑ Ⓒ Ⓓ Ⓔ	80. Ⓐ Ⓑ Ⓒ Ⓓ Ⓔ

Model Advanced Placement European History Examination No. 1

**Section I
Multiple-Choice
Questions**

Time—60 minutes for 80 questions

Directions: Each of the following questions has five suggested answers. Choose the one that is best in each case.

---

1. Which of the following is NOT true of the "Glorious Revolution" of 1689?
    (A) It established, once and for all, the right of Parliament to levy taxes.
    (B) It established that the monarchy and Parliament ruled England together.
    (C) It reflected the theories of government of Thomas Hobbes.
    (D) It was supported by the theories of John Locke.
    (E) It marked the supremacy of constitutionalism in England.

2. Religious toleration by the English government from 1534, when the English Reformation began, to 1689, when the Toleration Act was passed
    (A) guaranteed the right to worship to all Christian sects
    (B) denied the right to worship to all except Anglicans
    (C) denied only the right to worship to atheists
    (D) periodically denied to Catholics the right to worship
    (E) was varied, at times denying then guaranteeing freedom of worship to different sects

3. Which was NOT a goal of Christian humanists like Erasmus and Thomas More?
    (A) To recapture the moral force of early Christianity
    (B) To reform the Roman Catholic Church
    (C) To criticize the pomposities of leaders and inequities of society
    (D) To support Protestantism
    (E) To emphasize the religious aspects of classical literature

4. Regiomontanus and Nicholas of Cusa helped lay the foundations for Copernicus's radical theory of astronomy by their work in
    (A) telescopic observation
    (B) physics
    (C) mathematics
    (D) empirical science
    (E) philosophical disputation

5.   Machiavelli's *The Prince* was significant because
       (A)   it became the "Bible of 20th-century dictators"
       (B)   it was one of the first reality-based treatises on political behavior
       (C)   it was written with the goal of unifying Italy
       (D)   it was based primarily on empirical observation
       (E)   all of the above

6.   In the 14th and 15th centuries, mystics, such as Meister Eckhart, Thomas à Kempis, and the founder of Brothers of the Common Faith, Gerard Groote
       (A)   preached rebellion against the papacy
       (B)   stressed the importance of the sacraments
       (C)   laid the foundations for Protestantism's personal approach to worship
       (D)   argued the necessity of adhering to dogma
       (E)   had a universal and popular appeal

7.   An important accomplishment of the Treaty of Utrecht (1713–1714) was
       (A)   that it allowed a Bourbon monarch to rule both Spain and France
       (B)   it established a French empire in North America
       (C)   it set up an independent and unified Netherlands
       (D)   it ousted the Austrians from Italy
       (E)   it helped restore the balance of power on the continent

8.   The Massacre of St. Bartholomew's Day in 1572
       (A)   marked the renewal of religious civil war in France
       (B)   resulted in the slaughter of Catholic leaders
       (C)   marked the end of Protestantism in France
       (D)   restored religious toleration in France
       (E)   was perpetrated by Huguenot mobs

9.   Which of the following is NOT a major tenet of Lutheranism?
       (A)   Salvation is by faith and faith only
       (B)   The Bible is the final authority for Christian Doctrine
       (C)   Absolution from sin comes only through the grace of God
       (D)   Baptism is the only valid sacrament
       (E)   Only the inner grace of God, not indulgences or absolution, can free one from sin

10.   Which of the following is a significant difference between medieval and Renaissance sculpture?
       (A)   The shift from Old Testament to New Testament themes
       (B)   The use of stone rather than wood
       (C)   Renaissance sculpture was devoid of religious subjects
       (D)   Renaissance art represented the visible world rather than conventional symbolism
       (E)   Renaissance sculpture was no longer commissioned by the popes

11.   Calvin, a Frenchman, established a theocratic government in
    (A)   France
    (B)   Scotland
    (C)   Sweden
    (D)   Switzerland
    (E)   England

12.   "The church is not subordinate to the state, but rather must be ruled according to God's plan. The chosen few should not only govern the church but also the state." An adherent of what religious group is likely to have believed this in the 16th century?
    (A)   Lutheran
    (B)   Calvinist
    (C)   Roman Catholic
    (D)   Millennarian
    (E)   Anabaptist

13.   During the 16th century, which dynasty ruled a dominion that stretched from the Atlantic to Eastern Europe, from the Baltic to the Mediterranean?
    (A)   Valois
    (B)   Hohenzollern
    (C)   Bourbon
    (D)   Tudor
    (E)   Hapsburg

14.   All of the following are accurate depictions of the Thirty Years' War (1618–1648) EXCEPT
    (A)   it was fought mostly in Germany
    (B)   it involved the major states of Europe
    (C)   it was a religious struggle between Protestants and Catholics
    (D)   it was a political struggle between the German princes and the Holy Roman Empire
    (E)   it allied the French with the Austrian Hapsburgs

15.   Choose the correct chronology.
    (A)   Peace of Augsburg, Thirty Years' War, Peace of Westphalia
    (B)   Thirty Years' War, the Reign of Charles V as Holy Roman Emperor, Peace of Westphalia
    (C)   Ministry of Cardinal Richelieu, Diet of Worms, Thirty Years' War
    (D)   Reign of Louis XIV, Council of Trent, regency of Mazarin
    (E)   Regency of Mazarin, Treaty of Utrecht, Thirty Years' War

16. Philip II of Spain (1556–1598)
    (A)   championed religious toleration of Spanish Jews and Moslems
    (B)   granted independence to the Spanish Netherlands
    (C)   abolished the Alcabala, a 10 percent tax on all sales that inhib-
          ited commerce
    (D)   dedicated his reign to establishing Catholic orthodoxy
    (E)   was defeated by the Turks at Lepanto

17. The 17th century witnessed the rise in Central and Eastern Europe of
    two states:
    (A)   Austria and Prussia
    (B)   Poland and Austria
    (C)   Prussia and Russia
    (D)   Poland and Prussia
    (E)   Russia and Poland

18. The above map shows acquisitions of Peter the Great from 1682 to 1715.
    The territories were gained from
    (A)   Poland, Sweden, and the Ottoman Empire
    (B)   Prussia, Austria, and Poland
    (C)   Poland, Prussia, and the Ottoman Empire
    (D)   Sweden, the Ottoman Empire, and Austria
    (E)   Prussia, Poland, Sweden

19. Prussia has been called "a state built around an army," meaning that
    (A) the kings were recruited from the High Command
    (B) in a nation of separate states, the army was a unifying force
    (C) the Junkers were militarists
    (D) the army ruled the monarchy
    (E) universal conscription was the rule

20. Joseph II of Austria (1780–1790) has been called the "ideal Enlightened Despot" for all of the following EXCEPT
    (A) he abolished serfdom
    (B) he fostered freedom of the press
    (C) he granted religious freedom to most Christian sects and to Jews
    (D) he abolished the secret police
    (E) he suppressed the influence of the Roman Catholic Church

21. Louis XVI of France convened the Estates General in 1789 for the first time in over 150 years because
    (A) he wanted to show support for the growing democratic movement
    (B) he wanted approval to exempt the First and Second Estates from taxation
    (C) he wanted approval for taxing all landowners in the realm
    (D) he needed funds to help support the American cause against the British
    (E) he needed a legislative body to check the powers of Parlement of Paris

22. When the French people drew up cahiers (lists of grievances) in 1789 for the Estates General to consider, which of the following would NOT have been likely?
    (A) The peasants wanted relief from feudal dues.
    (B) The bourgeoisie called for access to high office in the military and government.
    (C) Shopkeepers wanted an end to unnecessary taxes on commerce.
    (D) The nobles wanted an expansion of royal power.
    (E) The clergy wanted protection of monastic lands.

23. The Age of Napoleon spanned what years?
    (A) 1799–1815
    (B) 1803–1815
    (C) 1789–1815
    (D) 1795–1814
    (E) 1799–1814

24.   Choose the correct chronology.
      I.   Congress of Vienna first assembles.
     II.   The Concert of Europe is formed.
   III.   The First Treaty of Paris is signed by Louis XVIII.
   IV.   The "Hundred Days" brings Napoleon's return and defeat.

   (A)   I, IV, II, III
   (B)   III, I, II, IV
   (C)   I, III, II, IV
   (D)   II, IV, I, III
   (E)   III, I, IV, II

25.   Why is it significant that Napoleon crowned himself as emperor of the First French Empire in 1804?
   (A)   He was the first of his line.
   (B)   It was a symbolic gesture to show his independence.
   (C)   Because of the Concordat of 1801, the clergy refused to participate.
   (D)   Because the Senate had named him "Emperor of the French" rather than "Emperor of France."
   (E)   It had no significance.

26.   All of the following were results of the Industrial Revolution EXCEPT
   (A)   it created two new social classes
   (B)   it displaced the landed aristocracy as the dominant social class
   (C)   it brought great wealth to factory owners
   (D)   it subjected workers and their families to low wages, long working days, and oppressive living conditions
   (E)   it created poverty much worse than that in the countryside

27.   According to Ricardo's Iron Law of Wages
   (A)   workers in pig iron production must earn subsistence wages
   (B)   population will outrun the food supply
   (C)   a ten-hour workday was most productive
   (D)   variations in the supply and demand of labor will lead to eventual mass starvation
   (E)   poverty will end only with the public ownership of the means of production

28.   How did Edward Jenner's development of a vaccine against smallpox influence the Industrial Revolution?
   (A)   It increased the food supply by protecting farmers from developing the disease through exposure to infected cows.
   (B)   It led indirectly to a population increase that provided more workers for urban factories.
   (C)   It improved the health of milkmaids and increased the supply of dairy products.
   (D)   Used on cattle, it increased the yield of meat.
   (E)   It had no influence.

"The Age of Reason diminished the human spirit by denying the emotionality that flows from the soul. Miracles are acts of God, not illusions for the senses. Mystery is at the core of existence. The tiller of the soil is purer at heart than the factory laborer, and science will never uncover the ultimate meaning of life."

29. The passage above would most likely have been written in the first half of the 19th century by
    (A) a Socialist
    (B) a materialist
    (C) a Romantic
    (D) a rationalist
    (E) a liberal

30. The writings of which of the following adhered to the themes of the movement reflected in the above passage?
    (A) Marx and Engels
    (B) Charles Darwin
    (C) Byron and Goethe
    (D) Edmund Burke
    (E) Freud

31. Hapsburg rule in the Austro-Hungarian Empire prior to World War I was most threatened by
    (A) the growth of socialism
    (B) liberal reformers
    (C) German aggression
    (D) the Pan-Slavic movement
    (E) a decline of the fine arts

32. Rejection of Romanticism and the adoption of realism in the arts and literature in the mid-19th century was affected by
    (A) the impact of industrialization
    (B) the impact of various scientific discoveries and theories such as Darwin's Natural Selection
    (C) the failure of the Revolutions of 1848
    (D) the "power politics" of national unification
    (E) All of the above

33. A revolution in psychology at the end of the 19th century popularized the notion that human behavior springs from irrational forces and unconscious urges. It was pioneered by
    (A) Auguste Comte
    (B) Leopold von Ranke
    (C) Sigmund Freud
    (D) William James
    (E) Carl Gustave Jung

34.   Monet, Renoir, and Pissarro pioneered which style of painting?
      (A)   Romanticism
      (B)   Impressionism
      (C)   Realism
      (D)   Abstractionism
      (E)   Cubism

35.   Who was the most influential statesman in Europe for the two decades
      before 1890, and why was he so powerful?
      (A)   Prime Minister Cavour because a united Italy had become a
            major player on the world stage
      (B)   Kaiser Wilhelm I because Germany had become the world's
            leading industrial power
      (C)   Chancellor Bismarck because the unification of Germany had
            upset the European balance of power
      (D)   Emperor Franz Joseph because he headed the rejuvenated
            monarchy of Austria-Hungary
      (E)   Prime Minister William Gladstone because England had
            acquired an empire upon which "the sun never set"

36.   Which of the following were strongholds of Protestantism by 1600?
      (A)   Northern Italy and Southern Germany
      (B)   Poland and Austria
      (C)   Hungary and Northern Germany
      (D)   Scandinavia and Northern Germany
      (E)   Austria and Germany

37.   All of the following are accurate assessments of the New Imperialism
      EXCEPT
      (A)   it degraded the subject peoples
      (B)   it created immensely profitable markets for European goods in
            the colonies
      (C)   it introduced progressive economies to the non-Western world
      (D)   it helped precipitate World Wars I and II
      (E)   it encouraged the non-West to modernize its social and politi-
            cal systems

38.   The transition from colonialism to independence was LEAST chaotic in
      which of the following?
      (A)   The Philippines
      (B)   The Belgian Congo
      (C)   The Dutch East Indies (Indonesia)
      (D)   Algeria
      (E)   Indochina

39.   The Open Door Policy was issued by the United States in 1899 to
    (A)   open China to trade with the West
    (B)   enable the United States to acquire territory in China
    (C)   protect China's territorial integrity
    (D)   counter Japanese imperialism in China proper
    (E)   restrict trade to those powers that had already established spheres of influence

40.   Which was NOT a provision of the Treaty of Versailles?
    (A)   Germany accepted sole responsibility for starting World War I.
    (B)   Austria was required to pay reparations to the Allies.
    (C)   Germany was effectively disarmed.
    (D)   The Rhineland was demilitarized.
    (E)   Germany was to pay the cost of damage done to the property of Allied civilians.

41.   All are important reasons for the failure of the League of Nations EXCEPT
    (A)   each member nation of the Assembly got one vote regardless of its power
    (B)   the United States never joined
    (C)   economic sanctions could be ignored by member nations
    (D)   the league could but never did raise an international force to repel aggression
    (E)   Italy and Japan's defiance of league mandates in the 1930s reduced its credibility

42.   All were weapons first employed in combat during World War I EXCEPT
    (A)   armored tanks
    (B)   poison gas
    (C)   observation balloons
    (D)   diesel-powered submarines
    (E)   fighter aircraft

43.   Cultural relativism—that the validity of a society's values depend upon its political and economic context—was encouraged in the 20th century by the theories of
    (A)   Herbert Spencer
    (B)   Sigmund Freud
    (C)   Albert Einstein
    (D)   Thomas Huxley
    (E)   Isaac Newton

44.   The peace settlements at the end of World War I helped cause World
       War II for all the following reasons EXCEPT
       (A)   the newly established independent states of Eastern Europe left
              a power vacuum in the region
       (B)   the establishment of Communism in Russia led to eventual
              conflict between Germany and the U.S.S.R.
       (C)   reparations and the war guilt clause provided grounds for
              Hitler's propaganda
       (D)   Italy's and Japan's resentments of the settlements created inter-
              national instability
       (E)   the collapse of the Ottoman Empire created a belligerent and
              aggressive independent Turkey

45.   The photo above is of a structure that has been called the greatest monu-
       ment to absolutism and self-aggrandizement. It was
       (A)   the Hermitage of Catherine the Great
       (B)   the Schonbrunn Palace of the Hapsburgs
       (C)   the Palace at Versailles of Louis XIV
       (D)   Sans Souci of Frederick the Great
       (E)   The Blenheim Palace of the Duke of Marlborough

46.   The German composer whose grandiose operas had nationalistic themes
       and who, long after his death, was a favorite of Adolf Hitler was:
       (A)   Robert Schumann
       (B)   Franz Schubert
       (C)   Ludwig Von Beethoven
       (D)   Richard Wagner
       (E)   Franz Liszt

47. Which of the following are valid generalizations about the rise of Communism in Russia from 1917 to 1939?
    (A) Corruption in the czar's government and war reverses brought Communism to power.
    (B) The disunity of both their internal and their foreign enemies solidified the original successes of the Communists.
    (C) Central economic planning and brutal repression industrialized Russia's agrarian economy within two decades.
    (D) None of the above
    (E) All of the above

48. What was the condition of the Soviet economy on the eve of World War II?
    (A) It was in a shambles due to the political repression of the labor force.
    (B) It was one of the world's most productive.
    (C) It had been ravaged by depression unemployment and underproduction.
    (D) It depended heavily on foreign investment and imports.
    (E) While healthy, its technology and productivity were far behind that of the capitalist nations of the West.

49. What is the social significance of women working in factories during World War I?
    (A) Due to the wartime shortage of male workers, even the supervisors were women.
    (B) Women were found to be more adept than men at close detail work.
    (C) Universal suffrage had been granted with the outbreak of war, and women used the vote as leverage for getting industrial jobs.
    (D) The vital contribution of women to the war effort helped in their liberation from narrow social roles.
    (E) Only women in those days would accept such tedious, menial work.

"'God is on our side,' each claimed and fervently believed as they marched off in 1914. They denied themselves the freedom to learn the truth and speak out against the insanity of it all, and they sent a whole generation of their young men to the slaughter."

50. The "they" in the passage above refers to
    (A) the kaiser's military High Command
    (B) the British General Staff
    (C) the leaders of the Central Powers
    (D) the czarist government of Russia
    (E) the belligerent nations of World War I

51. Had the above passage been written in 1914 in one of the warring countries, its writer would likely have been
    (A) published in the mainstream press
    (B) applauded by the general public
    (C) publically debated by an official of the government
    (D) ostracized and censored
    (E) a member of Parliament

52. After Lenin's death, how was Stalin able to succeed to the leadership of Communist Russia?
    (A) His heroic exploits during the Civil War of 1918 to 1922 earned him universal respect.
    (B) He was Lenin's heir apparent.
    (C) As secretary of the Soviet Communist party, he had appointed many of his supporters to positions of power.
    (D) He had his closest rival, Leon Trotsky, assassinated soon after Lenin died.
    (E) Most party members supported his policy of "building socialism in one country."

53. Adolf Hitler became chancellor of Germany in 1933 by
    (A) engineering a putsch against the Weimar Republic
    (B) setting fire to the Reichstag Building and using it as a pretext to restore order
    (C) being invited by the president to form a coalition government after the Nazis won a plurality of Reichstag seats
    (D) being directly elected by a clear majority
    (E) assassinating the chancellor of the Weimar Republic and seizing the office

54. The Nuremberg Laws of 1935
    (A) imprisoned known Communists in concentration camps
    (B) denied the Jews of Germany all their rights as citizens
    (C) outlawed labor unions and strikes in Germany
    (D) made Hitler German president for life
    (E) repealed the Treaty of Versailles

55. Which best characterizes the foreign policy aims of the major powers before World War II?
    (A) The United States, France, and Britain wanted to maintain the status quo as defined by the peace settlements after World War I.
    (B) Germany, Italy, and Japan wanted to revise the peace settlements that ended World War I.
    (C) The U.S.S.R. wanted to guarantee its security and expand its influence.
    (D) None of these
    (E) All of these

56. The first European country to grant women suffrage, in 1906, was
   (A)   Britain
   (B)   France
   (C)   Germany
   (D)   Norway
   (E)   Finland

57. Which of the following nations consistently urged the world community to take up "collective security" in the 1930s?
   (A)   The United States
   (B)   Britain
   (C)   France
   (D)   China
   (E)   The U.S.S.R.

58. Hitler's rule in Germany was popular with most of the German people until
   (A)   the Nuremberg Laws were enacted
   (B)   Dachau concentration camp was opened
   (C)   Germany suffered serious reversals in World War II
   (D)   the abuses of the SS were publicized
   (E)   Germany entered World War II

59. What is the best estimate of the number of Jews and non-Jews systematically murdered by the Nazis by such measures as gassing, shooting, starvation?
   (A)   600,000
   (B)   1,000,000
   (C)   6,000,000
   (D)   12,000,000
   (E)   25,000,000

60. Which of the following profoundly changed the traditional domestic role of European women?
   (A)   Industrialization
   (B)   Feminism
   (C)   Birth control
   (D)   None of these
   (E)   All of these

61. "Functionalism," founded by Walter Gropius and taught at the German *Bauhaus* was
   (A)   a philosophical movement espousing the expansion of women's roles in modern society
   (B)   a style of clothing that dispensed with frills
   (C)   a trend in postmodern painting that used limited colors and set modes of execution
   (D)   a school of literary critique that argued for precision in language in the age of "doubletalk"
   (E)   a style of architecture that argued that beauty will follow once a building is well designed to serve its purpose

62. There is strong evidence that the German Army might have toppled Hitler from power if the Western democracies had made a firm stand in 1936
    (A) against the *Anschluss* with Austria
    (B) at the Munich conference against the German annexation of the Sudetenland
    (C) against the Nazi-Soviet Nonaggression Pact
    (D) against the remilitarization of the Rhineland
    (E) against the invasion of Poland

63. What is the best estimate of the total cost in human lives of World War II?
    (A) 55 million, of whom approximately two thirds were civilians
    (B) 40 million, of whom approximately half were civilians
    (C) 30 million, of whom three quarters were civilians
    (D) 25 million, of whom two fifths were civilians
    (E) 15 million, of whom one third were civilians

64. The German blitzkrieg tactic, used against Poland in 1939 and France in 1940, included all EXCEPT
    (A) frontal infantry assaults against heavily fortified positions
    (B) a spearhead of fast armor on a narrow front
    (C) tactical air support of ground forces
    (D) mobile infantry units transported by motorcycles and fast vehicles
    (E) the clearing of enemy mines and obstacles by combat engineers

65. *Guernica*, a masterpiece of propaganda expressing outrage at the slaughter of innocents by a Fascist terror-bombing of a town during the Spanish Civil War, was painted by one of the most famous and controversial artists of the 20th century
    (A) Salvador Dali
    (B) Piet Mondrian
    (C) Marcel Duchamp
    (D) Edvard Munch
    (E) Pablo Picasso

66. The Soviets were able to repel and defeat the Nazi invaders in World War II for all of these reasons EXCEPT
    (A) the Germans were never prepared for combat in the brutal Russian winter
    (B) the Russians mounted heroic resistance
    (C) the enormous front overextended German defenses and supply lines
    (D) Soviet war production surpassed that of the Germans
    (E) the Soviets moved most of the industry of European Russia hundreds of miles east out of range of the Germans

67. Which was the MOST important contribution of the United States to the defeat of the Axis?
    (A) The superiority of its aircraft
    (B) The development of atomic weapons
    (C) The brilliance of its military commanders
    (D) The productivity of its industries
    (E) The abundance of its natural resources

68. The devastation of Europe after World War II was far worse than after World War I for which of the following reasons?
  (A) The technology and tactics of the First World War limited the damage to specific regions.
  (B) Saturation bombing of cities during World War II destroyed or severely damaged nearly all the major industrial areas of the belligerents.
  (C) The scorched-earth policy leveled hundreds of thousands of structures in the U.S.S.R. during World War II.
  (D) None of the above
  (E) All of the above

69. When they rejected Western aid in the form of the American Marshall Plan in order to rebuild their wartorn land, the Soviets
  (A) were unable to repair the damage for decades
  (B) commandeered the tools of industry from their satellites in order to rebuild their own damaged factories and left an agrarian economy in Eastern Europe
  (C) scoured the Third World for investors
  (D) repaired the damage within a decade under Stalin's Five-Year Plans
  (E) never did fully rebuild after the war

70. By the 1920s, the theories of Sigmund Freud, developed before World War I, had become widely known and by midcentury all of the following were true EXCEPT
  (A) his emphasis on the sex urge had been modified by his successors
  (B) new schools of psychology offered vastly different explanations of human behavior
  (C) Freud was criticized for his less than rigorously scientific methods
  (D) his theories were criticized for interpreting male behavior by standards more appropriate to females
  (E) watered-down versions of his creative and complex theories had crept into the popular culture

71. Which is the most valid generalization about the response of the Soviet satellites to the de-Stalinization program of the Soviet Communist party after Stalin's death?
  (A) They branded it as revisionist and rejected it.
  (B) They followed the "party line."
  (C) They responded in varying degrees; some were encouraged to openly revolt against Soviet domination.
  (D) They demanded and were granted liberalization of their Soviet-dominated governments.
  (E) They turned to the West for guidance.

72. In 1957, the West grudgingly accepted the technological advancement of the Soviets, who
    (A) tested their first atomic bomb
    (B) perfected an intercontinental missile capable of striking the United States
    (C) developed a hydrogen bomb
    (D) launched the world's first artificial satellite
    (E) installed indoor plumbing in all public housing in the U.S.S.R.

73. All of the following are valid generalizations about academic philosophy in the period before World War II EXCEPT
    (A) it attempted to adopt the methodology of science
    (B) it was often limited to linguistic analysis
    (C) it attempted to answer the traditional problems posed by philosophers
    (D) it was detached and remote from the ethical concerns of modern life
    (E) its concerns were remote for most people

74. Which was NOT true of the Brezhnev Doctrine?
    (A) It stated that the U.S.S.R. had the right to intervene in the internal affairs of any of its satellites where Communism was threatened.
    (B) It was applied to suppress the Hungarian Uprising of 1956.
    (C) Its promulgation marked the end of Soviet leadership of the Communist world.
    (D) It diminished the role of the U.S.S.R. as a model for other Communist states.
    (E) It alienated many Third World nations.

75. Which of the following is true of organized religion after World War II?
    (A) Protestantism attempted a closer understanding with Roman Catholicism through ecumenicalism.
    (B) Christianity adjusted to new challenges such as secularism and Communism.
    (C) The newly created state of Israel received support from Jews all over the world in response to the Holocaust.
    (D) Hinduism, Buddhism, and Islam drew new adherents in the West.
    (E) All of the above

76. Choose the correct chronology of Cold War events.
    I.   The Berlin Wall is built.
    II.   NATO is established.
    III. The Korean War breaks out.
    IV.   The Truman doctrine is announced.
    V.   The death of Stalin leads to a "thaw."

    (A) II, III, IV, V, I
    (B) V, IV, III, I, II
    (C) I, IV, III, II, IV
    (D) IV, II, III, V, I
    (E) IV, III, II, V, I

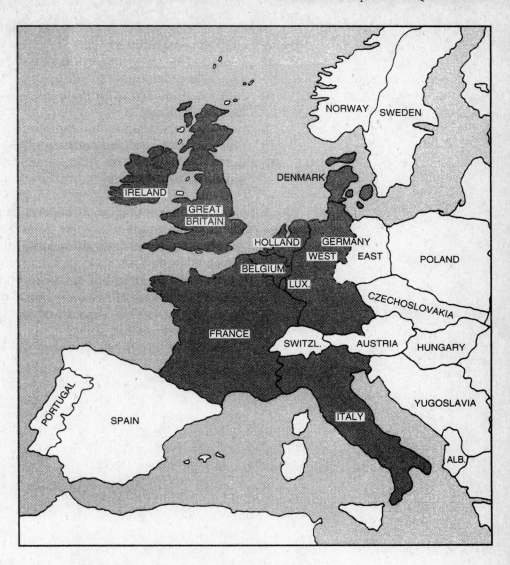

77. On the above map, the shaded countries
     (A) indicate the European members of NATO in 1949
     (B) indicate the members of the European Coal and Steel
          Community
     (C) show the Common Market members in 1973
     (D) show the recipients of U.S. military aid in 1947 under the
          Truman Doctrine
     (E) indicate the original members of the Common Market

78. The policy of détente—the peaceful coexistence of the Western and
     Communist blocs—was most actively pursued during the administra-
     tion of which of the following U.S. presidents?
     (A) Harry Truman
     (B) Dwight Eisenhower
     (C) John Kennedy
     (D) Lyndon Johnson
     (E) Richard Nixon

79.   The youth rebellion that developed worldwide in the 1960s had all of the following characteristics EXCEPT
    (A)   it tended to point out the failings of modern technological society and underplay its advantages
    (B)   it glorified rebels against the status quo such as Fidel Castro and Ho Chi Minh
    (C)   it attacked materialism and tradition
    (D)   it looked to Soviet Communism for guidance
    (E)   it drew on neo-Marxist theories and often resorted to violence to further its programs

80.   The militant contemporary phase of the Women's movement that began in the 1960s
    (A)   sought an end not only to legal but also to social barriers to gender equality
    (B)   had the greatest appeal in the Third World
    (C)   argued that gender differences were inborn
    (D)   found that gender discrimination was a problem rarely found in Communist societies
    (E)   originated in the United States and had little appeal in Europe

<table>
<tr><td>

Section II
Free-Response
Questions

</td><td>

Part A: *Document-Based Essay Question (DBQ)*

Writing time—45 minutes; 45 percent of Section II score

Directions: The essay question that follows is based on the accompanying documents. Write the essay in response to the question by analyzing the documents, considering their sources and biases, referring to appropriate historical information not cited, and integrating all these into your answer. (Some documents have been edited.)

</td></tr>
</table>

1.   Describe and analyze the ways the personal aims of Adolf Hitler and the doctrines of the Nazi party evolved into the policy of genocide. *Historical Background:* During the existence of the Third Reich and under the leadership of Adolf Hitler, an estimated 6 million of Europe's estimated 11 million Jews were murdered simply for being Jews. By 1942, concentration camps, more accurately "death factories," gassed thousands of people a day and cremated their bodies.

Document A

I began to hate them.... For me this was the time of the greatest spiritual upheaval I have ever had to go through. I had ceased to be a weak-kneed cosmopolitan and became an anti-Semite.

> Adolf Hitler recalling his days as a struggling artist in pre-World War I Vienna
> *Mein Kampf*

Document B

The Party.... combats the Jewish-materialist spirit within us and without us, and is convinced that our nation can only achieve permanent health from within on the principle: THE COMMON INTEREST BEFORE SELF.

> From the first Nazi party Program, 1920

Document C

In opposition to the bourgeois and the Marxist-Jewish worlds, the *Volk* philosophy.... by no means believes in an equality of the races, but.... feels itself obligated to promote the victory of the better and the stronger.... the subordination of the inferior and weaker.

> Adolf Hitler, *Mein Kampf*

Document D

Sign at the entrance to a Jewish-owned store. Sign reads: "Germans beware! Do not buy from Jews!"

Document E

"The Jew: supplier of war, prolonger of war."

>Widely distributed propaganda poster in the Third Reich.

Document F

"Juden unerwuenscht" ("Jews not welcome")

>Signs posted in public places all over the Third Reich.

Document G

If international Jewish financiers should succeed once more in plunging the nations into a world war, then the result will not be the Bolshevization of the world and a victory of Jewry, but, on the contrary, the destruction of the Jewish race in Europe.

>Adolf Hitler, Speech to the *Reichstag* soon after *Kristallnacht.*

Document H

I.... charge you to submit to me.... measures already taken for the.... *final solution* of the Jewish problem.

>Reich Marshal Hermann Goering to Chief of the Gestapo Reinhard Heydrich, July 1941.

Document I

The Jews should now in the course of the Final Solution be brought to the East ....for use as labor..... A great part will fall through natural diminution. The remnant that finally is able to survive all this ....must be treated accordingly.

>Heydrich to members of various Gestapo and SS agencies, Wannsee Conference, January 1942.

Document J

Still another improvement we made over Treblinka (Concentration Camp) was that.... we endeavored to fool the victims into thinking they were to go through a delousing process.... At Auschwitz [Concentration Camp], I used Zyklon B [gas].... which we dropped into the death chamber from a small opening. It took from three to fifteen minutes to kill the people.

Rudolf Hess, former commandant at Auschwitz.

**Section II
Free-Response
Questions**

Part B: *Two Essay Questions*

Writing time—70 minutes for two essays; 55 percent of Section II score

Directions: Answer *two* of the following, one from Group A and one from Group B. Be sure to cite relevant historical information to support your answer. Number your answer as the question below is numbered. Use extra time to check your work.

GROUP A

1. Explain why the Anglican Church broke with Roman Catholicism before adopting any of the tenets of Protestantism.

2. "The Congress of Vienna aligned the European balance of power effectively, but it restored the old order clumsily." Assess the validity of this statement.

3. To what extent and in what ways had Western Europe recovered economically from the effects of World War II a decade after it had ended?

GROUP B

4. Contrast and compare the French Revolution of 1789 with the Russian Revolution of 1917.

5. "The most profound revolutions are in the realm of ideas." Analyze this statement by making reference to the influence upon their age of TWO of the following thinkers: Copernicus, Calvin, Newton, Adam Smith, Darwin, Freud, Einstein.

6. "Japan's successes up to 1942 served as a model for subject peoples in the European colonial empires." Defend or refute this statement.

Answers and Comments for Questions on Model Advanced Placement Examination No. 1

Answer Key

1. C	2. E	3. D	4. C	5. E
6. C	7. E	8. A	9. D	10. D
11. D	12. B	13. E	14. E	15. A
16. D	17. C	18. A	19. B	20. D
21. C	22. D	23. A	24. E	25. B
26. E	27. D	28. B	29. C	30. C
31. D	32. E	33. C	34. B	35. C
36. D	37. B	38. A	39. C	40. B
41. A	42. C	43. C	44. E	45. C
46. D	47. E	48. B	49. D	50. E
51. D	52. C	53. C	54. B	55. E
56. E	57. E	58. C	59. D	60. E
61. E	62. D	63. A	64. A	65. E
66. A	67. D	68. E	69. D	70. D
71. C	72. D	73. C	74. B	75. E
76. D	77. C	78. E	79. D	80. A

Answers Explained

1. (C) Hobbes's works supported absolutism.

2. (E) Catholics and some Protestant sects were denied religious freedom at various times.

3. (D) They wanted to reform but not dismantle Roman Catholicism.

4. (C) Their work allowed Copernicus to develop a more elegant and simple model of the universe than that of Ptolemy.

5. (E) It was not a moral tract based on the Church law or dogma; it attempted to evaluate real politics and then offered a prescription for divided Italy.

6. (C) The mystics' personal approach to communion with God and the simple piety preached by Groote set the tone for Luther's tenets.

7. (E) France's overwhelming strength and Louis's penchant for war had disturbed the balance of power for decades.

8. (A) Catholic plotters and Catholic mobs slaughtered Huguenot leaders, and the religious civil war broke out with renewed fervor and brutality.

9. (D) Baptism and Holy Communion were both considered sacraments by Luther.

10. (D) It shows emotion, anatomic accuracy, humanity. It was religious but lacked the symbolic representation of medieval art.

11. (D) Zwingli and Calvin preached in Geneva, a Swiss city.

12. (B) Theocracy was a feature of Calvinism, which argued that religious morality should influence the state.

13. (E) The fabled Hapsburg family was one of the oldest and most powerful in Europe.

14.   (E)   Cardinal Richelieu got into the war in order to nullify Austria's power and influence among the German states.

15.   (A)   Another crusty chronological identification.

16.   (D)   He forcibly converted or expelled the Jews and the Moors, Spain's most productive and educated groups; he crushed resistance in the Spanish Netherlands; he put a restrictive tax on all sales; he helped defeat the Turkish invaders.

17.   (C)   Prussia and Russia modernized and expanded under wise leadership.

18.   (A)   He chewed into the possessions of these once-powerful states.

19.   (B)   A Christian buffer state between the West and the Russians, its army was always its focal point.

20.   (D)   The secret police actually helped Joseph to extend his reforms by making centralization of his government easier.

21.   (C)   The high court, the Parlement of Paris, declared it was necessary if he was to initiate a tax on the exempted First and Second Estates.

22.   (D)   The battle for power between a centralized monarchy and the nobility was a familiar theme all during the growth of the nation-state.

23.   (A)   Chrono madness! But again it is open to analysis. Napoleon made a comeback in 1815 after exile on Elbe. That rules out choices D and E. The French Revolution began in 1789; that makes choice C inappropriate. Napoleon was in power before 1803, so choice B is out.

24.   (E)   Here we go again. If you don't know it, avoid it.

25.   (B)   Beholden to no one and nothing but his own abilities. That was his point.

26.   (E)   Poverty was a normal condition before the generalized prosperity of the 20th century. Country people were as poor as urban dwellers, sometimes more so. The difference was that the Industrial Revolution concentrated the poverty in the city slums so it could not be ignored and had to be dealt with.

27.   (D)   He tried to explain why Adam Smith's "natural law" economy did not bring about the general prosperity that he had promised in *Wealth of Nations*.

28.   (B)   Healthier people work harder, live longer. His original experimental innoculation of a diluted solution containing a cowpox scab was into the arm of a small boy. An interesting moral issue.

29.   (C)   The Romantic movement was a reaction to the rationalism of the Enlightenment.

30.   (C)   Lord Byron, the English poet, and Johann von Goethe, the great German poet and dramatist, personified the movement.

31.   (D)   Of the many non-German minorities that were part of the empire, the Slavs were most vocal in their anti-German, anti-Hungarian nationalism.

32.   (E)   All of these.

33.   (C)   Freud's view of human irrationality revolutionized attitudes.

34.   (B)   Romanticism flowed from the reactions to the French Revolution, realism from the the ugly realities of the industrialized world, abstract art and cubism developed during and after the First World War.

35.   (C)   Head of a powerful united Germany, victor over France, he was the most influential man in Europe during that period. His masterful diplomacy kept a balance but helped incite World War I decades after his death because he tried to isolate France with a network of alliances.

36.   (D)   England was also an important center.

37.   (B)   The non-European peoples in the colonies did not have wealth enough to provide a rich market for European manufactured goods. The most profitable trade was between industrialized nations.

38.   (A)   It was slated for independence in 1946, and, despite the ravages of World War II, which ended in 1945, the schedule was kept. However, the Islands are wracked today by guerrilla war and economic instability.

39.   (C)   The United States was probably more interested in protecting its markets in China from the kind of partition that Africa suffered than in protecting Chinese culture and autonomy.

40.   (B)   It was required to pay indemnities but not under the Treaty of Versailles. The Treaty of Saint-Germaine settled the peace with Austria.

41.   (A)   The big powers got representation in the council.

42.   (C)   Observation balloons were used as far back as the U.S. Civil War.

43.   (C)   It was another of those broad applications of a revolutionary theory in a specific field, like social Darwinism following along on the coattails of Natural Selection.

44.   (E)   Turkey modernized, regained some territory lost after the peace settlements, but then maintained its neutrality during World War II, even though it leaned toward the Axis.

45.   (C)   The Palace at Versailles of Louis XIV cost huge sums of money that severly drained the French treasury. It was a monument to Louis XIV's glorified view of himself and his position.

46.   (D)   In the Third Reich, Wagnerian music served as a tool of propaganda, and there is strong biographical evidence that Wagner himself was an anti-Semite.

47.   (E)   Russia was ripe for revolution; the enemies of the Bolsheviks—the czarists, middle classes, Allied powers, and others—could not unite; modernization cost as many as 30 million Soviet citizens their lives.

48.   (B)   Stalin's Five-Year Plans had made it so despite the appalling costs to the people in terms of political repression.

49. (D)   War expediency drastically altered the idea that women—even middle-class women—belonged in the home. Their efficiency and dedication helped win them the vote in many European nations.

50. (E)   They all believed that God supported their cause.

51. (D)   Pacifists were not only publically reviled; they were often jailed.

52. (C)   Trotsky was the organizer of the victorious Red Army and Lenin's heir apparent, despite Stalin's claims to the contrary in the creative propaganda and historical revision after he had gained power. Stalin had Trotsky assassinated in 1940, more than a decade and half after ascending to power. The party was split on the issue of expanding the revolution outside the U.S.S.R.

53. (C)   He won the leadership of the democracy he swore to destroy, democratically.

54. (B)   They couldn't hold office, vote, own newspapers, marry non-Jews, work for the government, or carry on most business. It was the first step in the "final solution."

55. (E)   "Haves" versus "have-nots" and the consequences. Only the Soviets, for their own purposes, pushed for collective security measures during the 1930s.

56. (E)   Finland and then Norway granted women the vote before World War I. Britain and Germany instituted women's suffrage soon after World War I. France did not do it until after World War II.

57. (E)   The U.S.S.R. feared the Fascist militarists to the point of supporting the republican cause in the Spanish Civil War. Since the democracies were both afraid of Communism and absorbed by the depression, they ignored Soviet pleas.

58. (C)   When the bombs began to drop on their cities, they began to question the regime. By then, it was too late.

59. (D)   Six million Jews and six million non-Jews—Russian POWs, political enemies of the Nazis, minorities, underground fighters, clergy, and many others—were exterminated.

60. (E)   Industrialization brought them into the work force; feminism gave them the vote and opened new opportunities; birth control lengthened their lives and gave them biologic freedom.

61. (E)   "Form follows function" was the idea.

62. (D)   Hitler gambled that the French, with thousands of well-armed troops, would not oppose his token force. Anti-Nazi commanders in the Wehrmacht intended to depose him if the gamble had failed. The French sat behind their defenses and let him violate the Treaty of Versailles.

63. (A)   There is new evidence that the toll was even higher.

64. (A)   This was the deadly and futile tactic of the First World War.

65. (E)   The great Picasso was a Spaniard.

66.   (A)   After suffering the ravages of the winter of 1941–1942, the German military trained and equipped their troops and adopted tactics appropriate to the severe weather conditions.

67.   (D)   It was the "arsenal of democracy" and its industrial output surpassed that of all the other belligerents put together.

68.   (E)   It was, by far, the worst war in human history.

69.   (D)   It was a spectacular feat considering the destruction and death caused by the war.

70.   (D)   For interpreting female behavior by male standards.

71.   (C)   Armed resistance broke out in Poland and Hungary in 1956. Accommodations were made by the Soviets with the Communist government of Poland; the Hungarian Revolt was brutally and ruthlessly crushed.

72.   (D)   Sputnik shook the West out of its complacency.

73.   (C)   According to Ludwig Wittgenstein, philosophy could not deal with "God, death, and what is higher."

74.   (B)   It was used as a pretext to suppress the Czechoslovakian Uprising in 1968.

75.   (E)   All of the above.

76.   (D)   Some dates you simply have to learn.

77.   (C)   Britain, Ireland, and Denmark were added to the original six members. There are now twelve members.

78.   (E)   Despite, or maybe because of, his ardent anti-Communism, Nixon used personal diplomacy to improve U.S. relations with not only the U.S.S.R. but with Communist China.

79.   (D)   It rejected the Soviet leadership as encrusted bureaucrats out of touch with the real issues facing the planet, the Third World, and humanity.

80.   (A)   The gender issues in the Third World are powerful effects of tradition and poverty; subtle conditioning was identified as an important cause of sexual stereotyping; gender discrimination respects neither national boundaries nor ideology; it had wide appeal throughout the industrialized world.

Comments on the DBQ Section II; Part A

Refer to "DBQ Do's and Don'ts" on pages 18–19.

Read and interpret the question: To "describe and analyze" requires that you determine the relationships between Hitler's personal aims and the Nazi party's program and the murder of Europe's Jews, and that you trace the steps in the process. An "evolution" is a gradual process and not necessarily an intended result.

Read and analyze each of the documents in turn: Do they offer a schema to answer the question? Are they all pertinent to your answer? Are some more useful than others? How are they organized—by chronology, by contrast, by cause and effect?

Read the question again and relate specific documents to framing an answer: What were Hitler's aims? What doctrine of the Nazi party can you identify? What connection can you make between them and the remaining documents? Do you discern an evolution? If so, of what is it an evolution?

Outline your essay: Interpret the documents in order to analyze and describe how the aims of Hitler and the doctrine of the Nazi party that you have identified gradually led to the murder of 6 million innocent people. Refer to anything else you know about the period that is relevant to your answer. You may cite all or some of the documents. Be sure not to cite them by number or to simply summarize them. Use them to answer the question!

Before writing the essay: Read the question again. Glance through the documents. Check your outline to make sure it addresses the question.

Sample Answer for the DBQ

One of the most disturbing issues of the 20th century is how the Germans, an educated people who contributed mightily to Western civilization, could have allowed and, in too many cases, actively participated in the murder of 6 million people who were singled out simply because they were Jewish. An estimated total of 12 million people were "exterminated" by the Nazis: Soviet POWs, dissenters, homosexuals, clergy, various others chosen for various reasons, and Jews. The difference between the Jews and most other victims was that the Jews were killed in pursuit of a government policy that sought to eradicate their existence as a people. They were victims of genocide.

Why the Jews were slaughtered seems obvious. Hitler hated them. Why he hated them is the subject for psychohistorians. How he could translate this hatred into a government policy in a powerful, technologically advanced nation is not easily understood. The documents offered show a clear evolutionary process, but only careful analysis of their context in the period will reveal why one step led to the other. We see the step-by-step process from one demented soul's hatred of a group to its elevation as an aim of a political party to its dissemination through propaganda and political action to its terrible crystallization as a bureaucratic policy for genocide. The real issue that begs for analysis is how this process could take place, why sanity and decency did not nip it in the bud.

When you read the excerpt from Hitler's rambling autobiography, *Mein Kampf*, you begin to wonder what kind of young man—he was in his early twenties during his "Vienna Days"—could equate ethnic hatred with a "spiritual upheaval" and a decisive act of strength. One whose inferiority complex could only be mastered by finally finding people he could loathe as more loathsome than himself? Biographers and psychoanalysts have grappled with the question and offered insightful if contradictory answers. "He envied the Jews for their imagined wealth (most he met were poorer than he)." "He saw in their powerlessness a reflection of his own." "He needed victims." "If the Jews didn't exist, I would have had to invent them," he purportedly said. Whatever the root cause of his bigotry, how did he spread it like a plague among the German people?

One platform in the program of the early Nazi party was to combat "the Jewish-materialist spirit." Anti-Semitism existed long before Hitler and all over Europe. German greats such as Luther and Wagner perpetuated the medieval xenophobia that ghettoized and victimized Jews over the centuries.

The Nazi party existed before Hitler was part of it. It consisted of a small group of ten or so crackpots seeking solace for, and solutions to, Germany's humiliating defeat in World War I. Ironically, Hitler was sent by the army to spy on it as a subversive group. He sat in, listened and was fascinated, got to his feet and made one of his hypnotic, half-coherent speeches that dazzled the party members into immediately making him their leader. He had a career. He had an organization—however humble and harebrained—to help carry out his twisted aims. He helped hammer out the 1920 Party Program.

Mein Kampf (My Struggle), written while he was serving a sentence for the failed Beer Hall Putsch of 1923, reeks of Social Darwinism. "Survival of the fittest" is spelled out in "victory of the better and the stronger" and "subordination of the inferior and the weaker." Not just the Jews fit this later category; he wanted to enslave the Slavs of Poland and Russia. But the Jews were easier victims: There were less than 500,000 of them in Germany proper, 11 million in all of Europe. The ludicrous part of the Nazi accusation of a Marxist-Jewish "spirit," of a conspiracy of Jewish bankers who hoped to Bolshevize the world, is that Bolshevism, Communism, is the natural enemy of any capitalist, especially a banker.

The message was being delivered to the general populace. Boycott. Strong-arm tactics. They were used even before Hitler got into power. What should German buyers have been wary of when they patronized a Jewish store? High prices and low quality? More likely the thug in uniform at the door. Third Reich propaganda—radio talks, dramatic films, news distortions, vivid posters, doctored newspapers, even children's schools—spread and intensified the terrible bigotry, the infamous stereotypes. It wasn't the Jews who would profit from war and prolong its agony. It was the Nazis.

Discrimination is bigotry in action. "Jews not welcome." It wasn't just in government buildings; it was nearly everywhere. In hardly three years after Hitler took office, the Nuremberg Laws began to deny Jews the means to live, if not necessarily their lives. The public went along. Some didn't care. Some thought it would pass. Some agreed. The economy was booming. Unemployment was down. The war hadn't begun yet.

The saddest part of Hitler's promise of the destruction of the Jews in his speech to the Reichstag is that he could get away with the shabby jargon, internal contradictions, and veiled threats in front of the "Parliament of the People." It was already too late for decent people to stand against him and his Nazis. They had all the power. "The Night of Broken Glass" marked the beginning of the Holocaust. Not only did the Nazi mobs break the glass in every Jewish temple, shop, and home, but they began to murder. There were protests from the international community, but few nations—not even the great democracies—were willing to open their doors to Germany's beseiged and endangered Jews. It was a signal to Hitler that nobody cared enough to act.

The "final solution," a bureaucratic euphemism, a secretive reference to the terror ahead? How did it all go from discrimination to mass murder, from bigotry to genocide? Why did Reich Marshal Hermann Goering, second to Hitler, drug addict, sexual deviate, glutton, set into motion one of the worst deeds of history? Many people hate others for their physical characteristics or their religion or the group they belong to. Few resort to murder. Goering's order to "Hangman" Heydrich—the personification of the Aryan SS superman, a blindly obedient, heartlessly efficient bureaucrat and sadistic murderer—is the fruition of Nazism. One man's demented psyche was given voice by the program of a bunch of fringe people who got into power because German order collapsed after the First World War and the world collapsed with the depression. Hitler and the Nazis needed "scapegoats" to blame for Germany's and the world's ills. "Get rid of the scapegoat; solve the problem." Simple solutions to complex problems. They may not work, but they play well to a desperate audience.

Why genocide, though? Why not deportation, resettlement, anything else? The "final solution" to the "Jewish problem" was Hitler's insane legacy to the world, one of the contributions he thought would make him one of history's all-time greats. It was an expedient measure to provide scarce labor to a nation at war. It was a method of slavery whereby the slaves need not be cared for if they starve to death. There seemed to be an endless supply of them. It was another official order to obedient civil servants of the Nazis and of the German war machine. "The remnant... must be treated accordingly." The Wansee Conference was a meeting of the heads of the various SS and Gestapo bureaus—supermen, they thought themselves; bureaucrats, they were. Did they drink coffee and eat sweets while they decided the fate of 6 million souls?

The Nazis thought they could get away with anything because when it could have, the world didn't care to act; when it needed to, it couldn't. (Of course, there are those disturbing possibilities that were never acted out: bombing the tracks to the death factories or the crematoria; making it all public; promising retribution.)

Commandant Hess, a living god to the inmates at Auschwitz, a pathetic shell of a man at Nuremberg. Tricks to fool the victims into an easier slaughter. Deadlier gas. How proud he must have been to improve productivity. Did Heinrich Himmler, bespectacled head of the SS who fainted during his only visit to a concentration camp, award him for his efficiency?

They had to have detached themselves from the humanity of their victims. Everyone from the guard at the gates of Treblinka to Adolf Hitler had to pretend that they were "exterminating vermin" when they transported millions of men, women, and children across Europe to the death factories in Poland and Germany. There is no way around it. You cannot exterminate human beings. When you take a life intentionally, you commit the worst of all deeds. Why they didn't see that? Too many of them came to believe that anti-Semitism, that bigotry, that the disease of the disordered young man who wrote *Mein Kampf* was a "spiritual upheaval" to make them stronger.

Comments on the Sample Answer for the DBQ

5—Extremely well qualified

This essay demonstrates how the DBQ should be answered. It avoids the major Don'ts.

It doesn't simply list, refer to by number, or summarize the documents.

It doesn't forget to draw on the documents, if not necessarily all of them, to support its answer.

It doesn't fail to address the question in its effort to incorporate the documents.

The essay is a well-written, intelligent piece that responds to the question while drawing on the document and enriching the approach by knowledge-able references to the period. Its use of facts is appropriately restrained, interesting, and convincing:

"total of 12 million people exterminated"

"Hitler's rambling autobiography"

References to his "Vienna Days," his psychological problems, and their varied interpretations, "If the Jews did not exist"

References to the types of propaganda, to the Nuremberg Laws, to *Kristallnacht*

An understanding of the identity and roles of various personages—Goering, Heydrich, the bureaucrats at the Wansee Conference.

Above all, this essay reflects a profound understanding of the reasons for, and the effects of, this horrible period in human history:

"One of the most disturbing issues of the 20th century"

"he could translate this hatred into the governmental policy"

"a bureaucratic policy for genocide"

"anti-Semitism existed long before Hitler"

"He had an organization . . . to help carry out his twisted aims."

"reeks of Social Darwinism"

"The ludicrous part of the Nazi accusation"

"The message was being delivered to the general populace"

"Discrimination is bigotry in action"

"The *final solution*, a bureaucratic euphemism, a secretive reference to the terror that lay ahead?"

"Simple solutions to complex problems."

"when it could have, the world didn't care to act; when it needed to, it couldn't."

"Tricks to fool the victims into an easier slaughter."

"They had to have detached themselves from the humanity of their victims."

It is a logically connected and intelligible essay that incorporates document analysis into its consideration of the subject.

Comments on the Essay Questions Section II, Part B

In answering these questions, be sure to follow the "Simple Procedures" for writing an essay:

First, ask yourself what the question wants to know.

Second, ask yourself what you know about it.

Third, ask yourself how you would put it into words.

GROUP A ESSAYS

---

1.   *Explain* why the Anglican Church broke with Roman Catholicism before adopting any of the tenets of Protestantism.

What does the question want to know? "Offer the reason for and detail" why the Church of England declared its independence from Rome and the papacy before it had adopted any of the dogmas of Protestantism.

What do you know about it? In 1521, Henry VIII was awarded the title "Defender of the Faith" by Pope Clement VII for his anti-Lutheran tract. Six years later, when he decided to divorce Catherine of Aragon—to get a male heir and because he loved Anne Boleyn—the Pope denied him. Why did he deny him? What was his personal response? What was the role of Thomas Cranmer? Why did Parliament pass the Act of Supremacy in 1534? Why can it be said that the Statute of the Six Articles, 1539, completed the break with Rome?

How should you put it into words? The Anglican Church is the only Protestant sect to break with Rome before adopting Protestant ideas. Use a chronological approach to the events in order to explain why it happened.

---

2.   "The Congress of Vienna aligned the European balance of power effectively, but it restored the old order clumsily." *Assess the validity* of this statement.

What does the question want to know? "Determine the truth of" whether the Congress of Vienna laid out a design for peace better than it provided for a return to the systems of government that ruled European nations before the French Revolution.

What do you know about it? There was no continent-wide war in Europe for nearly a century after the Congress of Vienna. What is a balance of power? How had France upset it during the Wars of the Revolution and the Napoleonic Wars? How did the Congress nullify future French aggression with a system of "buffer states"?

What was the old order? How had the ideals of the French Revolution conflicted with absolutism, and how had they been spread over Europe? How did the Revolutions of 1832 and 1848 manifest many of these new ideals of government, such as nationalism, liberalism, republicanism?

How would you put it into words? Decide whether the statement is true or not. Build your essay accordingly. If you think it is true, demonstrate how the Congress designed the balance of power but failed to complete and maintain a restoration of the old governmental order.

> **3.** *To what extent and in what ways* had Europe recovered economically from the effects of World War II a decade after it had ended?

What does the question want to know? "How and how much" had Europe rebuilt its devastated cities, factories, transport systems, housing by the mid-1950s?

What do you know about it? What was the role of the United States in this reconstruction? What were the goals, accomplishments, and limitations of the Marshall Plan? How did the Soviet Bloc rebuild? How did the Five-Year Plans transform not only the U.S.S.R. but Eastern Europe? What part did the policy of containment play? What were the first steps taken toward a European economic union? What measures were there of economic revival?

How would you put it into words? Explain how Europe rebuilt and how far the reconstruction had gotten by 1955. Describe the progress, the agents of that progress, the innovations, the limitations.

GROUP B ESSAYS

> **4.** *Contrast and compare* the French Revolution of 1789 with the Russian Revolution of 1917.

What does the question want to know? "Show differences" between the French and Russian Revolutions, and "examine them for similarities." How were they different? How were they alike?

What do you know about it? Differences: The French Revolution occurred in the 18th century, a product of the Age of Enlightenment; the Russian in the early 20th century, an effect of World War I. What differences were there in the economic, social, and political conditions of each? How were they precipitated?

Similarities: They each had the classic three stages, although the third or reactionary stage was carried out in one by the group that had effected the second stage; they had far-reaching effects; they gave rise to radical ideologies; they helped define their times.

How would you put it into words? This is a difficult and comprehensive question, and the best approach is to follow the inherent structure: Show differences; show similarities.

> **5.** "The most profound revolutions are in the realm of ideas." Analyze this statement by making reference to the influence on their age of TWO of the following thinkers: Copernicus, Calvin, Newton, Adam Smith, Darwin, Freud, Einstein.

What does the question want to know? It requires you to "examine in detail" and to "explain" how new ideas create great revolutions. You have no choice here of evaluating the statement; you must show how a "profound revolution" can occur without a political change. Determine the meaning of "revolution" in this context, and then demonstrate how two of the thinkers helped bring one about in their respective historical periods.

What do you know about it? Copernicus developed the heliocentric view; Calvin formulated a new dogma of Protestantism; Newton described the universe according to "natural law"; Smith described the perfect laissez-faire economy; Darwin formulated the theory of Natural Selection; Freud defined human behavior by introducing the concept of the Unconscious; Einstein introduced the theories of Relativity.

How would you write about it? Each of these thinkers came up with ideas that shattered age-old assumptions or deeply held attitudes. What were these? What new perspective did the thinkers provide? How did it effect a revolution of belief, a crisis of belief?

---

6. "Japan's successes up to 1942 served as a model for subject peoples in the European colonial empires." *Defend or refute* this statement.

What does the question want to know? Argue for or against the idea that Japan was a role model for colonial peoples up to the time when it began to lose World War II.

What do you know about it? How was Japan's response to European imperialism different from that of most non-European nations? How were its industrialization, modernization, and maintenance of tradition an inspiration to the captive peoples of colonialism? How did its initial successes in World War II foster nationalism in the colonial world? How did its own colonial policies toward the Asians it conquered—the Co-Prosperity Sphere—alienate them? How did their wars against the Japanese invaders foster later independence?

How would you put it into words? Make your choice to argue for or against. The case for is very strong and easily defended. The case against has little to support it.

ANSWER SHEET FOR THE MODEL
ADVANCED PLACEMENT EXAM NO. 2

Name _____

Date _____

Grade _____

FOR SECTION I — MULTIPLE CHOICE

Sample: 1. The Reformation began in

    (A)   1450
    (B)   1492
    (C)   1507
    (D)   1517
    (E)   1618

1. Ⓐ Ⓑ Ⓒ ● Ⓔ

Box D is filled in since the correct answer for the sample question 1 is D.

---

1. Ⓐ Ⓑ Ⓒ Ⓓ Ⓔ	21. Ⓐ Ⓑ Ⓒ Ⓓ Ⓔ	41. Ⓐ Ⓑ Ⓒ Ⓓ Ⓔ	61. Ⓐ Ⓑ Ⓒ Ⓓ Ⓔ
2. Ⓐ Ⓑ Ⓒ Ⓓ Ⓔ	22. Ⓐ Ⓑ Ⓒ Ⓓ Ⓔ	42. Ⓐ Ⓑ Ⓒ Ⓓ Ⓔ	62. Ⓐ Ⓑ Ⓒ Ⓓ Ⓔ
3. Ⓐ Ⓑ Ⓒ Ⓓ Ⓔ	23. Ⓐ Ⓑ Ⓒ Ⓓ Ⓔ	43. Ⓐ Ⓑ Ⓒ Ⓓ Ⓔ	63. Ⓐ Ⓑ Ⓒ Ⓓ Ⓔ
4. Ⓐ Ⓑ Ⓒ Ⓓ Ⓔ	24. Ⓐ Ⓑ Ⓒ Ⓓ Ⓔ	44. Ⓐ Ⓑ Ⓒ Ⓓ Ⓔ	64. Ⓐ Ⓑ Ⓒ Ⓓ Ⓔ
5. Ⓐ Ⓑ Ⓒ Ⓓ Ⓔ	25. Ⓐ Ⓑ Ⓒ Ⓓ Ⓔ	45. Ⓐ Ⓑ Ⓒ Ⓓ Ⓔ	65. Ⓐ Ⓑ Ⓒ Ⓓ Ⓔ
6. Ⓐ Ⓑ Ⓒ Ⓓ Ⓔ	26. Ⓐ Ⓑ Ⓒ Ⓓ Ⓔ	46. Ⓐ Ⓑ Ⓒ Ⓓ Ⓔ	66. Ⓐ Ⓑ Ⓒ Ⓓ Ⓔ
7. Ⓐ Ⓑ Ⓒ Ⓓ Ⓔ	27. Ⓐ Ⓑ Ⓒ Ⓓ Ⓔ	47. Ⓐ Ⓑ Ⓒ Ⓓ Ⓔ	67. Ⓐ Ⓑ Ⓒ Ⓓ Ⓔ
8. Ⓐ Ⓑ Ⓒ Ⓓ Ⓔ	28. Ⓐ Ⓑ Ⓒ Ⓓ Ⓔ	48. Ⓐ Ⓑ Ⓒ Ⓓ Ⓔ	68. Ⓐ Ⓑ Ⓒ Ⓓ Ⓔ
9. Ⓐ Ⓑ Ⓒ Ⓓ Ⓔ	29. Ⓐ Ⓑ Ⓒ Ⓓ Ⓔ	49. Ⓐ Ⓑ Ⓒ Ⓓ Ⓔ	69. Ⓐ Ⓑ Ⓒ Ⓓ Ⓔ
10. Ⓐ Ⓑ Ⓒ Ⓓ Ⓔ	30. Ⓐ Ⓑ Ⓒ Ⓓ Ⓔ	50. Ⓐ Ⓑ Ⓒ Ⓓ Ⓔ	70. Ⓐ Ⓑ Ⓒ Ⓓ Ⓔ
11. Ⓐ Ⓑ Ⓒ Ⓓ Ⓔ	31. Ⓐ Ⓑ Ⓒ Ⓓ Ⓔ	51. Ⓐ Ⓑ Ⓒ Ⓓ Ⓔ	71. Ⓐ Ⓑ Ⓒ Ⓓ Ⓔ
12. Ⓐ Ⓑ Ⓒ Ⓓ Ⓔ	32. Ⓐ Ⓑ Ⓒ Ⓓ Ⓔ	52. Ⓐ Ⓑ Ⓒ Ⓓ Ⓔ	72. Ⓐ Ⓑ Ⓒ Ⓓ Ⓔ
13. Ⓐ Ⓑ Ⓒ Ⓓ Ⓔ	33. Ⓐ Ⓑ Ⓒ Ⓓ Ⓔ	53. Ⓐ Ⓑ Ⓒ Ⓓ Ⓔ	73. Ⓐ Ⓑ Ⓒ Ⓓ Ⓔ
14. Ⓐ Ⓑ Ⓒ Ⓓ Ⓔ	34. Ⓐ Ⓑ Ⓒ Ⓓ Ⓔ	54. Ⓐ Ⓑ Ⓒ Ⓓ Ⓔ	74. Ⓐ Ⓑ Ⓒ Ⓓ Ⓔ
15. Ⓐ Ⓑ Ⓒ Ⓓ Ⓔ	35. Ⓐ Ⓑ Ⓒ Ⓓ Ⓔ	55. Ⓐ Ⓑ Ⓒ Ⓓ Ⓔ	75. Ⓐ Ⓑ Ⓒ Ⓓ Ⓔ
16. Ⓐ Ⓑ Ⓒ Ⓓ Ⓔ	36. Ⓐ Ⓑ Ⓒ Ⓓ Ⓔ	56. Ⓐ Ⓑ Ⓒ Ⓓ Ⓔ	76. Ⓐ Ⓑ Ⓒ Ⓓ Ⓔ
17. Ⓐ Ⓑ Ⓒ Ⓓ Ⓔ	37. Ⓐ Ⓑ Ⓒ Ⓓ Ⓔ	57. Ⓐ Ⓑ Ⓒ Ⓓ Ⓔ	77. Ⓐ Ⓑ Ⓒ Ⓓ Ⓔ
18. Ⓐ Ⓑ Ⓒ Ⓓ Ⓔ	38. Ⓐ Ⓑ Ⓒ Ⓓ Ⓔ	58. Ⓐ Ⓑ Ⓒ Ⓓ Ⓔ	78. Ⓐ Ⓑ Ⓒ Ⓓ Ⓔ
19. Ⓐ Ⓑ Ⓒ Ⓓ Ⓔ	39. Ⓐ Ⓑ Ⓒ Ⓓ Ⓔ	59. Ⓐ Ⓑ Ⓒ Ⓓ Ⓔ	79. Ⓐ Ⓑ Ⓒ Ⓓ Ⓔ
20. Ⓐ Ⓑ Ⓒ Ⓓ Ⓔ	40. Ⓐ Ⓑ Ⓒ Ⓓ Ⓔ	60. Ⓐ Ⓑ Ⓒ Ⓓ Ⓔ	80. Ⓐ Ⓑ Ⓒ Ⓓ Ⓔ

Model Advanced Placement European History Examination No. 2

Section I **Multiple-Choice** **Questions**	Time—60 minutes for 80 questions *Directions:* Each of the following questions has five suggested answers. Choose the one that is best in each case.

1. The first literary and artistic expressions, as well as the highest cultural achievements, were centered in what Northern Italian city-state?
   - (A) Milan
   - (B) Florence
   - (C) Venice
   - (D) Naples
   - (E) Rome

2. The artistic brilliance of the *quattrocento* and the *cinquecento* was spurred in both Florence and Rome by
   - (A) the patronage of both civic groups and the Church
   - (B) artist guilds
   - (C) the Medicis
   - (D) the *popolo*
   - (E) foreign financiers

3. Which is true of Humanism?
   - (A) It set limits on what human beings could accomplish in this world.
   - (B) It emphasized the study of Greek and Roman classical literature.
   - (C) It sought to understand human nature exclusively by means of studying the writings of the early Christian philosophers.
   - (D) It promoted a medieval lifestyle.
   - (E) It discouraged a study of pagan writers.

4. Secularism during the Renaissance can best be described as
   - (A) a repudiation of the Roman Catholic faith
   - (B) a concern with the nature of individuality
   - (C) an emphasis on money and pleasure
   - (D) a belief in individual genius
   - (E) a literary movement centered primarily in the Northern states of Europe

5. Which is NOT true of the Northern Renaissance?
   (A) It was focused more on religion than on the Italian Renaissance.
   (B) It stressed social reform based on Christian teachings.
   (C) It began in the last three decades of the 15th century.
   (D) It preceded the Italian Renaissance.
   (E) Its art was more religious and less influenced by classical themes than Italian art.

6. During the early 16th century the need for reform within the Roman Catholic Church was indicated by all of the following EXCEPT
   (A) clerical immorality
   (B) the lack of education of the ordinary clergy
   (C) the growth of The Brethren of the Common Life
   (D) the extravagant lifestyle of prelates and popes
   (E) clerical pluralism

7. One of the tenets of Protestantism as stated in the Confession of Augsburg was that religious authority rests with
   (A) The pope
   (B) the Bible
   (C) The Ecumenical Councils
   (D) The Holy Roman Emperor
   (E) The German princes

8. What was the political impact of the Protestant Reformation on Germany?
   (A) It thwarted the designs of the French kings.
   (B) It strengthened the hold of the Hapsburgs over the region.
   (C) It aroused nationalism in Germany.
   (D) It enabled the Holy Roman Emperor to determine the religion of the various German principalities.
   (E) It led to a more united Germany.

9. One of Calvin's central ideas in The Institutes of Christian Religion was that
   (A) the Church was subordinate to the state
   (B) all Christian sects should be tolerated
   (C) "man is the measure of all things"
   (D) Calvinism should be confined to the theocratic city of Geneva
   (E) salvation is predestined

10. Which was one of the most important accomplishments of The Council of Trent (1545–1563)?
    (A) Reconciliation with the Protestants.
    (B) Reforms led to a spiritual renewal of the Roman Catholic Church.
    (C) The sale of indulgences was encouraged.
    (D) Simony and pluralism were established.
    (E) The Roman Inquisition was instituted.

11. One of the most significant long-term effects of Spain's establishment of a New World empire was that New World gold and silver
     (A) helped make Spain militarily superior in Europe
     (B) gave the Portuguese hegemony in the Atlantic
     (C) created a massive inflation that ended Spain's European empire
     (D) created a glut of precious metal jewelry among the upper classes in Europe
     (E) ruined manufacturing in the Spanish Netherlands

12. The Great European Witch Hunt through the 16th and 17th centuries resulted from
     (A) the region-wide religious struggles of the era
     (B) increased social and intellectual conformity
     (C) a general misunderstanding of women
     (D) a rise in the belief in the evil power of witches
     (E) all of these

13. The religious conflicts of the 1500s and 1600s led to
     (A) religious toleration between Roman Catholicism and the major Protestant sects
     (B) a unified Christian society in Europe
     (C) unremitting religious riots and civil war in Spain
     (D) a virtual end to Hapsburg hegemony in Germany
     (E) the establishment of Roman Catholicism as the state religion of the United Provinces of the Netherlands

14. Which of the following possessed *sovereignty* in the absolutist states of the 17th century?
     (A) Monarchs
     (B) Parliaments
     (C) Nobles
     (D) The Church
     (E) The wealthy

15. What is the most significant difference between absolutism and modern totalitarianism?
     (A) Totalitarian dictators lacked the political power of the absolutist kings.
     (B) Absolutism sought to subordinate only the nobility.
     (C) Absolutist states lacked the total control of their citizens "from cradle to grave."
     (D) State bureaucracies were absent in absolutist states.
     (E) Standing armies are an invention of modern totalitarianism.

16. Louis XIV employed which of the following to maintain his absolutist state?
     (A) The *intendant* administrative system
     (B) The Palace at Versailles as a "gilded cage" for the nobility.
     (C) A policy of regional wars for state aggrandizement
     (D) The Revocation of the Edict of Nantes to establish a state religion
     (E) All of these

17. Constitutionalism in BOTH 17th century England and the Netherlands
    (A) was established with the formation of long-lasting republics in both states
    (B) was protected exclusively by unwritten constitutions
    (C) limited the powers of the state by law
    (D) came about as the result of bloody revolutions in both countries
    (E) lacked protection of the rights of individual citizens

18. Choose the correct chronological order of the following events:
    I. Establishment of the Protectorate under Cromwell
    II. Execution of Charles I
    III. English Civil War breaks out in 1642
    IV. The Glorious Revolution
    V. Restoration of the Monarchy

    (A) III, II, I, V, IV
    (B) V, III, I, II, IV
    (C) I, III, II, IV, V
    (D) III, II, IV, I, V
    (E) II, IV, V, I, III

19. The political philosophy of which of the following argued that governments are set up to protect the life, liberty, and property of the people?
    (A) Thomas Hobbes
    (B) Bishop Laud
    (C) Oliver Cromwell
    (D) James II
    (E) John Locke

20. Cardinal Richelieu extended the power of French royalty with the *intendant system*:
    (A) a centralized administrative system
    (B) a medal of honor for the *musketeers*
    (C) a series of fortified cities in France
    (D) a tax that local nobles could levy
    (E) a standing army of 400,000 trained troops

21. Monarchial absolutism
    (A) was absent from Eastern Europe during the 17th century
    (B) lasted longer in Western than in Eastern Europe
    (C) abolished serfdom in 16th century Eastern Europe
    (D) lasted longer in Eastern Europe than in Western Europe
    (E) ended in Prussia and Russia by the early 1700s

22. The reforms of which Russian monarch helped to modernize many of Russia's institutions and made it a major European power?
    (A) The first prince of Kiev
    (B) The Mongol Khan
    (C) Frederick the Great
    (D) Peter the Great
    (E) Ivan III

23. Which revolution caused a greater change in the world-view and in the evolution of Western society?
    (A) The French Revolution
    (B) The Commercial Revolution of the 16th through 18th centuries
    (C) The American Revolution
    (D) The Scientific Revolution of the 17th century
    (E) The Price Revolution of the 16th century

24. The Scientific Revolution can be said to have begun with the heliocentric astronomy of Copernicus and to have culminated with the scientific synthesis of
    (A) Kepler
    (B) Newton
    (C) Galileo
    (D) Tycho Brahe
    (E) Bacon

25. As a result of the scientific theories developed through the 16th and 17th centuries, Europeans developed a conception of the universe
    (A) as governed by natural laws
    (B) as geocentric
    (C) as guided in every physical realm by a personal God
    (D) as chaotic, reflective of chance
    (E) as Aristotelian in makeup

26. The new science encouraged
    (A) critical thinking
    (B) repudiation of faith
    (C) questioning of traditional institutions
    (D) critique of governments
    (E) all of these

27. Which is the most accurate statement pertaining to the *philosophes* of the 18th century?
    (A) They were exclusively French.
    (B) They promoted radical revolution in the political sphere.
    (C) They were primarily reformers.
    (D) They were universally condemned by the monarchs of Europe.
    (A) They appealed only to the intellectual elite.

28. The Enlightenment
    (A) was based upon the assumption that science and reason can explain all things
    (B) was diametrically opposed to the Newtonian concept of natural law
    (C) was widely attacked by the royalty and nobility of Europe
    (D) regarded human progress as an impossibility "in this best of all possible worlds"
    (E) rejected the claims of modern science

29. The Enlightenment concept of a remote God who chooses not to interfere in the operations of his creation is
     (A) theism
     (B) pantheism
     (C) deism
     (D) atheism
     (E) Protestantism

30. Many philosophes believed that governmental reform would be accomplished by
     (A) the introduction of democracy
     (B) benevolent absolutist monarchs
     (C) empowering the nobles at the expense of the kings
     (D) revolution
     (E) trusting the masses

31. The agricultural revolution of the late 17th and 18th centuries came about because of all of the following EXCEPT
     (A) crop rotation
     (B) the Enclosure Movement
     (C) establishment of the open field system
     (D) establishment of capitalist farming
     (E) disappearance of common land

32. Why was there an explosive growth in the population of Europe during the 18th century?
     (A) Disappearance of the plague
     (B) Improvements in sanitation
     (C) Better nutrition
     (D) Fewer deaths
     (E) All of these

33. The putting-out system
     (A) created the urban craft industry
     (B) reduced rural poverty
     (C) eliminated the need for merchant-capitalists
     (D) destroyed cottage industry
     (E) replaced factory manufacturing

34. Premarital sex in preindustrial Europe
     (A) was rampant
     (B) resulted in a high percentage of illegitimate births
     (C) was more common than it is today
     (D) was suppressed by the social controls of village life
     (E) did not exist

35. "Liberty," in 18th century thought, can best be described as
    (A) human rights and the sovereignty of the people
    (B) equality of opportunity
    (C) an offshoot of the divine right of kings
    (D) generally opposed by the intellectual elite
    (E) receiving widespread popular support before the French Revolution

36. The roots of the French Revolution can be traced to which of the following?
    (A) Enlightenment ideas of liberty and equality
    (B) The example of the American Revolution
    (C) The corruption and inefficiency of the old order
    (D) Class resentments
    (E) All of these

37. Which best describes the Third Estate prior to the French Revolution?
    (A) It consisted of the peasantry.
    (B) The First and Second Estates outnumbered it in terms of population.
    (C) It included the middle class, peasants, and urban workers.
    (D) It had the right to tax peasants for its own profit.
    (A) It was exempt from the tithe.

38. Which event occurred during the radical stage of the French Revolution?
    (A) Formation of the national assembly
    (B) The Great Fear
    (C) Napoleon's military dictatorship
    (D) The Terror
    (E) The Storming of the Bastille

39. Napoleon has been characterized as a "son of the Enlightenment" because during his reign
    (A) he supported freedom of speech and the press
    (B) his civil code granted legal equality to the middle class
    (C) he conquered most of the autocratic regimes in Europe
    (D) the Napoleonic code established women's rights
    (E) he was a liberal emperor

40. Which Revolution had a greater impact on contemporary life?
    (A) The French
    (B) The American
    (C) The Industrial
    (D) The Commercial
    (E) The Glorious

41. All are important reasons for the Industrial Revolution beginning in England EXCEPT
     (A) agricultural improvements
     (B) increased demand for manufactured goods
     (C) adequate transportation
     (D) sufficient oil reserves
     (E) a banking system

42. The proponent of the theory that population would always exceed food supply was
     (A) Thomas Malthus
     (B) David Ricardo
     (C) Adam Smith
     (D) Karl Marx
     (E) Jeremy Bentham

43. Which of the following is an effect of the Industrial Revolution upon the common people?
     (A) The gradual improvement of general nutrition
     (B) The large scale use of child labor
     (C) The legal limitation of child labor
     (D) An improvement in the standard of living after 1850
     (E) All of these

44. What new sexual division of labor emerged as a result of industrialization in the 19th century?
     (A) Women became the family's primary wage earner.
     (B) Married women with children were most likely to work in factories.
     (C) Women were confined to low-paying jobs with little chance for advancement.
     (D) "Mr. Moms" often provided child care while their wives worked.
     (E) African slavery was introduced in the newly industrialized nations of Europe.

45. Which of the following ideologies had its roots in the French Revolution and the conquests of Napoleon?
     (A) Marxian socialism
     (B) *Laissez-faire* economic liberalism
     (C) Political conservatism
     (D) Nationalism
     (A) Utopian socialism

46. Which is the best characterization of the romantic movement?
     (A) It emphasized order and reason.
     (B) It stressed individualism, emotionality, and imagination.
     (C) It viewed nature as a force to resist.
     (D) It rejected the study of history.
     (E) It reflected the ideals of the Enlightenment.

47.   All of the following are important British literary romantics EXCEPT
         (A)   William Wordsworth
         (B)   George Sand
         (C)   Walter Scott
         (D)   Percy Shelley
         (E)   Samuel Taylor Coleridge

48.   Which is the most accurate appraisal of the Revolutions of 1830 and 1848?
         (A)   They established democratic republics in both Britain and France.
         (B)   They overthrew the conservative regimes of central Europe.
         (C)   They were largely unsuccessful.
         (D)   They brought about German unification.
         (E)   They established parliaments in both Russia and Austria.

49.   Urbanization and industrialization in 19th century Europe
         (A)   created new social classes
         (B)   increased class conflict
         (C)   changed family life
         (D)   encouraged the development of preventive medicine
         (E)   all of these

50.   Before the work of Pasteur, Koch, and Lister, the prevailing theory of disease in the 19th century was that
         (A)   it was caused by bad odors
         (B)   it could be controlled by vaccination
         (C)   it was caused by microorganisms
         (D)   it could be prevented by the sterilization of wounds
         (E)   it was brought about by an imbalance of the humors

51.   In the latter half of the 19th century, the preindustrial pattern of women working outside of the home continued primarily for which group?
         (A)   Middle class women
         (B)   Social elites
         (C)   The wives of urban professionals
         (D)   Working class women
         (E)   Young urban professionals

52.   Which literary movement, stressing the influence of heredity and environment on human behavior, replaced romanticism in the last decades of the 1800s?
         (A)   Humanism
         (B)   Rationalism
         (C)   Relativism
         (D)   Utopianism
         (E)   Realism

53. The scientific theory that all life had evolved from a common origin, by a process of struggle for survival, and was applied by social thinkers to human affairs was developed by
    (A)   Charles Darwin
    (B)   Gregor Mendel
    (C)   Herbert Spencer
    (D)   Jean Baptiste Lamarck
    (E)   Auguste Comte

54. Between 1850 and 1914, which principle of organization became supreme by appealing to all of Europe's social classes?
    (A)   Urbanization
    (B)   Socialism
    (C)   Nationalism
    (D)   Industrialization
    (E)   Internationalism

55. The Second Empire from 1852 to 1870 of which leader demonstrated how the programs of a national state could have an appeal by cutting across class and political lines?
    (A)   Otto Von Bismarck
    (B)   Camillo Cavour
    (C)   David Lloyd George
    (D)   Giuseppe Garibaldi
    (E)   Louis Napoleon

56. The failure of the Frankfurt Conference in 1848 to unify this nation, encouraged the growth of authoritarianism and militarism?
    (A)   France
    (B)   Germany
    (C)   Italy
    (D)   Austria
    (E)   Russia

57. The rulers of these ethnically diverse empires regarded nationalism within their borders as a threat:
    (A)   Britain and France
    (B)   Germany and Austria
    (C)   Italy and Russia
    (D)   Russia and Austria
    (E)   Prussia and Russia

58. The "new imperialism" by Europeans from 1880 to 1914 differed from the imperialism of earlier periods in that
    (A)   it was primarily economic
    (B)   its goal was the establishment of peaceful trading empires
    (C)   it involved the political domination of masses of people in Asia and Africa
    (D)   it was limited to the Pacific region
    (E)   it focused mainly on the Middle East

59.   Which are considered causes for the "new imperialism?"
   (A)   A search for markets for European manufactured goods
   (B)   European racism
   (C)   Acquisition of colonies for prestige and national security
   (D)   Missionary zeal
   (E)   All of these

60.   Which is not considered a long-term cause of World War I?
   (A)   The assassination of the Austrian Archduke
   (B)   A system of rival military alliances
   (C)   Nationalism
   (D)   A naval arms race between Germany and Britain
   (E)   Competition for colonies and markets

61.   Which of the following empires DID NOT collapse as a result of World War I?
   (A)   The Russian
   (B)   The British
   (C)   The German
   (D)   The Austro-Hungarian
   (E)   The Ottoman Turk

62.   During World War I, mobilization for war and planned economies helped set the stage for which of the following?
   (A)   Post-war democratic gains
   (B)   An increase in wartime strikes by unions
   (C)   The entrance of women into the workplace after the war
   (D)   Totalitarianism
   (E)   The establishment of laissez-faire economies in Europe

63.   Which is the best characterization of the Treaty of Versailles that ended World War I?
   (A)   In the League of Nations, it established an effective deterrent to future wars.
   (B)   It rejected the principle of national self-determination.
   (C)   It sowed the seeds for the growth of Nazism.
   (D)   It served as a foundation for the post-war alliance between Britain and France.
   (E)   It ended European imperialism.

64.   Choose the correct chronology of events in the Russian Revolution of 1917.

    I.   Under the military leadership of Trotsky, the Bolsheviks seize power.

    II.   Kerensky heads a provisional government.

    III. There is widespread public support for Russia's participation in World War I.

    IV. Food riots lead to the Czar's abdication.

    V.   The Petrograd Soviet gave authority to ordinary soldiers.

    (A) IV, III, II, V, I
    (B) III, IV, V, II, I
    (C) I, III, II, V, IV
    (D) III, IV, II, V, I
    (E) I, II, IV, III, V

65.   Because World War I tested the belief in traditional ideas and institutions, the post-war period is often referred to as
    (A) "the roaring 20s"
    (B) "the age of anxiety"
    (C) "The Great Depression"
    (D) "the era of angst"
    (E) "the age of appeasement"

66.   The deficit spending theories of this economist were employed by governments attempting to boost GNP during the Great Depression:
    (A) Gustav Stresemann
    (B) John Maynard Keynes
    (C) Charles C. Dawes
    (D) Bertrand Russell
    (E) Aristide Briand

67.   The philosopher whose ideas that Christian humility and rationalism had caused a decline in Western Civilization was
    (A) Friedrich Nietzsche
    (B) Henri Bergson
    (C) Ludwig Wittgenstein
    (D) Max Planck
    (E) Georges Sorel

68.   The work of Max Planck and Albert Einstein undermined belief in the natural laws and rational worldview of what earlier scientist?
    (A) Ernest Rutherford
    (B) George Orwell
    (C) Werner Heisenberg
    (D) Isaac Newton
    (E) Soren Kierkegaard

69. The psychoanalytical theories that fostered the belief that human behavior is basically irrational belonged to
     (A) Sigmund Freud
     (B) Aristotle
     (C) Charles Darwin
     (D) Jean-Paul Sartre
     (E) Oswald Spengler

70. The modern style of painting that focused on mood and imagination rather than on portraying nature or real objects was
     (A) baroque
     (B) expressionism
     (C) impressionism
     (D) romantic
     (E) functionalism

71. All of the following mass media were used both for entertainment and propaganda in the period between World Wars I and II EXCEPT
     (A) newspapers
     (B) television
     (C) radio
     (D) motion pictures
     (E) popular journals and magazines

72. Which is true of the Great Depression?
     (A) It began with a financial crisis in the United States.
     (B) Virtually all of the nations in Europe, except the U.S.S.R., suffered massive unemployment.
     (C) Government programs in France, Britain, Germany, and the United States attempted to foster economic recovery.
     (D) It ended largely because of arms production prior to World War II.
     (E) All of these.

73. The pessimism and alienation of the Age of Anxiety influenced writers such as James Joyce and Virginia Woolf to experiment with a literary technique in which emotions and thoughts from the unconscious surfaced randomly. It was called
     (A) dadaism
     (B) surrealism
     (C) stream of consciousness
     (D) Bauhaus functionalism
     (E) Ashcan realism

74. The radical dictatorships that grew in Europe during the 1920s and '30s and were characterized by a rejection of democratic ideals and by extreme control over every aspect of their citizens' lives were known as
     (A) communistic
     (B) fascistic
     (C) conservative authoritarian
     (D) totalitarian
     (E) militaristic

75. The economic programs that brought about dramatic gains in productivity and enabled the U.S.S.R. to catch up with the West in the growth of heavy industry during the 1930s were called
    (A) five-year plans
    (B) collectivization
    (C) the New Economic Policy (NEP)
    (D) the Russian New Deal
    (E) the Young Plan

76. The alliance of the United States, the U.S.S.R., and Great Britain was able to defeat Nazi Germany during World War II because
    (A) it demanded the unconditional surrender of the Axis powers
    (B) of the extraordinary sacrifices made by the British and Russian peoples
    (C) it left political issues to be settled after the war
    (D) it drew upon the American "arsenal of democracy"
    (E) all of these

77. Which of the following marked a post–World War II move toward European unity?
    (A) establishment of the League of Nations
    (B) the Warsaw Pact
    (C) the six-nation Coal and Steel Community
    (D) the policies of Charles de Gaulle
    (E) a resurgence of nationalism in the 1960s

78. All of the following are examples of decolonization following World War II EXCEPT
    (A) the work of Mahatma Gandhi and the Indian Congress Party
    (B) the political aims of Ho Chi Minh
    (C) Nasser's nationalization of the Suez Canal
    (D) the struggle between the communists and nationalists in China
    (E) the Pan-Arab movement

79. Reform and "de-Stalinization" in the U.S.S.R. was begun in 1956 when this Soviet leader denounced Stalin's "cult of personality":
    (A) Mikhail Gorbachev
    (B) Nikita Khrushchev
    (C) Leonid Brezhnev
    (D) Yevgeny Yevtushenko
    (E) Leon Trotsky

80. Which has been the most significant outcome of the collapse and breakup of the Communist governments in the U.S.S.R. and Yugoslavia?
    (A) The establishment of vibrant democratic governments among the new republics.
    (B) Ethnic conflict.
    (C) A dramatic increase in the standard of living.
    (D) The re-establishment of conservative authoritarianism in the newly independent states.
    (E) The universal adoption of Russian cultural institutions.

Part A: *Document-Based Essay Question (DBQ)*

Writing time—45 minutes; 45 percent of Section II score

Directions: The essay question that follows is based on the accompanying documents. Write the essay in response to the question by analyzing the documents, considering their sources and biases, referring to appropriate historical information not cited, and integrating all those into your answer. (Some documents have been edited.)

1. While comparing economic and social gender roles during the decades from 1850 to 1914 with those during World War I, analyze the factors that promoted change.

Historical Background: Prior to 1850, the pre-industrial pattern of men and women working together and then sharing household and childcare duties predominated in Europe. From 1850 to 1914, industrialization drastically changed sex roles in European society. This new social and economic pattern was then influenced by the outbreak of World War I in 1914.

Document A

"No wife of mine is going to work outside my home. A real man makes enough of a living to keep a wife and family."

> Skilled laborer, latter half of 19th century.

Document B

"The tobacconist works side by side with his wife in their little shop. He hand rolls the cigarettes while she deals with customers. It is a quaint *Mom and Pop* operation, reminiscent of the days before industrialization when husband and wife shared the labor of the cottage industry."

> Human interest piece in a popular European journal of the 1870s.

Document C

"In law, husband and wife are one person, and the husband is that person."

> 18th century English jurist, William Blackstone.

Document D

"Women have few legal rights, but we rule our homes. We determine how our husband's money is spent; we run our household; most important, we raise our children."

European feminist, 1890.

Document E

Home sweet home . . .

An immensely popular ballad in the 1870s.

Document F

"Not only are women last to be hired and first to be fired, but they almost always get a fraction of a man's pay for doing the same work as he."

From an 1865 report by a European socialist party on employment opportunities for women.

Document G

"Where have the men gone?"

The title of a 1916 British magazine piece about the entrance of millions of men into military service.

Document H

"WOMEN, HELP YOUR MEN WIN THE WAR! WORK IN A WAR PLANT!"

French 1916 propaganda poster.

Document I

"All male workers, between the ages of 17 and 60, as well as able-bodied women, are henceforth ordered to perform labor essential to the war effort."

From a German government edict of 1916.

Document J

"In the year before the 1917 Revolution, nearly half the labor force of Russia was made up of women."

Findings of a special committee of the Soviet government, 1922.

Document K

"The *Law of unintended consequences* has manifested itself in the use of women as industrial laborers for the recent war effort. While their skills and energy contributed to final victory, their experience in the work force has aroused a fierce and frightful independence among young women. Many have chosen to cut—bob—their traditional feminine locks, to smoke cigarettes like men, to shorten their skirts, and to adopt a free-thinking set of attitudes that will inevitably foster promiscuity."

> From a 1922 report by a European society founded to protect traditional moral codes of behavior.

Document L

"Within months of the Great War's end, women in Austria, Britain, and Germany have been granted the right to vote."

> Part of a 1919 memo to founding members of a suffragette organization.

Section II **Free-Response** **Questions**	Part B: *Two Essay Questions* Writing time—70 minutes for two essays; 55 percent of Section II score *Directions:* Answer *two* of the following, one from Group A and one from Group B. Be sure to cite relevant historical information to support your answer. Number your answer as the question below is numbered. Use extra time to check your work.

GROUP A

1. "During the *Age of Anxiety,* the 1920s and '30s, both psychology and the new physics contributed to the breakdown of traditional values." Assess the validity of this statement.

2. Contrast and compare the Italian Renaissance and the Northern Renaissance.

3. Explain why the *Opening of the Atlantic* led to a shift of political and economic power from the Mediterranean Basin to Western Europe.

GROUP B

4. To what extent and in what ways was Romanticism in art, literature, and music a reaction against the Enlightenment?

5.   Describe how the public health movement and urban planning during the latter half of the 19th century changed life in Europe's cities.

6.   "Religious differences caused the greatest disruption in 16th century Europe, ideological differences the greatest disruption in 20th century Europe." Defend or refute this statement.

Answers and Comments for Questions on Model Advanced Placement Examination No. 2

Answer Key

1. B	2. A	3. B	4. C	5. D
6. C	7. B	8. C	9. E	10. B
11. C	12. E	13. D	14. A	15. C
16. E	17. C	18. A	19. E	20. A
21. D	22. D	23. D	24. B	25. A
26. E	27. C	28. A	29. C	30. B
31. C	32. E	33. B	34. D	35. A
36. E	37. C	38. D	39. B	40. C
41. D	42. A	43. E	44. C	45. D
46. B	47. B	48. C	49. E	50. A
51. D	52. E	53. A	54. C	55. E
56. B	57. D	58. C	59. E	60. A
61. B	62. D	63. C	64. D	65. B
66. B	67. A	68. D	69. A	70. B
71. B	72 E	73. C	74. D	75. A
76. E	77. C	78. D	79. B	80. B

Answers Explained

1. (B)   The city-state of Florence is considered the center of the Italian Renaissance.

2. (A)   Both the Church and civic groups, often led by powerful families, sponsored the artists of the Renaissance.

3. (B)   The secular literature of the ancient world was "rediscovered" by European thinkers.

4. (C)   While the people and elites of the Italian Renaissance were by and large committed to Roman Catholicism, a life of activity was stressed, as opposed to the medieval ideal of monastic contemplation.

5. (D)   The Northern Renaissance borrowed from the Italians and gave Renaissance ideals religious flavor and national interpretations.

6. (C)   The Brethren of the Common Life, which supported the idea of living "a life based upon that of Jesus," was itself a reform movement.

7. (B)   Replacing the "final authority" of the Pope and Church Council with the Bible was one of the basic tenets of Protestantism.

8. (C)   It gave a focus to the aspirations of the German princes against the Holy Roman Emperor.

9. (E)   Predestination—the idea that God has "chosen" the few who will attain salvation at the beginning of time—is central to Calvinism.

10. (B)   Both doctrinal and administrative reforms of the Council inspired renewal.

11. (C)   The influx into Spain and Europe of New World precious metals created a demand for goods that the limited productivity could not match.

12. (E)   This complex phenomenon had many causes.

13.   (D)   The wars of religion evolved into national struggles and the HRE lost power and influence.

14.   (A)   All other segments of society were subordinated to the monarchy.

15.   (C)   Limited technology and the autonomy of traditional institutions, such as the Church, curtailed the power of the absolutist monarchs.

16.   (E)   A master manipulator on the domestic and diplomatic scene, Louis employed many tactics to maintain and extend his power.

17.   (C)   This is the essence of constitutionalism.

18.   (A)

19.   (E)   Locke's political philosophy serves as the doctrinal basis for constitutionalism.

20.   (A)   This extended the power of the monarchy over the nobles and local institutions.

21.   (D)   The absolutist traditions of Eastern Europe help explain the roots of contemporary economic, social, and political issues in that region.

22.   (D)   His reforms imposed modernism upon the reluctant institutions of his realm.

23.   (D)   The Scientific and concomitant Technological Revolution continue to affect the nature and quality of life.

24.   (B)   Newton was the great synthesizer: "If I have seen further . . ."

25.   (A)   A direct result of Newton's physics.

26.   (E)   A secular intellectuality prevailed.

27.   (C)   While they railed against the social, economic, political, and religious institutions of their day, they did not advocate revolution.

28.   (A)   A direct descendant of Newton's "natural laws," the Enlightenment assumed that humans could progress through reason and the scientific method.

29.   (C)   Voltaire, who was not an original thinker, promoted this idea as an antidote to the biases and intolerance of the organized religion of his day.

30.   (B)   Absolutism was still a powerful institution on the continent, and the so-called "enlightened despots" cultivated the *philosophes* while paying lip service to their ideals.

31.   (C)   The replacement of the traditional open field system increased productivity through an efficient competitive system.

32.   (E)   No one development brought it about.

33.   (B)   The rural workers, who produced goods from the raw materials provided by merchant-capitalists, found work.

34.   (D)   Restraints were encouraged and enforced by local communities.

35.   (A)   These were the very specific 18th century meanings of the term.

36. (E)   Complex events have complex causes.

37. (C)   It made up more than 90 percent of the total pre-revolutionary population of about 24 million.

38. (D)   It was precipitated by war and the perceived threat of counter-revolution.

39. (B)   an autocrat and self-proclaimed emperor, he put this aspect of the *philosophes'* program into law.

40. (C)   Industrialization changed the economic, social, and political structure of modern life.

41. (D)   Petroleum was not a significant energy source in the 18th and 19th centuries.

42. (A)   After Malthus, economics was referred to as "the dismal science."

43. (E)   The Industrial Revolution had positive and negative effects.

44. (C)   The shared labor of the farm and of the cottage industry was replaced.

45. (D)   Napoleon's successes inspired emulators of French nationalism among other peoples.

46. (B)   It broke with the Enlightenment's optimistic investment in reason.

47. (B)   Sand, a woman, was French.

48. (C)   They were suppressed, thousands of revolutionaries were killed, jailed, or exiled, but their nationalistic and socialistic aims were largely realized in subsequent decades.

49. (E)   These were two of the most powerful forces for change in the 19th century.

50. (A)   It was the "miasmatic theory."

51. (D)   Low family incomes required working class women to supplement their husband's pay.

52. (E)   The "new" sociology and psychology promoted its growth.

53. (A)   Like Newton before him, Darwin was a pure scientist whose theories were applied and misapplied to the social sciences.

54. (C)   Nationalism cut across class lines in its appeal.

55. (E)   He is in many ways the first "modern" politician with a program to appeal to the masses.

56. (B)   Prussia, with its military and autocratic traditions, led the movement for German unification.

57. (D)   Both were polyglot empires whose dynastic rulers were threatened by ethnic separatism.

58. (C)   The "new imperialism" imposed European political, religious, and social institutions on non-European peoples.

59.   (E)   Many segments of European society were drawn to imperialism.

60.   (A)   It was an *immediate cause*.

61.   (B)   Its economic and social institutions were weakened, but its governmental system survived.

62.   (D)   Planned economies and national war efforts prepared many European states for the mass mobilization of totalitarianism.

63.   (C)   In failing to address the issues that precipitated World War I, and in blaming the Germans for the war, it gave the Nazis a political lever for gaining popular support.

64.   (D)

65.   (B)   This pervasive anxiety manifested itself in art and literature, and it was exacerbated by the findings of physics and psychology.

66.   (B)   His deficit spending policies were to be employed in the United States as well as in Europe.

67.   (A)   He is one of the most misinterpreted philosophers of modern times.

68.   (D)   Newton's "natural laws" inspired the Age of Reason.

69.   (A)   His theories fit and fostered "the age of anxiety."

70.   (B)   Picasso is perhaps the most famous exponent of this school.

71.   (B)   Invented between the wars, TV came into popular use in the 1950s and '60s.

72.   (E)   It lasted for more than a decade with disastrous effects on the stability of the industrialized world.

73.   (C)   The character's train of association enabled the writer to delve into his/her unconscious.

74.   (D)   "From cradle to grave."

75.   (A)   The emphasis on heavy industry was at the cost of the ordinary Russian's standard of living.

76.   (E)   The fight against a common enemy held together this alliance of "strange bedfellows" for the duration.

77.   (C)   It was the forerunner of the Common Market and the European Union.

78.   (D)   This was a civil war.

79.   (B)   While his policies failed and he was ousted from power, Khrushchev started the liberalization that reached full fruition under Gorbachev.

80.   (B)   The West's dream of the collapse of Communism has created a fluid and even more dangerous world.

Comments on the DBQ Section II; Part A

Refer to "DBQ Do's and Don'ts" on pages 18–19.

Read and interpret the question: To "compare" involves demonstrating similarities and changes, in the economic and social gender roles, between the two periods. To "analyze" requires that you identify and explain the causes for these changes.

Read and analyze each of the documents in turn: Which are pertinent? Which are redundant? Which are related?

Read the question again and relate specific documents to framing an answer. What were the gender roles? How did they differ from one period to the next? What caused these differences?

Outline your essay: Use only the pertinent documents to make your case. Contrast the gender roles; explain the reasons for the changes. Use any information, aside from the documents, that may help you to make your case. Use the documents to answer the question; you may use all or some. Don't ever simply summarize them.

Before writing the essay: Read the question once again and check your outline and document references to be sure that you will answer the question.

Checklist for using the documents to answer the question effectively:

1. Which of the documents reveal the gender roles in the decades before the war? What were those roles?

2. Which reveal the roles during the war? How did the roles change?

3. Which documents offer the clearest reasons for the changes? Can a generalization be framed to explain the changes?

4. Which documents seem redundant? Of those that "overlap," which are the most relevant to answering the question?

5. Have you used each document to which you've referred to make a point that helps answer the overall question?

Comments on the Essay Questions Section II, Part B

Be sure to follow the "Simple Procedures" for writing an essay:

First, ask yourself what the question wants to know.

Second, ask yourself what you know about it.

Third, ask yourself how you would put it into words.

GROUP A ESSAYS

---

1. "During the Age of Anxiety, the 1920s and '30s, both psychology and the new physics contributed to the breakdown of traditional values." Assess the validity of this statement.

What does the question want to know? Decide whether these "new" sciences did indeed, help to erode peoples' fundamental beliefs, then describe how.

What do you know about it? This period followed World War I and was characterized by the dissolution of great empires, economic boom and bust, a disruption of class and gender roles, the rise of radical dictatorships. How and why did Freudian psychology and the physics of Einstein help shake peoples' faith in the traditional values and institutions of European civilization?

How should you put it into words? Describe the political, economic, and social disruption caused by the war; explain how the scientific theories contributed to a climate of cynicism.

---

2.   Contrast and compare the Italian Renaissance and the Northern Renaissance.

What does the question want to know? Describe similarities and differences in these two developments. Show how they were related.

What do you know about it? The essential difference between the Italian and Northern Renaissance is the emphasis placed on religion. Although, they shared themes—humanism, individualism, secularism, materialism—and cultural developments—artistic, architectural, scientific, and literary innovations—the Northern Renaissance flowered later and stressed Christian ideals and social reforms based upon them.

How should you put it into words? Describe the features and accomplishments of the Italian Renaissance, then explain how they influenced the Northern Renaissance, but were interpreted with an emphasis on Christian values.

---

3.   Explain why the *Opening of the Atlantic* led to a shift of political and economic power from the Mediterranean Basin to Western Europe.

What does the question want to know? How did exploration and colonization in the 15th and 16th centuries enable the countries that bordered the Atlantic Ocean to achieve economic, political, and military dominance in Europe?

What do you know about it? "Geography is destiny." For centuries, Italy dominated European trade with the Far East due to its strategic location in the Mediterranean. New trade routes with Asia—established by Portuguese explorers—and the discovery of the New World—by Spanish and other explorers whose nations had Atlantic access—offered new routes and new products.

How should you put it into words? With "geography is destiny" as your theme, describe how and why the power shifted in the 15th and 16th centuries.

GROUP B ESSAYS

> **4.** To what extent and in what ways was Romanticism in art, litera-
> ture, and music a reaction against the Enlightenment?

What does the question want to know? What were the values, expressions, and accomplishments of the Enlightenment and how much did Romanticism repudiate these in the various arts?

What do you know about it? The Enlightenment was characterized by a climate of progress and a fervid faith in reason as the tool for humanity to move to its highest fruition. The Romantic Movement emphasized emotion, glorified nature, and looked to the past.

How would you put it into words? Identify the assumptions and aims of the Enlightenment; show how Romantic art, literature, and music repudiated these.

> **5.** Describe how the public health movement and urban planning dur-
> ing the latter half of the 19th century changed life in Europe's
> cities.

What does the question want to know? What was the condition of Europe's cities in the 19th century? What were the public health movement and urban planning? How did they improve life in the cities?

What do you know about it? Haphazard growth and industrialization had resulted in overcrowded, filthy, unhealthy urban centers built on or around Europe's ancient cities. Reformers—in the health field and in urban planning—put their new theories into practice, thereby transforming many of Europe's cities into more livable, economically viable, and beautiful centers.

How would you put it into words? Describe the squalor and chaos that prevailed. Identify specific reformers and their theories. Detail specific improvements. If you have the facts, you could use a specific city as an illustration.

> **6.** "Religious differences caused the greatest disruption in 16th
> century Europe, ideological differences the greatest disruption in
> 20th century Europe." Defend or refute this statement.

What does the question want to know? Is the statement true or false? Make an argument that is supported by facts.

What do you know about it? The schism of the Christian world brought about by the Protestant Reformation and the subsequent political, social, cultural, and economic upheaval lasted for well over a century. The collapse of the political order that followed World War I affected every sphere of life in Europe, almost to the end of the 20th century.

How would you put it into words? The statement is most easily defended. Compare the realms of disruption in both centuries; contrast the religious issues of the 16th century with the ideological issues of the 20th.

Index

THERE'S ONLY ONE PLACE TO TURN FOR TOP SCORES...

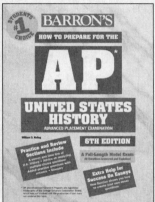
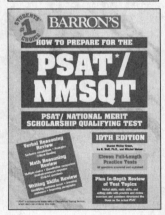
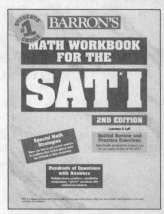
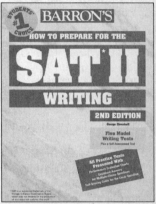

CHOOSING A COLLEGE

For every question you have, Barron's guides have the right answers.

BARRON'S COLLEGE GUIDES

AMERICA'S #1 RESOURCE FOR EDUCATION PLANNING.

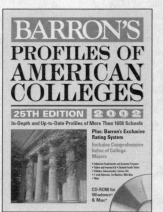
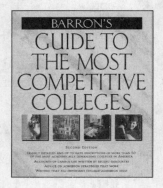

Success on Advanced Placement Tests Starts with Help from Barron's

Each May, thousands of college-bound students take one or more Advanced Placement Exams to earn college credits—and for many years, they've looked to Barron's, the leader in Advanced Placement test preparation. You can get Barron's user-friendly manuals for eleven different AP subjects. That includes two—in French and Spanish—that come with audiocassettes to improve your listening comprehension skills. Every Barron's AP manual gives you—

- **Diagnostic tests**
- **Extensive subject review**
- **Full-length model AP exams**
- **Study help and test-taking advice**

Model exams are designed to reflect the actual AP exams in question types, subject matter, length, and degree of difficulty. All questions come with answers and explanations. All books are paperback.

AP: Biology, 6th Ed.
0-7641-1375-5, 430 pp., $14.95, Can$21.00

AP: Calculus, 7th Ed.
0-7641-1790-4, 624 pp., $16.95, Can$23.95

AP: Chemistry, 2nd Ed.
0-7641-0474-8, 672 pp., $16.95, Can$23.95

AP: Computer Science
0-7641-0546-9, 600 pp., $14.95, Can$21.00

AP: English, 7th Ed.
0-7641-1230-9, 464 pp., $15.95, Can$22.50

AP: Environmental Science
0-7641-2161-8, 688 pp., $16.95, Can$23.95

AP: European History, 2nd Ed.
0-7641-0458-6, 240 pp., $14.95, Can$21.00

AP: French with Two Cassettes, 2nd Ed.
0-7641-7159-3, 450 pp.,
cassettes 90-min. each, $24.95, Can$32.50

AP: Macroeconomics/ Microeconomics
0-7641-1164-7, 496 pp., $14.95, Can$21.00

AP: Physics B, 2nd Ed.
0-7641-0475-6, 460 pp., $15.95, Can$22.50

AP: Physics C
0-7641-1802-1, 500 pp., $16.95, Can$23.95

AP: Psychology
0-7641-0959-6, 320 pp., $16.95, Can$23.95

AP: Spanish with Three CDs, 3rd Ed.
0-7641-7397-9, 480 pp., cassettes 90-min. each, $24.95, Can$34.95

AP: Statistics, 2nd Ed.
0-7641-1091-8, 432 pp., $15.95, Can$22.50

AP: U.S. Government and Politics, 3rd Ed.
0-7641-1651-7, 512 pp., $16.95, Can$23.95

AP: U.S. History, 6th Ed.
0-7641-1157-4, 336 pp., $15.95, Can$22.50

AP: World History
0-7641-1816-1, 512 pp., $16.95, Can$23.95

All prices are in U.S. and Canadian dollars and subject to change without notice. Order from your bookstore—or directly from Barron's by adding 18% for shipping and handling (minimum charge $5.95). New York State residents add sales tax to total after shipping and handling.

Visit our website at:
www.barronseduc.com

Barron's Educational Series, Inc.
250 Wireless Blvd.
Hauppauge, NY 11788
Call toll-free: 1-800-645-3476
Order by fax: 1-631-434-3217

In Canada:
Georgetown Book Warehouse
34 Armstrong Ave.
Georgetown, Ontario L7G 4R9
Canadian orders: 1-800-247-7160
Order by fax: 1-800-887-1594

(#93) R11/02

This book belongs to ALeRiQuE dArIsO